About the Author

Lucy Moore was born in 1970 and educated in Britain and the United States before reading history at Edinburgh University. She is the author of several books, including the critically acclaimed *Maharanis*. She lives in London.

LIBERTY

LIBERTY

The Lives and Times
of Six Women
in Revolutionary France

LUCY MOORE

HARPER PERENNIAL

NEW YORK • LONDON • TORONTO • SYDNEY • NEW DELHI • AUCKLAND

HARPER ● PERENNIAL

First published in Great Britain in 2006 by
Harper Press, an imprint of HarperCollins Publishers.

A hardcover edition of this book was published in 2007 by HarperCollins Publishers.

P.S.™ is a trademark of HarperCollins Publishers.

FIRST HARPER PERENNIAL EDITION PUBLISHED 2008.

Maps by Leslie Robinson

The Library of Congress has catalogued the hardcover edition as follows:

Moore, Lucy.
    Liberty : the lives and times of six women in revolutionary France / Lucy
Moore.—1st U.S. ed.
        xiii, 464 p. : ill. (some col.) , maps ; 24 cm.
    "First published in Great Britain in 2006 by HarperCollins Publishers."
    Includes bibliographical references (p. [417]–424) and index.
    ISBN: 978-0-06-082526-3
    ISBN-10: 0-06-082526-X
    1. Women revolutionaries—France—History—18th century. 2. France—
History—Revolution, 1789–1799—Women. I. Title.
DC158.8 .M64 2007
944.04092'2B 22   2006052595

ISBN 978-0-06-082527-0 (pbk.)

HB 04.06.2021

for Justin

CONTENTS

LIST OF ILLUSTRATIONS

INTEGRATED PICTURES

FIRST COLOUR PLATE SECTION

SECOND COLOUR PLATE SECTION

Tallien, brandishing the dagger Thérésia gave him, challenges Robespierre before the National Convention on 9 Thermidor (Blanchard, engraving after Tony Johannot. Hulton Archive/Getty Images)

The closure of the Jacobin Club in November 1794 (The Art Archive/Marc Charmet)

The women of the people storming the National Convention in May (Prairial) 1795, calling for 'Bread and the Constitution of 1793' (Nicolas Sebastien Maillot. The Art Archive/Musée Saint Denis, Reims/Dagli Orti)

La Chaumière, the rustic cottage Thérésia made into a masterpiece of Directory style (Martial Adolphe Potemont. Photothèque des musées de la Ville de Paris)

Thérésia in about 1805, as exquisite and statuesque as ever despite her exclusion from imperial society (François Gérard. Château de Versailles/The Bridgeman Art Library)

The caricaturist James Gillray's depiction of Thérésia in 1795 ('La Belle Espagnole', or 'La Doublure de Madame Tallien', published by Hannah Humphrey in 1796) and dancing with Joséphine in front of her lover Barras and Napoléon, 1799 ('Ci-devant Occupations', or 'Madame Talian and the Empress Josephine Dancing Naked before Barrass in the Winter of 1797') (Both © Courtesy of the Warden and Scholars of New College, Oxford/The Bridgeman Art Library)

Joséphine and her ladies in Italy, 1797 (Hippolyte Lecomte. Versailles, châteaux de Versailles et de Trianon © Photo RMN/© Rights reserved)

Thérésia's lovers: Gabriel Ouvrard. . . (Hulton Archive/Getty Images)
. . . and Paul Barras (Versailles, châteaux de Versailles et de Trianon © Photo RMN/© Rights reserved)

Germaine de Staël, wearing her trademark turban and holding one of the twigs she habitually played with as she spoke (Anne Louis Girodet de Roucy-Trioson. Château de Versailles, France/The Bridgeman Art Library)

The most visited bedroom in Paris: Juliette Récamier was so proud of her bedchamber she invited all her guests to admire it (Louis-Martin Berthault, French architect, engraving from Krafft and Ransonette collection. The Art Archive/Bibliothèque des Arts Décoratifs, Paris/Dagli Orti)

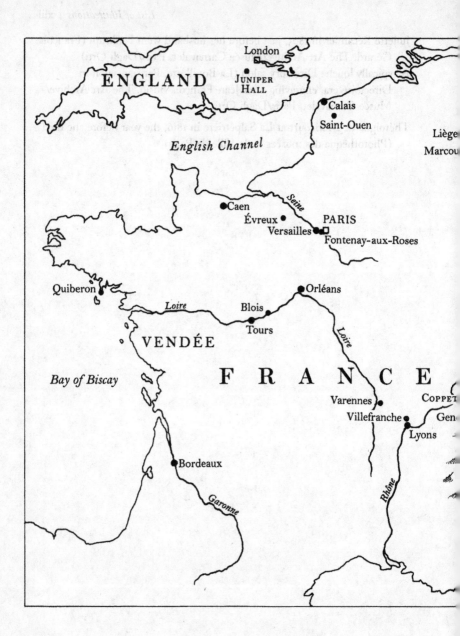

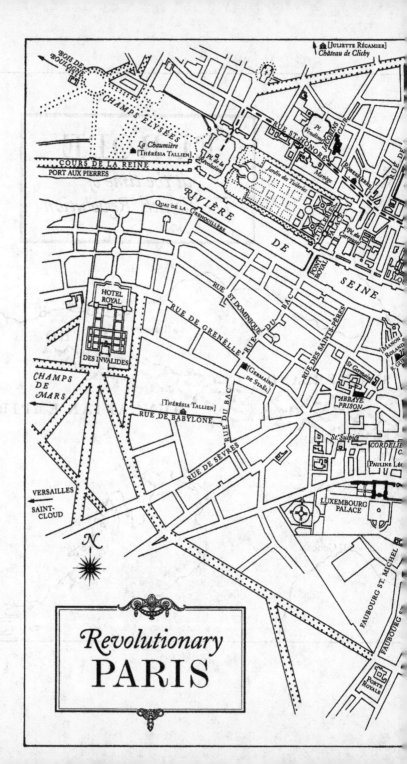

Revolutionary
PARIS

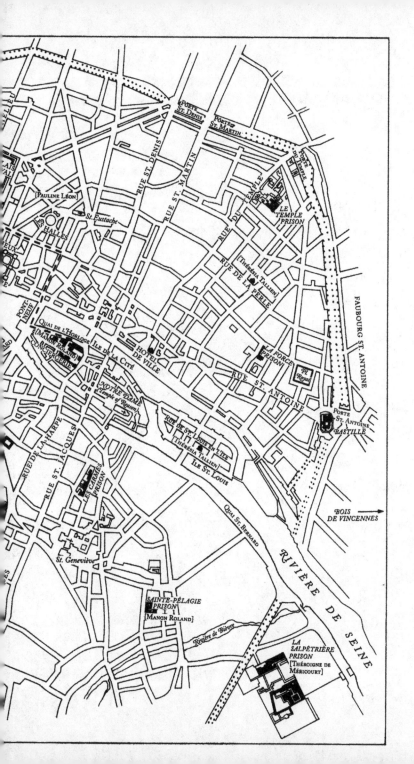

From my earliest days I had a feeling
that adventures lay in store for me.

Lucy de la Tour du Pin

INTRODUCTION

CITOYENNES

> The women have certainly had a considerable share in the
> French revolution: for, whatever the imperious lords of the
> creation may fancy, the most important events which take
> place in this world depend a little on our influence; and we
> often act in human affairs like those secret springs in
> mechanism, by which, though invisible, great movements
> are regulated.

HELEN MARIA WILLIAMS

THE NATIONAL ASSEMBLY – France's first constitutional government – met between October 1789 and September 1792 in the covered
riding-school of the Tuileries palace in Paris. The long, narrow *manège*
[see 'Words and Phrases' p. 437] had been remodelled to accommodate
the deputies with a classical austerity intended to correspond to the
gravity of their new political responsibilities.

Although women did not possess the rights either of voting or of
holding office, they were permitted into the hall's galleries to observe
and marvel at the workings of the administration and the debates on
France's future. On any given day in the spring of 1791, four women
might have been sitting among the onlookers gathered to watch the
Assembly's proceedings.

The first was a dark-haired, red-faced woman of twenty-five, looking perennially dishevelled despite her expensive, extravagantly dé-
colleté dress. As she watched the men below her debate, it was clear
that several of them were her friends and that she was well acquainted
with every argument they put forth. She leaned eagerly forward to

catch every word, fiddling distractedly with a twisted scrap of paper that showed off her fine hands.

This was Germaine de Staël, one of the richest women in Europe, daughter of Louis XVI's former Finance Minister Jacques Necker [see 'Secondary Figures' p. 425], whose dazzling intelligence never quite consoled her for not being beautiful.

She was at the heart of a group of progressive aristocrats she believed would shape a new, reformed France ruled by a constitutional monarchy; her centrist coterie included the hero of the American War of Independence, the marquis de Lafayette, toeing an uneasy line between his liberal principles and his loyalty to the king.

Her critics found her overbearing and even her friends called her self-centred, but such was the power of Germaine's intellect and conversation that within half an hour of meeting her most people, despite themselves, were utterly captivated. 'I know of no woman, nor indeed any man, more convinced of his or her own personal superiority over every other person,' wrote one of her lovers, Benjamin Constant, 'or who allows this conviction to weigh less heavily on others.'

Staël, as a novelist, social commentator and literary theorist, left behind a wealth of source material that, unusually, spans the entire period before, during and after the revolution. She is not only the best and most consistently documented of this book's six women, in terms of her own letters and of being mentioned in other people's correspondence and memoirs, but also the one who wrote the most eloquently about the revolution itself.

Germaine had little time for other women, but one acquaintance who might have been sitting nearby was the delectable Thérésia de

Fontenay. Just eighteen years old, already married for four years and the mother of a little boy, tender-hearted Thérésia was the toast of Parisian society; the only thing she enjoyed more than pleasure was attention. She would have been wearing fashionably simple, patriotic clothes – a white muslin dress with a tricolour sash fastened with a brooch made out of one of the shards of the fallen Bastille. At her side was her radical lover whose brother, a former marquis, was closely allied to

the most extreme-left deputies including Maximilien Robespierre.

Manon Roland, the thirty-seven-year-old wife of a provincial

civil servant, sat in another part of the gallery, well away from the world of high society. Demurely dressed, eyes downcast, her virtuous exterior concealed an ardent, rebellious heart. Drawn to Paris in 1791 by the events taking place there, she and her husband became central members of a group of middle-class republican lawyers and journalists who included Robespierre and the progressive journalist Jacques-Pierre Brissot. Unlike Thérésia de Fontenay,

Manon had chafed at the old order of things. When the revolution came it was the fulfilment of all her dreams.

Manon watched the debates as keenly as Germaine, knowing the deputies speaking, and their arguments, because many of them met regularly in her drawing-room. But while Germaine would have given her guests champagne; Manon proudly served sugar-water. With her love of order, she deplored the chaos of the Assembly's sessions: the uncontrollable deputies shouted over one another to make their voices heard, preventing the business of the day from being accomplished.

Pauline Léon had no such scruples. She heckled from the galleries,

shouting down moderates like Lafayette and cheering her hero Robespierre. No portrait of her survives – if one was ever made – but as a thirty-three-year-old single woman of the streets, who helped her widowed mother run the family chocolate-making business and look after her five younger brothers and sisters, it is likely that she was well made and strongly built. A fresh white handkerchief covered her hair, pinned up with a tricolour rosette, and she was wearing a blue woollen waistcoat over a white chemise, the sleeves pulled up to expose her tanned forearms; a red and white striped skirt with an apron; and wooden clogs.

Sixty-five per cent of French women of the late eighteenth century could not write their names; the illiterate would have been slightly fewer in Paris. Pauline Léon could read and write – she had been educated by her father – but she was a woman of the people and, as with most of them, it is harder to build up a rounded picture of her life because the sources concerning her are so scarce. No onlookers described her behaviour as a child; she left no diaries or letters. In a rare document produced while she was in prison in 1794, Léon testified to roaming Paris from 1789 onwards, frequenting political assemblies, demonstrating on the streets as well as 'manifesting my love for the fatherland'. She was less forthcoming about harassing and beating up passers-by for not being good 'patriots' – a synonym for devotion to the revolution.

A notable absence from the galleries on this imaginary afternoon was the former courtesan Théroigne de Méricourt, who before leaving Paris in the late summer of 1790 had been such a regular observer of the Assembly's sessions that she had her own seat reserved for her. She was known for always wearing a riding-habit of an austerely masculine cut, either in red, black or white. Although she had intended her trademark costume to compel men to treat her as an equal rather than as a woman, by wearing it she became one of the feminine icons of the revolution.

Abandoned by a faithless lover and reviled for having lost her reputation, Théroigne was very much alone in the world. She had suffered more at the hands of men than any of the other women here, and she was the most passionate and lonely campaigner for the liberties which the revolution seemed to promise women but ultimately failed to deliver. For nineteenth-century historians the image of pretty Théroigne in her red riding-habit, her bloody sword held aloft, represented all the savage excesses of the popular revolution; but this portrait of her bore very little relation to the earnest young woman whose early hopes were so disappointed by that revolution.

Another figure completes the sextet described in this book, but in the spring of 1791 Juliette Bernard, the future Madame Récamier, was still a bourgeois schoolgirl of thirteen, absorbed in studying English, Italian, dancing and the harp.

One further feminine image appears and reappears throughout these pages: not a real woman, but a constant, ghostly presence alongside her six flesh-and-blood sisters. Throughout this period Liberty – the ideal, or hope, that inspired the revolution – was represented as a goddess and exalted, pursued, manipulated and betrayed by turns.

The world of these six women, centred on Paris, was a small and intimate one. Less than six hundred thousand people lived in the capital in 1791 and their lives touched tangentially, crossed over without pausing and sometimes intersected. Respectable Manon Roland would never have received Théroigne de Méricourt at her salon, but one of her dearest friends fell hopelessly in love with her; Thérésia de Fontenay would not have known who Pauline Léon was, but before she met him her future husband gave a speech at a popular political club of which Léon was a member; despite the gap in their ages and backgrounds, Juliette Récamier would become one of Germaine de Staël's most intimate friends.

From the start, the revolution coloured every facet of their daily lives. It politicized everything, from clothing to modes of address to what was taught in schools to slang to food. Women, who had no direct influence over the political changes taking place around them, were intimately involved with these cultural changes; after all, they had read the same books and been inspired by the same ideas as their brothers. As the nineteenth-century historian Alexis de Tocqueville wrote of the period leading up to the revolution, even 'women, amidst their petty household tasks, sometimes dreamed about the great problems of existence'. Many found that they were swept away by the exhilaration and optimism that infused French society, and became as absorbed by the revolution as their husbands and lovers.

The six women whose experiences form the basis of this book were each transformed by their experiences during the revolution. As Simon Schama writes in his book *Citizens*, the revolution 'had the deepest craving for heroes' embodying the abstract principles they were trying to make real. It also created heroines.

Although they came from a range of backgrounds and, like looking through different sides of a prism, each illuminates different aspects of the period − from the tomboy Pauline Léon with a brace of pistols tucked into her belt, haranguing the deputies of the National Convention, to the exquisite Juliette Récamier abandoning her inhibitions on the dance floors of the public balls during the Directory − these six women had in common courage, vitality, a youthful energy and a passion that marked the revolution as much as it marked them. Each of them, in her own way, burned to distinguish herself in the great drama unfolding in front of her.

1

SALONNIÈRE

Germaine de Staël

May–October 1789

Mme de Staël's salon is more than a place where one
meets for pleasure: it is a mirror in which we see reflected
the image of the times.

Adam de Custine

Germaine de Staël, after a portrait by
her friend Elisabeth Vigée-Lebrun

EVERY TUESDAY EVENING in the early years of the revolution, Germaine de Staël held a small dinner at her *hôtel* in the rue du Bac, on Paris's left bank. She invited a catholic assortment of liberal, anglophile nobles, their glamorous wives and mistresses, and ambitious young men of middling rank. 'Go hence to Mme de Staël's,' wrote Gouverneur Morris, the one-legged American envoy to Paris, in his apple-green journal in January 1791. 'I meet here the world.'

For Germaine's guests, these evenings were a chance to discuss the latest news: books, plays, affairs and, above all, politics, the shared obsession of the day. Thomas Jefferson, a frequent visitor to the rue du Bac, called Paris in 1788 a 'furnace of politics . . . men, women and children talk nothing else'. In the words of a foreign observer, the entire country felt 'that they were on the eve of some great revolution'. For Germaine, her salons, combining her three passions – love, Paris and power – were 'the noblest pleasure of which human nature is capable'.

'We breathed more freely, there was more air in our lungs,' she wrote of this optimistic period; 'the limitless hope of infinite happiness had gripped the nation, as it takes hold of men in their youth, with illusion and without foresight'. If her friend the marquis de Talleyrand could say that no one who had not lived before 1789 could know the true sweetness of living, then Germaine could equally truly declare that for her, nothing could compare to the exquisite flavour of those days between 1788 and 1791 when she was in love and believed a new France was being created within the four gold-embroidered walls of her drawing-room.

Germaine de Staël was twenty-three in July 1789, the month that her father Jacques Necker, on-and-off Finance Minister to Louis XVI, was sacked by the king. Louis's powers permitted him to appoint, dismiss and banish ministers at will, so there was nothing unusual in this; what was unusual this time was the response it provoked.

Necker had made himself unpopular at court by advising the king to make wide-ranging changes to his archaic administration, urging modernization (particularly of the system of taxation, which weighed most heavily on the poor) and greater accountability to the French people. He had encouraged the king to summon the Estates-General, France's only national representative assembly, for the first time since 1614 and, partly at his daughter's urging, argued that the three estates (clergy, nobles and commons, known respectively as the First, Second and Third Estates) should vote individually - thus preventing the nobles and clergy from grouping together to block the Third Estate's demands.

Hard-line royalists, who feared the changes sweeping France, were convinced Necker would betray the king to his people, and welcomed his downfall. In the royal council, two days before Necker was dismissed, the king's brother, the comte d'Artois, told the minister to his face that he ought to be hanged; on the same day, in Paris, a well dressed woman was publicly spanked for spitting on his portrait.

Necker's defiant attitude towards the king had prompted his discharge and cemented his status as a popular hero; his reputation for financial acumen was matched only by his reputation for probity. Reformers who idolized him saw his expulsion as a manifestation of outmoded arbitrary power and an unwelcome confirmation of the king's distaste for reform. They rallied to the cause of their champion.

News of Necker's dutifully silent departure from Versailles reached Paris on Sunday, 12 July. A large crowd had gathered in the Palais Royal, as it did every Sunday, to eat ices, buy caricatures, ribbons or lottery tickets, ogle scantily dressed *femmes publiques* and magic lantern shows, and listen to orators declaiming against the government. The Palais Royal, owned by the king's cousin the duc d'Orléans, was a vast, newly built piazza surrounded by colonnaded shops, theatres and cafés. By the mid-1780s, protected from police regulation by its royal owner and encouraged by that owner's well known antipathy to the court party at Versailles, it had become a city within a city, a place where anything could be seen, said or procured, and the centre of popular opposition to royal abuses.

On that July afternoon the crowd gathered around a passionate young journalist, Camille Desmoulins, who stood on a table urging his fellow-citizens to rise up against the king's 'treachery' in sacking Necker. 'To arms, to arms,' he cried; 'and,' seizing a leafy branch from one of the chestnut trees that edged the Palais Royal, 'let us all take a green cockade, the colour of hope.' With Desmoulins carried triumphantly aloft, the shouting, clamouring, bell-ringing mob surged on to the streets to search Paris for the weapons that would transform them into an army.

The king was not unprepared for this type of rising; indeed, one of the underlying causes for the popular uproar that greeted Necker's dismissal was distrust of the troops – about a third of whom were Swiss or German soldiers rather than French – with which Louis had been quietly surrounding Paris during late June and early July as preparation for a show of force that would silence his critics for good. But the democratic germs of patriotism and reform that had infected the French people had penetrated as far as the lower ranks of the army, for so long a bastion of aristocratic privilege and tradition, and their leaders' response to the crisis was hesitant. The Palais Royal mob, by evening numbering perhaps six thousand, met a cavalry unit of the Royal-Allemands at the Place Vendôme and the Place Louis XV (later, Place de la Révolution, and still later Place de la Concorde) just to the north-west of the Tuileries palace, and, reinforced by the popular Paris-based *gardes françaises*, forced the German and Swiss soldiers, in the early hours of 13 July, to retreat from the city centre. After a day of chaos and plunder, on the 14th the people's army reached the Bastille, and the revolution received its baptism in blood.

The storming of the Bastille was by no means the first act of the revolution. Since 1787, extraordinary developments had been witnessed in government. France was a nation trembling on the brink of change. Its causes were many and varied: ideological, fiscal, constitutional, personal, economic, historical, social, cultural. 'The Revolution must be attributed to every thing, and to nothing,' wrote Germaine. 'Every year of the century led toward it by every path.' In the summer of 1789 the fateful mechanism that would exchange absolute for representative government (and back again) was already in motion. Nor was Necker's dismissal the sole cause of the Bastille's fall. But Germaine de Staël can be forgiven for thinking that her adored father – and through him, she herself – was at the heart of events.

It was no accident that green, the colour Camille Desmoulins chose as the emblem of hope in the Palais Royal, was the colour of Necker's livery – and typical of the confusion inherent in the revolution itself that it should be replaced soon after with the tricolour because it was also the livery colour of the king's unpopular brother, the comte d'Artois. The tricolour contained within it a multitude of references: red and blue for Paris, combined with white for the Bourbon dynasty; red and blue were also the colours of the popular duc d'Orléans. Like everything during this period, these colours were laden with symbolism: white for the revolutionaries' purity, blue for the heavenly ideals they were pursuing, red for the blood which was already seen as the necessary price of France's liberation. The tricolour was immediately invested with an almost mystical aura. It became a sacrosanct emblem of the new France that the revolution was creating, materially revered in bits of ribbon representing the fatherland.

Germaine had been dining with her parents in Versailles when Necker received Louis's notice on 11 July. Saying nothing, but squeezing his daughter's hand beneath the table, Necker got into his carriage with his wife as if for their regular evening drive; instead of idling round the park in Versailles, they headed straight for the border with the Low Countries. Germaine returned to Paris that night (fourteen kilometres, a carriage journey of about two hours) and found there a letter from her father informing her of his departure and advising her to go to his country house at Saint-Ouen. Ignoring, despite herself, the crowds already gathered in the rue du Bac to hear news of Necker, she rushed to Saint-Ouen with her husband, only to find there another letter summoning them to Brussels, where they arrived on the 13th. There she found her parents, still wearing the same clothes in which they had sat down to dinner two days earlier.

After a week Necker received a courier from the king recalling him to Versailles. He deliberated for three days and then began the journey back to Paris with his wife, daughter and son-in-law. Fifteen years later, Germaine remembered how intoxicated she was by the accolades showered on her father, the bliss of basking in his popularity. Women working in the fields fell to their knees as the Neckers' coach passed by; as they entered each town, their carriage was unhitched from the horses and drawn through the streets by the inhabitants. When they reached the Hôtel de Ville in Paris, where a massive crowd was waiting to greet the man on whom their hopes for reform and prosperity rested, Germaine fainted, feeling she had 'touched the extreme limits of happiness'.

The excitement even made her write affectionately to her husband, uncharacteristically sending him in a note, soon after they returned to Paris, '*mille et mille tendresses*'. The same letter concluded, more characteristically, with a message for her father: 'Tell my father that all of France does not love or admire him as much as I do today.'

It was in this heady atmosphere that Germaine de Staël's salon became the most important in Paris. The tradition of the salon, in which an intelligent woman (never her husband) held regular 'evenings' for a circle of friends and acquaintances, was a long-established one in France and had ordained Woman, according to the Goncourt brothers a century later, as 'the governing principle, the directing reason and the commanding voice' of eighteenth-century high society. The salon may have brought women extraordinary behind-the-scenes influence; but this influence came at a price.

On the surface, salons might seem nothing more than parties attended by bored, frivolous socialites whose daily lives were governed by their toilettes – aristocratic women changed their clothes several times a day, often while receiving favoured visitors – but the details of these lives in fact reveal the social developments of the times. In an age of rigorous formality, for example, in which behaviour itself seemed bound up in whalebone stays, the ritual of the toilette provided a release, allowing people to see each other in relaxed circumstances. In an age that had almost institutionalized extramarital affairs, it also gave women the chance to display themselves to current or potential lovers beyond the citadel of their petticoats, hoops and corsets: in 1790 it was fashionable to receive friends from the luxury of one's milk-bath.

Although she was famously badly dressed, Germaine never lost the ancien régime custom of receiving visitors during her toilette, all through her life carrying on metaphysical conversations with a horde of people while one maid dressed her hair and another did her nails. Her doctor in England in 1792 was surprised to be greeted by Germaine in her bedroom wearing 'a short petticoat and a thin shirt', and astonished by her energy. She talked and wrote all day long, he reported, her green leather portable writing-desk permanently open on her knees, whether she was in bed or at dinner. Even when she gave birth there were fifteen people in her bedroom and within three days she was talking as much as ever.

Before the revolution, every different outfit served a different purpose, and each one minutely indicated the wearer's status. Wearing unsuitable clothes was an implicit rejection of the hierarchy that controlled society. Inelegant Germaine, who always showed too much flesh – even her travelling dresses had plunging necklines – was by these criteria deeply suspect. Riding-habits were worn to ride or drive in the Bois de Boulogne or go out hunting with the court; day dresses were worn to receive guests at home, to go shopping in the Palais Royal or to attend lectures in the thrilling new sciences of electricity and botany; in the evening, to attend the theatre or a court ball, three-inch heels, heavy makeup and elaborate, pomaded headdresses, snowy-white with powder and sprinkled with jewels, flowers and feathers were de rigueur. Their hair arrangements were often so tall that women had to travel crouching on the floor of their carriages.

Fluttering a fan in a certain way or placing a patch near the eye as opposed to on the cheek revealed a person's character without them having to speak. The sociologist Richard Sennett observes of this period that it is hard to imagine how people so governed by 'impersonal and abstract convention [can] be so spontaneous, so free to express themselves . . . their spontaneity rebukes the notion that you must lay yourself bare in order to be expressive'. Contemporaries were fully aware of this dichotomy between word and action. 'A man who placed his hand on the arm of a chair occupied by a lady would have been considered extremely rude,' wrote the comtesse de Boigne, looking back on the pre-revolutionary period of her youth, and yet language 'was free to the point of licentiousness'.

But by the mid-1780s contemporary medical and philosophical views were transforming women's fashions and habits. In 1772 one doctor described corsets as barbarous, impeding women's breathing and deforming their chests, and especially dangerous during pregnancy; he was also concerned about the moral effects they produced by displaying the bosom so prominently. His advice was echoed by Jean-Jacques Rousseau, prophet of naturalness and sensibility in *Émile* and *La Nouvelle Héloïse*, who recommended that children wear loose clothes that would not constrict their growing bodies.

For the first time, women's clothes allowed them to breathe and eat freely: the new fashions quite literally liberated their bodies from an armour of stays, panniers and hoops at the same time as the ideological implications of the change in fashion began to liberate their behaviour. In *A Vindication of the Rights of Woman* written in 1792 Mary Wollstonecraft declared that stiff, uncomfortable clothes, like the 'fiction' of beauty itself, were a means by which society kept women submissive and dependent. Shedding these restrictions would empower them. By this definition Germaine, who rose above her plainness (Gouverneur Morris thought she looked like a chambermaid) and paid scant attention to her dress, was already halfway to emancipation.

Perhaps the most celebrated proponent of these progressive ideas was the queen, Marie-Antoinette, who was painted by Élisabeth Vigée-Lebrun in 1783 in a simple white chemise dress tied at the waist with a satin sash. This seemingly innocent act raised eyebrows for a number of reasons. Chemises were muslin shifts, previously worn only in the intimacy of a toilette (or by prostitutes), so to eighteenth-century eyes Vigée-Lebrun had painted the queen in a shocking state of undress. Furthermore, for the queen herself to reject the formality of court custom – she was traditionally portrayed in carapace-like court dress – carried seditious undertones of disrespect to the traditions she represented. Finally, the *chemise de la reine* (as it came to be called) was a style anyone could afford. As Mary Robinson, the courtesan who popularized the *chemise de la reine* in England, commented, 'the duchess, and her *femme de chambre*, are dressed exactly alike'. Dress, which had once distinguished between people, was becoming dangerously democratic.

Manners, too, were changing. As with clothing, the fashion for informality initially came from the top down: in the artificial world of the salon, being able to give the impression of naturalness and ease had long been considered the highest of the social arts. 'Do not people talk in society of a man being a great actor?' asked the philosopher Denis Diderot. Just as the cut flowers in her headdress were kept fresh with tiny glass vases hidden in her hair, the salonnière achieved the sparkling effect of spontaneity in conversation through study and discipline. Every day, Mme Geoffrin, celebrated pre-revolutionary hostess to the great Enlightenment philosophers, wrote two letters (in those days an art form) to keep her brain sharp.

Germaine de Staël's favourite game was called the Boat, in which everyone present was asked who they would save from a sinking ship. She asked her first lover, Talleyrand, who he would rescue, her or his other mistress Adèle de Flauhaut. He replied that she was so talented she could extricate herself from any predicament; gentility would oblige him to save the resourceless Adèle. Another version of this story has Germaine and Talleyrand actually in a boat, talking about devotion and courage. To her question as to what he would do if she fell in, he reportedly replied, 'Ah, Madame, you must be such a good swimmer.'

Word games, jokes, debates, making up poems and proverbs and amateur theatricals were salon pastimes designed to stimulate and heighten conversation, which Germaine described as an instrument the French above all other nations liked to play, producing a sublime 'intellectual melody'. Conversation, she said, was

> a certain way in which people act upon one another, a quick give-and-take of pleasure, a way of speaking as soon as one thinks, of rejoicing in oneself in the immediate present, of being applauded without making an effort, of displaying one's intelligence by every nuance of intonation, gesture and look – in short, the ability to produce at will a kind of electricity.

Naturally, Germaine herself excelled at this art: 'If I was queen,' said a friend, 'I should order Mme de Staël to talk to me always.' When she spoke, constantly fiddling with a small twig or twist of paper which the unkind said was a way of drawing attention to her fine hands, her captivated listeners forgot her scruffy clothes, red face and large frame, noticing only the beautiful expression in her eyes.

These showers of sparks, as Staël defined the words and ideas that brought a salon to life, showed the importance to French society of writers and philosophers. Salonnières acted as confidantes, editors, muses and patrons to their talented guests, corresponding with them, intriguing to have them elected to the Academy or appointed to political office and erecting statues in their honour. Women were, according to a 1788 pamphlet entitled *Advice to the Ladies*, 'the arbiters of all things . . . Business, honours, everything is in your hands.' These roles set a dangerous precedent by giving women powerful identities outside marriage and motherhood.

Another dangerous precedent set by the salons was the relatively open access to them. Women who wanted to have the best thinkers in Europe at their feet were unconcerned about their breeding, and willing to run the moral and political risks of being exposed to their exciting new philosophies. It was at Versailles and in the most exclusive salons in Paris that the 'bourgeois' works of Diderot, Rousseau and the artist Jean-Baptiste Greuze were celebrated.

Contemporary opinion was divided over the wisdom of women occupying such a prominent place in society. On the whole, the philosophers who frequented salons and benefited from their hostesses' efforts on their behalf were liberal-thinking, although many believed that trying to impose uniformity on men and women was to challenge nature's own distinctions. To equalize men and women, wrote the novelist Restif de la Bretonne in 1776, 'is to denature them.' Implicit in all this was the understanding that of the two sexes, the masculine was undoubtedly the superior. Diderot held that 'beauty, talents and wit' would in any circumstances captivate a man, 'but these advantages peculiar to a few women will not establish anywhere a general tyranny of the weaker sex over the robust one'.

Many reformers saw the influence women wielded as evidence of the corruption of the ancien régime. Boudoir politics, as it was called, when women manipulated their family, friends and, still worse, their lovers, to gain personal influence in the political world from which they were theoretically excluded, was held up before the revolution as one of the chief problems with the French system. Thomas Jefferson told Washington in 1788 that women's solicitations 'bid defiance to [natural] laws and regulation' and had reduced France to a 'desperate state'. The fact that women could play a role in politics at all was, for reformers of all stripes, one of the essential justifications for change.

'The influence of women, the ascendant of good company, gilded salons, appeared very terrible to those who were not admitted themselves,' conceded Germaine de Staël. While she acknowledged that ancien régime women 'were involved in everything' on behalf of their husbands, brothers and sons, she maintained they had no effect on 'enlightened and natural intelligence' like that her father possessed; in this as in everything, she believed herself an exception.

The prevailing view, propounded by the great naturalist Georges-Louis Leclerc, comte de Buffon, was that women, inherently more gentle and loving than men, played a valuable social role by moderating masculine energies. Germaine agreed, arguing that French women were accustomed to take the lead in conversation in their homes, which elevated and softened discussions on public affairs. This more temperate view did allow that wives and mothers were essential elements of a civilized society, and some radical thinkers went so far as to suggest that if women were educated they would make their husbands happier and their sons more successful. Mankind would enter into 'all its vigour, all its splendour', wrote Philibert Riballier in 1779, if women could be made 'strong, robust, courageous, educated and even learned'.

Riballier's 'even learned' is crucial, because it reveals, even in works that were outwardly sympathetic to women, a belittling tone beneath the praise. The duchesse d'Abrantes commented that before the revolution women seemed to be esteemed but in fact had only the appearance of influence. In 1785 Mme de Coicy said that although France was called 'the paradise of women' its female subjects were 'unworthily scorned and mistreated', despite their superiority to all other European women. The privileged few who became powerful, like Mme de Pompadour, Louis XV's mistress, generally acquired that power at the cost of their reputations.

Although strong women had been tolerated and even appreciated through French history, there was an equally potent strain of misogyny to which Germaine de Staël, as gauche as she was eloquent, frequently fell victim. In her writings, throughout her life, she railed against the double standards that permitted women to be judged by different standards than men. Women, as she put it in her novel *Corinne*, were fettered by a thousand bonds from which men were free. Every man of her acquaintance might, as she did, take lovers, neglect his spouse, write books or involve himself in politics; they were not criticized for doing those things at all, but for doing them well or badly, while she would always be castigated for her looks or her private life. In *On Literature* she wrote feelingly of the 'injustice of men towards distinguished women', their inability to forgive 'genuine superiority in a woman of the most perfect integrity'. The knowledge that she was as intelligent as any man of her generation but could never truly have a public life tortured her, and only at her salon was she consoled.

But Germaine was extraordinary, and her contemporaries did recognize it. 'The feelings to which she gives rise are different from those that any woman can inspire,' observed one, unwittingly providing a list of the feminine qualities her age considered ideal. 'Such words as *sweetness, gracefulness, modesty, desire to please, deportment, manners*, cannot be used when speaking of her; but one is carried away, subjugated by the force of her genius . . . Wherever she goes, most people are changed into spectators.'

Her friends (and enemies) were united in praise of her ability to talk, but also of her skill in drawing out whomever she was talking to. One left Germaine 'in admiration', spellbound by her knowledge and persuasiveness, but also 'entirely pleased with oneself'. She could be overpowering, egotistical and embarrassingly unselfconscious, and she preferred 'to dazzle rather than to please', but she was good-natured and generous to those she loved.

This group did not include her husband, whom she charitably described as being, 'of all the men I could never love . . . the one I like best'. Éric Magnus de Staël was an affable Swedish diplomat seventeen years Germaine's senior who had begun pursuing the greatest heiress in Europe when she was twelve. Her parents made it a condition of their betrothal that Staël be appointed ambassador to France for life; King Gustavus of Sweden conveniently made his betrothal to Germaine a condition of his appointment as ambassador. The wedding took place in Paris on 14 January 1786, the contract signed the day before by the king and queen.

Staël married Germaine for her money, and she married him for her freedom. As Claire says to Julie in Rousseau's *Nouvelle Héloïse*, 'If it had depended on me, I would never have married, but our sex buys liberty only by slavery and it is necessary to begin as a servant in order to be a mistress someday.' After their wedding day her husband was a virtual nonentity to her although for the first few years, almost surprised to be wooed by him, she did try to treat him kindly.

Germaine's first lover was probably Charles Maurice de Talleyrand-Périgord. A refined, cynical libertine, thirty-four-year-old Talleyrand was so amoral that his own mother opposed his appointment as Bishop of Autun in 1788. Like Germaine, Talleyrand skilfully deployed his abundant charm and subtle wit to make people forget his appearance; this was quite a feat, since he had been crippled since childhood and was described in 1805 as having the complexion of a decomposed corpse. Their relationship did not deepen into passion – besides, Talleyrand already had an 'official' mistress – but the love and the friendship endured.

In 1788 Germaine fell deeply in love with a friend of Talleyrand's, Louis de Narbonne, the man she called her magician. The sophisticated Narbonne, illegitimate son of Louis XV (and, it was whispered, of his own sister, Mme Adélaïde), united, according to Fanny Burney, 'the most courtly refinement and elegance to the quickest repartee'. Narbonne was as celebrated for his wit as for his looks – 'the inexhaustible treasures of grace, absurdity, gaiety, and all the seductions of his conversation' – and, at thirty-three, had already run through three fortunes (those of his mother, the comtesse de Narbonne; his god-mother, Mme Adélaïde; and his wife) and fathered at least two illegitimate children.

'He is a miracle,' wrote a young German acquaintance, some time later, marvelling at Narbonne's sparkling intelligence, courtesy, courage and modesty. 'It is no surprise that Madame de Staël should be so attached to this friend, even more so, as she was lumbered with a husband incapable of creating a recipe for potatoes, let alone gun-powder.' Her uninspiring husband was the man tradition and society had dictated that she marry, but Narbonne was her choice, her heart's partner, her soulmate, and Germaine dedicated herself to him and to their love with all the ardour and idealism of youth. The strength and purity of her feelings for Narbonne were all the justification she needed for a crime (infidelity) she considered society's, not her own.

A constant interchange of notes between Germaine and her hus-band, to and from her parents' lodgings in Versailles (where she stayed when she was called upon, as she often was, to play hostess for her father) and their house in the rue du Bac, indicates how rarely they were together during this period, and how often she would have been able to entertain Narbonne alone. When Staël accused her of doing so, she did not hesitate flatly to deny it: 'stop your famous jealousy,' she insisted. 'You will lose me if you continue [to make demands on me],' Germaine wrote in another letter, 'and it will only be your fault.' Personal freedom was evidently as important to her as abstract political liberties.

To outside eyes, the union between Staël's wife and the elegant courtier, Narbonne, was a strange one: 'her intellectual endowments must be with him her sole attraction,' wrote the naïve Fanny Burney, on being told that Germaine and Narbonne were lovers. 'She loves him even tenderly, but so openly, so simply, so unaffectedly, and with such utter freedom from coquetry, that, if they were two men, or two women, the affection could not, I think, be more obviously unde-signing.'

By July 1789, the month the Bastille fell, their relationship was public enough for Gouverneur Morris – who was chasing Talleyrand's mistress, Adèle de Flauhaut, with some success – to refer to Narbonne in his diary as 'the friend of Mme de Staël'. Another suitor, Stanislas de Clermont-Tonnerre, was not deterred from declaring his love for Germaine that autumn, but her relationship with Narbonne did allow her to reject him gently, telling him how much she loved 'le comte Louis' who had 'changed his destiny' for her the moment he saw her, breaking off his other attachments and consecrating his life to her.

By this she meant politically as much as emotionally. The aristocratic but relatively liberal Narbonne told Morris that July that he feared a civil war was inevitable; he was considering rejoining his regiment. He felt trapped between his duty to the king – his godfather and probably his nephew – and his political principles, urged upon him by Germaine. The American Morris, safe in his self-righteous republicanism, could smugly reply that he knew 'of no duty but that which conscience dictates', and speculate that Narbonne's conscience would 'dictate to join the strongest side'; but he was underestimating both the conviction that lay behind the progressive views of Germaine and her friends and the genuine conflict of interest they faced as they watched the revolution gather momentum. Narbonne allowed himself to be convinced by his mistress's eloquence, and remained in Paris with her to pursue glory through, rather than against, reform.

Germaine welcomed the early changes of the revolution with all the passion of her nature. Her upbringing had been a strange one. The only child of cool, ambitious, rather selfish parents, worshipping her father and jealous of her beautiful prig of a mother, she had lived among adults all her life. She was taught elocution by the greatest actress of the day, Mademoiselle Clairon (who later became her husband's mistress). Instead of playing, she watched Diderot, Gibbon, Voltaire, Grimm and Buffon spar in her mother's Friday salons; she did not have a friend her own age until she was twelve.

Germaine's intellectual brilliance, like her emotional intensity, was evident early on, and at twenty-two she published her first important book, *Letters on Jean-Jacques Rousseau*. Her passion for Rousseau was an indication both of her personal veneration of romantic love and of the philosophical atmosphere of the times. He was the most popular author of the second half of the eighteenth century, and probably the most important ideological inspiration to a generation of revolutionaries from Germaine herself to Robespierre. Even Marie-Antoinette had made a pilgrimage to his grave.

Rousseau's most celebrated and incendiary phrase comes from his treatise *The Social Contract* – 'Man is born free, but is everywhere in chains' – but his influence was far more than just political. He created a cult of sentimentality, exalting love not as a fashionable diversion indulged in outside marriage but as a noble, all-consuming calling: as Julie, the gentle but ardent heroine of *La Nouvelle Héloïse*, says, love became 'the great business of our lives'. In Julie, Rousseau gave Frenchwomen a new role model; her lover, sensitive, introspective Saint-Preux, provided a new romantic ideal.

Implicit in Rousseau's ideas about love was a rejection of conventional ideas about society's constraints, about status and about individual worth. 'I am not speaking of rank and fortune,' the commoner Saint-Preux tells his noble mistress Julie proudly, 'honour and love suffice for want of all that.' Germaine knew only too well that the bonds imposed by society meant nothing beside the bonds imposed by the heart.

Because of Rousseau, wrote the English traveller Mary Berry, 'maternal love became as much the fashion as soon afterwards balloons and animal magnetism'. Rousseau called motherhood a woman's highest responsibility. His works reunited a generation of mothers with their children, encouraging them to breast-feed (hitherto rare; middle- and upper-class babies had usually been handed almost immediately after birth to wet-nurses) and take an interest in their children's education. Before Rousseau, children had been treated as miniature adults. They were not allowed to run around or ask questions, and were dressed in stiff adult clothes. Rousseau recommended that they be allowed to play outside, that their curiosity be encouraged and their innocence nurtured. The exquisitely intimate, informal mother-and-child portraits of the late eighteenth century were direct responses to this new philosophy.

Rousseau, in glorifying women as wives and mothers, denied them any role outside the home. 'There are no good morals for women outside of a withdrawn and domestic life,' he wrote. 'A woman outside her home loses her greatest radiance, and is shorn of her true adornments, shows herself indecently. If she has a husband, what is she out seeking among men?' For him, as for so many of his generation, sexual inequality created an ideal equilibrium: men were dominant, active and reasoning, and their role was public; women were emotional, modest and loving, and their role was private. 'A taller stature, a stronger voice, and features more strongly marked seem to have no necessary bearing on one's sex, but these exterior modifications indicate the intentions of the creator in the modifications of the spirit,' he reasoned in *La Nouvelle Héloïse*. 'The souls of a perfect woman and a perfect man must not resemble each other more than their appearances.' According to this argument, the complementary differences between the sexes were essential to maintaining social harmony.

Despite the fact that her own ambitions were thwarted by his way of thinking, Germaine was typical of Rousseau's female readers in disregarding his prejudices because the vision he offered of love as redemption was so powerful, and the importance he attached to the domestic role so flattering. She conceded that 'Rousseau has endeavoured to prevent women from interfering in public affairs, and acting a brilliant part in the theatre of politics,' but while he attempted 'to diminish their influence over the deliberations of men, how sacredly has he established the empire they have over their happiness!' Even the committed campaigner for women's rights, Mary Wollstonecraft, famously described by Horace Walpole as a 'hyena in petticoats', was not immune to Rousseau's allure: she admitted she had 'always been half in love with him'.

Part of the reason for this is the hidden currents lying beneath the surface of Rousseau's work. Although he told women they should be subservient to men, his heroines were in fact often more capable and passionate than the men in their lives. In *Émile, ou De l'éducation*, Sophie 'sought a man and . . . found monkeys'. When Émile falls in love with her, he recognizes that she must be his guide, just as in *La Nouvelle Héloïse* Julie tells Saint-Preux that she will direct their common destinies. For all its melancholia and high-mindedness – Germaine said that he had made 'a passion of virtue' – Rousseau's writing was also thrillingly erotic. He himself said his books 'can only be read with one hand'.

The duality in his books echoed that in his life. Although he idealized motherhood, Rousseau abandoned his own children; although he wrote about pure, innocent love he openly admitted to masochism and masturbation; although he praised submissive women his own first mistress, with whom he lived in a *ménage à trois* alongside her herbalist, was a speculator, adventuress and sometime spy. His *Confessions*, published posthumously, revealed vanity, vices and frailties but only added to his appeal.

While he explicitly excluded women from political life, Rousseau's writings inadvertently made women political creatures. They may have read his works for pleasure, but they also found in them rejections of tyranny and pleas for justice so persuasive that they came to believe the inequalities and constraints of society that they had once unquestioningly accepted were absurd.

Rousseau's philosophy, both public and private, set the tone for salons like Germaine's of the late 1780s. Her circle rejected the ancien régime world for its hollowness, its arbitrariness and its superficiality. 'It laughs at all those who see the earnestness of life and who still believe in true feelings and serious thought,' she lamented later. 'It soils the hope of youth.' The French, she said, were 'too civilised in some respects', their rigmarole of manners and conventions grading 'people instead of uniting them'.

But while Germaine's salon was notable for its liberalism and lack of prejudice, and welcomed newcomers if they had something to offer, its habitués were largely drawn from a small group of aristocrats who, in Germaine's words, 'preferred the generous principles of liberty to the advantages which they enjoyed personally'. Despite her democratic ideas, Germaine lived and entertained on an almost royal scale: two rows of footmen flanked the anteroom through which her fashionably free-thinking guests entered the gold and marble salon. Victorine de Chastenay was thinking of Germaine's friends when she said that at the start of the revolution the most progressive nobles were generally 'not the provincial gentry and those least qualified, but the most brilliant youth, men whose families had been the most loaded with gifts and honours at the Court'. 'It was the fashion to complain of everything,' wrote one of the queen's ladies-in-waiting. 'Unnoticed, the spirit of revolt was rampant in all classes of society.'

Many of Mme de Staël's friends had served in the American army during the late 1770s and early 1780s when the French government supported the United States against the British (the burden of its spending there precipitating the financial crisis of the mid-1780s) and saw in the United States a republican idyll of freedom, simplicity and virtue. The marquis de Lafayette had fought beside George Washington and considered him his adoptive father. He and Washington were also united by their freemasonry, one means by which the enlightenment philosophies that inspired the revolution were disseminated; the writer Louis-Sébastien Mercier called masons' lodges in the 1780s 'a kind of school for oratory'. Germaine remarked that the love of liberty 'decided every action' of Lafayette's life.

Another idealistic American veteran was Mathieu de Montmorency, a friend of Lafayette's and a prominent member of the Estates-General, who demanded a Declaration of Rights and happily relinquished his aristocratic privileges in August 1789. A year later, he called for the abolition of titles themselves and all marks of nobility, like servants in livery and coats of arms on carriages, façades and church pews. 'All Frenchmen shall wear from henceforth the same ensigns,' he declared, 'those of Liberty.' Like Germaine he looked on Rousseau as a hero, petitioning for him to be honoured by the French nation in 1791.

As well as Frenchmen who had served in America, Germaine knew several Americans in Paris, including Thomas Jefferson (who advised Lafayette on his drafts of the Declaration of the Rights of Man and the Citizen before leaving Paris in September 1789) and Tom Paine. One of her most regular American guests was Gouverneur Morris, who admitted he felt very stupid in the rue du Bac. His pursuit of Talleyrand's mistress did not stop him making eyes at the wild, enchanting Aimée de Coigny. 'We have some little compliments together, Mme de Coigny and I,' he confided to his diary after a dinner in 1791 at Lady Sutherland's, – the British ambassadress was another member of Germaine's set, – 'and I think it possible we may be pretty well together, but this depends on the Chapter of Accidents for she must be at the Trouble of bringing it about. Stay late here.'

Morris was not entirely in agreement with the politics of Germaine's salon. Soon after his arrival in Paris in early 1789 he described Germaine's friend and Lafayette's cousin Mme de Tessé, a member of the queen's household, as a republican 'of the first feather'; a week later he was told her friends saw him as an 'aristocrat', with ideas 'too moderate for that company'. This was partly true. Morris thought the French too depraved for liberty – but perhaps he was simply intoxicated by the pleasures of the ancien régime and did not want them replaced by republican austerity before he had drunk his fill.

The most radical aristocrat of Staël's group was the marquis de Condorcet, a mathematician and philosopher. Reserved and painfully timid, Condorcet lacked social polish – he was said always to have hair-powder in his ears – but his passion for modernity illuminated his views. The first stirrings of reform confirmed all his faith in the perfectibility of mankind. 'Everyone tells us that we are bordering the period of one of the greatest revolutions of the human race,' he wrote optimistically. 'The present state of enlightenment guarantees that it will be happy.'

Condorcet, married to a celebrated intellectual (and another celebrated salonnière) twenty-one years his junior, Sophie de Grouchy, known as *la Vénus lycéenne*, was one of the rare feminists of the age. In his political writings of the late 1780s he called repeatedly for the franchise, when it came, to be extended to women as well as men. 'Either no individual in humankind has genuine rights,' he declared in *On the Admission of Women to Civil Rights* in July 1790, 'or all have the same ones.' Excluding women from political life, he argued, violated the entire principle of natural rights on which the first revolutionaries were basing their calls for reform. The right to participate in the government of their country is a right men hold by virtue of their reason, not their gender; thus women, who also possess reason, cannot be deprived of those rights. Furthermore, he insisted, women's active contribution to society could only be of benefit to it.

According to the historian Madelyn Gutwirth, Condorcet was so concerned to avoid the 'posture of bogus rococo gallantry' that marked so much eighteenth-century writing about women that he lamented his lack of it. 'Sighing philosophically, he observes that in robbing women of their myth by speaking of their "rights rather than their reign", he may fail to earn their approval, for he saw all about him the stampede among women to Rousseauist views', which granted them dominion over men's hearts but no political rights.

Although the constitution of the newly formed United States had not granted rights to women, its democratic example was an inspiration to Condorcet. 'Men whom the reading of philosophic books had secretly disposed to love liberty were filled with passion [during the War of Independence],' he wrote in a eulogy to Benjamin Franklin. 'They seized with joy this occasion to publicly confess sentiments that prudence had obliged them to maintain in silence.'

England provided Germaine's circle with another social and political model; collectively, they were known as 'Anglomaniacs'. Helen Maria Williams described the French in 1789 and 1790 as 'mad about the English'. So-called English pastimes of racing and betting preoccupied the upper classes' leisure time; young aristocrats affected English accents and a deliberate awkwardness of manner, because the English were famously clumsy. 'Everything had to be copied from our neighbours, from the Constitution to horses and carriages,' wrote Lucy de la Tour du Pin, whose Irish blood and fair English looks made her a sensation at court.

In the first half of the eighteenth century, the political philosopher Montesquieu had applauded Britain's well balanced, representative government. English customs were seen as an ideal combination 'of privilege and liberty, elegance and easy informality, tradition and reform', and English men and women were praised by French visitors for their cleanliness, motivation and industry. Germaine thought England had 'attained the perfection of the social order', with its division of power between Crown, aristocracy and people. But even to speak of the English constitution at court 'seemed as criminal as if one had suggested dethroning the king'.

Away from court, beneath the Gobelin tapestries on the walls of the dining-room in the rue du Bac, there were no such restrictions on speech or thought. In her favourite stance with her back to the fireplace, Mme de Staël, 'young, brilliant [and] thoughtless', would captivate her own coterie of dazzled youths by proclaiming 'in strokes of fire the ideas they thought they held'.

On 5 May 1789, from a palace window, an ecstatic Germaine watched the deputies of the Estates-General process into their opening session at Versailles. They had last gathered together 175 years earlier. Among the deputies Germaine's rejected suitor, Stanislas de Clermont-Tonnerre, represented the royalist centre right; her friend Lafayette was a moderate constitutional monarchist; the three Lameth brothers and Mathieu de Montmorency, all of whom had fought beside Lafayette in America, were slightly more liberal; on the extreme left were the lawyers Maximilien Robespierre, François Buzot and Jérôme Pétion.

Perhaps the most celebrated deputy in 1789 was Honoré-Gabriel de Mirabeau, the debauched Provençal count who represented his region in the Third Estate, the commoners, instead of sitting with the peers. The inspiring beauty of his oratory was almost enhanced by its contrast with his physical brutishness and coarse, pock-marked face. Germaine despised him: he was her father's rival for the hearts of the people. Blinded by his weaknesses – egotism and immorality – she could not see the political talents he possessed in abundance. Necker dismissed Mirabeau as 'a demagogue by calculation and an aristocrat by disposition'.

On the streets of Versailles, crowds 'drunk with hope and joy', according to another observer, lined the route to wish the Estates-General well, but Mme de Montmorin, the wife of a royal minister standing beside Germaine, was pessimistic. 'You are wrong to rejoice,' she said to Germaine. 'This will be the source of great misfortune to France and to us.' She was right, as far as she and her family were concerned: she would die on the scaffold beside one of her sons; another son drowned himself; her husband and one daughter died in prison and another daughter died before she was thirty.

Maximilien Robespierre was invited to Necker's Versailles residence later that summer. Deputies to the National Assembly* were much in demand in the grand salons of Paris and Versailles. 'His features were ignoble, his skin pale, his veins of a greenish colour,' Germaine recalled. 'He supported the most absurd propositions with a coolness that had the air of conviction.' From the start, Robespierre saw himself as France's saviour. '*La patrie est en danger*,' he had written in April 1789. 'Let us fly to its aid.' A provincial lawyer from a modest but comfortable background (at the start of the revolution he signed his name using the aristocratic 'de'), he became a regular speaker at the National Assembly and was already attracting attention for his lofty democratic principles, arguing in favour of freedom of the press and insisting suffrage should be granted to all men, including servants and the poor; he did not mention votes for women.

Alongside Germaine's friends Lafayette and the Lameth brothers, Robespierre was a prominent member of a club formed at Versailles in the summer of 1789 by a group of progressive deputies with the purpose of debating issues before they came before the National Assembly. The Society of the Friends of the Constitution would become known as the Jacobin Club because, when the Assembly moved to Paris that October, they hired the hall of a Dominican (*Jacobin*, in French slang) monastery on the rue Saint-Honoré, almost opposite the *manège* where the Assembly met.

As her opinions of Robespierre and Mirabeau demonstrate, Germaine's view of politics was intensely personal, coloured by her first-hand observation of people and her sense of being at the centre of events. She called Clermont-Tonnerre 'my speaker', meaning speaker on her behalf in the Assembly, and in September 1789 she scribbled an urgent note to Monsieur de Staël in Versailles to find out whether or

---

* The Estates-General had changed its name to the 'National Assembly' on 17 June 1789, three days before the Tennis Court Oath in which the deputies swore to remain in session until France had a constitution; over the next three years it would become, successively, the Constituent Assembly and the Legislative Assembly. As contemporaries usually did, in the main I have referred to it as the National Assembly.

not 'my bill on the veto' (whether or not the king should have a veto over legislation in the new constitution, and if so how strong a veto) had been won; as she hoped, the 'Necker–Lafayette' partial veto had been adopted.

She had cause to feel possessive. In July, committees were created to compose France's first constitution, and on them sat many of Germaine's friends including Talleyrand, Lafayette and the Lameths. In August they produced the Declaration of the Rights of Man and the Citizen which established in its first article that all men are born and live free and equal. Torture and arbitrary imprisonment were abolished and innocence was presumed; freedom of the press and of worship was declared; citizens were to bear the weight of taxation according to their abilities; the army was defined as a public force and access to the officers' ranks opened up to non-nobles.

Even though the real work of composing a constitution was still to come, these basic liberties were exactly those for which Germaine had been agitating behind the scenes and, looking back on the achievements of this period, she remained certain that politics and society had never been so intimately or valuably connected. 'As political affairs were still in the hands of the elite, all the vigour of liberty and all the grace of old-fashioned manners were united in the same people,' she wrote. 'Men of the Third Estate, distinguished by their enlightened ideas and their talents, joined those gentlemen who were prouder of their own merit than of the privileges of their class; and the highest questions society has ever considered were dealt with by minds the most capable of understanding and debating them.'

This self-referential, unabashedly elitist idea of 'communication of superior minds among themselves' was the spirit of Germaine de Staël's salon, and, though it was instrumental in bringing the revolution into being, it would have little place in it in the years to come. As Germaine herself said, from the day that the National Assembly moved from Versailles to Paris in the autumn of 1789, 'its goal was no longer liberty, but equality'.

2

FILLE SANS-CULOTTE

Pauline Léon

Everywhere, just like warriors,
We carried off the laurels and the glory,
And roused hopes for the glory of France.

Poissard song, autumn 1789

La Femme du Sans-Culotte: what Pauline Léon may have looked like

LIKE A CAROUSEL abandoned to centrifugal force, with respect for
the government and tradition dissolving, France spun into revolution
in 1789. The harvest the previous year had been destroyed by late hail
storms and the winter was the worst for nearly a century. Bread prices
had doubled and people were dying of starvation. Bands of brigands –
and horrifying rumours of their brutality – swept through the countryside, taking advantage of the chaos caused by the abolition of feudal
rights and dues, and the vacuum once filled by the king's heavily
centralized government.

Alongside Germaine de Staël's gilded cocoon teemed another
world. Marie-Antoinette's friend, the painter Élisabeth Vigée-Lebrun,
was terrified in the summer of 1789 when she looked out of her window
to find sans-culottes shaking their fists at her from the street and
jumping on to the running-board of her carriage, shouting, 'Next year,
you'll be behind the carriages and we'll be the ones inside!' When
émigrés, including Vigée-Lebrun, began leaving France, the savage
insults of passers-by floated in the wake of their heavy-laden carriages:
'There go some more on the way out, those dogs of aristocrats.'

Although Germaine and her friends passionately believed in
reform, their ideas were largely conceptual. The aristocracy numbered
several hundred thousand in a population of twenty-eight million;
perhaps five thousand nobles lived in Paris, a city of about 550,000
inhabitants, in 1790. Isolated from the rest of France in their magnificent *hôtels* and crested carriages, the only common people with whom
they came into contact tame peasants or liveried servants, they had
little comprehension of what life was like for ordinary men and women.
Rich and poor viewed each other as utterly alien beings; it seemed all

they had in common was their cynicism and their disaffection with the king and his government. The rich saw the poor as barely human – savage beings for whom it was certainly not worth stopping one's carriage if they had had the bad luck to have been run over – while the poor viewed the rich as frivolous, mannered and cruel.

Popular responses to the political upheavals taking place in Paris were marked by a defiant, unrestrained combination of violence and delight: 'no riotous scene ... did not have its festive aspect,' writes Mona Ozouf in her study of revolutionary festivals, and there was 'no collective celebration without a groundswell of menace'. *Poissard*, the Parisian slang dialect of the markets, exemplified this peculiarly French juxtaposition of levity and deadly seriousness in 'comic and abusive verse, rhymed insults and a kind of tough, threatening talk'. Its jeering tone was fashionable among slumming aristocrats in the 1770s and 1780s, who performed *poissard* plays in their private theatres without any conception of the true resentment that lay beneath its rough mockery.

The typical *poissarde* woman, literally a fish-seller, but including other market women, seamstresses or laundresses, was described in the revolutionary newspaper *Père Duchesne* as a plain speaker, a frugal housekeeper and a chaste wife. She had an ugly face and despised finery, and was devoted to her family and capable of defending it savagely if need be. Her children were raised according to the political principles she and her husband held, a tradition of fierce egalitarianism and independence, and she claimed the right to sign petitions, fill the audience chambers of the National Assembly and denounce those she considered unpatriotic, deliberately addressing them by the familiar '*tu*' rather than the more formal '*vous*'. Although the revolution was marked by violent anticlericalism, these women often continued to revere Mary, '*la bonne petite mère*'. Many of them lived in the faubourg Saint-Antoine, just east of the Bastille on the outskirts of Paris.

Common women were praised by revolutionaries, generally from middle-class backgrounds themselves, for their shrewdness, swift judgement and moral fibre. 'The women of the people hide a fine character which finds expression when needed,' wrote one patriotic journalist in 1789. They were barometers of the political environment: if things were really bad, the market women would be restless.

The activist Pauline Léon came from a typical lower-middle-class faubourg background – not the poorest of the poor but far from prosperous. Her father was a chocolate-maker – an artisan working in a luxury market supplying the rich – and, she said, a philosopher, who had raised his children according to his principles and without prejudices. She could read and write, although her family's modest means had not allowed for much education; girls from her background might have learned to read the mass in French and vespers in Latin, and then begun working in their early teens. When her father died, her mother took over his business and raised their five children, with help from Pauline, apparently the eldest.

Pauline was thirty-one and unmarried at the start of the revolution, still living at home and working with her mother, when the new ideas inflamed her. Mothers with young children stayed at home, so the politically minded women on the streets were either young and single, like Pauline, or middle-aged, sometimes widows, perhaps with sons fighting the revolution's foreign enemies at the front while their mothers and sisters guarded against the fatherland's 'aristocratic' enemies at home. Unlike in the salons of the nobility, sans-culotte men and women, though in accord ideologically, led separate political lives during the revolution. Radical lower-class women protested together, went to political clubs together and watched the guillotine's blade falling together.

But the women of Paris began participating in the revolution long before Madame Guillotine cast her shadow over the city. In January 1789, the women of the Third Estate addressed a petition to the king, a mirror of the *cahiers* the men of the nation had been asked by the king to draw up at the same time, stating the grievances and expectations of their classes and regions. At a time 'when everyone is trying to assert his titles and his rights, when some people are worrying about recalling centuries of servitude and anarchy, when others are making every effort to shake off the last links which still bind them to the feudal system', they began, neatly summing up both the political situation and women's contradictory status in France, should not women, 'continual objects of the admiration and scorn of men . . . make their voice[s] heard?'

Common women, they explained, had no fortunes or education, and were doomed to becoming prey for seducers if they were pretty or to unhappy dowerless marriages if they were not. Their plight was exacerbated by parents often refusing to help their daughters financially, preferring to concentrate their resources on their sons. Because of these disadvantages, the women had three demands. First, they requested that women's trades, such as embroidery and dressmaking, be reserved for women; 'if we are left at least with the needle and the spindle, we promise never to handle the compass or the square'. Second, they asked that prostitutes, 'the weakest among us', be required to wear a mark of identification so that honest women were not mistaken for them. They added tartly that if prostitutes did wear distinctive dress, 'one would run the risk of seeing too many women in the same colour'. Finally, they implored the king to set up free schools where girls could learn religion and ethics. Science would not appear on the curriculum: teaching women such a 'masculine' subject would be flying in the face of nature, and would only make female students stupidly proud, not to mention producing unfaithful wives and bad mothers. 'We ask to be enlightened, to have work, not in order to usurp men's authority,' they assured Louis, 'but in order to be better esteemed by them.'

The escalation of the revolution's pace throughout the spring of 1789 thrilled working-class women as much as men. Inflamed by a potent combination of resentment, patriotism and the desire for change, Pauline Léon said she felt 'the liveliest enthusiasm' when the Bastille, symbol of royal despotism, fell. Even though she was a woman she 'did not remain idle'. She was on the streets from morning till evening, 'inciting citizens against the partisans of tyranny, [urging them] to despise and brave aristocrats, barricading streets, and inciting the cowardly to leave their homes to come to the aid of the fatherland in danger'. France was not yet at war; the danger Léon refers to came from counterrevolutionaries – internal, rather than external, enemies.

Pauline does not say whether she saw the prison taken and the few prisoners it contained liberated on 14 July, but many women were present. The idealistic young British writer Helen Maria Williams, who moved to Paris in 1790, heard that women had patrolled the streets, as Pauline described doing, and brought their sons and husbands at the Bastille food and drink, 'and, with a spirit worthy of Roman matrons, encouraged them to go on'.

Throughout the remainder of the summer of 1789, Parisian women and girls wearing the white dresses they reserved for ceremonies and wreathed in orange blossom paraded in thanksgiving for the Bastille's fall, demonstrating their gratitude 'for the happy revolution which had just taken place'. They made offerings of bouquets, bread, brioches and vines at their local churches, just as liberal bourgeoises donated their silver and trinkets to the nation's bankrupt treasury, as expressions of their patriotism.

On the feast of Saint-Louis at the end of August, the market women went to Versailles with the mayor and magistrates of the city of Paris, as they did every year, to present a bouquet to the king. Marie-Antoinette, well aware she was loathed by the common people for her foreignness, extravagance and perceived corruption, both physical and political, was cold and unfriendly to the deputations. Utterly resistant to the idea of reform, she was visibly shaking with rage when Lafayette presented the captains of the newly formed National Guard to her, and the fishwives also noticed how poorly they were received.

In the summer of 1789, aged thirty-two (a year older than Pauline Léon), Lafayette had been made commandant of the National Guard, but it was a complicated role to play. Despite his immense personal popularity, he found it hard to please both the royalists and the 'patriots'. As Germaine de Staël said, he supported the king 'more from duty than attachment', but he was drawn 'towards the principles of the democrats whom he was obliged to resist'. Neither group trusted him. Pauline Léon attested that she was suspicious of Lafayette from the time he took office. In her eyes he was one of the internal enemies of the state, a counterrevolutionary in disguise; aristocrats, who had oppressed the nation for so long, could not be trusted. Caught between two extremes, anxious to satisfy both his liberal principles and his responsibilities to his office, Lafayette would end by fulfilling neither.

The National Guard he commanded was made up of the members of various volunteer militias, especially former members of the *garde française*, gathered together as a regular force and charged with defending the decrees of the new National Assembly on the one hand

and protecting the people from revolution's excesses on the other. They had to pay for their own muskets and red, white and blue uniforms, so most were relatively prosperous. Progressive patriotism was their unifying sentiment. Germaine de Staël's army officer lover, Louis de Narbonne, would become commander of a regiment of the National Guard in Besançon the following summer.

The effects of recent failed harvests, droughts and bitter winters had accumulated and despite an adequate harvest in 1789 a flour short-age became cruelly evident on the streets of Paris as September wore on. In the public mind, the subsistence crisis was intimately connected to the political crisis. The despised representatives of the Crown were held responsible for the people's hunger; it was thought that bread was being withheld from them in order to crush their spirit of revolt. Lafayette, who was responsible for ensuring that supplies reached the Parisian markets, was a particular focus for their resentment.

Women began stopping carts of grain and dragging them to the Hôtel de Ville for distribution. On 17 September, after another morning when riflemen had been stationed at the bakers' to prevent rioting when the bread was handed out, they requested an audience with the mayor, saying 'men didn't understand anything about the matter [the lack of grain] and they wanted to play a role in affairs'.

The issue of the veto (what Germaine de Staël had described as 'her' veto – Louis was delaying his assent to his new constitutional role, approved by the National Assembly on 10 September) exacerbated popular discontent and suspicion of the king and queen, who were scathingly known as Monsieur and Madame Veto. In revolutionary newspapers, firebrand journalists like Jean-Paul Marat urged their readers to 'sweep away the corrupt, the royal pensioners and the devious aristocrats, intriguers and false patriots. You have nothing to expect from them except servitude, poverty and desolation.'

Given the atmosphere of starvation and destitution, an extravagant dinner held at Versailles on 1 October by the royal bodyguard was ill conceived. An additional regiment from Flanders had been summoned to Versailles as a precautionary measure, and the royal forces extended to them their traditional welcome of a banquet. Unusually, the king and queen made an appearance, bringing the gold-ringleted dauphin with them; toast after toast was drunk, royalist songs were increasingly blurrily sung, and court ladies handed out cockades in white and black, respectively – the Bourbon (for Louis) and Hapsburg (for Marie-Antoinette) colours.

The next day, the liberal press denounced this royalist 'orgy', repeating the words of one officer who had said, 'Down with the cockade of colours [the tricolour]; may everyone take the black, that's the fine one.' It was said the guards had stamped underfoot the tricolour cockade, since the fall of the Bastille in July the potent emblem of a new, reformed France. Marie-Antoinette later expressed her 'enchantment' with the guards' banquet, and this was taken to mean that she was enchanted by the insult offered to France. Black and white cockades seen on the streets of Paris began provoking fistfights; the people grew still hungrier.

At dawn on the morning of 5 October, a young market woman began beating a drum in the street in central Paris. By seven o'clock, perhaps two thousand women had gathered in front of the Hôtel de Ville, calling out for bread and for the punishment of the royal bodyguard. They broke into the building, threatening to burn all the council's papers, combing it for weapons, blockading the doors – refusing to let any men inside on the grounds that the city council was made up of aristocrats – and denouncing the mayor Jean-Sylvain Bailly, and Lafayette, who they said deserved to be strung up from streetlights for not ensuring that Paris had bread. They declared that 'men were not strong enough to be revenged on their enemies and that they [the women] would do better'.

This violent appropriation of previously proscribed places 'was the first delight of the revolution': 'the beating down of gates, the crossing of castle moats, walking at ease in places where one was once forbidden to enter'. For ordinary women, restricted by their gender as well as by their status, these new liberties were all the more potent. What is evident in the accounts of these October days is that the women revelled in their own boldness and determination. They were driven to act by desperation, but they seem to have surprised even themselves, and they were proud of what they did.

Men, who had failed in their duties as administrators and providers, were deliberately barred from the Hôtel de Ville. The only man the women allowed in was a National Guardsman called Stanislas Maillard. At first, because of his black coat (members of the Third Estate wore plain black coats), they thought he was a councillor; but then they recognized him as a *vainqueur*, one who had participated in the sacking of the Bastille, and opened the doors to him.

Despite Maillard's initial efforts to dissuade them, the women insisted they were going to Versailles to present their demands to the king and the National Assembly. Maillard decided to go with them, explaining to a colleague that in this way warning could be sent ahead of the crowd of angry women and control maintained over them. He was also sympathetic to their cause, as were many National Guardsmen who were husbands or sons of those protesting. Lafayette, knowing this, tried to keep the National Guard under his command from joining up with the marchers for as long as possible, fearing violence.

Another Guardsman, known as Fournier 'l'Américain', who defied 'the sycophant Lafayette' to assemble troops to follow the women to Versailles, believed, like the women, that royalists were plotting to starve the nation into submission. Writing during the Reign of Terror, he remembered rallying straggling women in Paris with the words, 'Your children are dying of hunger; if your husbands are perverted and cowardly enough not to want to go look for bread for them, then the only thing left for you to do is to slit their throats.'

Maillard began beating a drum to call the women to order, but the area in front of the Hôtel de Ville was too small to hold them all and they moved their assembly point first to the Place Louis XV at the end of the Tuileries gardens and then spilled over into the open Place d'Armes on the Champs Élysées. Children blowing bugles and ringing bells went round the market area of Les Halles to assemble the throng. Women converged on the site carrying makeshift weapons like pitchforks and broomsticks as well as pikes, swords and muskets. 'The town is in alarm,' reported Gouverneur Morris. 'All carriages were stopped', and any passing woman was swept along by the crowd and 'obliged to join the female mob'. Later, respectable bourgeois women would testify that they had been forced to join the crowd; onlookers were surprised to catch sight of pale-complexioned women in fine clothes alongside the rough market women.

Numbering by this stage about six thousand, the women set off for Versailles, fourteen kilometres distant, through driving rain. Maillard and six drummers headed the procession alongside two cannon, ridden by women. The cannon were taken for effect; they had no powder, but all the same Maillard persuaded the women to place them at the back of the cavalcade when they reached Versailles so as not to intimidate the townspeople. The marchers wore tricolour cockades and carried leafy branches, just as Camille Desmoulins's mob had three months earlier when they stormed the Bastille. They sang *poissard* songs such as the 'Motion of the Market Women of La Halle', which just tipped the balance between coarsely amusing and threatening:

> If the High-ups still make trouble
> Then the Devil confound them,
> And since they love gold so much
> May it melt in their traps –
> That's the sincere wish
> Of the Women Who Sell Fish.

With cries of '*Vive le roi!*' the women reached Versailles at about five in the afternoon, just as dusk was beginning to fall, marching down the broad *allée* that leads straight up to the palace. Germaine de Staël, who had driven to Versailles by the back roads as soon as she heard news of the march, had already arrived, but a reluctant Lafayette, at the head of the seditious National Guard, was some hours behind her. The great gates had been drawn across the palace entrance for the first time in its history. 'Every eye was turned towards the road that fronts the windows of the palace of Versailles,' recalled Germaine. 'We thought that the cannon might first be pointed against us, which occasioned us much alarm; yet not one woman thought of withdrawing in this great emergency.' Both inside and outside the palace women were preparing themselves to participate in history.

After much discussion, fifteen were chosen to appear with Maillard before the National Assembly. Maillard spoke for them, raising rumours of grain hoarding, which the women believed was an aristocratic plot. Deputy Robespierre, immaculate as usual, rose to his feet to confirm the rumours of hoarding. Maillard took the floor again, this time asking that the royal bodyguard be requested to adopt the tricolour cockade to make amends for the insult they were said to have made to it.

As he spoke, the women waiting outside flooded into the assembly hall, declaring that the bodyguards in the palace courtyard had fired on them. The mood in the hall became riotous, almost carnivalesque: the marchers levelled hostile remarks at the Bishop of Paris, threatened to murder a guard, derided the king's failure to sign the Declaration of Rights and spread their wet clothes out to dry. One woman sat in the chair reserved for the president of the Assembly; others tried to participate in the debate and vote with the deputies. They mocked the rituals of government, shouting insults so as to disrupt proceedings, some dropping off to sleep on the deputies' benches.

Outside, the town of Versailles had shut down. One of Marie-Antoinette's ladies-in-waiting tried to get back into the palace at about nine on the evening of the 5th, but a National Guard sentry from Versailles recognized her at the gates and sent her back to her lodgings. 'You must not be seen in the street,' he told her. 'You have nothing to fear for your friends, but there will not be a single lifeguardsman [royal bodyguard] left tomorrow morning.'

Meanwhile the Assembly's president, Jean-Joseph Mounier, had taken a deputation of women to see the king himself. Much impressed by Louis's paternal sympathy and concern (he fetched smelling-salts for a seventeen-year-old flower-girl, chosen as spokeswoman, who fainted at his feet), they returned to the assembly hall bearing a signed order for any delayed wheat to be delivered to Paris immediately. Mounier and some of the women now went back to Paris to inform the people of the king's promises; the remainder stayed in Versailles, the lucky ones finding beds in stables and coach-houses, others huddling in the lee of buildings wrapped in their damp clothes. Many of them wept with exhaustion and confusion, saying they 'had been forced to march and did not know why they were there', miles from home and without shelter on a cold, damp night.

The king then agreed without qualification to sign the Declaration of the Rights of Man and the Citizen, which he had delayed doing for almost a month. He consulted his ministers about whether he should resist the hostile approaching National Guard by force, or flee, and decided to do neither. 'Habits of formality' stopped him escaping, then or later, according to the daughter of an aristocrat who urged flight.

When Lafayette arrived with the factious Guard it was almost midnight. Versailles was quiet, but wide awake: the tinderbox still smouldered. Alone and unarmed, the general was permitted into the palace to see the king, and told him – after swearing to die at his feet – that if Louis would guarantee food for Paris, allow the patriotic National Guard to replace the royal bodyguard, and agree to move his family, court and government from Versailles to Paris, the National Guard would be satisfied and a clash between them and the royal bodyguard would be averted. The king said he needed to think about the last proposal. Lafayette reported back to the National Assembly, then to his soldiers and officers, and spent the next few hours trying to maintain calm before snatching a few hours' sleep on a sofa at his grandfather's house.

Just before dawn, a crowd of armed men and women broke into the palace compound. Storming into the royal apartments, they called for the blood of the 'Austrian whore' (Marie Antoinette had been an Austrian princess before she became the French queen). Two soldiers were killed and their heads paraded around the courtyard on pikes. They chased the barefoot, frantic queen through the Hall of Mirrors to the king's apartments, where the terrified royal family were reunited; outside, the National Guard finally turned against the mob and stemmed their advance.

Lafayette, awoken by the mayhem, ran to the palace. At his suggestion Louis took his family on to the narrow balcony outside his grandfather's state bedroom and, addressing the crowd, promised to entrust himself to the love of his subjects, to their cheers below. Then Lafayette persuaded Marie-Antoinette to step out in front of the crowd alone, turned to her, and kissed her hand; the volatile crowd suddenly turned royalist, and erupted with cries of 'Long live the queen!' as well as, brandishing loaves on pikes, 'We have bread!'

For the moment, the crisis had been averted.

Later that morning, Lafayette escorted the royal family back to Paris through the rain at the heart of a procession of perhaps sixty thousand people flanked at either end by the National Guard. Ministers and deputies marched too, alongside flour wagons from the king's own stores and triumphant market women arm in arm with Guardsmen whose caps they were wearing. Green branches were tied to rifle butts, the two cannon brought from the Hôtel de Ville the morning before were wreathed in laurel, and the two murdered bodyguards' heads were carried aloft on pikes beside bloody loaves of bread. Many women lifted their skirts and flashed their bottoms as they passed, a traditional expression of female mockery and contempt. They were bringing the baker, the baker's wife and the baker's boy (the king, queen and dauphin) to Paris, sang the mob.

The harlequin makeup of the crowd during those October days excited much comment at the time. The eight-year-old daughter of a courtier remembered the streets of Versailles flooded with 'horrible-looking people, uttering wild cries'. Edmund Burke, from the safety of England, denounced the 'horrid yells, and shrilling screams, and frantic dances, and infamous contumelies, and all the unutterable abomin-ations of the furies of hell, in the abused shape of the vilest of women'. 'Probably,' responded Mary Wollstonecraft icily, 'you mean women who gained a livelihood by selling vegetables or fish, who never had any advantages of education.'

Some of the October women undoubtedly were violent, blood-thirsty and deliberately intimidating. On the way to Versailles, a few shouted that they were going to the palace 'to bring back the queen's head'. When the palace was stormed, some were heard calling for the queen's liver to be fricasséed. On the whole, though, it was not until the National Guard arrived late on the night of the 5th that the mood turned bloody.

Mme de Tourzel, governess to the royal children, thought that many of the 'women' who entered the palace early on the morning of the 6th were men in female clothing. It was not unusual for eighteenth-century Frenchmen to adopt women's clothes and women's names, such as Mère Folle, when demonstrating for political or economic purposes; peasants had dressed as women and blacked their faces to attack surveyors during a land dispute in the Beaujolais in the 1770s. Like *poissard* humour, like the joy taken in entering forbidden places and challenging long-established authorities, this grim fancy dress was another element of black carnival, the combination of festivity and menace that characterized the popular revolution.

Most of the marchers were proud of their participation, and saw the precedent set by women seizing the political initiative as a positive one. The following month, a woman writer in *Les Étrennes Nationales des Dames* hailed the Parisiennes for proving that they were at least as courageous and enterprising as the men. 'We suffer more than men who with their declarations of rights leave us in the state of inferiority and, let's be truthful, of slavery in which they've kept us so long,' she continued. 'If there are husbands *aristocratic* enough in their households to oppose the sharing of patriotic honours, we'll use the arms we've just employed with such success against them.'

The *poissardes*, for their part, had a new song:

> To Versailles, like braggarts,
> We dragged our cannon.
> Although we were only women,
> We wanted to show a courage beyond reproach.
> We made men of spirit see that just like them, we weren't afraid;
> Guns and musketoons across our shoulders . . .

Pauline Léon did not say whether she had been in Versailles on 5 and 6 October, but she did say that Lafayette's behaviour on those days, the evident conflict between his political principles and his loyalty to the king, and his efforts to bring about a compromise between the royalists and the populists, had confirmed her mistrust of him. She saw him as a traitor, and her words echo Fournier l'Américain's portrait of a wretched, perfidious general stalling for time to save his king at the cost of his countrymen: 'Since that time [the women's march] I have sworn eternal hatred of him, and I have used all possible means to unmask him.'

The march on Versailles gave the women of Paris like Pauline Léon a new political self-confidence. The guts and initiative they had shown gave credence to their demands. Ceaselessly they urged the continuance of the work of the revolution. Eighteen months later a group from Saint-Germain, mostly widows and single women, addressed the Cordeliers' Club, a popular revolutionary assembly which had met, since April 1790, on the rue des Cordeliers. Léon may have been among them: she lived in Saint-Germain and regularly attended the club, which met at the bottom of her street.

'Watch with more exactitude and severity than ever over the governing of the state,' they exhorted the Cordeliers. If Frenchmen failed in their duty, if they trusted perfidious tyrants – like Lafayette – who hoped to return the French people to slavery, the women swore that they themselves would defy established social roles to fight in defence of liberty.

> We have consoled ourselves for our inability to contribute to the public good by exerting our most intense efforts to raise the spirits of our children to the heights of free men. But if you deceive our hope, then indignation, sorrow, despair will impel and drag us into public places . . . Then we shall save the Fatherland, or, dying with it, we will uproot the torturous memory of seeing you unworthy of us.

Like Germaine de Staël, these women made a point of accepting feminine political passivity as essential to society's greater good; but they were utterly committed to the revolutionary cause. They did not want rights for themselves, but they wanted rights for all Frenchmen. If men failed to deliver the new liberties they had promised, they insisted, women would not be afraid to step on to the public stage as they had in October 1789.

All over France, common women gathered together in clubs of different types to demonstrate their patriotism and their devotion to the revolution. Some dared call for girls to be better educated; others demanded the privilege of fighting for the *patrie*, or rights of consent over marriage and inheritance. In Saint-Sever, a Mme Lafurie argued that custom did not prove the law: contrary to popular belief, she declared, women were neither too weak to work nor too depraved to play a role in public life.

Twenty-seven cities had auxiliary clubs of the Fraternal Society of the Friends – calling themselves *Amies* rather than *Amis* – of the Constitution. In Breteuil in August 1790 a group of unmarried 'Sisters of the Constitution' offered a hand-sewn national flag to the town; the women of Alais formed a Patriotic Club which met to read the decrees of the National Assembly to their children. Female companies of the National Guard were formed across the country: at Creil, at Angers, at Villeneuve-la-Guyard, Aunay, Bergerac and Limoges. In the summer of 1791, the women of Les Halles, Paris's central market, donated to the National Assembly their guild treasure, in silver plate and cash, amounting to almost fifteen hundred livres. Before the revolution, they said, 'all politics and all refinements' had been foreign to them; since then, 'the idea of liberty [had] enlarged souls, inflamed spirits, electrified hearts', and they were willing to make any sacrifice to acquire and safeguard it.

Most rural Frenchwomen were not revolutionaries; all they wanted was bread to feed their children and fuel for their fires. Counter-revolutionary sentiments were strong in the west of the country. In September 1790, women protesting at the price of bread cried, 'We want to save the monks! Long live the clergy! Long live the nobility!' A royalist newspaper, *L'Ami du Roi*, reported in 1791 that 'a Frenchwoman inflamed with love for her country' had suggested forming a club of female 'Amazons' to defend France and the king.

Louis-Marie Prudhomme, editor of the left-wing *Révolutions de Paris*, wrote in November 1791 that many of his female readers were complaining of being excluded from participating in the revolution. Some claimed that in ancient Gaul women had had a voice in government and questioned why these rights were not returned to them. Prudhomme responded savagely: 'we do not venture to come and teach you how to love your children, spare us the trouble then of coming to our clubs and expounding our duties as citizens to us'. His chauvinism was not unusual, and would only become more widespread. Jacobin Clubs across the country increasingly resisted women's attempts to participate in their activities, fearing what they saw as their corrupting influence; in Tonneins, the local Jacobins succeeded in segregating the men and women watching their debates and in banning women and men from conversing with each other on their premises.

The month after the women of Saint-Germain addressed the Cordeliers, Pauline Léon presented to the National Assembly a petition bearing over three hundred signatures. In the event of a foreign war, she argued, women would be left defenceless at home; they needed weapons in order to defend the *patrie* from its hidden, internal enemies. 'Your predecessors deposited the Constitution as much in our hands as in yours,' she argued. 'Oh, how to save it, if we have no arms to defend it from the attacks of its enemies?'

Women did not want to abandon their homes and families, she insisted, but having been 'raised to the ranks of *citoyennes* [citizennesses]', having 'sampled the promises of liberty', they could never again submit to 'slavery'; the irony of her argument was that the 'rank' of *citoyenne* carried with it neither civic liberties nor political rights. Politicized by the march to Versailles in October 1789, Léon and her associates claimed not the vote but a greater role in the defence of the nation. She demanded 'the honour of sharing their [men's] exhaustion and glorious labours and of making tyrants see that women also have blood to shed for the service of the fatherland in danger'.

3

CLUBISTE

Théroigne de Méricourt

July 1789–August 1790

[Théroigne] crossed the Assembly floor with the light
pace of a panther and mounted the tribune. Her pretty,
thought-filled head seemed to shine among the
depressing, apocalyptic figures of Danton and Marat.

CAMILLE DESMOULINS

Mademoiselle Théroigne

ONE WOMAN popularly thought to have been willing to shed her own blood on behalf of the fatherland, as Pauline Léon hoped to, was the former courtesan Théroigne de Méricourt. Although she was mentioned only five times, in contradictory reports, in the nearly four hundred official depositions on the women's march to Versailles in October 1789, Théroigne was described again and again by nineteenth-century historians of the revolution as having been at the vanguard of the mob storming the palace, astride a jet-black charger and dressed in a riding-habit 'the colour of blood', with her sabre unsheathed – as the poet Baudelaire later put it, '*amante de carnage*'. For these romantics, she represented all that was most savage and most noble about the revolution: passionate and untamed, and ultimately crushed by the forces she had helped unleash. Michelet called her 'the fatal beauty of the revolution', '*la belle, vaillante, infortunée Liégoise*'; and so she was, although he exaggerated most of the facts of her life.

Anne-Josèphe Terwagne (or Théroigne) was born into a family of prosperous peasants in 1762 in Marcourt (or Méricourt) near Liège, in the Ardennes region of the Low Countries, at the time just over the French border in Austria. Anne-Josèphe's childhood was a desperately unhappy one. Her mother died when she was five, and the little girl was initially sent to live with an aunt in Liège, a hundred kilometres from her home, where her two younger brothers remained. The aunt sent her to a convent to learn dressmaking, but soon stopped paying Anne-Josèphe's keep there and took her in as a maid, treating her cruelly. Anne-Josèphe returned home when her father remarried, but her stepmother, busy with children of her own, did not make her welcome; her father's fortunes were also declining rapidly.

At thirteen, Anne-Josèphe sent one of her brothers to one branch of her mother's family and she and her other brother went to live with her mother's parents. Again she found herself unloved, forced to do heavy work, the victim of injustice and neglect. She returned to her aunt's, but received the same ill-treatment as before, and ran away once more.

This time she set out alone, working as a cowherd and then as a nursemaid before finding a post as companion to a woman in Anvers. Mme Colbert was the first person to show the sixteen-year-old Anne-Josèphe any kindness. She taught her to write, encouraged her to read, and arranged for her to study singing and the pianoforte, at first so that she could accompany her daughter and then because she showed talent. In an atmosphere of affection and comfort, Anne-Josèphe blossomed, and dreamed of a glorious musical career.

When she was twenty, a young English army officer seduced her and then reneged on his promise to marry her when he came of age, instead making her his mistress and living with her between London and Paris. He did provide well for her, giving her 10,000 louis which she invested carefully, but, in the language of the day, she was ruined, and could no longer hope for marriage and respectability. For the next few years Anne-Josèphe lived uneasily, as her modern biographer puts it, 'suspended between literary bohemianism, polite society and moral degradation'. Although she knew she would never change her lover's libertine ways, their liaison continued; she was also kept in some style by the rich, elderly and unpleasant marquis de Persan, whose advances she later insisted she had evaded. She called herself Mlle Campinado, after a branch of her mother's family, and regularly attended the opera alone, 'covered in diamonds, in a large box'.

Her air of melancholy mystery was not contrived. She gave birth to a daughter, whom her English lover refused to acknowledge and who died in 1788 of smallpox. An affair with an Italian tenor ended badly; then she fell in love with another Italian singer, a celebrated castrato and, somewhat surprisingly, seducer, called Ferdinand-Justin Tenducci, who encouraged her hopes for a musical career. She followed him to Genoa, and although their connection ended in the courts, stayed there alone for a year.

Anne-Josèphe returned to Paris in May 1789, just before the Bastille fell. Although as yet she knew no one involved in the coming revolution and was unfamiliar with the ideas behind it, her unhappiness with her lot in pre-revolutionary France had prepared her to love liberty instantly and instinctively. She was enthralled by the 'general effervescence' she sensed around her, recognizing that her chance to change her own life could come at this moment of crisis and opportunity.

While the nineteenth-century poet Lamartine described her 'descending into the streets' on 14 July, 'her beauty like a banner to the multitude', in fact she said she did not witness the main events of those days. On the evening of the day the Bastille fell, she and her maid went down on to the streets of Paris – her lodgings were a five-minute walk from the Palais Royal – and saw the crowds of men, some armed, some searching for arms. Afraid of attracting their attention, she returned to her rooms, unaware of what had taken place on the other side of the city. The next day she heard the news, and first saw people with green cockades. She immediately began wearing one herself, tucking the green leaves into her hat-band as a mark of support for Desmoulins and then, when leaves were replaced by the tricolour rosette as the sign of reform, she took the tricolour instead.

When the king came to Paris on 17 July and pinned the tricolour cockade to his hat outside the Hôtel de Ville, demonstrating his surrender to the forces of change, Anne-Josèphe walked in the rapturous crowd ahead of him. She was wearing the costume that was to make her famous, a white riding-habit, or *amazone*, and round-brimmed hat. This choice of severely masculine dress was deliberate: she wanted 'to play the role of a man, because I had always been extremely humiliated by the servitude and prejudices, under which the pride of men holds my oppressed sex'.

Anne-Josèphe's resentment was not unusual. Even Germaine de Staël, an only child, an heiress, a member of the most progressive society in the land, as privileged and free as a woman could be in eighteenth-century France, railed against the discrimination that restricted her; many others, like Anne-Josèphe, had more to complain about. In 1788, the teen-aged Lucile Duplessis, before her marriage to the journalist Camille Desmoulins, had expressed her frustrations in her journal: 'How the months, the days, seem long to me, what a sad fate is woman's and how much do we suffer! Slavery, tyranny, that is our lot ... Nothing is fair for us! Ah! That they [men] would worship us less and set us free!' An unhappily married Mme Morel from Choiseul had 'set up the tricoloured cockade and preached liberty before her husband's face' in 1789, explicitly associating public with domestic tyranny. For women, the revolution's rejection of the paternal authority of the ancien régime state carried within it an implicit rejection of the private injustices they endured in their own lives.

For Anne-Josèphe, whose family had not wanted her, whose lovers had abandoned and betrayed her, the impression of being trapped by her sex was doubly strong. She was a fallen woman, living outside society and despised by decent women like the workers who had petitioned the king at the start of 1789. Men had tried only to buy or to use her. Her adored daughter's death and her own struggle, while she was in Genoa, with severe venereal disease, can only have increased her antipathy to her former life.

From the summer of 1789, Anne-Josèphe Terwagne, formerly Mlle Campinado, became simply Théroigne, using her real name as if to express a sense of coming into her true self. She sold some shares she had and pawned her jewels to fund her newly modest existence, proudly recoiled from any suggestion of impropriety – even, according to one report, scorning personal cleanliness, a mark of the 'professional coquette', as a political statement – and turned her back on her past. The revolution offered her a new life: 'the kept woman,' as Simon Schama phrases it, 'had become a free person'.

Nearly every day Théroigne walked in the Palais Royal, absorbing the new ideas of liberty and equality that she heard there. 'What most impressed me was the atmosphere of general benevolence; egoism seemed to have been banished, so that everyone spoke to each other, irrespective of distinctions [of rank],' she marvelled. 'During this moment of upheaval, the rich mixed with the poor and did not disdain to speak to them as equals.' Her private transformation was mirrored on the faces of the people she saw around her. 'Everyone's countenance seemed to me to have altered; each person had fully developed his character and his natural facilities,' she wrote. 'I saw many who, though covered in rags, had a heroic air.' Heroism seemed possible even for a woman with a past like hers; humiliation had been displaced by equality and opportunity.

So stirred was she by this spectacle that she decided to move to Versailles, where the National Assembly met, to watch their debates on the Declaration of the Rights of Man and the Citizen. She was overcome by the beauty and grandeur of the Assembly. Every day, wearing her *amazone*, Théroigne sat in the same seat in the visitors' gallery, or tribune; every day she was the first to arrive and the last to leave. Although initially she could hardly follow the debates, little by little she began to understand the issues. 'My devotion to the revolution increased as I grew better informed and became convinced that right and justice were on the people's side.'

Théroigne was in her usual place in the tribune of the National Assembly on the afternoon of 5 October 1789 when the market women entered Versailles. She left before the session ended, perhaps unamused by the sight of the marchers debasing the hall she so revered with their *poissard* banter; but, wanting to see what was going on, she walked with a friend to her street corner and saw the Flanders regiment, the royal bodyguard and the female marchers with their cannon pass by. On her way home she saw three or four unhappy people who had not eaten for several days; she brought them some bread, and then went back to her lodgings for the night.

When she returned to the Assembly as usual at about six or half past the following morning and heard that it had been in session throughout the night, she went out into the crowds gathered in front of the palace to hear what they were saying. Dressed in a riding-habit, as usual – she had one in scarlet, one in white, and one in black – she mingled with the market women and soldiers before taking her seat in the tribune again.

In 1791, when she was held prisoner in Austria, Théroigne was cross-examined about those October days. The Austrian government, fearful of upheaval in their own territories and keen to defend Marie-Antoinette, wanted to know whether the duc d'Orléans had paid the women to go to Versailles and cause trouble. Théroigne, surprised at the allegation, replied that although she did not know Orléans she believed him to be a good patriot. They were also curious about stories of men dressed as women, but Théroigne had not seen any. When they asked her what she thought had caused the demonstration, she replied the people's enthusiasm for liberty and their devotion to it. It was clear from her deposition that it was not she who had led the bloodthirsty mob into the palace, bribed the marchers on behalf of Orléans or plotted to assassinate the queen, the crimes of which the Austrians and the French royalists, keen to find a scapegoat, suspected her.

When the National Assembly reopened in Paris later in October of 1789, Théroigne was in the tribune. She was becoming acquainted with the men whose newspaper articles and speeches she admired so fervently: Camille Desmoulins, the progressive journalist Jacques-Pierre Brissot and the handsome lawyer Jérôme Pétion.

Two other men now assumed a particular importance in her political life, neither of whom was likely to cause her to blush angrily, as she was known to do, at whispered insinuations. The Abbé Sieyès was a reserved, uncompromising intellectual much respected in the Assembly who bridged the gap, as did several of Théroigne's friends, between the aristocratic liberals of Germaine de Staël's salon and the more democratic milieu of men like Desmoulins, Pétion and Brissot. A passionate constitutionalist, his 1789 pamphlet *What Is the Third Estate?*, in which he argued that France's prosperity was derived solely from the people while the nobility and the clergy were just parasites on the nation, sold three hundred thousand copies and became the battle cry of the early radicals. To Théroigne, Sieyès was of all the deputies 'the most worthy of the recognition and esteem of the public'.

But it was with the sober mathematician Gilbert Romme, whom Théroigne had met in the gallery of the Assembly and who became a quasi-father figure to her, that she founded the short-lived Society of the Friends of the Law in January 1790. The association, which never numbered more than about twenty members, was dedicated to disseminating the Assembly's work to the people and teaching them their rights – exactly what Théroigne had had to learn herself when she began attending the Assembly's debates. It met first in Théroigne's lodgings near the Palais Royal and later in Romme's larger apartment. Théroigne was its only female member and its secretary. While the National Assembly struggled to create a workable constitution from the principles established by the Declaration of the Rights of Man and the Citizen, Théroigne and the Friends of the Law met to discuss the issues themselves.

From the Assembly's earliest debates, the issue of 'active' and 'passive' citizenship had been a provocative one. Active citizens had the right to vote for representative assemblies and to sit in them themselves; they had the freedom to make moral choices and to act independently. Passive citizens had to allow other people to think, speak and act for them. In order to sit in the National Assembly, a man had to pay annual taxes of a silver mark, or fifty days' wages for an unskilled worker; those who paid ten days' wages' worth of taxes qualified to sit in local government; those who paid three days' wages in tax were eligible to vote. It was not just the poor who were counted as passive citizens: even if they paid taxes, women, blacks, non-Catholics, domestic servants and actors were all forbidden the vote and considered incapable of participating in public life.

Robespierre was one of the earliest champions of universal male suffrage, arguing against the Abbé Sieyès's contention that property should define civil status. When the question of Jewish citizenship was raised in December 1789, Robespierre spoke out against persecution. 'We should bear in mind that it can never be politic,' he said, 'to condemn to humiliation and oppression a multitude of men who live in our midst.' In January 1790, after this debate, the Society of the Friends of the Law denounced discrimination against Jews. They called the law of the silver mark unjust and expressed the hope that an alternative way of distinguishing between citizens be found. They backed the complete freedom of the press, also being debated in the Assembly at the time.

At the last session of the month, in a discussion on natural rights, one member of the Society asserted that a man's rights over his wife and children 'are those of a protector over his protégés'. Despite Romme's progressive views on women's rights, Théroigne was the only member of the group to voice her objections to this statement; like Robespierre, most revolutionaries were too busy defending men's rights to concern themselves with women's. Although she never drafted her views on the matter, as she had intended, she put down in her notebook her thoughts on 'the liberty of women, who have the same natural rights as men, so that, as a consequence, it is supremely unjust that we have not the same rights in society'. The prejudice and discrimination she had encountered in her own life made her desire for freedom and equality all the more poignant.

One member of the Society of the Friends of the Law was Augustin Bosc d'Antic, a mineralogist and botanist. He had seen Théroigne in the galleries of the National Assembly in Versailles and written to a friend about a beautiful, patriotic stranger who had captured his imagination. A few months later, he joined the Society and may have confessed his feelings to her. If so, the former courtesan Théroigne, who in her new incarnation rejected any amorous advances 'with Spartan pride', did not respond.

Because of her regular attendance at the National Assembly, and because of her remarkable appearance which had so fascinated Bosc d'Antic – Théroigne's slight figure and delicate, gentle face contrasted unintentionally picturesquely with the strict cut of her signature *amazone* and plumed hat – she became a celebrity. The people and the deputies respected her, she said proudly, 'because of my patriotism and my personal conduct'. By the end of 1789, she was popularly known as '*la belle Liégoise*'.

The royalist press had different words for her: trollop, nymph, second-rate courtesan, *débauchée*, whore. The name Théroigne de Méricourt (which she never acknowledged) was first used in a November 1789 article in the royalist paper the *Apostles*: 'One might call her the muse of democracy, or else think of her as Venus giving lessons in public right. Her company is itself a college; her principles are those of the Porch. She would adopt those of the Arcades [the prostitutes' haunt in the Palais Royal], if the need arose.'

Théroigne was also the heroine of a satirical play entitled *Théroigne et Populus, ou le triomphe de la démocratie*, in which she was linked to a deputy to the National Assembly whose name, Populus, made him a cypher for the average Frenchman. Although the pair did not know one another, their names were often joined by journalists implying that Théroigne sold her favours to the entire French nation. Another royalist newspaper described her in lurid detail giving birth to the 'National embryo', with labour brought on by her excitement at Robespierre's eloquence, and suggested Talleyrand, Mirabeau or the young orator Antoine Barnave might be the imaginary infant's father.

It was at this time, too, that the rumours of Théroigne as a bloodthirsty warrior who had stormed the Bastille in July, then Versailles in October, became current. She was depicted in an engraving wearing, inevitably, the *amazone* in which, sword aloft and pistols smoking, she supposedly 'bested a brigade of bodyguards [at Versailles] . . . She was ever to be found where the unrest was greatest.' While the attacks against Théroigne in the press demonstrate the prominence she had attained – in a 1791 etching she represented French women alongside a generic cleric, nobleman and peasant as witnesses to the birth of France's new constitution – they are also evidence of how threatening emancipated women were to the majority of Frenchmen, from members of the political elite to the man in the street.

Women who were outsiders and did not have reputations to protect were practically the only ones who dared speak out against the social injustices women faced, and to which they were especially vulnerable – fallen women like Théroigne or Mary Wollstonecraft, living in Paris in the early 1790s with an American merchant to whom she was not married and with whom she had a child; actresses, who were viewed as little more than prostitutes; and foreigners.

It was no accident that Théroigne, although she counted among her male acquaintances friends of both the liberal aristocrat Germaine de Staël and the republican bourgeoise Manon Roland, never met either woman. She would not have been welcome in their worlds. The aristocratic adulteresses Germaine de Staël and Thérésia de Fontenay were, arguably, greater sinners than the newly virtuous Théroigne, who had rejected her degrading past; but while they were embraced by society, she was despised by it.

Their already ambiguous moral roles freed female outsiders to express discontent with the status quo. This was partly because they had less to lose – no families to disown them, no legitimate children to disgrace, no respectability to sacrifice in the name of idealism – and partly because any woman who did have a voice in eighteenth-century France, from the queen down, was denounced for immorality.

Marie-Antoinette had been married at fourteen to the future Louis XVI, who had a medical condition that made sex almost impossible; their union was unconsummated for seven years. Despite living in a society which considered love affairs completely normal, she might in twenty years of marriage have taken a single lover (Axel von Fersen). Her actual sins were thus completely incommensurate with those of which she was accused by the revolutionary scandal-sheets: of sleeping with her brother-in-law and various ministers, not to mention fleets of footmen, and of lesbian orgies with her ladies-in-waiting during which she committed incest with her prepubescent son. These egregious crimes were salaciously reported alongside her real political 'crimes' – her influence over the king and her fear of the changes taking place in her world. The association between politics and pornography, which were sold alongside each other in the stalls lining the Seine and the shops of the Palais Royal, was a long-standing one; in 1748 Diderot had attacked Louis XV through the lubricious tale of a king who owned a magic ring that made women's vaginas speak.

Attacking the ancien régime meant, in one sense, attacking the power women were thought to wield from behind the scenes. Politically involved women, who were seen as preventing politics from being disinterested by promoting their favourites, were believed to contaminate both society and the state. For most revolutionaries, cleansing France of corruption could only be accomplished by preventing women from playing any kind of public role. Influenced by Rousseau, they believed that a society dominated by women was fundamentally tainted. In the ideal republic, according to their 'natural' roles, men would lead and women would serve. 'The reign of courtesans brought on the ruin of the nation; the power of queens consummated it,' wrote the journalist Prudhomme in 1791. Women, who 'are born for perpetual dependence and are gifted only with private virtues', should not be allowed to enter into public life.

By this thinking, any politicized woman, regardless of her private behaviour, was depraved and unnatural, and inventing lurid stories about her was a legitimate way of undermining her reputation and public influence. Although Théroigne was a revolutionary, and at this stage women's rights of citizenship were still on the constitutional table, her conduct was every bit as suspect as Marie-Antoinette's because they were both women. Théroigne became such a prominent figure because the idea of a former courtesan becoming a revolutionary campaigner was almost inconceivable at the time – and offered her opponents such irresistable ammunition with which to attack her.

The actress and writer Olympe de Gouges was another woman held in contempt by the press at the start of the revolution. Like Théroigne, she came from a humble background and had washed up as a kept woman in 1780s Paris – just as Lamartine had said of Théroigne, 'as the whirlwind attracts things of no weight'. Like Théroigne, she saw the revolution as an opportunity to jettison her unhappy past, reinventing herself as a prolific and enthusiastic political pamphlet-writer. As an animal-lover and a believer in reincarnation, her campaigns were occasionally eccentric but always benevolent. Gouges advocated the abolition of slavery, rights for illegitimate children (a cause close to her heart – she claimed to be the bastard daughter of a marquis) and cleaner streets, and proposed setting up maternity hospitals, a national theatre for women and public workshops for the unemployed. But both the republican and the royalist papers reviled her.

Actors and actresses like Olympe de Gouges, inhabiting the same demi-monde as Théroigne in her incarnation as Mlle Campinado, were until 1789 not only automatically excluded from political life but excommunicated from the Church. Because of this treatment, many were immediately sympathetic to the revolutionary cause. The theatre's new star, François-Joseph Talma, used his traditional end-of-season speech in the spring of 1789 to speak out against prejudice and servitude and express the hope that the Estates-General (soon to be the National Assembly) would rid France of the last vestiges of feudalism. Marie-Joseph Chénier, an habitué of Germaine de Staël's salon and a new friend of Théroigne's, wrote Talma's footlights speech as well as the hit play of 1789, *Charles IX*, in which Talma played the murderous, manipulative, imbecile monarch. Although the play was suppressed after only thirty-three performances, patriotic audiences continued to clamour for the crucial scene in which the king acknowledged his betrayal of his country and his honour.

Talma's politicization was tacit as well as outspoken, evident as much in the way he interpreted roles, the way he moved and dressed, as in the words he spoke. Ancien régime theatre and festivals were seen as tawdry and elitist; revolutionaries, again taking their cue from Rousseau, idealized naturalism, innocence and purity. In popular celebrations, this meant replacing artificial tableaux with pastoral *fêtes* modelled on village life: country dancing, fresh, simple food, branches of greenery and bunches of flowers instead of tinsel. In the theatre, it meant Talma.

He was the first actor to play his roles in authentic costumes rather than the tights and doublets of traditional theatre-wear. His friend the painter Jacques-Louis David, who often collaborated with Talma in set-design, congratulated him for making his Charles IX look like a Fouquet painting; when Talma played Rousseau's ghost to celebrate the fall of the Bastille, he wore the same clothes in which Rousseau was pictured in his memorial portraits; as Proculus in Voltaire's *Brutus*, in November 1790, David designed him a short toga modelled on antique statues, with bare legs, sandalled feet and cropped hair.

This desire to be genuine and uncontrived was revolutionary in itself. The liberal press contrasted Talma's Roman haircut with the powdered ringlets of the court party. Brissot's publication the *Patriote Français* declared it the only suitable republican hairstyle, praising its economy of money (hair-powder, made of flour, was unpatriotically wasteful) and time (elaborate aristocratic hair-dos took hours to perfect). 'It is care-free and so assures the independence of a person,' the paper continued, 'it bears witness to a mind given to reflection, courageous enough to defy fashion.' Even liberal society women stopped powdering their hair, letting it fall on to their shoulders in loose curls. Théroigne's iconic riding-habits were demonstrations of this same impulse towards free-thinking, simplicity and classlessness in appearance, with an added frisson of transgression – the idea of a woman in a man's clothes. By wearing such a deliberately masculine outfit, Théroigne imagined that she would be better respected by men: seen as a public woman, not a *femme publique*. She hoped looking less feminine would compel people to respond not to her appearance but to her words and conduct.

Under the ancien régime, people had been identified by their dress; in the new France, people were still defined by what they wore. Even though the ceremonial costumes of the three governing estates were abolished in October 1789, republican men continued to take pride in the unadorned black coats, breeches and shoes they had been required to wear as members of the Third Estate, in contrast to the glowing colours, velvet and lace of the other two estates. Théroigne urged her fellow-women to give up their luxuries, which were 'incompatible with liberty'.

Several ironies were concealed behind the cult of naturalism. In the first place, it was often as artfully contrived as any ancien régime salonnière's conversation: the great revolutionary orator Hérault de Séchelles had lessons in declamation from the actress Mlle Clairon, Germaine de Staël's elocution teacher; later Napoléon would be tutored by Talma. Secondly, when republicanism became stylish – Théroigne's *amazones* soon adorned many society figures – its original intention of being outside fashion was defeated.

The unhappiest side-effect of this craze for simplicity was the destruction of the stay-making, embroidery and silk-making industries, which put thousands of workers, principally women, out of work. Starchers and laundresses saw less business when plain muslin cravats replaced stiffened lace jabots; coiffeurs became redundant when smart ladies no longer wanted model ships to float in their headdresses. Lace-makers rioted in Normandy and Velay in 1793; Lyon, centre of the textile industry, was defiantly anti-revolutionary. After the revolution, the duc d'Orléans's mistress Félicité de Genlis recounted a conversation she overheard between an old stay-maker and an old hoop-maker bemoaning the new fashions. 'As soon as they began to introduce bodices, instead of whalebone stays,' concluded the stay-maker darkly, 'I immediately prophesied the revolution.'

Théroigne's riding-habit had not been intended as a fashion statement, but it soon became one. When she arrived at the newly formed
Cordeliers' Club in February 1790, the sight of her crimson *amazone*
and her sword provoked a flattering reaction. Camille Desmoulins
greeted her: 'It is the Queen of Sheba, come to see the Solomon of the
sections [the Paris wards].' Théroigne delivered her speech in her soft
Walloon accent, proposing that a temple dedicated to Liberty, a home
for the National Assembly and an altar to the fatherland be built on
the ruins of the Bastille. It prompted wild applause.

Although a committee was set up to consider her suggestion, the
conclusion to Desmoulins's article on her appearance at the Cordeliers'
demonstrated her fellow-patriots' true attitude to women involving
themselves in politics. With her Society of the Friends of the Law
dissolving, Théroigne had requested membership of the Cordeliers'
Club, which would allow her a consultative vote in the Assembly.
While she was granted the honours of the session for her address,
Desmoulins evaded her demand for an official political voice as a
member of the Cordeliers':

> Mlle Théroigne and those of her sex will always be at liberty to
> propose whatever they believe to be advantageous to the fatherland,
> but as regards the question of state, as to whether Mlle Théroigne
> should be admitted to the district with a consultative vote only, the
> assembly is not competent to take sides on this question, and this
> is not the place to settle it.

Other clubs were more receptive to women members; indeed,
'women were the soul of the societies and of the democratic movement',
according to the historian Alphonse Aulard. The first Fraternal Society
of Patriots of Both Sexes was formed in February 1790 with the intention of 'reading and interpreting the decrees of the National Assembly',
and welcomed women from the start. Its female members would
include Théroigne, Pauline Léon, Manon Roland and Thérésia de
Fontenay; Germaine de Staël did not join, but many of her friends
did. Olympe de Gouges was another member, as was Louise Robert,
a writer married to a lawyer (from Liège, like Théroigne) and deputy
to the Convention. François and Louise Robert were ardent republicans

and active members of the Fraternal Society; Louise Robert believed that it and associations like it would bring about the final destruction of despotism. In late 1790 the Roberts founded the *Mercure National*, one of the hundreds of new journals that appeared between 1789 and 1792, for which their friend Manon Roland would write.

One of the most eloquent of the Fraternal Society's women members was the Dutch baroness Etta Palm d'Aelders. In December 1790 she addressed the Social Circle, another club which welcomed male and female members and met weekly in the Palais Royal. She urged the government to extend full citizenship to women.

Six months earlier Condorcet had written on the same topic:

> He who votes against the rights of another, whatever that person's religion, colour or sex may be, has by the same token forsworn his own. Why should creatures subject to pregnancies and to passing indispositions not be able to exercise their rights [a common argument against women participating in public life], when no one has ever contemplated depriving people who have an attack of gout every winter, or who readily catch a cold?

He advised that unmarried women and widows should be granted the vote and called for all women to use their talents to benefit the society in which they lived.

Not every member of the Fraternal Society or the Social Circle shared Condorcet's unusually egalitarian views, but most were progressive thinkers committed to improving women's status in society through legislation, to legalize divorce, to provide protection for battered wives, and to reform inheritance and property laws. A committee was established by Etta Palm d'Aelders's club, the Confederation of the Friends of Truth, to distribute aid to ill and indigent women and children in Paris.

Most men tolerated their wives' and daughters' new-found interest in politics, but the Jacobin Club was wary of women from the start. The Fraternal Society met in 1790 in various rooms of the same former monastery as the Jacobins, and the two clubs shared some members, many of whom also had connections with Théroigne, Germaine de Staël, Thérésia de Fontenay and Manon Roland: Condorcet, Brissot, the Lameth brothers, Mirabeau, Georges Danton and Jean-Lambert Tallien. Despite these links, however, the Jacobins displayed their reluctance to treat the Fraternal Society seriously from the start. In the autumn of 1790, they told the Society that they would only receive a deputation from them if it were composed entirely of men. The journalist Marat used the Fraternal Society to attack the Jacobins that December, snidely saluting 'the club of women which providence seems to have placed beneath the Jacobins [the Society sometimes met in the monastery's crypt] to repair their faults'.

It was this type of revolutionary misogyny that prompted Théroigne to leave Paris at the end of the summer of 1790. The idealism with which she had greeted the early months of the revolution had been disappointed. It was becoming clear to her that her fellow-revolutionaries were campaigning for the rights of men, not the rights of humanity; her struggle was unimportant to them. In prison in Austria the following year she said it had been her dearest wish to have been able to destroy 'the tyranny which men exercise over my own sex', but her efforts had been in vain.

Neither of the progressive associations she had formed had taken off as she had hoped. The Society of the Friends of the Law had disbanded in the spring of 1790. In February Théroigne had watched the deputies of the National Assembly process to Notre Dame to hear a mass celebrating their oaths of citizenship. She recognized some of them, and they asked her to join them; the honour of walking with them and of seeing such a spectacle made her say yes, but when onlookers exclaimed at there being a woman in the deputies' midst she was forced to withdraw, even though many others marching were not deputies either. What the people had found so curious, she said, was the thought that a woman should wish to be a part of the procession.

Théroigne acknowledged that her lack of talent and experience hindered her efforts to play an active political role, but her greatest weakness in the eyes of her fellow-revolutionaries was her sex. She was hassled in the Assembly's tribunes, mocked on the streets and lampooned in the press, but her most bitter disappointment stemmed from the men with whom she hoped to work. 'The patriots, instead of encouraging me and treating me justly, ridiculed me,' she said; this was why she became disenchanted with politics, despite her devotion to the cause of reform, and left Paris 'without too much regret'. For the moment, Théroigne's hopes of being allowed to participate directly in France's new government had been dashed.

4

MONDAINE

Thérésia de Fontenay

MAY 1789–APRIL 1791

We continued to dance,
as they do in camp on the eve of a battle.

AUGUSTE-FRANÇOIS DE FRÉNILLY

Thérésia de Fontenay

If for Théroigne de Méricourt the revolution was a sacred event, regenerative and transformative both publicly and privately, for Thérésia, marquise de Fontenay, seventeen years old and three years married, it was just the new backdrop to her normal life. Instead of attending dull court parties in stiff tight-laced dresses, she wore frilled chemises to picnics in the woods; otherwise, eighteen months after the Bastille had fallen, not much seemed different. 'The tranquillity of France is but little disturbed, notwithstanding the wonderful changes that have of late happened,' Lady Sutherland, the English ambassadress, wrote home in January 1791, complaining that Paris had grown very dull.

Thérésia de Fontenay moved in the same worldly circles as Lady Sutherland and Germaine de Staël. Her father François Cabarrus was a successful Basque banker at the Spanish court, who in 1782 had founded the state bank, the Banco San Carlos. Thérésia had been brought up in rural Spain before joining her mother in Paris and attending, as girls of her class did, an exclusive Parisian convent. When she was fourteen she was married to twenty-six-year-old Jean-Jacques Devin de Fontenay who came from a family of recently ennobled merchants. Like Germaine Necker's marriage to Éric Magnus de Staël, Mlle Cabarrus's match with Fontenay was arranged – a union of new money with, in this case, new aristocracy. Thérésia's dowry included a substantial chunk of Parisian real estate, but the young couple lived in the Fontenay *hôtel* on the Île Saint-Louis.

Thérésia was married for the first time, according to her daughter long afterwards, '*sans joie comme sans chagrin*'. 'Her good and tender soul' would have grown attached to her husband's, lamented Mme du Narbonne-Pelet, but for his 'revolting behaviour, inconstancy and profound immorality'. Her parents, ambitious but inexperienced in Parisian ways, and according to Thérésia's later descriptions of her childhood, neglectful, seem to have found Fontenay's personal unsuitability for marriage less important than his title. He was a gambler and a roué, utterly debauched, who kept a mistress and travelled with a guidebook containing details 'of all the *filles de joie* to be found on the road'. Thérésia, still a child, was 'prostituted' to an infamous rake.

This, of course, was the way of the pre-revolutionary *haut monde*; all that was unusual was the degree of Fontenay's dissipation, and the fact that his mistress was a lowly shop-girl rather than an actress or a friend's wife. The same society that reviled the lonely, idealistic Théroigne de Méricourt as a prostitute sold the young Thérésia de Fontenay into an unhappy marriage and expected her to console herself with lovers.

In *Letters to Jean-Jacques Rousseau*, written two years after her own marriage, Germaine de Staël lamented the hypocrisy that brought up young girls in the closest seclusion only to marry them off to men who had no intention of forming an emotional attachment to them, thrusting them unprepared into a world where everything they had been taught to value was denigrated. 'Even the men, with their bizarre principles, wait until a woman is married before they speak to her of love,' she observed. 'At that point, everything changes: people no longer seek to exalt their minds with romantic notions but to soil their hearts with cold jests on everything they have been taught to respect.' Custom only legitimized these practices. 'What social disaster for a husband to consider himself invited to a house simply because his wife was invited!' remembered Lucy de la Tour du Pin of the habits of her pre-revolutionary life. Corruption had become natural. 'Virtue in men and good conduct in women became the object of ridicule and were considered provincial.'

Many husbands encouraged their brides to take lovers, aware that if their wives were busy elsewhere their own activities would escape attention. Accomplished libertines were masters of amorality. 'There is nothing in love but the flesh,' held the naturalist Buffon, and Rousseau's *Confessions* substantiate the ancien régime's institutionalized cynicism.

His independent, older mistress, Mme de Warens, was taught by her first lover that the moral importance of marital fidelity lay only in its effect on public opinion. According to this argument, 'adultery in itself' was nothing, and was only called into existence by scandal ... every woman who appeared virtuous by that mere fact became so'.

Perhaps because her husband was so unlovable, Thérésia made little effort even to appear virtuous. Although she produced a son, Théodore, in May 1789, she was more interested in social than domestic life and quickly became part of the louche, liberal circuit of Germaine de Staël and her friends. By the summer of 1790, in an aptly revolutionary analogy, Thérésia was said to have 'dethroned' the 'delicious' blonde Nathalie de Noailles as the most beautiful woman in Paris.

Thérésia's dark loveliness and foreign riches made her a celebrity. Raven-haired, with flashing eyes, she was much in the mould of Germaine de Staël, 'but extremely *en beau*'. Mme de la Tour du Pin compared her to the goddess Diana – though no doubt in her aspect as huntress rather than virgin – enthusing that 'no more beautiful creature had ever come from the hands of the Creator'. Thérésia's statuesque looks were enhanced by 'matchless grace', 'radiant femininity' and a peculiarly charming voice 'of caressing magic', husky, melodious and slightly accented.

She was self-centred, but generous and passionate, taking delight in pleasing others as much as herself. The secularism of the early days of the revolution, its philosophical and political exaltation of liberty and the pursuit of happiness, had loosened private moral strictures; high-spirited Thérésia enjoyed these new freedoms to the full. The personal philosophy she would develop combined the worldliness and sexual licence enjoyed by married noblewomen before the revolution with the secular amorality of the new republic. Pleasure was her only responsibility, and Thérésia was as happy to find it in 1791 at revolutionary *fêtes* as she had been at royal receptions in 1788. Although she was not at first personally transformed by the revolution in the way that her friend Germaine, or Théroigne de Méricourt, were, Thérésia's entire adult existence was coloured by the revolution and its upheavals. Fifteen years old in 1789, she knew nothing but change. The great lessons of her youth were opportunism and adaptability.

Thérésia's whirl of parties and gossip continued, but imperceptibly every aspect of daily life, private as well as public, assumed political overtones. 'When they converse, liberty is the theme of discourse; when they dance, the figure of the cotillion is adapted to a national tune; and when they sing, it is but to repeat a vow of fidelity to the constitution.' Even the slang reflected the changing times, according to Helen Maria Williams. 'Everything tiresome or unpleasant, "*c'est une aristocracie!*" [sic] and everything charming and agreeable is, "*à la nation*".' Jean-Jacques Devin de Fontenay may have been debauched, but he was sufficiently fashionable to keep up with politics, attending meetings at the Jacobin Club in December 1790.

Since it was stylish for women to take an interest in politics too, it is likely that Thérésia attended the National Assembly's opening session in Paris, after the women's march to Versailles, in the late autumn of 1789. Théroigne de Méricourt must have been present, taking the place in the tribunes of the *manège* that she had claimed as her own in Versailles; Germaine de Staël was sitting in the front row of the women's galleries; nearby was Rose de Beauharnais, wife of a progressive aristocratic deputy and the future Empress Joséphine, and Félicité de Genlis, mistress of the liberal duc d'Orléans and governess to his children, one of whom, the future King Louis-Philippe, sat beside her.

The Assembly's meetings were chaotic. Every deputy seemed 'more inclined to talk than to listen', recorded Helen Williams, but that did not stop women of all classes crowding the galleries at every session. Rosalie Jullien, wife of one of the deputies, went so regularly that she only mentioned *not* attending the Assembly in her letters. English visitors like Williams, Mary Wollstonecraft and Mary Berry rushed to request tickets when they arrived in Paris. Lucy de la Tour du Pin said her sister-in-law, the former marquise de Lameth, watched the Assembly's sessions every day.

Thérésia attended meetings of the Fraternal Society of Patriots of Both Sexes, branches of which counted among its members Théroigne and Pauline Léon. She also became a sister at the Olympic Lodge of freemasons, following in her friend Lafayette's footsteps, and was a member of the liberal Club of 1789 whose patron was the duc d'Orléans. Like other women of her background, Thérésia probably observed the early proceedings of the Jacobins many of whom, in 1790 and early 1791, were her friends.

A list of putative members of a 1790 Club of the Rights of Man* numbered not Thérésia herself but several of her most intimate friends, and demonstrates the milieu in which she lived. Members were said to have included Thérésia's best friend from convent days, Mme Charles de Lameth, and her husband; his brother Alexandre, close to both Thérésia and Germaine de Staël; Mathieu de Montmorency, also linked to Germaine; and the brilliant, lecherous comte de Mirabeau, with whom Thérésia toured the ruins of the Bastille.

True salonnières like Germaine de Staël and Félicité de Genlis had little time for popular societies. Their interest in politics was strictly personal and entirely exclusive. Genlis went just once to watch the Jacobins, and thought the more radical Cordeliers' Club, because 'women of the lower orders spoke in it', was 'a sight at once striking, shocking and ridiculous'. The young chocolate-maker Pauline Léon was a regular attendant of the Cordeliers' sessions; she was exactly the kind of loud-mouthed working woman who would have offended Genlis's elitist sensibilities. The political involvement of the lower classes of either sex worried Germaine de Staël, whose steady advocacy of a constitutional monarchy became less and less radical as the goal-posts shifted past her. 'The Revolution naturally descended lower and lower each time that the upper classes allowed the reins to slip from their hands, whether by want of wisdom or their want of address,' she lamented.

In the summer of 1789 Thérésia held a dinner at the Fontenay château in Fontenay-aux-Roses just outside Paris. The theme and decorations were inspired by the Rousseauesque pastoral ideals of simplicity and nature so valued by liberals. Girls dressed in white handed guests bunches of flowers as they arrived, '*comme dans une pastorale*

---

* Her French accusers said Théroigne de Méricourt had boasted of forming this club.

antique'; they dined on the grass beneath spreading chestnut trees, '*comme en Arcadie*'. Thérésia was toasted not as queen but as goddess of the *fête*. Her guests, she remembered later, were the progressive aristocrats of her circle, like Mirabeau, as well as a sprinkling of political radicals including Camille Desmoulins and his old schoolfriend Maximilien Robespierre; she lacked the elitist scruples of Mme de Staël. 'That day was the true celebration of my youth,' Thérésia recalled, years later. 'They did not yet call me Notre Dame de Thermidor, but nor did the cowards call me Notre Dame de Septembre: I was simply Notre Dame de Fontenay.'

These pastoral idylls were a fashionable way for the liberal elite to demonstrate their virtuous sentimentality and their solidarity with the 'people'. In the 1780s, when the celebrated lawyer Guy-Jean Target had won back for the villagers of Salency in Picardy the right to choose their own *rosière*, or annual rose queen (instead of their lord, who claimed the right for himself), Félicité de Genlis had gone to Salency to play the harp at their *fête*. The song based on that popular victory, 'La Rosière de Salency', was played at Thérésia's own *fête champêtre*.

The following summer, a similar festival was held to celebrate the anniversary of the so-called Tennis Court Oath. The deputies of the National Assembly processed to Versailles bearing the oath of allegiance inscribed on a bronze tablet alongside stones from the fallen Bastille. They renewed their oaths in the palace's tennis court, then returned to Paris, stopping in the Bois de Boulogne for a feast held under the trees at which they were attended by women dressed as shepherdesses. The Declaration of the Rights of Man and the Citizen was read as grace. Georges Danton, crowned like the rest of the deputies with an oak-leaf wreath, proposed a toast to the liberty and happiness of the entire world. In one of the elaborately symbolic set-pieces so beloved of the revolutionaries, a model of the Bastille was set on the table and smashed, hopefully with great care, since revealed inside lay a real baby swaddled in white, representing oppressed innocence liberated by the revolution. A red Phrygian cap, modelled on those given to Roman slaves when they were freed, was placed on its head.

In Paris, meanwhile, rapturous preparations for the anniversary of the Bastille's fall were under way, as men and women of all ages and classes, 'inspired by the same spirit', helped turn the Champs de Mars into a vast amphitheatre. Even the king took his turn with a spade. The worksite became the backdrop for scenes of revolutionary virtue and brotherhood as Parisians competed with one another to contribute to the cause of freedom and the *patrie*. Women and men saw themselves as equal contributors to the effort: 'I honour no less that multitude of citizens and citizenesses who do not think that they have consecrated those works by their hands but their hands by those works,' wrote Camille Desmoulins. The atmosphere was fervently emotional. It would have been impossible, wrote Louis-Sebastien Mercier, to have beheld the scene without being moved.

Women of gentle birth were eager to be a part of Federation Day. 'Ladies took the instruments of labour in their hands, and removed a little of the earth,' wrote Helen Williams, 'that they might be able to say that they had assisted in the preparations.' Pauline de Laval – beloved by Thérésia's and Germaine's friend Mathieu de Montmorency – caught pneumonia after spending the whole night before the celebrations helping cart dirt on the Champs de Mars, and died a few days later, 'victim to an excess of patriotic zeal'.

Their unpowdered hair falling loosely on to their shoulders, wearing blue military-style jackets with red collars and cuffs based on National Guard uniforms, or straw bonnets and white muslin dresses trimmed with tricolour ribbons and sashes, or riding-habits *à la* Théroigne – all as expressions of their modish political sympathies – fashionable ladies like Thérésia de Fontenay brought drinks to the men toiling at the Champs de Mars. Even the colours of their clothes echoed the mood of the times: a shade of red known as 'Foulon's blood' was named after an unpopular minister killed in the aftermath of the Bastille's fall.

On 14 July the statue of the king most admired by the revolutionaries, Henri IV, sported a tricolour scarf. Priests and National Guardsmen in their bright new uniforms of red, white and blue danced in the streets with white-clad girls. Lamps hung in the trees lining the Champs-Élysées, the palace of the Louvre was illuminated and the site of the Bastille had been turned into a park. Representatives from the newly created French regional departments processed beside the deputies of the National Assembly, the National Guard and the king and queen. Talleyrand celebrated mass on the monumental Altar of the Fatherland while Lafayette administered the oath to the people, who, right arms upheld, swore 'to be faithful forever to the nation, the law and the king'. Fireworks fizzled in the pouring rain, and the hundreds of thousands of patriotic onlookers cried, 'The French revolution is cemented with water, instead of blood!' 'What is it to me if I'm wet,' sang the *poissardes*, 'for the cause of liberty?' As one historian comments on the ecstatic mood of the day, 'no fatal gap had yet opened up between principles and reality'. Only the queen could not hide her ill-humour.

The air of celebration permeated the nation. 'This memorable day was like an experiment in electricity,' wrote Mercier. 'Everything which touched the chain partook of the shock'. Helen Williams thought it 'the most sublime spectacle' ever witnessed, while her countryman William Wordsworth, landing in Calais on Federation Day, was struck by how 'individual joy embodied national joy'. Everywhere, 'benevolence and blessedness spread like a fragrance'.

Although Parisian women had been refused permission by the Constitution Committee to take part in the main ceremony – they were permitted instead to organize a tableau representing the confederation being offered to St Genevieve – across the country women celebrated alongside the men. In Beaufort-en-Vallée, eighty-three women disappeared during the ceremony and returned, as a surprise, in costumes representing the eighty-three departments; the women of Dénezé-sous-le-Lude received the municipality's reluctant consent to hold their own Federation Day celebrations. As an expression of the benevolent atmosphere of the day in Angers, 'each of the municipal officers insisted on taking the arm of one of those women that are called women of the people'.

Motivated by the same spirit that led fine ladies to pick up shovels for the first time in their lives, donating one's jewels to the *caisse patriotique* became far more chic than wearing them. Félicité de Genlis had the ultimate revolutionary accessory: a polished shard of the fallen Bastille made into a brooch. Her stone was set in a wreath of emerald laurel leaves tied at the top in a jewelled tricolour rosette, and inlaid with the word *Liberté* in diamonds.

'Every man seems at pains to show that he has wasted as few moments as possible at his toilette,' wrote Helen Williams, commenting on the trend for negligence in dress, 'and that his mind is bent on higher cares than the embellishment of his person.' There was an element of fancy dress in all this artful simplicity that characterized every stage of the revolution except the darkest moments of the Terror. It was almost as if people were trying on new identities with each change of their political faith, or struggling to define themselves through their appearance when everything around them was shifting and uncertain. Talma's classical costume for his role in Voltaire's *Brutus*, combined with the early revolutionaries' hero-worship of the Greeks and Romans, made a craze of antiquity. 'We were transformed into Spartans and Romans,' remembered the actress Louise Fusil. Helen Williams even took lessons in Roman history from a private tutor. When *Brutus* was performed, with its noble revolutionary theme of a father sacrificing his sons to save the Roman republic, the subject was considered so incendiary that weapons were banned from the theatre and extra police forces were marshalled in case of trouble.

David's monumental history painting, *The Lictors Bringing Back to Brutus the Bodies of his Sons*, had been shown for the first time at the Salon of August 1789. Louis XVI, David's patron, had requested for the exhibition a painting of Coriolanus, the fifth-century Roman leader who had safeguarded the rights of the aristocracy over the people. When David defied him by submitting the Brutus painting instead, at first the king banned it, but then submitted to public pressure. Art students wearing the uniform of the newly created National Guard watched over it in the gallery. It caused a sensation: as the newspaper *Père Duchesne* observed, David's paintings 'had inflamed more souls for liberty than the best books'.

In the background of David's drawing of the Tennis Court Oath, exhibited in the Salon of 1791, a bolt of lightning – symbol of liberty – strikes the Chapel-Royal at Versailles. Félicité de Genlis's response to this sketch demonstrated the underlying conservatism of her liberal views. She challenged him about it, arguing that it seemed to show 'the destruction of the royal family'; he responded that it was meant to indicate merely 'the destruction of despotism'. They never spoke again.

Helen Williams later commented on the hypocrisy of nobles like Félicité de Genlis, who claimed to be revolutionaries, but who despite their genuine enthusiasm for change never betrayed their class. 'I have found out that an *aristocrate* always begins a political conversation assuring you he is not one – that no one wished more sincerely than him for reform,' she wrote in 1794. They would continue, she said, by protesting, 'But to take away the King's power, to deprive the clergy of their revenues, is pushing things to an extremity, at which every honest mind shudders. If the National Assembly had made a reform without injuring these orders of the State, they would have been applauded by the world.'

Thérésia would have frequented Mme de Genlis's Thursday salon at Bellechasse in Saint-Germain as well as Germaine de Staël's salon in the nearby rue du Bac. There was no love lost between the two hostesses although their politics were similar and their circles of friends overlapped. Genlis, twenty years older than Germaine, had known her since childhood and thought her ill-bred and 'altogether a most embarrassing person'. Like Germaine, Félicité was well known for her intelligence and what Talleyrand called her 'career of gallantries'; Thérésia cited both their names when she later bemoaned the loss of her virtue in the drawing-rooms of the capital. Whereas Germaine was unrepentant about her passion for Narbonne, Félicité affected 'the height of prudery'. 'To avoid the scandal of coquetry,' continued Talleyrand, she 'always yielded easily to powerful, useful men', the latest and longest-lasting of whom was the king's liberal cousin, the duc d'Orléans.

'Though her eyes and smile were fine,' said Elisabeth Vigée-Lebrun, who thought Genlis a spellbinding conversationalist, 'I do not think her face would have adapted easily to the expression of kindness.' Genlis's ten volumes of memoirs bear out Vigée-Lebrun's conclusion. A typical anecdote begins, 'One praise I may venture to give myself, because I am quite sure I deserve it . . .' Félicité presents herself as an unrivalled beauty (everybody else's looks are judged and found wanting), a celebrated authoress, a gifted musician, a talented rider ('I was thought to look so well on horseback'), a skilled nurse who can let blood and set wounds 'to perfection', and an expert on education. She seems unaware of her lack of generosity or humour.

Those who attended Félicité's salon in Saint-Germain and her lover's dinners at the Palais Royal were as influenced by England and America as were Germaine's friends in the rue du Bac, but their tone, as Evangeline Bruce points out, was derived less from Rousseau than from Choderlos de Laclos, author of the cynical masterpiece *Les Liaisons Dangereuses* and the duc d'Orléans's best friend. Orléans himself, charming, lighthearted and vain, 'corrupted everything within his reach'. He flattered himself as a liberal patriot, selling paintings to feed the poor in the harsh winter of 1788 and opening the Palais Royal in the spring of 1789 for a night of carousing to celebrate the release of members of the *garde française* who had been imprisoned for refusing to fire on their fellow-citizens, but he was not at all unhappy to be increasingly often suggested as a constitutional replacement for his absolute cousin Louis on France's throne.

Orléans was quick to relinquish his title in 1790, choosing instead the shamelessly populist name of Philippe Égalité, and reducing his establishment at the Palais Royal in order to demonstrate his modesty and attachment to reform. Félicité began calling herself Citoyenne Brûlart (one of her family names), embracing, like Thérésia, yet another of the fashionable trappings of the revolution. She made more of an effort than Germaine de Staël to cultivate the young radicals of the National Assembly, including Théroigne's friend the future mayor of Paris, Jérôme Pétion, for whom she 'had a real esteem', and another progressive deputy, Bertrand Barère, who admired her writing and sent her his own pamphlets. She was seen at a ball in Paris at this time with boldly unpowdered hair, wearing a dress of red, white and blue, dancing wildly to the revolutionary anthem 'Ça Ira'.

This stirring song, dating to the summer of 1790, would accompany the revolution through all its incarnations – later with lyrics calling for the stringing up of all aristocrats. For the moment, its words celebrated the revolution's victories and aims: despite the traitors, the people would triumph; aristocrats and priests regretted their mistakes; the enemies of the state were confounded; equality, liberty and patriotism would prevail. It was a dangerous tune for a woman in Félicité de Genlis's position to sing.

Although Mary Berry, visiting Paris from London in 1790 for the first time in five years, found it neglected and empty, with carts instead of carriages filling the streets, for Thérésia, Félicité and their friends the social seasons of 1790–1 and 1791–2 were particularly glittering. Paris 'had never been so brilliant. One might have thought that people were accumulating joy to last them all the time they were about to sorrow,' wrote the marquis de Frénilly afterwards. 'There was something prophetic in this surfeit of pleasures. We had the art of amusing ourselves out of foresight, like people who lay in a supply of food against famine.'

This frenetic aristocratic hedonism took place against a backdrop of increasing popular menace, directed as much against women as men. Mary Berry was surprised and shaken in the spring of 1791 to find a group of six or seven *poissardes*, market women, demanding entrance to her room, ostensibly to give her a bouquet but in fact to demand money of her. She gave them six francs, 'which they desired to have doubled', and one insisted on embracing her. Afterwards she discovered that her experience was fairly common. Travellers, who the women knew would have ready money on them, were frequent targets, although even the king's brother had been accosted in this way. 'It seems these *ladies* now make a practice of going about where or to whom they please ... and neither porters nor servants dare to stop them.'

At about the same time a large band of men, some in women's clothes, invaded the convents of Paris, many of which had ties to aristocratic families, stripping and beating nuns of all ages and running them out of their sanctuaries in a brutal rite of humiliation. Even the anticlerical Manon Roland would later lament the fate of her friend Agatha, a nun expelled from her convent in 1791, suffering on her wretched pension 'when age and ill health make that asylum [the convent] more necessary than ever for her'.

Many royalist aristocrats, marginalized by their views and fearing for their safety, simply left France. After the Bastille fell in 1789, 'emigration became all the vogue': people raised money from their estates to take with them; many even welcomed the chance to travel. As Germaine de Staël said, emigration was 'an act of party', a statement of aristocratic honour and loyalty to the royal family rather than (at this stage) a flight from active persecution. Elderly men who had retired to their country houses received small parcels containing white feathers, emblems of cowardice, as reproaches for sanctioning the revolution by remaining behind.

Although she respected the émigrés' attachment to the king, in hindsight Germaine was horrified by their desertion of their country. In politics, as in morals, she later wrote, there are certain responsibilities one must never abjure, the first of which is that one must never abandon one's nation to foreigners. She thought the nobility's desertion of France – seeing their country as 'as a jealous lover wishes his mistress – dead or faithful' – gave the masses more reason to hate aristocrats, as well as demonstrating how unnecessary they were to the running of society.

The pace of change accelerated as 1791 progressed. Germaine, alarmed on the one hand by the increasing radicalization of the Assembly and on the other by the continued resistance of the king and his party to change, published an article called *How Can We Determine What Is the Opinion of the Majority of the Nation?*, in which she called for moderation, a balance between liberty and order. The central position, she argued, would be 'stronger, more distinct and more vigorous than the two opposed extremes'. Her efforts were in vain: a poem satirizing her attempts to reconcile all the parties showed her receiving royalists and Jacobins at intervals through the day, 'and at night, everybody'. In both Jacobin and royalist newspapers she was called a *'nouvelle Circé'*, and her husband was depicted as a foolish cuckold. A play entitled *The Intrigues of Mme de Staël* appeared, in which she was shown as a nymphomaniac stirring up riots to help advance her lovers' careers.

Despite her desire for a constitution, Germaine was sympathetic to the monarchy and hoped to preserve it. In February 1791, her lover Louis de Narbonne accompanied the king's two aunts, Mmes Adélaïde and Victoire (and perhaps his own great-aunts), to exile in Rome. The king and queen never trusted Germaine. Her radical reputation had stuck, although she was in 1791, by comparison with the Jacobins, a political moderate. Gouverneur Morris shared a mistress with Talleyrand, the intimate friend of Germaine and her lover Narbonne; Morris reported what he learned about Germaine's set from Adèle to his friends in the king's party. In the summer of 1791 Morris was placing royalist spies in the Jacobin Club and urging the king to stand firm against the revolutionaries.

Almost inadvertently, as a member of the set which included intriguers like Germaine and Morris, the young marquise de Fontenay became politicized. Even a girl with a life as defiantly superficial as hers could not remain immune to the chaos swirling around her. Thérésia's close friends and lovers were all passionately involved in politics. Her name was linked to all three of the liberal Lameth brothers, whose shared passion for her was said to have prevented any one of them seeking to make her his own. But her great love from this period was the more radical Félix Lepeletier, with whom she started an affair in 1789, when she was fifteen.

In April 1791 Thérésia's name appeared for the first time in the counterrevolutionary press. As with other women in the public eye, such as Théroigne de Méricourt, Germaine de Staël and Marie-Antoinette, her 'corrupt' private life was associated with the political corruption of her supposed lovers. Thérésia apparently took the unusual step of writing directly to the *Journal de la Cour et de la Ville* professing her patriotism and denying their claims that she was 'a little too much' involved with the brothers Lameth and Condorcet, among others. The letter was probably a fake, intended to compromise her still further, but it is marked by the naïve faith in others' good nature that always characterized Thérésia's behaviour.

Thérésia and her friend Mme Charles de Lameth – since schooldays nicknamed Dondon because of her precocious bosom – became regular features of the royalist gossip sheets. The *Chronique Scandaleuse* presented Thérésia in the autumn of 1791 as a worshipper of Priapus, 'the other god', each week entertaining eight lovers, including such unlikely candidates as Robespierre and Mirabeau, who had died suddenly earlier that year. 'How could I resist his eloquence?' she asks. But although these alliances were fabricated, one young radical had indeed caught the beautiful former marquise's eye.

Jean-Lambert Tallien was born in Paris in 1767, the son of the marquis de Bercy's butler. Bercy – who some believed was the boy's father – had paid for his education, and Tallien worked initially as a secretary to the Bercy family. In 1790, aged twenty-three, he was tutoring his own cousins, daughters of a Paris merchant. This job left Tallien plenty of time to pursue his revolutionary interests: he was a National Guardsman; his name was on the first known list of Jacobin Club members in December 1790; he attended sessions of the Cordeliers' Club, across the Seine near the Church of Saint-Sulpice. Tallien founded a branch of the Fraternal Society which met at the former convent of the Minimes in the Place Royal (now the Place des Vosges) near his home in the Marais; this was the division of the Fraternal Society attended by Pauline Léon. On his twenty-fourth birthday, 23 January 1791, he addressed the Society on the historical causes of the revolution.

Two months later, Alexandre de Lameth hired Tallien as his secretary. One day soon afterwards, Tallien, looking for Alexandre, was admitted to the house of his brother Charles, husband of Thérésia's girlhood friend. Alexandre was not there, but Dondon de Lameth asked Tallien to go out into the garden to cut some white roses for Mme de Fontenay. Tallien, tall and blond, offered them with a flourish to Thérésia; a single flower fell from the bouquet and Tallien self-consciously kept it rather than putting it back with the others. As he left, Thérésia turned to Dondon and demanded to hear all she knew about Tallien. She replied that he was witty and lazy and ran after girls, but for all that he was the best secretary in the world and was rapidly making himself indispensable to Alexandre. Thérésia's interest was piqued.

An unverifiable anecdote suggests that this may have been their second encounter. Apparently, while Thérésia was having her portrait painted by Vigée-Lebrun before the painter left Paris in 1789, Tallien arrived at the studio; he was working for a printer at the time and looking for the journalist Antoine Rivarol, one of Vigée-Lebrun's guests. A small group was standing around the portrait debating how well it had captured its sitter's beauty. Vigée-Lebrun, fed up with their comments, turned to the young messenger and asked him what he thought of it. Tallien examined the painting and, provocatively slowly, the model herself. Eventually he delivered his critique: Vigée-Lebrun had made the eyes a little too small and the mouth a little too big, but she had almost captured Thérésia's expression and character, and the play of light reminded him of Velázquez. He bowed and withdrew. It is a romantic story, as so many stories about Thérésia are, particularly the ones she told herself – one of her early-twentieth-century biographers called her penchant for embroidering her life story her '*curieuse mythomanie*'* – but no painting of Thérésia by Vigée-Lebrun survives and in her memoirs she describes meeting Thérésia for the first time in 1801, with no mention of this incident.

Regardless of when they first laid eyes on each other, in 1791 Tallien the ambitious messenger-boy and Thérésia the former marquise still inhabited worlds so far apart that there was no possibility of their coming together on equal ground. All that would have changed by the time they met again.

---

* Thérésia's account of her birth is just one example of this tendency: she claimed to have been born in Madrid at a grand ball given by the French ambassador, although records show she was actually born in Carabancel, just outside Madrid.

5

RÉPUBLICAINE

Manon Roland

FEBRUARY 1791–MARCH 1792

My spirit and my heart find everywhere the obstacles of
opinion and the shackles of prejudice, and all my force is
spent in vainly rattling my chains.

MANON ROLAND

Manon Roland

SEVENTEEN-YEAR-OLD Thérésia de Fontenay inhabited a world in which politics was a fashion; for thirty-six-year-old Manon Roland, wife of a provincial civil servant and recently arrived in Paris, politics was an all-consuming obsession.

Manon Roland returned to Paris, the city in which she had grown up, in February 1791. Living for the most part outside the capital since her marriage eleven years earlier, she had devoted herself to realizing Rousseau's ideal of the *citoyenne* as a wife and mother whose political passivity was her patriotic duty. Although she acted as her husband's secretary, according to Rousseau's strictures she did not interest herself in public affairs. In 1783 she boasted to her friend Augustin Bosc d'Antic, Théroigne de Méricourt's future admirer, that she never bothered herself with politics; as late as 1787 she described herself as 'yawning over the papers'.

But the revolution, as she phrased it, 'engulfed' her. By May the following year, when the the royal administration was challenged for the first time, all her indifference had dissolved. 'But how can one speak of . . . private troubles,' she demanded, 'when there are public ones?' In August 1789, writing to Bosc d'Antic again, she had to remind herself how to address him on a subject other than politics, but concluded, 'We do not deserve to have a country if we are indifferent to public affairs.'

From the start, Manon was convinced the monarchy would have to go. She had emerged fully formed like Athena, clothed in her armour of uncompromising opinion, a republican from the outset. As she later wrote, 'I had hated kings since I was a child and I could never witness without an involuntary shudder the spectacle of a man abasing himself before another man.' In this she was more radical than her husband and their friends, most of whom were at first constitutional monarchists favouring the same type of reforms as the more progressive of Germaine de Staël's aristocratic friends.

She was also unashamedly belligerent. When her letters to Bosc d'Antic in Paris in 1789 and 1790 were intercepted and opened (as she imagined, by government spies), she responded by threatening the 'cowards' who had violated her rights: 'Let them tremble to think that she [Manon] can make a hundred enthusiasts who will in turn make a million others.' This was how she saw her role – as inspiration and support for the men who would destroy the crumbling edifice of the ancien régime and create a new, free France. The patriot, she told Bosc d'Antic, unwittingly describing her own effect on the men around her, should inflame people's courage, should 'demand, thunder, scare'.

When she and Roland reached Paris, Manon lost no time in gathering around her an informal *petit comité* of men with similar backgrounds and political views. Early in April she informed a friend that 'the society of which I just spoke to you will form, and the meetings may even be in our house'. The regular visitors to her salon at the Hôtel Britannique, on the rue Guénégaud on the left bank, were mostly in their thirties, provincial lawyers, journalists or civil servants drawn from the educated middle classes. Its members crossed the Pont-Neuf into the rue Guénégaud most afternoons between four and six, after the National Assembly (in which many of them were deputies) closed and before the Jacobin Club (in which many of them sat) opened.

Some of them, like Manon's husband Jean-Marie Roland de la Platière, had tenuous links with the lower rungs of the nobility but had been largely excluded from the social and political advantages peers enjoyed before 1789. At fifty-seven, Jean-Marie Roland was distinguished among their friends by his age. He was a tall, stiff, spare man habitually dressed in a threadbare brown or black suit, with no wig covering his thinning hair above a mild face. Before 1791 he had worked as an inspector of manufactures, earning the respect of his colleagues through his diligence, energy and integrity.

His wife, twenty years his junior, was animated and immaculate in her plain *amazone*, her rich brown hair cut simply but modishly '*en jockei*', and 'an expression of uncommon sweetness' (according to her friend Helen Maria Williams) in her full hazel eyes. Everything about Manon proclaimed her 'most ardent attachment to liberty': her self-control, her warmth, her penetration, her obvious virtue and modesty.

Even before they arrived in Paris Manon had been central to a set of men who shared her passionate commitment to reform, and who would form the core of the Brissotin (later known as Girondin) group coalescing at her salon in 1791. Bosc d'Antic and François Lanthenas had been friends with Manon and her husband for years; in their letters the quartet called each other brother and sister, a quiet statement of the ideals by which they hoped to live. Since 1787, Manon had been corresponding with Jacques-Pierre Brissot (from whom their loosely affiliated group, the Brissotins, would derive one of its names), and contributing anonymously to his *Patriote Français* under the byline, 'Letters from a Roman Lady'.

Brissot, who before 1789 styled himself, with an aristocratic flourish, 'de Warville', was the son of a cook from Chartres. Before the revolution he had been a jobbing pamphleteer, selling information to the police when times were hard and, when that expedient failed, spending time in a debtors' prison and in the Bastille. The man Manon called 'generous Brutus' had been agitating for change throughout the 1780s, campaigning for the abolition of the slave trade and forming a Society of the Friends of the Negroes.

Brissot exposed the Rolands to an international network of liberal reformers. The English republican historian Catherine Macaulay had given him a letter of introduction to George Washington when he visited the United States in 1788, recommending him as a 'warm friend to liberty'. Brissot's *Travels in the United States* was intended to hold up the American example as a model to Frenchmen. He called Americans 'the true heroes of humanity' because they had discovered the secret of preserving individual liberty by correlating their private morality with their public responsibility. But despite her respect for Brissot and for the way his private life reflected his ideals, Manon recognized that his political weaknesses were too much easy charm and too naïve a faith in mankind's goodness. His quiet wife 'admired his devotion to the cause' but was harder-headed: 'she thought France unworthy of liberty and that anyone who attempted to promote it was wasting his time'.

It was Brissot who introduced the Rolands to three deputies of the National Assembly who were in 1791 the focus of progressive hopes: the cheerful, vain lawyer Jérôme Pétion, who had escorted Théroigne de Méricourt back to her lodgings in Versailles on the day of the women's march in October 1789; another lawyer, Maximilien Robespierre, whose sneering watchfulness did not yet excite Manon's distrust; and the passionate, principled François Buzot. They were regular frequenters of the Jacobin Club which was fast becoming a political elite to whom, in the words of Camille Desmoulins, Robespierre's schoolfriend, 'only the witness of their conscience is necessary'. Manon nicknamed them the 'Incorruptibles'; and another left-wing wife, in the classical vocabulary of the day, called them the *bons et précieux Triumvirs*. All three were soon frequent visitors to the rue Guénégaud.

A few others added their voices to the radical chorus in Manon's salon, but she was sparing in her approval and favoured those who shared her morals as well as her opinions. Mme Roland admired Tom Paine, author of *Common Sense*, more for his bold, original political principles than for his ability to realize them; she and the radical aristocrat Condorcet, Germaine's friend, respected one another's views and intelligence, but she was contemptuous of his crippling timidity.

Given Manon's continued adherence to Rousseau's disapproval of women involving themselves in public life, it was hardly surprising that no other women were invited to these meetings. She respected Brissot's wife and liked Pétion's; hers was one of the few houses at which Manon deigned to call. Buzot's older, less attractive wife she considered unworthy of him.

'I knew the proper role of my sex and never exceeded it,' Manon wrote later, describing how she sat at a separate table from the men, silently sewing or writing letters as they discussed the events of the day. Listening submissively to visitors who thought their every word a revelation to her and considered her capable of no more than stitching a shirt gave her a secret thrill. But although she insisted she had accepted her 'proper role', she still had to bite her lip to stop herself speaking out of turn. While she admired her guests' honourable intentions, powers of reasoning and personal enlightenment, she admitted she sometimes longed to box their ears when she heard them wasting 'their time in pure cleverness and wit' and failing either to reach conclusions or to establish objectives.

Although her guests were often as frustrating as they were inspirational, Manon thrived. 'I loved political life, its talk, its intrigues,' she wrote. 'I do not mean the petty intrigues of a court or the sterile controversies of gossip and fools, but the true art of politics, the art of ruling men and organising their happiness in society.'

Having observed the events of the revolution from afar for so long, when she arrived in Paris Manon was hungry to witness for herself the new machinery of power. 'I went to all the meetings,' she remembered, watching among others 'the powerful Mirabeau ... [and] the astute Lameth' at the National Assembly. She was unimpressed by what she saw. The Assembly, she wrote in March 1791, less than a month after her arrival, was divided, weak and corrupt, the government was 'detestable' and the Jacobins, among whom she counted her husband and their friends, neglected their responsibility to serve the cause of liberty. Worst of all, the interests of the old regime profited from these divisions to inhibit the revolution's progress.

Acquainting herself with the political climate also meant attending a session of the Social Circle in the library of the Jacobin Club. Manon was 'very well satisfied with the meeting', she told a friend that March. 'I listened to the greatest principles of liberty outlined with force, warmth and clarity; I saw them applauded with delight.' Her detached tone – she did not applaud herself but, rather, was pleased that others were applauding – suggests that she, like the aristocratic salonnières Germaine de Staël and Félicité de Genlis, viewed the Social Circle as more useful for other women than for herself; she had no need of it. Even though her writing did appear in the *Mercure National* (anonymously, as in the *Patriote Français*) edited by François and Louise Robert, organizers of the Social Circle, Manon attended meetings only rarely. Her own coterie was infinitely more engrossing.

Manon Roland did not see herself as part of a feminist movement like the one Pauline Léon was trying to initiate; instead she saw herself as a personal inspiration to individual patriots and republicans. Her relationship to the inner workings of politics convinced her, like Germaine de Staël in 1789, that she could accomplish more through her private influence on the men who were shaping policy than through speaking or writing publicly as women like Pauline Léon and Théroigne de Méricourt, less well connected than her, were obliged to do. Their double handicap, of class as well as gender, forced them to act radically; Manon, whose friends were becoming among the most influential men in the nation, had no need to draw attention to herself in order to make her voice heard.

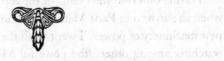

Five years earlier, a man or woman from Manon Roland's background would never have had access to the kind of power her 'petit comité' was contemplating in 1791. Manon herself came from a family of bourgeois Parisian artisans. She was born in 1754, the beloved only daughter of an ambitious engraver, Gatien Phlipon, and his gentle wife Marguerite, whom she described as 'plain, undistinguished people'. Manon spent her earliest years with a wet-nurse in the country, returning to her parents in Paris a precocious child of two.

Manon's upbringing was middle-class: while her mother did not work, she ran the household, and little Manon was often sent out to market in her linen smock to fetch a bunch of parsley or a head of lettuce that had been forgotten. She knew how to make an omelette and shell peas, to mend sheets and polish the silver. Although the adult Manon was proud of her bourgeois housekeeping skills, it is hard to escape the feeling that she considered them beneath her: when she described how capable she was of making her own supper she could not resist adding, 'yet no one who looked at me would have thought of burdening me with such a menial task'.

This sense of being somehow better than the circumstances into which she had been born was stimulated by her education. Unusually for a girl of the middling sort – probably because she was an only child – her parents indulged her obvious intelligence and aptitude for learning. As well as going to a parish catechism class on Sundays and receiving Latin lessons from her uncle, a priest, the young Manon was taught writing, geography, music and dancing by tutors in the family's first-floor apartment on the quai de l'Horloge, on the Île de la Cité, and her father taught her drawing and engraving. She was allowed to read anything she chose. Like Rousseau, she had absorbed the republicanism of Plutarch's *Lives* before she was ten; she wept to think that she had not been born in another time. 'I should have been born a Spartan or Roman woman, or at least a French man,' she lamented at twenty-two.

Manon's indomitable spirit and strong sense of self-righteousness were evident from an early age. If she was beaten unjustly by her father, she would bite his thigh. On one occasion, aged about seven, she refused to take some medicine; her father beat the hysterical child three times for refusing it, and still she would not give in. Finally a sort of 'stiffness' came over her, 'a new strength flowed through my veins'. Manon tucked up her chemise and again offered her back to her father's blows. Her terrified mother, seeing the little girl's extraordinary, stubborn stoicism, persuaded her father to leave the room and put Manon to bed. Two hours later, with tears in her eyes, she persuaded Manon to take the medicine for her sake. The child finally swallowed it, but instantly threw it up and lapsed into a much more serious fever than the one the medicine had warranted in the first place. Her father never dared beat her again.

This story, as she tells it, is revealing on several counts. First, its triumphant conclusion shows Manon's confidence in her own judgement; even thirty years later, and a mother herself, she did not doubt her right to have refused the hated medicine. Second, the importance she placed on the experiences of her childhood self and her highly intimate tone, with the narrator playing the role of the innocent victim of injustice, are directly derived from Rousseau's *Confessions*. Finally, the context in which she remembered the incident – while she waited in prison to be tried by the Revolutionary Tribunal, knowing her probable fate would be the scaffold – is vital. Calling to mind her youthful conviction and courage gave her strength to face the future, whatever it held. 'They can kill me,' she concluded, 'but they shall not conquer me!'

Manon's memories of the web of social relationships that dominated her childhood demonstrate the rigidity of ancien régime France, and her resentment of the invisible barriers that restricted her. She was never able to forget her place in society, describing in icy detail the humiliation she suffered when she was invited to dinner by a noble family only to be sent to the kitchen to eat their left-overs, and the fury she felt when, calling on an aristocratic connection of her grandmother's, she heard her beloved grandmother condescendingly addressed by her maiden name. When she visited Versailles she could not wait to leave: she resented seeing all that wealth and energy expended on 'individuals who were already too powerful and whose personal qualities were so unmemorable'. She knew if she spent any longer there she would 'detest these people so much that I shall not know what to do with my hatred . . . [it is] all so unfair and so absurd'.

Reading between the lines, though, a certain social fluidity is evident alongside the strict stratification. Manon was the daughter of an engraver, but her parents had such high hopes for her that they sent her to be educated at a convent, like the aristocratic Thérésia Cabarrus, and had her taught accomplishments like dancing and guitar-playing. She did meet rich, influential people, some of whom encouraged her intellectual pretensions. Manon may have resented not being the star of the literary salons and concerts to which she was taken, but she *was* taken to them. Compared to the childhood of someone like Théroigne de Méricourt, her perspective was far from enclosed; and it was from exactly this type of background that one of the most celebrated and powerful women of the ancien régime, Mme de Pompadour – Jeanne-Antoinette Poisson, daughter of a steward – had sprung. But for the young Manon, to whom virtue was as important as happiness, her station in life was as much an obstacle to her ambitions as her sex.

Her education and composure granted her access (albeit limited) to the nobility's exalted world at the same time as encouraging her to hope for its downfall. The ancients taught the young Manon to admire self-discipline, civic responsibility and virtue, and cast a critical light on the feckless aristocrats with whom she came into contact. Stories of courageous Roman matrons like Cornelia and Agrippina encouraged her to hope that she might one day be worthy of similar tales. 'I thought of my own duty and the part I could play in the future,' wrote Manon, revealing how far her ambition to play a role in history blinded her to the reality of her situation – for at fourteen what part could she have conceived of playing, other than wife and mother? 'If souls were pre-existent to bodies and permitted to choose those they would inhabit,' she told a friend in 1768, 'I assure you that mine would not have adopted a weak and inept sex which often remains useless.'

After a pious girlhood, during which she hoped at one stage to become a nun, Manon's reading led her to Voltaire. His belief in an aristocracy of intellect appealed to her, as did his profound scepticism. While she retained her faith in God, the Catholic Church became for her from her late teens nothing more than a hypocritical and often harmful institution – 'a scene where feeble-minded people . . . worship a piece of bread'. 'I cannot digest, among other things, the idea that all those who do not think like me will be damned for all eternity,' wrote Manon, 'that so many people will be cast into the eternal flames because they have never heard of a Roman pontiff who preaches a severe morality which he does not often practise.' Like Voltaire, however, she believed organized religion played an essential social role, the poor's only consolation for the deprivation of their lives. The Church, like the Social Circle, had its place; but she, Manon Roland, had no need of it.

Manon discovered Rousseau when she was twenty-one. His impact on her was as profound as Plutarch's had been when she was eight, putting into words feelings and ideas she had sensed before reading him but had never articulated herself. Looking outward, Rousseau's books validated her anger at the social injustice she saw around her, and allowed her to imagine challenging the accepted order of things; turning inward, with his exaltation of romantic and maternal love, he showed her 'the possibility of domestic happiness and the delights that were available to me if I sought them'.

So great was her devotion to Rousseau's principles that, like many other women of her generation, Manon accepted unquestioningly his belief that women should never venture outside domestic life. She would have agreed with the words of Germaine de Staël, another devotee of Rousseau's: 'it is right to exclude women from public affairs. Nothing is more opposed to their natural vocation than a relationship of rivalry with men, and personal celebrity will always bring the ruin of their happiness.' When someone predicted a future for Manon as a writer, she replied that she would chew her fingers off before publishing her work and pursuing renown. 'I am avid for happiness and I find it most in the good which I can do,' she wrote, much later. 'I have no need for fame. Nothing suits me better than acting as a sort of Providence in the background.'

While Manon argued that women should avoid public lives, her desire to play God, even from the background, belied her protestations. The paradoxical nature of Rousseau's philosophy fed Manon's conviction that intense sensibility was the mark of greatness. Her egotism, critical nature, moodiness and tendency to introspection were for her the necessary price of attributes she prized: spontaneity, candour and passion. As she wrote to Roland before their marriage, when she read a novel, she never played the secondary role: 'I have not read of a single act of courage or virtue without daring to believe myself capable of performing it myself.' 'Life was to her a drama in which she had been destined to play the main part,' comments a modern biographer. 'That this part was to turn out to be that of a tragic heroine she could not, at first, suspect, but when the time came to play that role, she would almost welcome the opportunity.'

The inescapable burden under which the young Manon laboured was her knowledge that despite her superiority to everyone she saw around her – in her intelligence, her good looks, her energy and discipline – nothing would change her fate as a woman of the middling ranks. 'I knew that I was worth more,' she wrote. Like Rousseau, she felt keenly the 'unbearable contrast between the grandeur of my soul and the meanness of my fortune'. Her only chance to shape her destiny lay in her choice of husband.

Bourgeois Parisians arranged marriages for their children as assiduously as aristocrats at Versailles, and with as little reference to those children's feelings. Manon, the pretty only daughter of respectable, prosperous parents, was an attractive prospect. When she reached her teens, men began writing to her father requesting the chance to make her acquaintance, but none of them appealed. M. Phlipon was concerned only about setting Manon up with someone rich and well established; Manon had a more stringent list of requirements. Despite her background, she refused to consider tradesmen, because she saw commerce as avaricious: 'having concerned myself since childhood with the relationships of men in society, having been nourished on the purest morality and steeped in the ideas of Plutarch and the philosophers, how could I possibly marry a merchant who would not think or feel like me about anything?'

Manon Phlipon did not meet the serious, intellectual Jean-Marie Roland de la Platière until she was twenty-two, by which time her mother had died, she herself had rejected a string of suitors and her father had gone through most of her dowry. Roland, the youngest of five sons from an ancient Beaujolais family which had claims to nobility (but no actual patent), was attracted to Manon but found her background and connections distasteful; it took him four years to propose.

The unflattering thought that Roland's love had taken so long to conquer his scruples was not lost on Manon, but, at twenty-six, few romantic illusions remained to her. She accepted Roland because she respected his morals and intellect; because the fact that he had overcome what she called 'the external disadvantages of an alliance with me' showed her that she could be sure of his esteem, once won; and because she could see no other role for herself than that of wife and mother. Just as Rousseau's heroine Julie had accepted her older suitor, Wolmar, Manon 'married in a spirit of solemn rationalism, without reservation, and devoted myself completely to the role'.

High-minded and cerebral, Manon was entirely innocent when she married. Her wedding night, she said later, disproved her theory that she could endure great suffering 'without crying out . . . though it must be said that surprise played a large part in that'. Roland did not awaken her sensuality and the desire to be a virtuous wife led her to suppress it. 'But of course, that does not protect one from the agony of a real passion,' she wrote, long afterwards. 'In fact, it may simply store up fuel for it!'

In her memoirs Manon would describe in bald detail her first sexual experience, at twelve years old, when one of her father's apprentices clumsily tried to seduce her – grabbing her hand and putting it into his trousers, pulling her down on to his lap. After the first incident, she wrote, 'the world began to seem a strange place', and she was curious. The second time, fear outweighed inquisitiveness and she confessed everything to her mother. Mme Phlipon 'skilfully exploited the repugnance which my youth and bashfulness had already made me feel', making the naïve, ignorant Manon feel she was 'the greatest sinner in the universe'. 'I did not dare to be passionate,' she wrote of her girlhood self.

Determined to find happiness in her domestic life even if it did not include romantic love or physical satisfaction, the young Mme Roland threw herself into her relationship with the husband she thought of as having 'no sex'. She honoured and cherished him 'as an affectionate daughter loves a virtuous father' and found, when his younger friends made advances to her, a 'voluptuous charm in remaining virtuous'.

The newly-wed Rolands moved to Amiens, where Roland was the local Inspector of Manufactures. In 1784, Manon spent some months in Paris trying to acquire for him the patent of nobility which his family claimed but had never purchased. It was typical of the way things were done under the ancien régime that Manon, rather than her husband, was entrusted with this responsibility. While she resented having to go to Versailles to solicit an honour for which she considered Roland's experience and knowledge more than qualified him, Manon pursued her objective with characteristic drive. The experience only confirmed to her the despicable nature of the system in which they lived: when she heard his suit had been rejected, she wrote to Roland, 'in truth, we are people too honourable to succeed!'

Although she did not achieve her original aim, Manon did manage to get Roland transferred to Lyon, near his family home, Le Clos. From 1784 they lived with his mother near Villefranche for most of the year, spending the winter months in Lyon. Manon acted as Roland's housekeeper, secretary, copyist and proof-reader; she ran the household and saw to the education of their daughter Eudora, born in 1781. The Rousseauian doctrine that governed this stage of her life was neatly summed up on the other side of France by the young Maximilien Robespierre in 1784: 'virtue produces happiness as the sun produces light'.

Like many men and women of their background who saw themselves as excluded from influence and privilege simply by virtue of their birth, and who chafed against the inequalities of the old system, during the 1780s the Rolands considered emigrating to the United States. The American War of Independence had inflamed them with the same sense of highly emotional anticipation as the liberal aristocrats who rushed to serve under Washington. It seemed to herald a momentous era of change: as Tom Paine wrote, 'the birthday of a new world is at hand'.

Early America, seen through European eyes, was stylized into a paradigm of revolutionary ideals, from pastoralism to the fashion for the antique. Brissot wrote with misty romanticism that he would have liked to have been born 'under the simple and rustic roof of an American husbandman'. It was said that the creators of the American nation had gathered in a peaceful wood, and on a grassy bank had chosen Washington as their leader. Washington's own rejection of an American crown was seen as surpassing the virtuous republicanism even of the Greeks and Romans. Brissot thought the Americans 'greatly *superior* to these ancients', and expressed the hope that Frenchmen would 'be capable of surpassing their ancestors when the circumstances are favourable'.

Even the American attitude to women was admired by French radicals in the 1780s. Their austere, masculine republic had no time for boudoir politics, despite Abigail Adams's vain plea to her husband John:

> I desire you would Remember the Ladies, and be more generous and favourable to them than your ancestors. Do not put such unlimited power into the hands of the Husbands [she wrote in 1776]. Remember all Men would be tyrants if they could. If particular care and attention is not paid to the Ladies we are determined to ferment

a Rebellion, and will not hold ourselves bound by any Laws in which we have not voice or Representation.

But events conspired to direct Brissot's and the Rolands' attention homewards. As Manon Roland told Brissot in 1790, 'We regret this promised land less now that we have hopes for our own country.'

A few months in Paris were enough to convince Manon of the fragility of her hopes. In May 1791, three months after her arrival, she expressed the revulsion she felt when she attended sessions of the National Assembly – a revulsion caused by the intensity of seeing her sublime expectations disappointed. As Alexis de Tocqueville observed in one of the great early studies of the revolution, 'disgust with the revolution and attachment to its results were almost contemporary with its birth'. 'We must make another insurrection, or we will lose happiness and liberty; but I doubt that there will be enough vigour in the people for this rising, and I see things are given over to the hazard of events,' Manon wrote bitterly to a friend in London. 'Adversity forms nations like individuals, and even civil war, as horrible as it is, brings the regeneration of our character and our morals.' More sacrifices were needed; more blood must flow. Behind her railing against the mediocrity of the revolutionaries, who cared more for 'their little glory than the great interests of their country', sounds relentlessly her own frustrated desire to act. 'It is not spirit they lack, but soul!' she exclaimed, sure that she possessed the soul required.

Manon's initial willingness to grasp the necessity of violence to the revolution was echoed by the radical journalist Jean-Paul Marat in his popular newspaper, *L'Ami du Peuple*. In the same month as Manon's tirade, he wrote that in 1790 '500 heads would have sufficed [to complete the revolution]; today 50,000 would be necessary; perhaps 500,000 will fall before the end of the year'. Even before the Reign of Terror the relationship between blood and liberty was direct and intimate: blood would make France free. As Simon Schama writes, violence 'was not just an unfortunate side effect' of the revolution, but its 'source of collective energy. It was what made the Revolution revolutionary.' Manon Roland was as aware of this brutal truth as was Marat himself.

On the afternoon of 21 June, the Rolands, Robespierre, Brissot and François Buzot were at Pétion's house when they heard news of the king and queen's flight from the Tuileries, where the royal family had been living in virtual house arrest since the autumn of 1789, increasingly horrified by the direction the revolution was taking and their powerlessness to halt it. According to Helen Williams, in 1790 when the king called Marie-Antoinette, in jest, Mme Capet (the French dynasty's family name – republicans would soon refer to him as Louis Capet), she replied wearily, addressing him as M. Capot – the word used at picquet, when the game is lost.

Across Paris on the same day, Pauline Léon, her mother and a friend, probably their neighbour Constance Évrard, were near the Palais Royal loudly protesting against the king's 'infamous treason'. She reported that they were 'almost assassinated' by Lafayette's '*mouchards*', or spies, and were saved by sans-culottes who succeeded in snatching them 'from the hands of these monsters', as she called the National Guardsmen.

Like Léon, Manon Roland despised kings and queens in general and the weak-willed Louis and his shallow wife in particular. The news that they had abandoned their pretence of accepting the revolution's changes electrified her and her friends: at last, the king had undone himself. The coterie at Pétion's on the 21st was convinced that the king's true attitude towards the revolution and the constitution had now been revealed to the people, and that advantage should be taken of this moment to prepare the ground for a republic. Robespierre, described by Manon as biting his nails at the thought that the king would only have dared escape if he had left orders for every patriot in Paris to be murdered, sneered at the others and 'asked what was meant by a republic'.

The result of that afternoon's discussion was the publication of a short-lived journal, *The Republican*, produced in association with Condorcet and Tom Paine as well as Manon's group. It proposed in its first issue, in July 1791, that the king's flight had released the nation from its loyalty to him. The king had abandoned his people; the people consequently owed him nothing. At the end of June, another member of this loose affiliation of republicans and a former soldier in the United States' War of Independence, Achille Duchastellet (former marquis du Chastellet), declared that the monarch was a 'superfluity'. Manon agreed: 'keeping the king on the throne is an ineptitude, an absurdity, if not a horror'. In the National Assembly, the king was declared *hors de cause* – irrelevant. Although no motion was passed against him, when the topic was debated 'three times the entire Assembly was lifted to its feet, arms lifted, hats in the air, with an indescribable enthusiasm'. Finally it was decided that the king's flight must be presented as an abduction, staged in order to re-establish his authority.

Jérôme Pétion was one of the two official representatives of the Assembly sent to Varennes to escort the royal family back to Paris. Louis was still king, but the mystique of royalty was gone for ever. Pétion and Antoine Barnave climbed into the coach and sat down between the king and queen without asking their permission. Barnave cast infatuated glances at the queen, and invited the dauphin to show him how well he could read by spelling out the revolutionary slogan 'Live free or die' on his buttons. A sign posted across Paris forbad onlookers from either applauding or insulting the king when he arrived back in the city, but the Jacobins recommended Parisians keep their hats on when he passed to demonstrate their disapproval of his attempt at escape.

On 24 June, a thousand people gathered between the faubourg Saint-Antoine and the Tuileries, where a sign had been hung reading, '*Maison à louer*' (To Let). The demonstration had the air of a festival: men carrying pikes, the traditional weapon of the common man, mingled with women singing the 'Ça Ira' and shouting out their desire to send the king and all aristocrats to the devil. Manon was impressed by the crude energy of the scene, and regretted the fact that instead of using it to their advantage 'the Jacobins [her friends] passed their time in pitiful discussions'. She described to her friend Henri Bancal, in London, the celebratory atmosphere on the streets, the chaotic sessions at the National Assembly, the Jacobins in the weeks following the flight to Varennes and the king's chastened return: 'one lives here ten years in twenty-four hours'. Twice in less than ten days she used the phrase 'sea of blood' when describing to Bancal the obstacles that needed to be surmounted before liberty could be achieved.

At the Jacobins' on the 22nd, the members cried, 'Live free or die!' as Robespierre took the floor. Manon's account of him at Pétion's, sneering and craven, was written later, with the benefit of hindsight; now, in June 1791, she described him as full of energy, courage and virtue, his noble heart oppressed by the vacillations and corruption of the Assembly. Their political styles and convictions at this time were similar: both Maximilien and Manon were tenacious, sentimental, fastidious and driven; both were suspicious of moderates and of the Church and detested the monarchy. By contrast Manon was concerned that Brissot, whose lightness of character she considered 'incompatible with liberty', would not prove worthy of the times.

Less than a month later, on 17 July, a crowd of fifty thousand men, women and children met in the Champs de Mars to deliver petitions demanding a referendum on the monarchy and declaring the people sovereign. Versions of similar petitions were circulated by different fraternal societies. On one, forty-one 'women, sisters, and Roman women' signed separately from the men. François and Louise Robert circulated another declaring that Louis's desertion of his 'post' was, in effect, an abdication.

Confirming all Pauline Léon's suspicions of him, Lafayette, who had persuaded the mayor to declare martial law in Paris, ordered the National Guard to open fire on the demonstrators. Perhaps fifty people were killed. There was talk of Robespierre being put on trial because of his role in writing the Jacobin Club's petition, which had been withdrawn by the Jacobins the day before, at the last minute, for being too radical. Late that night the Rolands had themselves driven to his house in the Marais to offer him asylum, but he was already in hiding.

Pauline Léon, her mother, and Constance Évrard were among the hundreds of people arrested in the aftermath of the massacre. Évrard was twenty-three, a few years younger than Léon, and lived in the same street as Léon and her mother; she had been working as a cook in the household of a former aristocrat since 1788. She was arrested for insulting the wife of a National Guardsman, and asked why she had been on the Champs de Mars. Évrard replied that she and the Léon women, '*comme tous les bons patriotes*', had been there to sign a petition calling for the reorganization of executive power.

Her interrogator wanted to know whether she attended political meetings and clubs, and what newspapers she read. Évrard's replies show the high level of politicization among working-class Parisian women. She answered that she did go sometimes to the open spaces of the Palais Royal and the Tuileries gardens, which became rallying points for protestors at certain crucial moments such as before the destruction of the Bastille; although she was not a member of the Cordeliers' she had sometimes watched sessions there – perhaps with Léon, who elsewhere declared she attended it 'without interruption'; and she read the incendiary newspapers of, among others, Jean-Paul Marat and Camille Desmoulins.

Léon's response to the Champs de Mars massacre was one of indignation. Just as during their demonstration on the day of the king's flight, she, her mother and Évrard were threatened by Lafayette's Guardsmen and, when they returned home, insulted by their neighbours and threatened with imprisonment by their local ward. Like Évrard, and along with Anne Colombe, the publisher of Marat's *L'Ami du Peuple*; a female cousin of Georges Danton; and the wife of the president of the Cordeliers' Club, Léon was arrested and interrogated in the days following the demonstration as part of a government crackdown on popular radicalism – made all the more terrifying, to the authorities, when women were the radicals.

The Dutch writer Etta Palm d'Aelders, who had spoken so passionately on behalf of women's rights at the Social Circle in 1790, was another woman arrested on 19 July, accused of subversive behaviour. Her arrest was seen as an effort to intimidate the club, and it was successful: within days the Social Circle's Confédération des Amis, and its female equivalent (des Amies) had shut down. Repressive measures taken against other popular societies like the Cordeliers' effectively declawed them too. 'I need to see my trees again after watching so many fools and scoundrels,' wrote Manon. By mid-August, an illusory calm had settled over Paris. 'Paris is as still as the surface of a pond,' wrote Rosalie Jullien de la Drôme, wife of the Jacobin deputy, 'apart from the individual fights that occasion tragic scenes every day.'

The Rolands left Paris in September when Roland's job was finished, returning to Le Clos, their home outside Lyon, to oversee the grape harvest. During their absence a rumour had spread that Roland had been arrested as a counterrevolutionary, and the once friendly villagers there initially greeted Manon with cries of '*Les aristocrates à la lanterne!*' Boundaries were being blurred: the word 'aristocrat' – like 'patriot', 'virtue' and 'popular will' – took on new meanings. Language was being used ritualistically, with totemic words invoked 'as absolute, moral concepts' that would somehow guarantee and preserve the revolution's integrity. Germaine de Staël was aware of this development, in 1791 attacking democrats (another word whose meaning was transformed in the 1790s) 'who desecrate words merely by using them'.

From Le Clos, Manon initiated a correspondence with two of her so-called Incorruptibles, François Buzot and Maximilien Robespierre. To Robespierre she wrote in a deliberately classical, self-consciously historical style, addressing him as 'one whose energy has not ceased to offer the greatest resistance to the claims and schemes of despotism and intrigue' and predicting for him a brilliant career. She tried to engage him in a discussion of political and philosophical theory, tacitly presenting herself as a correspondent with whom he could debate ideas and policies, his partner in the fight for France's liberty. 'One should work for the good of the species in the same manner as the Deity,' she wrote, 'for the satisfaction of being true to oneself, of fulfilling one's destiny and earning self-esteem, but without expecting either gratitude or justice from individuals.' Manon signed her name with republican austerity: 'Roland, *née* Phlipon'. There is no record of any response from Robespierre.

Buzot was more receptive. Manon 'had already singled him out in our little circle for his breadth of vision and confident manner'; she admired his compassion, integrity and courage. Although she did not think his wife deserved him – he had married a cousin some years older than himself – the Rolands and the Buzots lived close to each other in Paris and saw each other frequently in the spring and summer of 1791. Their relationship grew closer while the Rolands were in Villefranche, and Buzot back at home in Évreux, that autumn. Through their letters, recorded Manon later, 'our friendship became intimate and unbreakable'. Buzot came to represent for Manon a revolutionary ideal, vigorous and full of integrity. Beside his passion her worthy, pedantic husband faded to grey.

Louis XVI signed the constitution and the Declaration of the Rights of Man and the Citizen on 30 September 1791, while the Rolands were away from Paris. It created a constitutional monarchy in which only propertied men were active citizens. All women were passive citizens, although the laws governing marriage, divorce and inheritance were made fairer; early proposals to allow wives property rights equal to their husbands' had been rejected outright.

At the end of the last meeting of the Constituent Assembly, which was dissolved by Louis's signature on the constitution, Robespierre and Pétion were garlanded with oak-leaf wreaths and carried on the shoulders of the people from the *manège* to their lodgings. Pétion became the new mayor of Paris, defeating Lafayette in the election in October with the covert support of the queen, who had long despised the general. Félicité de Genlis, last seen in a tricoloured dress and dancing to the 'Ça Ira' as Citoyenne Brûlart, had decided that the time had come to flee France. Emigration was, after all, as much the fashion for aristocrats as revolution. Pétion, whom Genlis had befriended when popular politics were à la mode, found time to escort her, her adoptive daughter Pamela, Henriette de Sercey and the duc d'Orléans's daughter into exile in London in October.

The radical pamphlet-writer Olympe de Gouges published her own *Déclaration des droits de la femme et de la citoyenne* as a response to the new constitution. 'Women are now respected and excluded,' she wrote; 'under the old regime they were despised and powerful.' The first article stated unequivocally, 'Woman is born free and lives equal to man in her rights.' Gouges demanded that women share with men both the burdens and the privileges of public services, taxation and representation. 'Woman has the right to mount the scaffold; she must equally have the right to mount the rostrum,' she wrote.

Gouges's appeal was passionate, but marred by her over-identification with her ideas and a lack of intellectual focus. 'Woman, wake up; the tocsin of reason is being heard throughout the whole universe; discover your rights,' she exhorted in her postscript. 'Having become free, he [man] has become unjust to his companion. Oh, women, women! When will you cease to be blind? What advantage have you received from the revolution?' Her claims that women deserved rights because they were superior to men in beauty and courage; her unfashionable devotion to the queen, to whom she dedicated the document; and her insistence on demanding equal rights for children born outside wedlock (Gouges herself was illegitimate, so it was a cause close to her heart) clouded her message, diluting her call for equality and her lucid analysis of the prejudice of most male revolutionaries.

Gouges's pronouncements made little impact on her contemporaries. Later, when the walls of Paris were plastered with her posters, the government spies said they produced no effect on the public. 'One sees them, stops for a second, and says to oneself, "Ah, c'est Olympe de Gouges."'

The satire *Mère Duchesne* was published at about the same time as Gouges's *Déclaration*. It echoed the popular new journal *Père Duchesne*, published by Jacques Hébert, in its use of colourful street slang and coarse language, and its style, as if straight from the mouth of its speaker. 'Although I am ignorant and not lettered, like former judges or the deputies, I don't lack a brain when it comes to political matters,' held the fictional Mère Duchesne stoutly. 'Can you believe in good faith that I would hesitate to stuff some good reasons up the noses of aristocrats?' Although she stopped short at demanding political rights for her sex, she praised women for their readiness to fight for liberty, and called for them to be better educated. 'Women have imagination and penetration; they are fertile in resources and expedients . . . Women aren't doomed, damn it, to be geese.'

Germaine de Staël spent the summer of 1791 at her father's house, Coppet, in Switzerland, arriving back in Paris in September in time for the opening session of the new Legislative Assembly. A motion proposed by Robespierre, that no deputy who had sat in the Constituent Assembly should be eligible for election to the Legislative, had been adopted, and so all the deputies were new to their responsibilities. The majority of them were Feuillants, constitutional monarchists who, by virtue of France's new constitution, considered the revolution over. The Feuillants' club, which had broken away from the increasingly radical Jacobins earlier in the year. They commanded 360 seats on the right of the hall; on the left sat 130 Jacobins, Manon's friends; in the centre sat the undecided remainder.

On her return, Germaine began agitating anew for the promotion of her lover, Louis de Narbonne. After the king's flight and subsequent arrest, Gustavus of Sweden had demonstrated his sympathy for his fellow-monarch by ordering the embassy on the rue du Bac closed to all social functions. Germaine was forced to use her friend Sophie de Condorcet's influential salon as her base – giving rise to rumours that Narbonne had seduced Mme de Condorcet as well as Mme de Staël – but their alliance in Narbonne's cause was successful. Mary Berry, visiting Paris that autumn, was disappointed to find Germaine so preoccupied (as she thought) with Talleyrand that she had no time to spend with her old friend; in fact it was Narbonne who was distracting her. The newspapers reported Germaine in her petticoats, 'rushing around from nine o'clock in the morning to all the journalists to give them the official papers; the letters and reports which she herself has dictated to her darling lover'.

In December, Narbonne was made Minister for War. 'What a triumph for Mme de Staël and what a pleasure for her to have all the army at her disposal,' wrote the queen bitterly. 'What a happiness it would be if one day I might be powerful again to prove to all these rogues that I was not their dupe.'

A rapturous Germaine watched Narbonne address the Assembly for the first time on 7 December. Although she praised his talents and his love of honour, she entertained no illusions about the uphill struggle that Narbonne, a courtier and an aristocrat, faced before the increasingly populist Assembly, distrusted by the royalists for being too radical and by the radicals for being too moderate. He once made the mistake, she said, of appealing 'to the most distinguished members of this Assembly'. The radical deputies were enraged: all the Assembly's members, they yelled back at Narbonne, 'were equally distinguished'.

The Rolands returned to Paris from Lyon in the same month that Narbonne was promoted. Roland had missed the Legislative Assembly's elections in Lyon, and needed a job; with their friends increasingly prominent politically – Brissot as deputy to the Assembly, Pétion as mayor, Robespierre as public prosecutor – they saw more opportunities in Paris than Lyon, and Roland could also pursue his claims to a pension.

They took rooms at the Hôtel Britannique again, but this time a smaller, cheaper apartment on the fourth floor, and they did not resume their salon. The Brissotin group was meeting instead in the Place Vendôme, at the home of Mme Dodun, mistress of another member of the circle, but Roland attended only rarely and Manon never. Instead she was said to have gone occasionally to the home of Julie Talma, wife of the great actor, whose salon was another important meeting-place of the left-wing; but on the whole she kept herself to herself.

In March 1792, Brissot came to see Manon at the Hôtel Britannique. The Feuillants who dominated the current ministry, led by Lafayette and Alexandre de Lameth, among others, were in disarray. Narbonne, their Minister for War, had been dismissed for plotting (with Germaine's help) to become prime minister in his own right and, when that failed, to steal the post of Foreign Minister.

Rumour also had it that Narbonne, on the verge of bankruptcy because his wife's estates in the Caribbean had been torched, was using the profits from selling military supplies to repay his debts. Germaine was told that Narbonne would be arrested unless he could find 30,000 francs at once. She asked her husband to advance her the money. 'Ah! You overwhelm me with joy,' he replied. 'Judge of my happiness: I believe I have freed your lover!' Neither he nor Germaine would have known, at this point, that he was also freeing the father of her unborn child, their second (their first, Auguste, had been born in August 1790). It was the kind of exchange that, had she needed any encouragement, would have made Manon Roland more determined than ever to rid France of corrupt aristocrats.

Brissot told Manon that the court party, seeking to restore its popularity, had decided to appoint some Jacobins to government ministries. He asked her if Roland would consider joining the king's council. Manon replied that she thought Roland would be interested. They discussed it, and agreed he would accept if he were offered a place. Roland was made Minister of the Interior the next day, 23 March.

Manon's friend Sophie Grandchamp described visiting the Rolands early on the morning after they heard the news of his promotion. She found them in bed, pale and exhausted after a sleepless night. Excited tears, kisses and vows of friendship were exchanged and Sophie went off to do some errands for Manon. On her return an entirely different scene greeted her. The Rolands' small fourth-floor rooms were overflowing with callers: ministers, important deputies, other officials. Two lackeys were waiting outside the door. Roland looked on contentedly while a glowing Manon, who had seemed near death that morning, received their visitors' compliments.

When Roland made his first official call on the king, he wore his usual clothes: a shabby black suit, round hat, woollen stockings and plain laced shoes. The master of ceremonies was aghast: 'Imagine, my Lord,' he exclaimed to General Dumouriez, the Minister for Foreign Affairs, indicating Roland out of the corner of his eye, 'no buckles on his shoes!'

The Rolands moved out of their rented apartment into the magnificent Hôtel de l'Intérieur, the childhood home of Germaine de Staël. Venetian mirrors hung on panelled, painted and gilded walls; the Rolands slept chastely beneath a frothing canopy of ostrich feathers. Although Manon was obliged to give twice-weekly dinners for her husband's colleagues and associates, still she invited no women, served her guests only one simple course and provided them with sugar-water rather than wine. She was determined that her behaviour should set the tone for a new republic of virtue.

6

AMAZONE

Théroigne de Méricourt

AUGUST 1790–AUGUST 1792

And we would wish to earn a civic crown too, and court the honour
of dying for a liberty which is dearer perhaps to us [women] than it is
to them [men], since the effects of despotism weigh still more heavily
upon our heads than upon theirs.

THÉROIGNE DE MÉRICOURT

Revolutionaries: Louis-Pierre Manuel, Jérôme Pétion
and Pierre-Gaspard Chaumette

THÉROIGNE DE MÉRICOURT had left Paris in the late summer of 1790, disillusioned by the revolution. Frustrated by her inability to make her voice heard, running out of money, the object of insults and ridicule, and afraid of arrest, she wanted to go home; but the revolution itself had been the closest thing she had ever found to a home.

Her prospects were bleak. Although she had remained close to her two younger brothers, supporting them from her earnings as a courtesan, her father had shown no interest in her and her stepmother had never made her welcome. Her experiences since running away with an English soldier in the early 1780s – at first living in the demi-monde of London, Paris and Genoa, then trying to break into the world of music and theatre, finally seeking acceptance by radical revolutionaries – made her all the more unusual in the quiet farming community in which she had grown up. But Théroigne had nowhere else to turn.

Returning to Marcourt, she found solace as the autumn progressed in the peaceful patterns of rural existence that she had turned her back on eight years before: the harvest, the village fairs – simple, pastoral, virtuous pleasures. She decided to buy a small plot of land and settle near Liège, pawning her diamonds – the diamonds once worn to the Paris opera by the mysterious Mlle Campinado – to fund her new life there.

Théroigne's democratic idealism, despite her disillusion with individuals, was undimmed, encouraged by her reading of Plato and Seneca whose words she copied eagerly down into her notebook. She taught the village children revolutionary songs, gave stockings and skirts to the poor and quarrelled with the priest over his tithe and with the miller over his prices. Her beliefs were noted by those who lived in the area, and she began to dream again of helping to create a better society.

She made friends with the young wife of the local baron, who shared her progressive opinions. After Théroigne's visits to Mme de Sélys, though, her conservative husband would write to comte Maillebois, the French émigré agent responsible for the region (part of Austria at the time), informing him of Théroigne's activities; the local priest with whom she had clashed over tithes joined Sélys in denouncing her. The Austrian government, hearing of her presence in Liège and fearful of revolutionary ideas flooding across the French border and sweeping away their regime too, began to observe Théroigne more closely.

Confounded and alarmed by events in France, the Austrians became convinced that Théroigne was a Jacobin agent, sent to the area with vast sums of money to buy the loyalty of the Liégoises. The former Austrian ambassador to France, who had heard of Théroigne's alleged activities at Versailles in October 1789 and believed she had been at the centre of a plot to assassinate Marie-Antoinette, confirmed their suspicions to the Austrian emperor, Leopold II, Marie-Antoinette's brother. Théroigne, who through the autumn had been writing back to Paris in an effort to get her name cleared of the rumours still circulating about her activities during the October days, was once again the object of suspicion; this time it would be harder for her to escape.

Austrian troops entered Liège in January 1791 and Théroigne was arrested in the middle of the night of the 15th. She was asleep at an inn in a small village, surrounded by her books and papers, when three mercenaries burst into her room, saying that they were patriots who had come to rescue her from counterrevolutionaries. She was suspicious at first, but eventually agreed to go with them. The hired carriage, its curtains drawn, drove off into the night.

Over the next ten days, as the berline jolted and swayed across the Low Countries towards the Austrian Tyrol, Théroigne was questioned again and again by the three men – all ardent royalists and émigrés, two of them former officers in the French army – about her revolutionary activities. She was 'provoked and irritated by them in a thousand different ways, each of them more degrading and shocking than the last'. They subjected her to the sexual harassment she had come to regard as normal, speaking to her 'ineffectually of love' and telling her she would fetch them a better price on the street. One of the men, the Chevalier Maynard de la Valette – using the macho alias M. Legros – tried to rape her, but she successfully fought him off. On another occasion the men stopped their carriage to beat up a coachman, and when they climbed back inside they jeered at her, 'So much for your Rights of Man.' La Valette bragged of his desire to flog the entire 'left side of the National Assembly, and M. the abbé Sieyès at their head'.

When she realized her captors had deceived her about being patriots, Théroigne began exaggerating her role in the revolution, feeding them with lies just to see whether they were fools enough to believe her. They noted down her words as evidence to be used against her, building up a portrait of her exulting in bloodshed, longing for the deaths of the royal family, plotting the October days, speaking in front of the Jacobins and forming her own women's club – the latter two accusations, however untrue, considered as shocking as the first three.

The Parisian newspapers and satirical sheets were not slow to pick up on 'the famous Théroigne's' arrest. 'We have been assured that the Jacobin Club is going to threaten the emperor [Leopold] with an army of 500,000 National Guards if he refuses to hand over this heroine,' reported the *Journal général*, tongue in cheek, 'because its chief members are anxious lest she betray their secrets.'

Théroigne was taken to the immense, menacing medieval castle of Kufstein in the Austrian Alps, an impregnable fortress topped with squat towers and set on the crest of a forbiddingly steep hill. She was imprisoned under the name of Mme de Théobald: the Austrians considered her far too treacherous an agent provocateur to confine her using her real name. Count Metternich-Winneburg, Austrian minister plenipotentiary to the Low Countries, told the imperial chancellor Anton von Kaunitz that she was 'particularly dangerous for public order'. From Kufstein, Théroigne wrote to one of her brothers, begging him to come to Vienna to plead her case before the emperor. She was under no illusion about the gravity of her situation. Although her captors had not yet accused her of anything, they were 'making every effort,' she said, 'to prove that I was in part responsible for the events of the French revolution'. But her brother, whose allowance she still paid, remained in Paris, merely writing to her banker about his despair at having lost his *protectrice* before asking for more money.

Prince Kaunitz was convinced, as Théroigne thought, that his attractive prisoner could unravel the entire revolution for him. He sent the conscientious, scrupulously impartial civil servant François de Blanc to Kufstein to interrogate her formally. Kaunitz's extensive instructions revealed the importance he attached to her testimony and how his hopes of discovering through her the truth of events in France prevented him from assessing her real significance. He told Blanc to find out how central a role Théroigne had played in the revolution, which men had been her patrons (the implication being, lovers) and who had facilitated her rise to prominence. He wanted to know 'how it was possible for her to wield such enormous political influence', not dreaming that the influence she had actually wielded was negligible.

Through Théroigne's revelations – he suspected 'grave political crimes' although he was prepared for mere revolutionary propaganda – Kaunitz hoped Blanc would furnish him with detailed information 'on the main leaders of the revolution, on their personal characters and their ideas, and, finally, on their intentions and their ultimate aims'. He was particularly interested in these unspecified leaders' views on the royal family. Kaunitz told Blanc that Théroigne seemed 'an exceedingly enterprising person, possessed of an ardent desire to have some influence upon the masses'. Alongside this ruling passion he detected an almost fanatical vanity. Blanc was not instructed to treat 'the delightful person who is in our charge' with cruelty: the intention was not to punish Théroigne but to elicit from her everything she knew.

François de Blanc, rigorous and principled, devoted to the pursuit of truth and justice, would turn out to be Théroigne's saviour. At their first meeting, he read out to her the parts of Kaunitz's letter demanding a complete confession. Théroigne, who had absorbed the concept that freedom of thought and speech was a natural right and thus could not be criminal, willingly accepted this directive, believing that a man of principle would see the innocence of her words and actions. All through the month of June 1791, while the French king and queen tried and failed to reach the French border, Théroigne and Blanc laboured over her 'confession'. While he sifted through various reports on Théroigne as well as the papers seized with her when she was arrested, she spent her days laboriously writing a detailed account of her life up until her arrest. Blanc asked her to fill in gaps and respond to certain allegations, but otherwise she wrote what she thought was important. What she left out were the shaming or painful details of her past: the extent of her career as a courtesan, the severe venereal disease she had suffered from in Genoa, and her little dead daughter.

Blanc discovered what Théroigne did not tell him from her confiscated papers, which included a record of her political opinions and activities, her thoughts on the books she read, drafts of letters and some strange, dark, stream-of-consciousness writings. The coherence of her notes on patriotism and legislation ('As far as politics is concerned, the important thing is not to have a good king but to have a good government') was completely lacking from these private dream sequences. In one, she imagined building a bronze façade containing a black vault where a female figure stood, trampling tyranny underfoot. 'This tyranny will be represented by the figure of a man. This woman will reach out her hand to me and will cry out: help me or I shall succumb. I will then take hold of a dagger from nearby and I will strike the man.' These words were underlined in black.

When Blanc asked her what this troubling image meant, Théroigne replied that she had heard of a vault in Rome bearing a statue of a Fury with a dagger:

> This vision came to me because, having always been offended by the tyranny which men exercise over my own sex, I wished to find an emblem for it in this picture, in which the death of this tyranny would mark the downfall of the prejudices under which we groan, and which it was my dearest wish to have been able to destroy.

For Théroigne, the revolution's rejection of the paternal authority of the monarchy was explicitly associated with her personal rejection of any type of masculine domination and exploitation, from which she had suffered so much.

Blanc soon realized that her political importance and the contacts she was credited with were vastly exaggerated. He rejected the sensational 'statements' extracted from her by her abductors en route to Kufstein: 'I have to point out that they [the documents] were drafted and signed by French aristocrats,' commented Blanc, 'that is, by people who are plainly the prisoner's sworn enemies.' Théroigne's evidence about having both misled her abductors and been maligned by them was borne out by their own admissions. The responses to the enquiries that Blanc addressed to the courts in Paris showed that the evidence against her was so slim that the authorities there had not bothered to issue a summons.

At the beginning of July, Blanc summed up his preliminary findings to Kaunitz, saying 'the accused seems to be innocent, the accuser [La Valette] the opposite'. He recommended that Théroigne, whose health was deteriorating – she was depressed, could not sleep, coughed and spat blood and complained of terrible headaches – be released. He praised her enthusiasm for her country and 'luminous and surprising' intuitive understanding of events there, and compared the bullying La Valette and his henchmen to their prisoner in strikingly unfavourable terms.

In August, Blanc and a doctor accompanied Théroigne to Vienna. Although she had not been formally cleared or released, Blanc told her she would be freed when the case was closed. By the time she left Austria the two of them had spent six months together in a situation of extraordinary intimacy and had developed an affectionate mutual respect. With her usual admiration for austere, older men – like Romme and Sieyès in Paris – Théroigne saw Blanc as a father figure. Her letters to him, mostly concerning things she needed or wanted, or asking him to visit her, were signed '*votre toute dévouée*' and show the comfortable, rather touching trust that had grown up between the vulnerable former courtesan and the upright civil servant.

In October, Théroigne was granted an audience with the emperor Leopold, who gave her permission to return to Liège. Money for her return journey was advanced to her and she returned to the Low Countries at the end of November. Almost immediately, the rumours started flying again: Leopold's sister Marie-Christine, wife of the Austrian governor of the region, reported to him that Théroigne had been spotted in Brussels, boasting 'of having seen the emperor and of having converted him to her principles'.

By the end of January 1792, Théroigne was back in Paris. The political atmosphere was tense and divided, with royalists, Feuillants and Jacobins taking different sides over the issue of whether to declare war on Austria. The king and the court party advocated war, hoping a French defeat would allow the Austrians to re-establish the ancien régime. Among the Feuillant constitutional monarchists, Lafayette favoured war, hoping glory would advance his personal ambition, while Alexandre de Lameth thought even victory would only help the republican party. Brissot believed war would consolidate the revolution in France and spread its principles across Europe. Robespierre opposed him, arguing that victory would throw up a dictator while defeat would restore the king to his former powers; neither end, he said, would serve the revolution.

From this point onwards, the ideological division between Brissot and Robespierre would become an unbridgeable chasm. Manon Roland, rebuffed by Robespierre, attributed his antipathy towards Brissot and his associates to envy. In fact he saw that the Brissotins would be fatally compromised by the policies they were instituting. They urged war, but opposed the governmental control necessary for victory; they made the monarchy unworkable, but hesistated to dispose of the king; they championed moderation, but moderation always fell short of the revolution's ever-changing aims.

Théroigne, fresh out of her Austrian prison, backed Brissot's calls for war. Her first public appearance was in the galleries of the Jacobin Club – where both Brissotins and Jacobins still met – on 26 January. 'I can announce to you a triumph of patriotism,' declared the president. 'Mlle Théroigne, celebrated for her civic devotion and by the persecutions she has submitted to, is among us in the women's tribune.' She was carried down on to the floor, and invited to come back to give an account of her recent experiences.

On 1 February, Théroigne duly returned to address the Jacobins, urging war and declaring that the Low Countries were full of patriots waiting to be freed from Austrian rule. She also recommended the formation of regiments of female soldiers – not a home guard of women to defend the *patrie* against internal enemies of the revolution, like that for which Pauline Léon petitioned, but actual fighters, *amazones*, in the field of battle. She was granted, as 'president of her sex, seated today alongside our president', the honours of the session. Male-dominated society had once questioned whether women had souls, but this was just an effort 'to curse women in order to seem not to love them', said Louis-Pierre Manuel, who paid homage to the Amazon of Liberty. 'If our forefathers had so dim a view of women, it was because they were not free; for liberty would have taught them, just as it has taught us, that it is as easy for nature to create Porcias as Scaevolas.'*

Almost two months later, on 25 March, Théroigne addressed the Fraternal Society of the Minimes – the branch of the Fraternal Society founded by Alexandre de Lameth's handsome young secretary Jean-Lambert Tallien, who had perhaps already tucked Thérésia de Fontenay's fallen rose into the breast-pocket of his National Guardsman's jacket.

Théroigne called once again for women to show men that they were inferior to them neither in courage nor in virtue. 'Let us raise ourselves to the height of our destinies; let us break our chains,' she cried. 'At last the time is ripe for women to emerge from their shameful nullity, where the ignorance, pride and injustice of men had [sic] kept them enslaved for so long a time.' She recalled how the women of the ancient Gauls and Germans had debated in public assemblies and fought beside their men, and asked if men alone had the right to glory. Women too, who cherished liberty all the more because despotism weighed even more heavily on them than on men, had the right to earn laurels in defence of the *patrie*.

Her audience must have been receptive, not least because another

* Porcia Catonis was a Roman matron who committed suicide by swallowing hot coals when her husband Brutus was defeated in battle by Marc Anthony; Mucius Scaevola put his hand into a fire to demonstrate his patriotism. The implication is that women could also be patriots.

member of the Minimes branch of the Fraternal Society was the radical Pauline Léon. Only a few weeks before, the Society had re-addressed Léon's 1791 petition requesting for women the right to defend themselves, this time to the Legislative rather than the Constituent Assembly, and with Léon's signature among the names rather than at the head of them.

On the same evening that she addressed the Minimes, Théroigne attended a dinner given in the working-class faubourg Saint-Antoine for the market porters. Also at the party were revolutionary royalty: 'Queen' Audu, heroine of the women's march to Versailles, and Théroigne's friend Jérôme Pétion, mayor of Paris and nicknamed King Pétion. Two weeks after the dinner, the city of Paris gave commemorative swords to Audu and Théroigne. Pétion praised Audu, who had been imprisoned after the October 1789 protest, for her patriotic conduct during the demonstration and 'for having escaped the slavery of your sex's education'. When the *patrie* was in danger, he said, women 'do not feel any the less that they are *citoyennes*'. Someone in the crowd protested at such honours being granted to Théroigne, but he was told to shut up: 'she will serve her country better than you'.

Théroigne began trying to muster recruits in the faubourg Saint-Antoine, urging women to arm themselves and join her battalion of *amazones*. Her activities brought her name to the attention of the Jacobins again, but this time in a less favourable light. On 13 April a delegation to the Club accused Théroigne of stirring up trouble in the neighbourhood, of arranging thrice-weekly political meetings for local women and promising them a civic banquet at which Robespierre – whom she had never met – and other prominent Jacobins would be present. A Jacobin friend, Antoine Santerre, whose wife's signature Théroigne was accused of forging on a list of supporters for her proposed banquet, defended her cautiously, but suggested that the men of the faubourg preferred 'to find their household in good order rather than to await the return of their women from meetings [which] . . . rarely inculcate a spirit of docility in them'. For this reason, said Santerre, he had asked Théroigne to stop her meetings in Saint-Antoine.

Santerre's wary response to Théroigne's efforts to bring women into public life, especially when contrasted with Pétion's enthusiasm for female patriots, demonstrates reformers' wildly varying views on the issue of political women. Both men were considered progressive ideologically, and both were popular idols, but Santerre, following Rousseau, believed women could best support the *patrie* by creating a home for their husbands and children, while Pétion, closer to Condorcet ideologically, praised women who had risen above such limitations. As women, fired with enthusiasm for the revolution, moved into the public sphere, their actions were regarded with increasing mistrust by many male observers, however radical their views on other issues. The misogynist Robespierre, whose concern for universal suffrage was limited strictly to men, demonstrated his antipathy to women interfering in politics by refusing to dignify with a comment Théroigne's misappropriation of his name for her own uses.

At about the same time, on 1 April 1792, Etta Palm d'Aelders, who had been arrested after the Champs de Mars massacre the previous July, received permission to address the National Assembly. 'Women have shared the dangers of the revolution; why shouldn't they participate in its advantages? Men are free at last, and women are the slaves of a thousand prejudices,' she said. She asked the Assembly to educate girls and to grant them their majority at twenty-one, to make divorce legal, and to declare 'that political liberty and equality of rights be common to both sexes'. Once again, d'Aelders was granted the honours of the session, but her suggestions were not implemented.

That same spring of 1792, Théroigne persuaded Jean-Lambert Tallien, the radical actor and writer Jean-Marie Collot d'Herbois, the painter David and his frequent collaborator the playwright Marie-Joseph Chénier to head a delegation of 'our most illustrious patriots', requesting permission from the Paris Commune, the municipal body that governed Paris, to commemorate the soldiers of Châteauvieux at a Liberty *fête*. The Châteauvieux regiment had mutinied in August 1790 after their demands for back pay were refused, and their rebellion had been suppressed with savage brutality. The soldiers were seen by many as martyrs, and their rising had become a rallying-call for some who feared the revolution was being diluted by moderates. Others, like Marie-Joseph Chénier's poet brother André, and Camille Desmoulins who called it a 'celebration of insurrection', saw it as a counterrevolutionary plot.

Revolutionary festivals, as Mona Ozouf has described, 'provide a mirror in which the revolution as a whole may be viewed'. From the joyous hopefulness of the Federation Day celebrations in July 1790 to the uncomfortable primness of the Festival of the Supreme Being four years later (see page 290), they reflected the changing face of the revolution as each successive faction and regime sought an understanding of the events that had brought them to power, and tried to disseminate their interpretation of those events.

The unifying elements of revolutionary festivals – girls in simple white dresses, fresh flowers and greenery instead of tarnished tinsel for decorations, a move away from elaborate, creaking machinery and towards didactic speeches to provide the entertainment of the day – derived from Rousseau, who loathed the artifice of ancien régime festivals and theatre. 'Plant a stake crowned with flowers in the middle of a marketplace,' he recommended. 'It is in the open air, it is beneath the sky that you must assemble and give yourself up to the sweet spectacle of your happiness.'

Théroigne's Festival of Liberty was held on 15 April and the Jacobin deputy's wife Rosalie Jullien enjoyed it so much that in her diary the following day she exulted, 'I was there, I was there!' She thought it exemplified 'all the pomp, all the magnificent simplicity and all the profound tranquillity of a festival of the people'. Women dressed in white marched arm in arm with soldiers. The streets were full of people dancing and the strains of the 'Ça Ira' floated out of every window. Because of the protests made against her in Saint-Antoine two days earlier, Théroigne made no public appearance as the celebration she had initiated came to life.

At the beginning of June another *fête*, this one called the Festival of the Law, was held in honour of the mayor of Étampes who had been killed trying to maintain order during a food riot. The *Révolutions de Paris* criticized the women who participated in the celebrations, led by Olympe de Gouges who, the writer commented condescendingly, resembled nothing so much as a drum major in charge of unruly troops. A band of mothers in white, crowned with oak leaves, symbolically received the book of laws from the Constituent Assembly, but the theatricality of the performance grated with the *Révolutions*' contributor, who saw it as overly feminizing the masculine majesty of the Law. 'Whatever one may say,' he concluded, 'women seemed out of place on that great day.'

Given the prominence of Théroigne's activities after her return from Austria, it was only a matter of time before she would once again be the object of journalistic venom. In March, the *Journal général* announced the sale of patriotic playing-cards, in which Théroigne was the *dame de piques* (queen of spades) – a pun on her well known desire, as an *amazone*, to carry a pike (*pique*) herself. The pike was an emblem of independence, equality and surveillance, according to a February 1792 piece in the *Révolutions de Paris*. 'The pikes of the people are the columns of French liberty,' it proclaimed. But 'let pikes be prohibited for women; dressed in white and girded with the national sash, let them content themselves with being spectators'.

The king in Théroigne's suit was the duc d'Orléans, who was said to have paid her to rabble-rouse at Versailles in October 1789, and her knave was Antoine Santerre, the rich brewer who would shortly chastise her for trying to drum up support for her female regiment in the faubourg Saint-Antoine; both were well known womanizers and therefore, in the eyes of her political adversaries, apt partners for a former courtesan like Théroigne. The other queens in the pack were Thérésia de Fontenay's friend Dondon de Lameth, Sophie de Condorcet and Germaine de Staël.

Satirical attacks rained down on Théroigne: the 'Jacobins' strumpet' was depicted in the *Journal général* drilling a regiment of Les Halles market women wearing false moustaches; the *Chronique du manège* called her 'a manhunter, mad for men'; an etching showed her in her *amazone* leading an army of women including Mmes de Staël, Condorcet and Genlis against the Austrian troops, vanquishing them by showing them her '*république*'.

A miscellaneous and often sensationalist selection of revolutionary writings published in England in 1806 includes a speech Théroigne was said to have made at the Palais Royal in June 1792 extolling free love and calling for marriage to be banned. Its tone is so salacious that it must have been written by a royalist journalist – for whom Théroigne represented the most terrifying incarnation of womankind – seeking to associate political liberty with the worst excesses of immorality. The putative Théroigne asked if 'our shameful institutions, imposed by rogues and submitted to by fools', were not less natural than the unrestrained freedoms and equality enjoyed by lovers and seducers. 'Yes, I, Théroigne de Méricourt, rejoice in being among those called harlots by aristocrats; I rejoice in prostituting myself to everybody, without belonging to anybody,' she is said to have said. 'I am as free as the birds that wing the air, or the animals that range the forests.'

The most vicious misogynist amongst the royalist hacks was François Suleau, who in the most demeaning and revolting terms, described in April 1792 'the women who have harnessed themselves to the chariot (or, more exactly, to the dung-cart) of the revolution'. The young women – he did not specify Théroigne here, though she was the frequent butt of one of the newspapers he wrote for, the *Acts of the Apostles* – who 'have hurled themselves into the [frying pan] of the rights of man' were, according to Suleau, despite their 'pretty little faces', their 'frisky appearance and their air of being a proper little madam', covered with the marks of promiscuity and madness: 'itch, scabs, ringworm, *fleurs à la Pompadour*, scurf, yaws, blisters on the nape of the neck, suckers on the breast, ulcers on the thigh, and plasters on all their scars'. Théroigne, always so conscious of humiliating insults directed at her sex, would remember Suleau's name.

The dissension between Robespierre and Brissot over war with Austria was becoming increasingly overt, and even Théroigne's name was drawn into it as the political lines were drawn. In the days immediately following the declaration of war on 20 April 1792, Robespierre and his friends attacked Brissot and his political allies. Robespierre attacked

Lafayette at the Jacobin Club while Jean-Lambert Tallien, becoming more and more prominent politically, denounced Condorcet, who was accused at the same time of being dominated by his spirited young wife.

During one of these debates, someone said as an aside that he had heard Théroigne, at a café near the *manège*, angrily withdrawing her support from Robespierre because of his opposition to the war. The deputies burst out laughing at the thought that a woman's backing could count for anything in a debate of such gravity. Théroigne, embarrassed and furious, tried to insist on speaking, but her move towards the tribune caused such an uproar that the session had to be suspended. 'Since we cannot find men capable of being ministers, why don't we call on women, such as Mme Condorcet and Mlle Théroigne de Méricourt?' asked the right-wing *Petit Gautier* the next day. 'They have the vocation, the talent to be *femmes publiques* [literally, public women or prostitutes].'

Jean-Marie Roland, as Minister of the Interior, was at the heart of the Brissotin administration that had declared war on Austria. At this stage Roland hoped the king accepted that his interests would be best protected by their government, and he and his associates, believing in Louis's sincerity, were trying to work with him. But the temporary alliance between court and Brissotin parties was based on mutual mistrust. For his part, Louis welcomed war, numbly hoping he would be restored to his former powers in the aftermath of a French defeat, while Marie-Antoinette was doing her best to provide the Austrians with treacherous information about the French army. As Manon Roland said, Louis 'constantly undermined the arrangements which he was professing to support'. *Père Duchesne* put it more succinctly, calling the king '*Louis le Faux*'.

Germaine de Staël's view of the Brissotin ministry was that they were talented but inexperienced unknowns who 'aimed at a republic and succeeded only in overturning the monarchy'. She saw them as principled, but made hypocritical by their desire for power – 'some of them offered to support royalty, if all the places in the ministry were given to their friends' – and it did not occur to her that her own efforts to advance her friends might be interpreted in a similar light. Principles do not preclude ambition, and the Brissotins, like Germaine herself, would have countered that their principles were the best for France and that they were the only people capable of realizing them.

As the wife of a minister, Manon Roland found herself in the spring of 1792 'at the centre of affairs'. In her memoirs she attempted to emphasize her continued distance from public life, insisting that she did not join in political talk or distribute political favours, but her use of the pronoun 'we' when she described the events of Roland's ministry belied her efforts to demonstrate her non-involvement. Roland confided everything in her; and Manon, claiming that their methods, spirit and principles were as one, acted less as her husband's secretary than as his muse and inspiration. She guarded personal access to him from her little office, where friends and petitioners used her to sound out ideas or pass messages on to Roland. Manon wrote later that she found 'it hard to describe my agitation at that time. I was passionate for the revolution . . . I burned with zeal for my country. Public affairs had become a torment to me, a moral fever which left me no rest.'

Manon had backed war from the start – like Brissot she believed that it would cement the revolution and bring about the king's final demise – but she was anxious about the rift between Robespierre, whom she respected, and her friends. She knew that the resolution she desired could only come about through unity. As his political relations with Brissot and Roland were breaking down towards the end of March that year, Manon wrote to Robespierre, asking him to visit her and assuring him of her unalterable admiration for him. 'I hope only to be able to make some contribution to the common weal with the help of enlightened, devoted and wise patriots. You are for me at the head of this class.'

She wrote again a month later, five days after the declaration of war, repeating her request that he come to see her because she believed him 'an ardent lover of liberty, entirely devoted to the public good', and assuring him that she had nothing to do with 'those whom you regard as your mortal enemies'. Her appeals came to nothing. Robespierre was not interested in dealing with a woman – if anything,

Manon's interference would only have confirmed his dislike of Roland, Brissot and their friends – and he already recognized that he must take command of his political destiny.

The early stages of the war did not go well. At the beginning of May, the Assembly was in constant emergency session as unhappy news kept rolling in from the front. Fears of invasion were intense. Arms were distributed among the Parisian *sections* (wards) so that sans-culotte patriots could defend themselves. On 29 May the king agreed that his personal bodyguard, a privilege granted to him as a safeguard of his constitutional role, be disbanded, amid worries that it would rise to join an invading Austrian force.

Louis agreed to relinquish his bodyguard because his attention was focused elsewhere; he was determined not to allow two other proposals through the National Assembly. He used his hard-won veto once to reject a decree that would force into exile refractory priests, and a second time to prevent an armed camp of twenty thousand provincial soldiers, or *fédérés*, being established just outside Paris. Manon Roland was enraged by his presumption: the king's behaviour 'proved his lack of good faith' and she was determined that her husband, as the minister concerned, should resign in a blaze of publicity. A quiet withdrawal would not be enough – Roland 'must make his gesture openly and vigorously, so as to enlighten public opinion about the evils which had led to it and turn his resignation to good account for the Republic'.

On 11 June, Roland had delivered to the king a letter of resignation written entirely by his wife and in the most searing of tones. She castigated Louis for his policies and attitude to the revolution, and forcibly reminded him of his duties to France and of the risks of civil war. The revolution 'will be accomplished and cemented at the cost of bloodshed unless wisdom forestalls evils which it is still possible to avoid,' she warned. 'I know that the austere language of truth is rarely welcomed near the throne but I also know that it is because it is so rarely heard that revolutions become necessary.'

Two days later, without acknowledging the letter, the king dismissed Roland and the rest of the Brissotin ministers. Manon urged Roland to send a copy to the National Assembly so that the reasons for his leaving office – and the fact that it was a resignation rather than a dismissal – were made clear. The Assembly ordered the letter printed and sent out to all the regional departments of France. Manon's words were greeted with admiration by Roland's supporters. Condorcet praised it in the highest terms, saying Roland spoke 'the most pure language of probity, patriotism and reason'. Rosalie Jullien thought the letter immortalized him, and would win him the admiration and respect of the entire country.

Her experience of Roland's opponents and colleagues during the few days leading up to this crisis reduced still further Manon's already low opinion of most of the men involved in affairs of state. 'I would never have thought, if I had not seen it with my own eyes, that good judgement and firmness of character were such rare commodities and that so few men are fit to govern,' she remembered. Asking for those qualities to be combined with honesty was 'like asking for the moon'. What struck her most about the people Roland worked with was their 'universal mediocrity'. This realization gave her a new confidence in her own opinions and abilities. 'Really! I am not surprised that I was much sought after. They could see that I was worth something.'

After the king's dismissal of his ministers, a huge demonstration took place on 20 June in front of the royal palace of the Tuileries where the National Assembly met. With the Brissotin Pétion in the *mairie*, or mayor's office, there was little chance of official opposition to the protest. Popular leaders and activists – including the sans-culotte butcher Louis Legendre; Fournier l'Américain, one of the seditious National Guardsmen who had followed the women who marched on Versailles in October 1789; Théroigne's friend Santerre; Théroigne herself; and Pauline Léon – had spent several days mobilizing artisan and working-class Paris wards such as the faubourg Saint-Antoine to come out on the 20th to plant a 'liberty tree' in the Tuileries grounds.

The people gathered at the palace and asked permission to present their petition to the National Assembly, which, given the king's recent dismissal of the Brissotins, was sympathetic to their demands. Carrying pikes and wearing red caps – the Phrygian cap worn by freed Roman slaves, symbol of liberty – they planted a poplar in the Capuchins' garden; as Bertrand Barère said in front of the Assembly, 'the tree of liberty grows only when watered by the blood of tyrants'. They waited for a response to their request, according to Rosalie Jullien, who was sitting in the Assembly tribunes, 'in the most profound silence'. Finally they were admitted to the *manège*, singing the 'Ça Ira'. 'Never has the Assembly been so brilliant and so majestic,' recorded Rosalie. 'What a beautiful day! What a triumph!'

Afterwards, as the huge crowd swelled around the *manège*, the Tuileries gardens and up to the palace railings, the gates burst open and a multitude swarmed into the undefended palace and came face to face with the king, attended by only a few unarmed guards and courtiers. Some were said to have waved in his face a calf's heart, stuck on a pike, intended to represent 'the heart of an aristocrat'; others yelled insults at him. The butcher Louis Legendre, at the head of the mob, is said to have said to King Louis, 'Monsieur, you must hear us; you are a villain. You have always deceived us; you deceive us still. Your measure is full. The people are tired of this play-acting.'

The king, backed into an alcoved window, responded with dignity and composure. He was given a red cap which he put on, then toasted the Parisians and the French people, but he refused to declare that he would relinquish his right to the veto or that he would reinstate the Brissotin ministers. Marie-Antoinette was subjected to abuse, but kept out of sight: Rosalie Jullien, scathingly republican, reported that '*la femme du roi* [not *la reine*] was away in the morning, I don't know where'. Finally at six that evening, Pétion appeared: he had just been informed of what was going on, he told Louis. He managed to disperse the exultant crowd and the exhausted king was reunited with his terrified wife and children.

Although Pétion was briefly suspended from office and letters of support for Louis flooded into the Assembly, after 20 June the political momentum rested entirely with the people of Paris. They could smell the march of their own power. Lafayette made his final attempt to dominate events, returning to Paris to demand controls on the press and the closure of the popular societies, but when he was challenged in the Assembly about having left his troops without permission he was forced to back down and return to his command in Alsace. Marie-Antoinette, who hated Lafayette, had informed Pétion of his plans to rally his Guardsmen to support a *coup d'état*.

The atmosphere in Paris became steadily more disorderly throughout July 1792 as fears of invasion escalated, thousands of ardently revolutionary *fédérés* converged on the city, and the divided leaders of the weak National Assembly made and broke alliances with one another. On the 11th an emergency government was declared, requiring every council, ward and department to sit in permanent session, and the Assembly assumed the executive role, effectively removing from Louis the vestiges of his official duties as monarch.

Private life was changing too. From 5 July, every *citoyen* was required to wear a tricolour cockade as a demonstration of his devotion to the *patrie*. Five days earlier Catherine Grand, the future Mme Talleyrand, had ordered forty-six yards of tricolour ribbon. Gradually the wards and departments began formally to adopt a more egalitarian style of address, reflecting the common revolutionary usage between strangers of the unceremonious second-person-singular *tu* instead of the more polite second-person-plural *vous*.

Louis made what would be his last public appearance before his death on 14 July, the third anniversary of the Bastille's fall. Cheers of '*Vive Pétion!*' drowned out the few feeble shouts of '*Vive le roi!*', which sounded to Germaine de Staël 'like a last cry, like a last prayer'. She watched the king's old-fashioned embroidered court coat and his white head – conspicuously alone in a sea of plain black coats and patriotically unpowdered hair – as he mounted the steps of the altar with his touchingly shambling gait, to renew his oath to the constitution. 'He seemed,' she wrote, 'a sacred victim offering himself as a voluntary sacrifice.' The queen's eyes were red from crying.

A week later, the émigrés gathered in Mainz for the coronation of the new emperor of Austria, Francis II. Their hopes for victory were quixotically high. The politician Lord Granville Leveson Gower described the scene to his mother, and reflected that 'the pleasure of seeing these great people' was enhanced by the thought 'that they are preparing to crush the Democrats and to bring back the people of

France to their senses. The French here speak as confidently of living at Paris next year as if they were in actual possession.'

As Paris spiralled out of control and the power of the popular wards swelled, Manon Roland and her friends debated how to preserve the revolution and protect liberty if the Austrians did reach Paris. They were willing to try to harness popular energy to their cause, uniting the radical sans-culottes on the street with the patriotic soldiers newly arrived in the capital from the provinces. If they could not defeat the king's supporters, as a last resort the Brissotins were prepared to move the revolutionary government away from Paris.

A battalion of five hundred soldiers from Marseille marched into Paris at the end of July singing the stirringly patriotic 'War Song for the Army of the Rhine', which would become known as the 'Marseillaise'. Scuffles between rival groups of soldiers, sans-culottes and 'aristocrats' began to break out on the streets. The city's radical wards – in which any man, regardless of his wealth or property, was allowed a voice and a vote – were in constant session. Almost unanimously, they called for the establishment of a republic: 'Let us strike this colossus of despotism . . . let us all unite to declare the fall of this cruel king, let us say with one accord, Louis XVI is no longer king of the French.' One ward declared that if the Assembly did not accept their petition and declare Louis dethroned, they would sound the tocsin from nine until midnight. Even Robespierre, who hoped to see Louis removed from power by a legitimately elected Assembly rather than by a popular uprising, declared in the Jacobin Club on 29 July that the king had been overthrown.

'*Pauvre Louis XVI*,' wrote Rosalie Jullien, sympathetic to his plight despite her strident republicanism. Her husband had chastised her a few days earlier for writing to him (he was away from Paris) of nothing but politics. 'So you don't want me to talk politics to you?' she asked. 'In truth that is a great contradiction, because I think of nothing else, and public affairs become so personal that one can't stop oneself taking them to heart as that is what controls our fortune and our life.' A few weeks later, she wrote, 'the affairs of state are my love affairs; I do not think, or dream, or feel but of them'.

Prussia had allied itself with Austria by declaring war on France in early July. As their troops marched towards the French border, their commander, the Duke of Brunswick, issued a manifesto unwittingly demonstrating Louis's treasonous collusion with France's foreign enemies. Brunswick urged the French to rise up against the revolutionaries who controlled their nation and threatened to raze Paris to the ground and torture anyone who resisted his reimposition of the monarchy. Patriotic Parisians were drunk on a toxic combination of cheap wine, fear and defiance.

On 6 August, the travel writer and francophile Dr John Moore landed in Calais. As he and his party travelled from the coast to Paris, wherever they stopped they encountered more carriages full of people fleeing the capital, each giving alarming accounts of the mood there and urging Moore and his companions to turn back. 'They all seemed to be impressed with the notion that an important event is about to happen.' But when Moore's group got to Paris, they were surprised to find the general public there apparently unconcerned by the prospect of invasion or by the impending elections. An uninformed visitor, wrote Moore, would have imagined 'from the frisky behaviour and cheerful faces' of the people he met on the streets that this was a holiday 'appointed for dissipation, mirth and enjoyment' – not the day before one of the defining moments of the revolution.

On the night of 9 August, delegates from the forty-eight Paris wards overthrew the moderate municipal government and formed an 'Insurrectionary Commune' (replacing Paris's usual governing body), which immediately gave orders to march on the Tuileries palace the following day. Robespierre would sit on its new governing committee; Antoine Santerre was put in charge of the National Guard.

Before midnight, the alarm bells in the wards began to sound out their 'monotonous, mournful and rapid' toll. Carrying a musket, the journalist Camille Desmoulins set out for the Hôtel de Ville beside his bear-like friend Georges Danton, an important figure in Parisian city politics who had been instrumental in organizing the antimonarchist demonstration that provoked the massacre of the Champs de Mars the previous summer.

The tocsin rang throughout the night, and soon after dawn, while Louis reviewed his remaining loyal troops in the courtyard of the

Tuileries, the first blasts of cannonfire were heard in the faubourgs. As the people of Paris massed outside the palace, the king and his family were ushered to safety behind the bars of the National Assembly's cell-like press gallery. The Assembly, submitting to the demands of the pike-bearing sans-culottes, formally suspended the monarchy and instituted a provisional Executive Council which would rule until a National Convention could be elected by universal male suffrage. Equality had finally prevailed over liberty; but while all men possessed civil rights from this date, women were still 'citoyennes without citizenhood'.

Outside in the August sunshine, bands of sans-culottes and soldiers invaded the Tuileries and began murdering the Swiss guards still stationed in the palace. The fighting was frenzied, fierce and bloody. In the mêlée, any man in a red coat – the uniform of the Swiss guards – was a target; even the ultra-patriotic fédérés from Brest, who wore the same colour, were mistaken for them and blindly killed. People were 'stabbed, sabred, stoned and clubbed' to death, their bodies stripped and crudely mutilated, and then thrown on to either bonfires at the Tuileries or carts that took them to limed burial pits.

Some women fought alongside the men. Pauline Léon, who spent the night of 9 August at her local ward on the left bank while the decision was made to seize power, marched with her neighbours towards the Tuileries 'to fight the tyrant and his satellites' the next morning. Once there, she was persuaded to hand her pike over to a sans-culotte – but 'only after I admonished him to make good use of it in my place'. She might have been among the women in the courtyard seen stripping corpses of their clothes and rifling their pockets. Reine Audu, heroine of the October days, and Claire Lacombe, an actress recently arrived in Paris, were more successful than Léon: both were granted civic crowns for their bravery in the battle by the new National Convention when it convened in September.

Théroigne de Méricourt also received a civic crown. At last her chance had come to prove that women were as brave and as worthy of glory as men. Wearing a black plumed hat and a blue amazone, with a pair of pistols tucked into her belt, she was seen standing on a stone holding her sabre aloft, addressing the people:

Citizens, the National Assembly has declared that the fatherland is
in danger, that it was unable to save it, and that its safety depends
on your arms, your courage and your patriotism; take up arms, then,
and run to the château des Tuileries, for your enemies' leaders are
there. Exterminate this race of vipers, which for three years has
done nothing else but conspire against you. If you are not victorious
today, in a week's time you will be exterminated. Choose between
life and death, between liberty and slavery. Show due respect for
the National Assembly and for property, justice is in your hands.

Théroigne fought beside the Marseille regiment, and was at the
head of a gang which confronted the royalist journalist François Suleau
and eight others who had been arrested outside the Tuileries earlier
that morning and then seized by the mob. She recognized Suleau, or
at least recognized his name, and leapt at his throat. He fought back,
and was about to run her through with a sword he had grabbed out of
someone's hand when the crowd surged and brought him down. All
nine royalists were killed and decapitated, and their heads paraded
around on pikes.

Despite the brutality of the day, patriots and republicans counted
it as a triumph, a second revolution. Dr Moore, who had arrived in
Paris just in time to witness the events of 10 August, saw a weary
National Guardsman return home to his shop that evening to be
greeted by his wife and children. He went through the door 'carrying
one of his children in each of his arms; his daughter following with
his grenadier's cap in her hand, and his two little boys carrying his
musket'. Moore depicts not a murderer, but a dutiful family man,
defending his country and his children's future. 'Day of blood, day of
carnage, and yet day of victory,' wrote Rosalie Jullien, 'which was
watered by our tears.'

ÉMIGRÉE

Germaine de Staël

AUGUST–SEPTEMBER 1792

In twenty-four hours the aspect of Paris was changed . . .
Nobody dared to show himself to be rich, or to be
superior to anyone else.

AUGUSTE-FRANÇOIS DE FRÉNILLY

Louis de Narbonne

DURING THE RISING outside the Tuileries on 10 August Germaine de Staël – who was six months pregnant with their second child – heard that her lover Louis de Narbonne, as a member of the palace's exterior guard, had been slaughtered. She immediately got into her coach, and tried to cross the river to the palace to seek news of him. But she was held up for two hours because the streets were so full of raging *fédérés* and sans-culotte men and women. Some men signified to her green-liveried coachman with a silent, expressive gesture that anyone who did pass, especially in such a grand carriage, would probably have their throat cut. Finally Germaine heard that Narbonne was alive – he had rushed to fight at the king's side but the courtiers had not allowed him into the palace – and turned her horses homeward.

That night, this time on foot, stepping over drunken, half-sleeping men in doorways raising their heads only to utter curses, Germaine went out into the streets and found Narbonne and Mathieu de Montmorency in their hiding places, and brought them back to the embassy where she put them in the remotest room of the house. Warrants were out for their arrest; other friends had already been imprisoned, and one of the most brilliant of their number, Stanislas de Clermont-Tonnerre – the man Germaine had once called '*mon orateur*' and who had tried, in the early days of their affair, to woo her away from Narbonne and earned such a loving rejection – had been thrown out of a window at the Tuileries and trampled to death.

Although Dr Moore thought Narbonne 'as much distinguished by his talents as by his birth ... [and] a warm friend to freedom', the prejudice against his and his friends' noble origins was too strong for them to remain any longer in Paris. Brissot might have been able to believe 'that men were born equal; and that there was no birth either illustrious or obscure'; but the man on the street, who sensed his power growing through the late summer of 1792, wanted to punish aristocrats simply for existing. Nor did Narbonne want to stay. After Louis had been bullied and humiliated that June, he wrote to a friend in England that it was 'no longer possible for a man of honour to stay [in France], if the whole of France neither refutes nor avenges this act. As for me, I cannot hold on any longer.' Like many aristocratic liberals, Narbonne had favoured a constitutional monarchy, but he could not bear to see his king dishonoured and removed from the throne.

Overnight Paris was transformed. 'Not a carriage was to be seen . . . The city gates were closed. At night the red-capped members of the *sections* made domiciliary visits.' The word 'royal' was erased from shops, hotels and street names. Public statues, regardless of their historical or artistic value, were to be destroyed and replaced with monuments to liberty. Property belonging to émigrés was to be sold off. '*Liberté, Fraternité, Égalité ou Mort*' was scrawled on the walls.

When the local patrol arrived at the Swedish embassy late one August night, saying that they had heard Monsieur de Narbonne was hiding there, Germaine, 'with death in my heart', forced herself to greet them with her usual brio. She was alone: her husband had been recalled to Sweden by Gustavus for consorting with revolutionaries – his wife's friends. Narbonne crouched beneath the altar of the embassy's chapel while Mme l'Ambassadrice, pregnant with his child, lectured the sans-culottes in the hall on the inviolability of embassies, the sanctity of international law and the warlike vigour and might of Sweden – which, she said, was an easily roused nation just across the Rhine. The guards were confused, but when Germaine managed to joke with them about 'the injustice of their suspicions' they allowed themselves to be led to the door without searching the house. 'Nothing pleases men of this class better than jokes,' Germaine observed, with the very condescension for which the aristocracy were loathed, 'for in their boundless hatred of the nobles they enjoy being treated by them on an equal footing.'

This scare prompted Germaine to arrange Narbonne's escape as quickly as she could. She found a young German willing to provide him with one of his friend's passports and so, disguised as a German traveller, Narbonne reached England on 20 August. When she heard the news of his arrival five days later, Germaine laid aside the opium she had carried with her for the past four months, ready to kill herself if the worst should have befallen her lover. 'At last I can hope that I do not need it, that your baby will be born and that as long as I live I will hold in my arms his adored father, the object of such tender and passionate idolatry,' she wrote to him. To the young man who had escorted Narbonne to England she wrote simply, 'You have saved my life and more than my life.'

Germaine had also hoped to help the king and queen escape, having sent a message to them in July with her plan of buying a small estate at Dieppe, going there twice with servants resembling the royal family, and then one day going with the royal family themselves, disguised as her servants. Narbonne would drive the coach; Lafayette had promised to send support. But Marie-Antoinette refused to accept the help of Germaine, Lafayette and the constitutionalists; she sent a frosty message back saying that there was no very pressing reason for the royal family to leave Paris. Three weeks later, having narrowly escaped death, she and her family were moved from the ransacked Tuileries into imprisonment in the Temple, a former monastery on lands once owned by the Knights Templar, now transformed into the royal prison.

On the night of 11 August, Robespierre was elected to the Paris Commune as representative for the Place Vendôme ward in which stood the rooms he rented on the rue Saint-Honoré, a short walk from the Jacobin Club. He led the Commune in the last few weeks of August as they incarcerated the king and his family and defended their localized seizure of power against the outmanoeuvred Brissotins in the National Assembly, defying the national government to establish their own revolutionary regime.

When Dr Moore visited the Jacobin Club on the 17th, he found Robespierre's partisans there so vocal in support of their hero that whenever someone dared oppose Robespierre's views he was drowned out entirely and had to step down from the tribune. 'A little English phlegm would be of use in their councils,' observed Moore drily.

Women were very much in evidence in the galleries of the Jacobin

Club. 'Applauders and murmurers are to be had at all prices,' Moore's companion told him, 'and as females are more noisy, and to be had cheaper than males, you will observe there are generally more women than men in the tribunals [*sic*].' Ironically, most of the women were there because they revered the grave, priestly Robespierre, whose antipathy to their taking part in public life was unshakeable. Rosalie Jullien described him at this time as 'a man devoted to public affairs, with the generosity of the greatest men of antiquity'.

Moore saw only one woman enter the Jacobins' main hall and take her seat among the members. Although he did not name her, it is clear from his description that this was Théroigne de Méricourt: she was wearing a blue jacket modelled on the National Guard uniform, and Moore reported that she was known to have 'distinguished herself in the action of the tenth, by rallying those who had fled, and attacking a second time at the head of the Marseillois [the Marseille contingent]'.

The guillotine, which had been in sporadic use in front of the Hôtel de Ville since April 1792, mostly for forgers, was moved to the Place du Carrousel outside the Tuileries. Its first victims were scapegoats for the bloodshed at the Tuileries: royalists accused of instigating the violence on 10 August, convicted, significantly, in front of a newly created Communal Committee of Surveillance rather than by due process of law. Under the auspices of this radical revolutionary committee over a thousand people deemed unsympathetic to the new regime – from the dauphin's devoted governess to royalist journalists to refractory priests to admirers of Lafayette (dismissed from his post at this time, he crossed enemy lines and spent the rest of the revolution in an Austrian prison) – were imprisoned in the last weeks of August.

The National Assembly reinstated the Brissotin ministers dismissed in June (including Roland, back at the Ministry of the Interior) in the provisional Executive Council, and added two Jacobins to their number: the mathematician Gaspard Monge and the jovial lawyer Georges Danton, who became Minister of Justice.

Danton's powerful voice dominates this period. He had been an adored figure in the Cordeliers' Club from the start of the revolution, and had become a popular hero. In July 1791 at the Champs de Mars and in June, July and August of the next year, he had learned to use his influence with the people to instigate mass demonstrations. As minister, Danton authorized emergency police powers, including domiciliary visits. Heavily armed ward patrols, sometimes numbering up to ten people, were ordered to search houses – ostensibly for weapons, but also for counterrevolutionary suspects or for incriminating evidence against them.

The Prussian army crossed the French frontier on 19 August, and laid siege to Verdun on the 30th. Danton managed to use the enemy's approach as a spur to patriotism. 'Citizens, no nation on earth has ever obtained liberty without a struggle,' he declared, encouraging Parisians to meet their impending ordeal with courage and determination – even relish. 'You have traitors in your bosom; well, without them the fight would soon have been over.'

Newspapers and placards from the last weeks of August – many of them written by friends of Danton and Robespierre – emphasize not only the threat from external enemies, but also a more immediate threat from internal traitors. Dark rumours swirled about the 'ravening wolves' held in the prisons. It was said that as soon as the army left Paris to fight the Prussians, the counterrevolutionaries would escape to slaughter the wives and children the patriots had left behind. Before turning to foreign enemies, then, 'the first battle we shall fight will be inside the walls of Paris,' wrote Stanislas Fréron in his *Orateur du peuple*. On the 19th, Marat urged his readers to 'rise and let the blood of traitors flow again. It is the only means of saving the fatherland.' He instructed 'good citizens to go to the Abbaye [prison], to seize priests, and especially the officers of the Swiss guards and their accomplices and run a sword through them'.

A placard written by the poet and playwright Fabre d'Églantine echoed Fréron and Marat:

> Once more, citizens, to arms! May all France bristle with pikes, bayonets, cannon and daggers; so that everyone shall be a soldier; let us clear the ranks of these vile slaves of tyranny. In the towns let the blood of traitors be the first holocaust to Liberty, so that in advancing to meet the common enemy, we leave nothing behind to disquiet us.

Given the incendiary atmosphere, it was hardly surprising that when news reached Paris of Verdun's fall to the Prussians, the capital should ignite once again into violence. It was said that the Prussian army would be at the city's gates in three days. Black flags of distress were hung on the churches, and the tocsin rang out across the rooftops. The Paris wards began demanding 'the death of conspirators before the departure of citizens'. The streets were full of people every night.

Germaine de Staël, undaunted by the mood of impending tragedy, set out for the Hôtel de Ville on 28 August to plead for the lives of her friends Trophime-Gérard de Lally-Tollendal and François de Jaucourt, who were being held in the Abbaye prison in Saint-Germain. She had selected the literature-loving Paris procurator Louis-Pierre Manuel, who had proposed the honours of the session to Théroigne de Méricourt at the Jacobins earlier that year, as the most likely of the Commune's officials to be susceptible to her fame.

As instructed, she swept into his office at 7 a.m., notwithstanding that it was '*une heure un peu démocratique*'. Manuel was late, and as she waited, Germaine was pleased to observe a self-portrait on his desk. 'This made me hope, at least, that he might be vulnerable if he was attacked in his vanity.' She was right. The procurator told her that it would be difficult to be more compromised than she was, but he was still delighted to help the celebrated Mme de Staël; and Germaine's friends were released forthwith.

They got out just in time. The massacres began at the Abbaye three days after her meeting with Manuel, and spread quickly to the city's dozens of other prisons. A crowd outside the Abbaye demanded that a party of priests arriving under guard be put through a mob 'trial'. They were perfunctorily interrogated and then pushed into the prison's garden, where an armed rabble awaited them. Within an hour and a half nineteen of them were hacked to death by perhaps fifteen men.

For five days this pattern was repeated across Paris, the crowds watching the murders and National Guardsmen standing impotently by. The lucky ones were shot; most of the victims were stabbed through with pikes, beheaded by sabres or bludgeoned to death. 'All Paris saw it and all Paris let it go on,' raged Manon Roland later, having heard the shameful details from the surviving prisoners when she arrived at the Abbaye herself. 'It is impossible to imagine Liberty finding a home amongst cowards who condone every outrage and coolly stand by watching crimes which fifty armed men with any gumption could easily have prevented.'

Perhaps 70 per cent of the Abbaye's prisoners were killed over the subsequent days, their murderers returning day after day to complete the job, for which they had evidently been paid, though no one knew by whom. One survivor remembered how the horror was intensified by the 'profound and sombre silence' in which they worked.

Women were a particular focus of the killings because, like priests, aristocrats and speculators, they were seen as inherently counter-revolutionary and suspected of involvement in the most sinister conspiracies. Prostitutes, whose very existence undermined ideas of republican virtue, were especially despised. When the mob reached La Salpêtrière on 4 September, which doubled as a prison for prostitutes and a women's asylum, thirty-five women were killed and a further group, numbering anywhere between fifty and two hundred, were raped and released. There were predictably few witnesses to these atrocities, but Manon Roland heard 'the terrible details': 'women brutally violated before being torn to pieces'.

Marie-Antoinette's devoted friend, the princesse de Lamballe, had been placed in La Force prison earlier in August when the royal family were incarcerated in the Temple. In 1791, she had returned from exile to serve the queen in her hour of need. Their friendship, naturally, was transformed by the salacious revolutionary press into a lesbian affair; they were said to have encouraged the little dauphin to join in their orgies.

When the mob reached La Force on 3 September, the princess was summoned into a makeshift court in the records office and asked to swear an oath of loyalty to Liberty and Equality, and another of hatred to the royal family and the monarchy. She made the first oath but, refusing the second, she was hustled through an open door where men waited with pikes and axes. She was killed and stripped. Her naked body was dragged through the streets and her head was cut off and paraded through the Marais to the Temple, where the mob demanded that Marie-Antoinette look out of the window to see her friend's bloodied blonde curls. It was said, too, that her body was grotesquely mutilated, her guts worn as a belt and her genitals cut off and exhibited as a macabre trophy.

Mme de Lamballe and the whores of La Salpêtrière were the first female victims of the revolution. Although they had not been permitted to share the same civic rights and freedoms as men, from September 1792 women would be held accountable for their perceived crimes. It was equality of the the most unjust nature.

Sentences were meted out unevenly. The duchesse de Tourzel, the dauphin's governess imprisoned with the royal family in the days immediately following 10 August, who had sat beside Mme de Lamballe during her interrogation at La Force, was saved by a man previously unknown to her who had freed her daughter a few days earlier. As she left the prison at the end of the day, Mme de Tourzel was greeted by several sans-culottes who only a few hours before had been preparing to kill her. In one of the astonishing turnarounds so common during the revolution, they embraced the duchesse and congratulated her on her freedom. They insisted on accompanying her to her hiding-place, giving the coachman directions so as to spare her seeing the worst of the carnage on the streets.

Women thus became victims in September 1792, but they were also perpetrators: if not actual murderers, then supporters, hecklers, bearers of pikes on which heads were mounted, draggers of corpses through streets. The women of the faubourgs and marketplaces spoke the same shockingly savage tongue as their husbands and sons, what Louis-Sébastien Mercier later called the *idiome jacobin* of blood and carnage, vociferously announcing their desire to eat the 'naked, quivering bodies of their victims', or telling their children of 'nothing but cutting or tailoring heads and shedding ever more blood'. The fact that some women succumbed to the savage mob mentality allowed some men to make women in general into revolutionary Furies, feasting on flesh and drunk on blood. One observer said that in every crisis of the revolution, women invented and executed atrocities, inciting men 'to commit new tortures and bloody deeds'; this, he said, disgraced all womankind. 'The myth of the Maenads was not gratuitous,' writes Madelyn Gutwirth. 'It allowed men to emerge virtually unscathed in their own eyes in the wake of the massacre.'

Having seen Lally-Tollendal and Jaucourt safe, Germaine de Staël had finally made up her mind to abandon Paris; she hoped to meet Narbonne in London or tempt him to join her in Switzerland. On the morning of 2 September she ordered six horses harnessed to her big yellow travelling-coach, and set out for the city gates accompanied by her liveried postillions and servants. Later, she recognized that such magnificence was ill-judged; at the time, she thought her boldness would serve as a double bluff, disguising her true intentions. One historian has speculated that she was deliberately courting drama: 'asking for it', by daring to go out so brazenly, seeing how far she could rely on her wits to get her out of trouble.

The horses had not taken four steps before 'a swarm of old ladies, emerging from hell, threw themselves on my horses, and cried that I should be arrested, that I was taking the nation's gold with me, that I was going to join the enemies'. Their shouts attracted a crowd, and 'common people with savage faces' insisted that Germaine be taken to the ward office of the faubourg Saint-Germain.

The ward officials found her papers in disorder: one servant was missing. When she realized that her journey had been interrupted Germaine had sent a groom to inform a fugitive friend whom she was planning to pick up on her way out of Paris that she could not keep their appointment. She was dispatched to the Hôtel de Ville under police escort.

Moving slowly through the crowded streets, the caravan took three hours to reach the Hôtel de Ville, a distance that should have taken about half an hour to walk. The people on foot, seeing her fine clothes and equipage, screamed insults at her. Germaine's very obvious pregnancy only made matters worse. She appealed to the gendarmes accompanying her for help but they responded with 'the most scornful and menacing gestures'; only the policeman sitting beside her in the coach was sympathetic, promising to protect her with his life.

The Place de Grève, in front of the town hall, was packed.

Germaine was taken 'under a vault of lances' to the Hôtel, then mounted the staircase which 'bristled with spears'. One man pointed his pike at her, but her faithful gendarme drew his sword and she passed safely. She was told to wait. Soon afterwards, Louis-Pierre Manuel, whom she had visited three days earlier in the same building, happened to pass by. Understanding the danger she was in, he locked Germaine and her maid into his own office. He did not dare try to take her home in daylight. Despite his position, there was nothing he could do to halt the murders they both knew were taking place throughout the city. 'An abyss was opened behind the steps of every man who had acquired any authority,' wrote Germaine, 'and if he receded he could not fail to sink into it.'

The two women waited there for six hours, 'dying of hunger, of thirst, of fear', looking out over the throngs in the Place de Grève where the abandoned coach-and-six stood bizarrely untouched, protected from looters by a lone National Guardsman. This was the brewer Antoine Santerre, friend of Théroigne de Méricourt, who had led the men of the faubourg Saint-Antoine when they attacked the Tuileries in August. Although Germaine did not recognize him – she could not imagine why he was bothering with her carriage on such a day, she commented – Santerre knew exactly who she was. He came in later with Manuel to tell her that he had guarded her coach as a way of demonstrating his gratitude to her father, whose efforts to procure wheat for the people in times of scarcity he remembered. Germaine was unimpressed; her coach, she thought, had given him a useful excuse for avoiding the gaols.

As evening drew in, they saw the assassins making their way home from the emptied prisons, 'with their arms bare and bloody and uttering horrible cries'. When night fell Manuel returned and drove Germaine and her maid home in her own carriage, along unlit streets through which gangs of men carrying torches roamed. He promised her that the following day he would send someone to her with a new passport.

The man Manuel sent to Germaine on the morning of 3 September was Jean-Lambert Tallien. He had been working for Manuel since February 1792. In August he became secretary to the Commune and was elected to it as a ward representative. He also sat on its new

Committee of Surveillance, alongside the journalist Marat. When he arrived at the rue du Bac, he found wanted men in Germaine's rooms. She begged him not to give them away; Tallien gave his promise, and kept it. He took her to the city gates. For once, Germaine was silent. 'We parted without being able to tell each other what was on our minds.' The words, she said, were frozen on their lips. Leaving Tallien at the city's boundary, her carriage rolled away towards Switzerland and safety.

In the first five days of September 1792, 1,368 people including forty-three children were killed – about half of all the prisoners in Paris. Although no one person or group seems to have masterminded the massacres, it is clear both that most members of the Commune knew that they would happen – there was a rush in the last days of August to free or imprison certain individuals – and that, once begun, they could do nothing more than wait for them to end. Some militants, like Fournier l'Américain, personally saw to it that certain killings took place; many others were content to use the chaos to settle old scores.

'Is it possible that this is the accomplishment of a plan concerted two or three weeks ago?' wondered Dr Moore on the night of 2 September.

> That those arbitrary arrests were ordered with this view; that false rumours and treasons and intended insurrections and massacres were spread to exasperate the people; and that, taking advantage of the rumours of bad news from the frontiers, orders have been issued for firing the cannon and sounding the tocsin, to increase the alarm, and terrify the public into acquiescence; while a band of chosen ruffians were hired to massacre those whom hatred, revenge or fear had destined to destruction, but whom law and justice could not destroy? It is now past twelve at midnight, and the bloody work still goes on! Almighty God!

By the next day Moore was hearing rumours – rife on the streets of Paris since before the massacres began – that the Duke of Brunswick, commanding the Prussian and Austrian troops, was in league with certain unnamed traitors 'long concealed under the mask of patriotism' who were about to open the gaol gates, arm the prisoners and set them free to plunder, rape and murder all patriots. Robespierre himself accused Brissot of having been bought by Brunswick. Although Brissot's name was cleared, the taint of treachery was less easy to erase.

Moore saw Parisians not exulting in the bloodshed, but rather 'lamenting their fate'. The people he observed were terrified above all by the stories of conspirators and the sight of bands of assassins moving from prison to prison, their alarm heightened by the sound of the cannon and the tocsin and by fears of invasion. By 6 September the ardent Robespierrist Rosalie Jullien – who four days earlier had written of the people avenging 'three years of cowardly treasons' – was of the opinion that, 'inconceivable as it may seem', Paris had thrown a veil over the recent scenes of carnage and was preparing to meet the impending invasion. The streets were full of people marching to the noise of the drum and crying '*Vive la nation!*' 'We have the air not of a threatened people, or an embattled people; but of a great family which is in jubilation,' she wrote. 'If you have another idea of the capital, you do not know the French.'

Despite Mme Jullien's composure, during the first two weeks of September a wave of violence spread across France. On the 18th, a report from Neuville-aux-Bois, in the Loiret, was sent to Paris. 'Anarchy is rampant; there is no more authority,' it began. 'There is a state of frenzy that we can hardly describe to you. All we hear is threats to kill, break down houses and ransack them . . . Finally all these people are saying that they want no more administration, no more courts, that the law is in their hands and that they will enforce it.'

The elections for the new National Convention were held between 5 and 9 September, while the bloodstained streets and prisons of Paris were scrubbed down and doused with vinegar. The deputies to the Convention, which would replace the National Assembly, were elected for the first time by universal male suffrage. Despite this democratic opportunity, perhaps only 6 per cent of France's seven million eligible voters exercised their new right. Paris's deputies were chosen, according to a suggestion of Robespierre's, by open ballot at the Jacobin Club. Unsurprisingly, Robespierre was the first to be picked. Sixteen of Paris's twenty-four deputies were members of the insurgent Commune; all were Robespierrists, who would acquire the name Montagnards (*montagne*, mountain) from their usual seats in the Convention, high up at the left of the hall.

Prominent among the Parisian deputies were Georges Danton, Camille Desmoulins and Jean-Paul Marat. Jean-Lambert Tallien was rejected by Robespierre's electors because he boasted that 'he was neither Brissot nor Robespierre', although Robespierre, who had disapproved of the Châteauvieux festival Tallien had helped Théroigne de Méricourt to organize that spring, said it was because he 'blew hot when the people blew hot and cold when they blew cold'. Tallien was elected instead by the neighbouring district of Seine-et-Oise. At twenty-five he was among the youngest of the Convention's deputies; 46 per cent of them were under forty.

The other dominant group in the Convention were the Brissotins, elected from the provinces and from this point known as Girondins because several of them came from the Gironde region around Bordeaux. Roland was elected deputy for the Somme region, Brissot for the Loiret, and François Buzot for the Eure.

On 21 September, the day after the French army decisively turned back the Prussian advance at Valmy, the National Convention met for the first time. The following day it declared France a republic. 'Kings are to the moral order what monsters are to the physical order,' declared one deputy. Standardization and modernization were decreed: henceforth every Frenchman was to speak the same language and use the same money and the same measurements. The metric system was introduced. Gilbert Romme, Théroigne de Méricourt's partner in the short-lived Society of the Friends of the Law, would be one of the chief architects of the new revolutionary calendar, in which the first day of the first year was 23 September 1792. As Tom Paine had said of the American Revolution, it was indeed a new dawn.

The royal crown and sceptre – accoutrements of the Bourbons' majesty – were melted down into republican coins. Louis's personal seal was replaced by an abstract female figure of Liberty, new symbol of the Republic. On this first national seal (they were changed with each successive regime), Liberty is standing alert, youthful and vigorous, holding a pike topped by a red Phrygian cap.

Women were granted civil but not political rights by the Convention. After 1792, both men and women might marry without parental consent when they reached the age of twenty-one; hitherto it had been thirty. The Girondins, always more sympathetic to the cause of women's rights than the Montagnards, backed plans to allow women greater participation in public life when their standards of education had reached those of men.

Divorce was also made legal. Over three thousand couples in Paris alone took advantage of this new liberty in its first year. One of the law's early beneficiaries was Thérésia de Fontenay, who had been among the crowds of onlookers at the Champs de Mars on Federation Day in July 1792.

Étienne-Denis Pasquier remembered a conversation with her that day. 'She shared all my fears about the present and all my worries about the future,' he wrote later; given the timing, four months before she filed for divorce from Fontenay, it is more than likely that her worries centred on her unpleasant husband.

According to the unreliable Arsène Houssaye, Thérésia had watched Jean-Lambert Tallien speaking at one of the last sessions of the National Assembly before the massacres, and was impressed by his good looks and thrillingly patriotic views. Rosalie Jullien also saw Tallien speaking at this time, and approvingly noted his eloquence and energy. He was one of the men who had pressed, earlier in August, for the demolition of all 'symbols of despotism', calling for the replacement of statues of Louis XIV with statues of Liberty.

Tallien was beginning to develop a following among the tribunes of the Assembly, appealing to the crowds by speaking dramatically, like Robespierre, of the will of the people. Since 1791 he had published a newspaper, *L'Ami des Citoyens*, which informed readers that he could be found every morning until ten in his rooms at 17 rue de la Perle in the Marais, or at the Jacobin Club. Its tone was eager and idealistic. He addressed his readers as '*concitoyens*', and throughout the autumn of 1792 attacked the perfidious Philippe Égalité, former duc d'Orléans, as well as prominent Girondins including Jean-Marie Roland and François Buzot.

Despite his ardently revolutionary views – and his obvious ambition – Tallien was by no means prejudiced against aristocrats. As well as helping Germaine de Staël escape and not informing on her friends, he had also used his influential position in the Commune to save several other 'designated victims' of the September massacres, including the king's former valet François Hue, perhaps sympathetic to him because of his own father's role as butler in a noble household.

Thérésia applied for a divorce from her debauched husband on grounds of incompatibility in November 1792. While she waited for the decree to be approved she remained in Paris, although some fourteen thousand people fled the city that autumn and winter, forfeiting their fortunes by becoming émigrés, but too afraid to stay. Late that September in Calais, Dr Moore saw someone he knew waiting to board a boat for England. She was a 'woman of rank', but she was dressed as a maid; the maid was wearing her mistress's clothes. They were impatient, agitated, scared. Dr Moore turned away lest his acquaintance recognize him and fear exposure.

The frivolous, extravagant life Thérésia had once lived had vanished completely. From January 1792 fashion magazines had advised women to stop wearing conspicuous colours – even red, white and blue, however patriotic, drew too much attention to the wearer. By the winter, fashion magazines themselves were no longer being published. Women of all classes went hatless when they ventured on to the streets, wearing wooden clogs on their feet and shawls over their chemises; heavy rouge was their only concession to style. Lucy de la Tour du Pin's former maid, in her spotless white apron, was drawn aside one day on the street by a cook who told her she would be arrested as an aristocrat for going out in such unpatriotically clean clothes; she was advised to wear coarse cloth instead.

Aggressive beggars wore huge tricolour cockades. Men went

unwashed and unshaven. 'The visible signs of patriotism,' said Helen Williams, 'were dirty linen, pantaloons, uncombed hair, red caps or black wigs.' Radical deputies to the Convention wore rough pantaloons and short coarse jackets; the Girondins favoured floppy muslin cravats. Only Robespierre, who was said to resemble 'a tailor of the *ancien régime*', continued to appear '*poudré, frisé, parfumé* and a hundred times more *muscadin* [foppish] than any of us'.

Courtesy was seen as absurd and unpatriotic. Hand-kissing had long since gone out of practice. *Tutoiement* was now not only used universally, but made mandatory by several ward administrations: '*Toi* suits citizen, just as *vous* suits monsieur.' The Girondins protested against 'this breach of good manners' but many others approved of it. Helen Williams thought the ancien régime's gallantry had been replaced with something far better: 'a mutual estimation, a common interest in the great questions of the day'.

Another radical Englishwoman, Mary Wollstonecraft, arrived in Paris in the autumn of 1792 and found manners, which she called 'gay ornamental drapery', a thing of the past; and fashion, the badge of feminine slavery, no longer an obsession. She took up lodgings in the Marais, close to where Jean-Lambert Tallien lived. Between the beautiful *hôtels* of the area, the streets were dirty, narrow, and ill-lit: 'very disagreeable'. Unlike in London, there were no pavements. Carriages no longer bore the family crests of their owners, and there were a great deal fewer of them around, but their drivers still careened furiously over the cobbles heedless of pedestrians.

The last thriving remnant of ancien régime life was the theatre. That November, eight or ten theatres were still putting on plays four times a week. The subjects of these plays were, like Chénier's sensations *Brutus* and *Caius Gracchus*, adapted to the times: kings and princes were always voluptuous, corrupt and tyrannical; nobles were craven and insolent; priests were wicked and hypocritical. The only heroes were ordinary people.

Germaine de Staël arrived at Coppet, her father's house in Switzerland, on 7 September. No letter was waiting for her from Narbonne, and she sat down immediately to beg him to write. 'Do not kill me with your silence ... Do not forget one whose soul, heart and thoughts are entirely yours,' she wrote. 'God, how you toy with me!' She was determined to divorce Staël and fly to Narbonne's side as soon as she had borne their child. Increasingly hysterical, demanding and self-indulgent – especially as Narbonne's inadequate letters arrived so infrequently, sometimes even carelessly addressed to the wrong place – by turns she railed at his ungratefulness, forgave him all his sins, reproached him with his cruelty, threatened suicide and pleaded for his love. 'Frivolous man, what evil you do!' she wrote in October, after another anguished period during which she had had no news from him.

Narbonne, devastated by news from Paris of the imprisonment and trial of the king, made ineffectual attempts to discourage her from coming. He was staying with a congenial group of émigrés including Mathieu de Montmorency and Théodore de Lameth at Juniper Hall in Surrey, for which Germaine, through Narbonne as 'Sir John Glayre', paid the rent; Talleyrand made frequent trips from London to visit them. 'There can be nothing imagined more charming, more fascinating, than this colony,' wrote a dazzled neighbour, the novelist Fanny Burney. 'Between their sufferings and their *agrémens* [pleasures] they occupy us almost wholly.'

Perhaps twenty-five thousand French men and women were living in exile in England by 1794; after the revolutionary government passed a law confiscating the property of all émigrés, almost all of them were impoverished. Germaine was an exception because her assets were held abroad and because her husband's status conferred diplomatic immunity on her. Men and women who had dreamed of nothing more than ornamenting society now learned to make their livings teaching French or music; convent-educated ladies put to good use the skills of embroidery, fan-painting, tatting and dressmaking they had been taught as children. Félicité de Genlis, in Berlin, continued her career as an author while Talleyrand's mistress Adèle de Flauhaut alternated making straw bonnets with writing what became a bestselling romance,

Adèle de Sénange. Books, jewels, silver and works of art were sold off; luxuries like candles and sugar were hoarded and shared; conversation, which cost nothing, was more highly prized than ever.

In Switzerland, her disapproving parents tried to persuade Germaine to be reconciled with her husband, whom she had not seen for over nine months (making the baby she carried very obviously not his), but she refused. It was typical of her that when they sent a friend to reason with her, Germaine described her lover and their relationship with such ardent eloquence that instead of convincing her to remain with Staël he found himself lending her the money for her passage to England.

After long and heated arguments, Germaine agreed not to see Narbonne for three months on condition that if she still wanted to be with him at the end of that time, she and Staël could formally separate. 'I love you like a madwoman,' she wrote to Narbonne. 'I am frightened by your hold over me.' But Narbonne was no longer in love with the woman who hoped to give up everything for him. 'You are so cold in your letters and I am so passionate,' she wrote, distraught, after receiving a letter in which he urged her to delay her departure. 'You seem to have so little wish to see me again that my heart is withered by fear and open to every kind of doubt.'

Their second son, Albert, was born on 20 November. Leaving her children with her parents in Switzerland on 28 December, Germaine arrived in Surrey in January 1793. After only four months she returned to Switzerland. Narbonne saw her off at Dover, promising to join her as soon as he could; it would take him over a year.

FEMME POLITIQUE

Manon Roland

AUGUST 1792–MAY 1793

Always in the eye of the storm, always in the shadow of
the popular hatchet, we walk in the glint of lightening.

MANON ROLAND

The 'sea-green Incorruptible': Maximilien Robespierre

FOR MANON ROLAND, the pleasure of having her husband re-instated as Minister of the Interior in August 1792, following the storming of the Tuileries, was marred by the fact that his colleague on the provisional Executive Council was Georges Danton, newly created Minister of Justice. 'Ferocious in face and probably of heart,' she wrote of him. 'I could not apply the idea of a good man to that face.'

Danton represented to Manon the antithesis of all that she valued: discipline, discretion, virtue, self-sacrifice. She imagined him, dagger in hand, inciting the mob on to still greater deeds of butchery. She found Danton's boldness misplaced, his bonhomie and openness contrived and his extravagant physicality repellent. Her prim disapproval of the easy-going womanizer was heightened by her awareness of her own unfulfilled sensuality; this was a woman, after all, who would write of herself that 'no one so obviously made for voluptuous pleasure has known so little of it'.

Danton made every effort to win Manon over. He visited her almost daily during the last weeks of August, arriving at the Hôtel de l'Intérieur early before Council meetings or inventing excuses to stay late afterwards to chat to her of patriotism, and asking himself to dinner on evenings when no one else was invited. Although she admitted that 'no one could have shown more zeal, a greater love of Liberty or a stronger desire to agree with his colleagues in her service', Manon could not bring herself to accept or trust him. Every fibre of her judgemental soul revolted against Danton: political unity was not worth the price of consorting with a man like him. She whispered to her friends that the Council was tarnished by the presence of a man with such an 'evil reputation'.

Manon was not alone in her suspicions of Danton's integrity. 'If the gratification of his own ambition is to be had at no other price than the sacrifice of his country's good, he will not refuse the purchase,' wrote Dr Moore at this time, outlining the means by which Danton consolidated his power base among the deputies: by his own and Robespierre's eloquence, by bribery and intimidation. Others associated with the Rolands politically were more willing to build bridges, arguing that Danton had made a valuable contribution to the revolution, that he was loved by the people, 'and that there was no point in making an enemy unnecessarily'. Pierre Vergniaud, the most brilliant of the Girondin orators, admired the man, and tried to work towards a mutual understanding. Danton frequented Vergniaud's mistress Mme Dodun's salon in the Place Vendôme, as did Condorcet, who earned Manon's contempt for refusing to choose sides on the matter.

Mme Roland's arrogance was beginning to win her enemies. Paul Barras, a former count from Provence who sat in the Convention near the Montagnards, thought highly of Roland's patriotism and 'generous ideas' but found Manon impossible. When he was introduced to her, the bow with which she favoured him was imperious, and he disapproved of the 'obstinate assurance' of her occupation of Roland's office. Barras declined her invitation to dinner at the Hôtel de l'Intérieur.

By the end of August, Manon's haughty and undisguisedly censorious reserve had finally convinced Danton that she would not melt, and he stopped dropping in at the Hôtel de l'Intérieur. 'They [Danton and his friend, Fabre d'Églantine] had no doubt concluded that Roland was an upright man who would have no part in their enterprise and that his wife could not be used to influence him,' she wrote later, with satisfaction. 'They probably saw that she, too, had principles and a woman's instinct for recognising false knaves; and they will have conjectured, I little doubt, that she could on occasion use her pen.'

Roland, as Minister of the Interior, was responsible for maintaining public order, but when the massacres began on 2 September he had no forces with which to achieve it. Manon insisted in her *Memoirs* that as soon as he heard what was happening in the prisons that day, Roland wrote to the mayor Jérôme Pétion and to Antoine Santerre, head of the National Guard, requesting extra security for the gaols; according to her, he had these letters printed and posted up around the city to add extra authority to his words. However, no trace of these documents survives, and it seems likely that Roland's first public response to the killings was his weak declaration twenty-four hours later, in front of the National Assembly, that the Executive Council 'had been unable either to foresee or to prevent the excesses'.

At five on the afternoon of the 2nd, two hundred men appeared, drums beating, outside the Hôtel de l'Intérieur. They were demanding arms with which to set off to Verdun to fight the Prussians, and calling for Roland, who was in council session at another ministry. The demonstrators refused to accept that he was not at home, and seemed about to storm the building when Manon had ten of them shown in to see her. She managed to convince them that she had no hidden weapons, and directed them to the War Ministry. Finally they left, taking the *valet de chambre* with them as a hostage and complaining that all ministers were fucking traitors. Manon sprang into a coach and rushed to tell Roland and the Council, but met with a lukewarm response. 'Most of them thought it was a natural result of the prevailing conditions and of the public agitation.'

On the same day the Commune's Surveillance Committee, headed by Marat, issued warrants for the arrest of Roland, Brissot and other leading Girondins whom Robespierre had denounced, without naming them, in front of the Commune. Marat was especially determined to destroy Roland, who had in the past month refused him state funding for his newspaper. Danton recalled the warrants, saying, 'You know that I do not hesitate at such things when they are necessary, but I disdain them when they are useless.' Although she knew it was Danton himself who had countermanded the orders of what he called 'that fanatical cabal', still Manon attributed to him the worst of motives.

She was convinced that Danton, Robespierre and Marat had orchestrated the September massacres and that the mob that converged on the Hôtel de l'Intérieur on the 2nd had been sent to kill Roland. It is true that Danton, and perhaps most of France, saw the murders as an unfortunate but inevitable explosion of popular feeling – an exigency of revolution. Danton and his friends' incendiary words in the last few days of August had inflamed public fears. When he was informed that the massacres had begun, Danton responded, 'I don't give a damn for the prisoners. They can go to the devil.' Brissot recorded him saying, on 3 September, that the executions were the expression of common will and 'necessary to appease the people of Paris'. Danton made no effort to staunch the flow of blood; but then, neither did anybody else.

Roland, sallow, unable to eat or sleep and nursing a stress-induced rash, was in no position to condemn Danton. When he was told a week later that a warrant had been issued for his arrest (Manon had kept the news from him), the way he spoke of 'this personal predicament . . . enabled his enemies to suggest that his opposition to the executions was due to fear for his own neck'.

It must have been hard for Manon, so brave and spirited, to have been married to a man who so completely lacked her charisma and drive. Roland was upright, diligent and devoted to his wife and the revolutionary cause, but he could also be petulant, affectedly grave, suspicious, inflexible and timorous. As General Dumouriez, his former colleague, observed, he would have been better suited to a minor bureaucratic position than to the great office of state he held. Although she defended him loyally in her account of their life together and of his career, and declared she wanted nothing more in writing her memoirs than to 'see my husband's glory intact', Manon's frustration is at times almost palpable. Her husband's most glorious or courageous deeds resulted from courses she had advised him to take or letters she had written in his name; when he acted alone, he was always less than inspirational.

The sole man on whom she felt she could rely, after the horrors of early September, was François Buzot, one of the three Incorruptibles from her *petit comité* of spring 1791. Pétion was compromised by his vanity and Robespierre had distanced himself from the Rolands; Buzot alone remained to make Manon's political dreams a reality. He had spent the previous year, since September 1791, as president of the local criminal court at his home town in Normandy, but had kept in regular touch with the Rolands. On 13 September Manon wrote to beg him to get himself chosen as a deputy to the new National Convention and return to Paris so as to save Roland from the Commune; implicit in her appeal was her own desire to have him near her in such terrifying times. A week later, Buzot was in the capital.

Manon saw the Girondins, who held the majority in the National Convention, as true representatives of France, while the Paris Commune, ever more powerful, were a group of opportunistic villains who 'had nothing to lose and everything to gain by the revolution [and] . . . felt the imperative need to commit new crimes in order to cover up the old'. Through Roland, Manon began to press for a federal system like that in the United States in order to deprive the Commune – and the Parisian mob – of its power. Robespierre and his allies presented this as counterrevolutionary treason.

As Bertrand Barère said the following spring, the Girondins believed the revolution was achieved, whereas the Montagnards wanted to push it still further. As for Germaine and her friends in 1789–90, for the Girondins the revolution had been accomplished when they were granted access to power. The historian Alexis de Tocqueville described 'the unfortunate and almost ridiculous situation of the sincerely republican party [the Girondins], that honest third party, running after an ideal and ever receding republic, caught between those who wanted the Terror and those who wanted the monarchy'.

Although neither group was especially cohesive, and both were made up of men from similar backgrounds and professions, increasingly the Montagnards (who dominated the Jacobin Club, and whose power base was in Paris rather than the provinces) were a more effective political coalition than the Girondins. The latter were united by their political moderation, romantic devotion to liberty and high-minded principles – they saw themselves as '*honnêtes gens*' – but lacked the increasingly ruthless, focused energy of the Montagnards and their willingness to champion and harness the popular energy of the people on the streets.

Those people saw Robespierre as the epitome of fundamental revolutionary concepts such as patriotism and virtue. As the historian

François Furet observes, while the Girondins, who had not identified so deeply and personally with the stylized language of revolution, could not find a way to attack him, Robespierre was able to 'dispatch them in advance to a guillotine of their own making'. Monopolizing this new language and imagery made it easy for Robespierre, and Marat to a lesser extent, to portray the Girondin fears of popular involvement in politics as elitist and their moderation as faint-hearted and hypocritical.

One of the obvious differences between the Montagnards and the Girondins in the first weeks of the National Convention was that while the Montagnards were content to draw a veil over the events of early September, the Girondins wanted to bring the perpetrators to justice – hoping in doing so that they would implicate their political opponents. Many Girondins, like Roland, believed that they had barely escaped cold-blooded murder. Both sides cried conspiracy. When Roland stood up in the Convention on 22 September, its second day in session, and demanded an end to arbitrary power exercised by revolutionary committees, his words were applauded but nothing was done.

When the Convention was asked to punish the perpetrators of the massacres, the Montagnards justified their decision not to pursue them on the grounds that during revolutions 'very vigorous measures were necessary'. Jean-Lambert Tallien, secretary to the Commune's council and member of the Surveillance Committee during the massacres, insisted that existing laws were sufficient to protect people. The Girondins took the line that all those who would not condemn the murders were implicated in them. 'There can be neither esteem nor union between the heroes of August 10 and the assassins of September,' cried Buzot. 'There can be no union between virtue and vice.'

Buzot's first speech to the Convention, on 24 September, demonstrated his commitment to Girondin, and more particularly Manon Roland's, ideology. He proposed three resolutions: a reconciliation between the capital and the rest of the country; a law condemning the instigators of death and murder; and a project to create a new domestic force at the Convention's command and drawn from each of the Republic's eighty-three departments – a national rival, in effect, to the gangs of armed sans-culottes roaming the streets of Paris.

When the issue of Roland continuing as Interior Minister was

Above Germaine Necker, the future Mme de Staël, aged 14, in the stiff corset and elaborate headdress even children endured pre 1789, and her father, Jacques Necker.

Below The Neckers' home in Coppet, near Geneva, where Germaine spent much of her life.

Above and below, respectively, women march triumphantly
to and from Versailles in October 1789.
Opposite, the women of the people celebrate in the streets (*below right*)
while wealthier ladies donate jewels to the Caisse Patriotique (*above right*).

Above A pastoral idyll: worshipping at Liberty's altar.

Théroigne de Méricourt in an *amazone* modelled on the National Guard uniform (*left*) and receiving a whipping from a mob of Républicaines-Révolutionnaires in May 1793 (*below*).

Manon and Jean-Marie Roland.

Below Revolutionary playing cards with queens replaced by 'Libertés'.

Bottom Revolutionary fashions: a lady's shoe decorated with a tricolour rosette and a *bonnet rouge*.

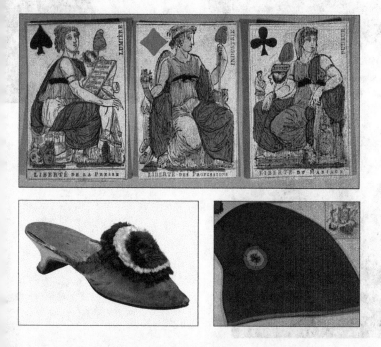

LIBERTÉ DE LA PRESSE   LIBERTÉ DES PROFESSIONS   LIBERTÉ DU MARIAGE

Hero and villainess, or villain and heroine? Charlotte Corday and her victim, Jean-Paul Marat, whom she stabbed to death with a kitchen knife.

Manon Roland is taken to Ste-Pélagie prison in June 1793.

Left Her lover François Buzot gazes longingly at her portrait.

Above The Festival of Reason, held in the deconsecrated cathedral of Notre Dame in November 1793, with Sophie Momoro starring as Liberty.

Right The prison of La Force, in the Marais, where Thérésia Cabarrus was held in solitary confinement in the summer of 1793.

brought before the Convention on the 29th – no government minister could also be a deputy to the Convention, so Roland (like Danton, if he was to remain as Minister of Justice) would have to choose between the two responsibilities – Buzot introduced the motion inviting him to stay on in office. Danton pushed back his chair and roared, 'No one is more fair to Roland than I, but I suggest that if you invite him to be Minister, you should also extend the invitation to Mme Roland, for everyone knows he was not alone in his department!' Buzot replied that he was proud to call Roland his friend.

Roland was reconfirmed as minister in late October, after more efforts on Danton's part to undermine him and a campaign of public accusations against him throughout the autumn. Tallien criticized his policies in *L'Ami des Citoyens*; Jean-Paul Marat went further in *Père Duchesne*. 'It was past midnight and the "virtuous" Roland slut was relaxing in the arms of the nigger Lanthenas from those pleasures which her bald old husband has to procure for her . . .' He called Manon a modern Circe, compared her to Lucrezia Borgia, accused her of seducing every Girondin associate of her husband's and, still worse, of running his ministry.

Roland's speeches were thought pompous and laboured by many younger deputies. Dr Moore overheard two of them discussing his rhetoric. The first said peevishly, 'His only object is to make us admire the beauty of his style.' The second replied, 'In which he sometimes succeeds, with the help of his wife.'

Moore was an admirer of Roland's, describing him, in his drab suit lined with green silk, as a thorough republican, scrupulous, modest and trustworthy. Although he had not met Manon, Moore had heard she was an agreeable woman of good taste. He thought Roland's fatal flaw was to show his enemies how shaken he was by the attacks made on him: 'this is one reason perhaps for their being continued with such spirit'. Some of these disputes were marked by mutual misunderstandings and small-mindedness. Moore reported in October that Roland protested to the Commune that a list of the addresses of the Convention's deputies had been approved for publication by a forgery of the mayor's signature. The Commune responded that Roland's complaints diminished public confidence in the government.

The Girondins, losing ground in Paris, were heartened by the news from the frontiers. The war had begun to go in France's favour. By 8 October, all foreign troops had been pushed back over the border, and at Jemappe on 6 November the French army won another significant victory. But in the Jacobin Club, Jean-Paul Marat croaked out criticism of the Girondin General Dumouriez, according to Moore, with 'affected solemnity' and 'eyes of menace, or contempt'.

On 29 October the editor of *La Sentinelle*, Jean-Baptiste Louvet – unlike Marat, one of the editors to whom Roland had granted government funds – accused Robespierre in print of creating a personality cult and conspiring to set himself up as dictator. Robespierre counterattacked by turning Louvet's criticisms on their head. He managed to make his obsessive personal identification with the popular will a virtue rather than a fault – he was simply the agent of France's destiny – and defended the recent surge of violence by explaining that the revolution required it and must not be judged by ordinary standards of morality. 'Do you want a Revolution without a revolution?' he asked dramatically.

Dr Moore, an eyewitness of the debates, observed that although many people like speaking about themselves Robespierre was exceptional, seeming 'as much enlivened by the eulogies he bestows upon himself, as others are by the applause of their fellow citizens'. The dispute had come to perhaps the worst possible conclusion for the interests of the nation, wrote Moore, 'for the parties remain too nearly equal in force, and likely to ruin the common interest by their mutual animosity'.

Once again, Moore commented on the heavy preponderance of women cheering Robespierre on from the visitors' galleries – five or six hundred women as opposed to perhaps two hundred men watched him defend himself against Louvet on 5 November. Some of these women admitted they were paid to be there; most simply worshipped his stance as impartial defender of the poor and the weak. When Robespierre had dinner at the home of Rosalie Jullien a few months later, despite his powdered hair and stiff silk coat, she found him simple and natural – the loftiest revolutionary praise – and, although a thinker, as 'sweet as a lamb'. 'I would like to believe that he wants the best for humanity, more from justice than from love,' she wrote. As Condorcet said,

Robespierre was like nothing more than the leader of a sect: the high priest of the holy revolution.

Moore agreed with Condorcet. He thought Robespierre was a zealot, ruled by his craving for popularity rather than avarice, and an arch-manipulator of events. 'He retires before danger, and nobody is so conspicuous as he when the danger is over,' said Moore; he 'refuses offices in which he might be of service, takes those where he can govern; appears when he can make a figure, disappears when others occupy the stage'. It was only with difficulty, he added, that Robespierre concealed 'the hatred and malice which is said to exist in his heart'.

In November 1792 the National Convention turned its attention to the problem of the king. With what some deputies found an infuriating smugness, Roland declared that incriminating documents had been found in a safe in Louis's former apartments in the Tuileries. His air of mystery – Roland hinted darkly that several deputies might also be compromised by the papers – caused rumours to fly. Roland was suspected of tampering with the evidence, because he had taken no witnesses from the Convention with him when he went to open the safe. The papers' most dramatic revelation was that before his death Mirabeau had been accepting money from the king for advice about how to regain his power. More damningly for Louis, they also showed he had had dealings with France's enemies and had unwillingly accepted the constitution he privately described as detestable in order to buy himself time.

The Convention began to debate the procedures for the trial of France's former king. Robespierre argued that he needed no trial – that, as the 'solitary rebel' of the Republic, he already stood condemned. 'Louis must die that the country may live,' he declared. His young follower, Antoine Saint-Just, echoed Robespierre: 'There is no innocent reign ... every king is a rebel and a usurper.' Tallien also called for Louis's death, but with a slightly different emphasis: 'He knows that he is condemned ... to keep him in suspense is prolonging his agony. Let us, in tenderness for his sufferings, decree his immediate execution and put him out of anguish.'

Olympe de Gouges, irrepressible champion of lost causes, offered to defend Louis and demonstrate that women were as capable of generosity of spirit and heroism as men. Although she said she was a republican, she saw Louis as a victim. 'The blood, even of the guilty, eternally defiles a revolution,' she said, arguing that deprived of his crown, Louis was no longer guilty of the faults he had committed as king. Furthermore, if he were executed he would become a martyr. 'To kill a king, you need to do more than simply remove his head, for, in such circumstances, he will live a long time after his death; he would only be really dead if he were to survive his fall.'

On the streets of Paris, where signatures (including Pauline Léon's) were being added to petitions calling for Louis's death, Gouges's plea for humanity provoked outrage. Her lodgings were besieged by a furious mob, and when she went downstairs to reason with them, she was grabbed by the waist and her distinctive white headdress knocked off. 'Who'll bid me 15 sous for the head of Olympe de Gouges?' cried her assailant. Her bold reply – 'I'll bid you 30, and I demand first refusal' – may have saved her life. The crowd's mood switched from menace to laughter, and they dispersed.

Gouges posted placards all over the city, calling for a referendum on Louis's fate and condemning all the Montagnard leaders but Danton, whom she admired. She called Robespierre an 'amphibious animal' and described the invalid Marat as having 'neither the physique nor the morals of a man'. As with Théroigne de Méricourt, her energetic, eccentric attachment to their cause only harmed the Girondins, whose tolerance of political women was criticized by the misogynist Montagnards and whose reluctance to condemn Louis to death was seen as weakness.

In early January 1793, having heard the arguments, the deputies to the Convention began to cast their votes on Louis's fate. At Marat's insistence, each man was required to stand before the bar and state aloud his judgement as to whether Louis was guilty and whether or not he should be killed. No one defended his innocence. Three hundred and sixty-one votes were cast for unconditional death; 319, for imprisonment followed by exile. Philippe Égalité voted for his cousin's execution.

The evening before Louis was killed, one of the best known of the Convention's Jacobin deputies was fatally stabbed in a café in the Palais Royal. Michel Lepeletier was a rich former marquis who from 1789 had become a committed reformer, drafting an impressive plan for free compulsory elementary education and contributing to the new penal code drawn up by the Constituent Assembly. Out of principle, Lepeletier had voted for the king's death; his murderer was a former royal bodyguard who believed that as a *ci-devant* noble Lepeletier had betrayed his former master. Lepeletier's last words were said to have been, 'I die content that the tyrant is no more.'

Jacques-Louis David painted Lepeletier as a revolutionary *pietà* and planned his funeral so as to present him as a martyr to the fatherland, happy to die if it furthered the causes of liberty and equality. The cortège paused outside the Jacobin Club, where Lepeletier's daughter was declared a ward of the nation. Walking at the head of the mourners was his younger brother Félix, Thérésia de Fontenay's first great passion.

Young aristocrats like Félix and Thérésia who had 'donned its [the revolution's] costume and borrowed its language' still believed that they were safe in Paris in the winter of 1792–3, but in most cases their sense of security would turn out to be illusory. Félix Lepeletier was one exception: he remained faithful to the Montagnard ideology espoused by his brother, and survived the Terror. Thérésia de Fontenay waited until her divorce came through in April and then, as Citoyenne Cabarrus, fled south towards Spain.

Mary Wollstonecraft watched Louis's carriage pass by her window on his way to the guillotine, which had been moved from the Place du Carrousel to the Place de la Révolution on a foggy January morning. The eerie silence of the empty streets was rendered more awful by the slow beating of drums. People 'flocked to their windows' to watch him go by, but at the Commune's order 'the casements were all shut, not a voice was heard'.

Louis looked more dignified than Wollstonecraft had expected, 'in a hackney coach, going to meet his death'. The sight made her cry. 'I want to see something alive; death in so many frightful shapes has taken hold of my fancy,' she wrote that night. 'I am going to bed – and, for the first time in my life, I cannot put out the candle.'

As soon as the blade fell on Louis's neck, a cheer went up, students lifted their hats up into the air, and the crowd rushed forward to dip their pike tips, handkerchiefs, and even their fingers into his blood. The executioner sold little packets of the king's hair and pieces of the rope that had bound his hands. Germaine de Staël's friend Mathieu de Montmorency, at the head of his band of National Guards, had witnessed the execution. Having made remarks that would incriminate him in revolutionary eyes, the once-liberal former aristocrat fled Paris, going into exile a confirmed royalist.

To many, it was hardly even an event. 'At half past ten, the gates were opened and the life of the city resumed its course, unchanged,' wrote Lucy de la Tour du Pin. After the execution Louis-Sébastien Mercier saw the onlookers, apparently unmoved, walking about arm in arm, talking and laughing as if it were a holiday. One city official said that many women were sad to see Louis die, explaining that 'it would be unreasonable of us [men] to expect them immediately to grasp the significance of political events'. 'There were perhaps a few tears shed; but we know that women abound in tears,' he continued. 'There were some reproaches also, and even some insults. All this is quite excusable, in a frail and light-headed sex, which has seen the radiant last days of a brilliant court.'

Louis had not been the only one to face the National Convention in December 1792. Manon Roland appeared before it on the 7th, accused of corresponding with French refugees – including, improbably, Germaine's friends Talleyrand and Louis de Narbonne – and of masterminding a royalist conspiracy. Her defence was eloquent, patriotic and restrained and her name was cleared; she received an ovation and was accorded the honours of the session.

But Manon's moment of glory did not guarantee their security.

Even before Roland gave up his portfolio, on 22 January, the Rolands had begun to fear arrest or assassination. Roland had his bed moved into Manon's chamber so that they would share the same fate if someone tried to murder them as they slept. Manon kept a pistol beneath her pillow 'to protect my honour if need be'. She tried to be stoical, writing to a Swiss friend the week before Roland resigned that 'if we did not possess that peace of conscience that resists everything, we might very well be weary of life. But ... one becomes accustomed to the most painful thoughts, and courage becomes only a matter of habit.'

Roland had become an object of controversy and public derision; the very mention of his name before the Convention provoked an uproar; he could no longer make his voice heard. When he decided to resign, it was 'because he was not prepared to share the blame for crimes and follies which he could not prevent'. Idealistic Helen Williams, who had known the Rolands since 1791, said that he 'retired from office for no other reason than that he was too pure to hold it'.

The Rolands moved back into their rooms at the rue de la Harpe and returned to their formerly modest existence. They arranged for her governess to take responsibility for eleven-year-old Eudora if anything were to happen to them. Although their friends advised them only to venture on to the streets in disguise, and to sleep away from home to avoid a midnight arrest, Manon scorned such defences. 'I am ashamed to have to act like this,' she declared. 'If they wish to murder me they can do it in my own house.'

According to her best friend Sophie Grandchamp, in the weeks following what Manon called not Roland's but 'our' removal from office, the inverse of her defiance was an all-consuming languor. The secret ambitions she had nourished of one day finding a 'theatre where she could deploy all her talents' had failed her. Sophie said Manon deplored 'the success of men who did not value her husband, [and] the unimportance to which she found herself reduced' and feared she would never 'recover her empire'.

For his part, Roland was devastated that his associates among the Girondins had not stood up before the Convention to support him against fabricated charges of treason. Still worse was a piercing private betrayal. The only man who dared defend him publicly was his friend François Buzot – with whom Manon had just dramatically informed her husband she was desperately in love.

The Rolands' friendship with Buzot and his wife dated back to the spring of 1791, when, newly arrived in Paris, they met a wide circle of like-minded people through Jacques-Pierre Brissot. They saw the Buzots a 'great deal' until both couples left Paris in September that year, although Manon commented that she did not think Buzot's wife good enough for him. For the next year, they corresponded from their respective homes – Buzot in Normandy, Manon near Lyon – until meeting again the following September when Buzot returned to Paris at Manon's request.

In the early winter of 1792 Manon and Buzot admitted their feelings to one another. While she was resolved to sacrifice herself by staying with Roland, in January 1793, like the heroine of a novel, she confided her passion to him, promising that she would not surrender to her feelings. But although she would be faithful to her wifely duties and was determined to be governed by virtue, having long since abandoned any hope of experiencing romantic love she could not hide her exultation at having found her soulmate. Roland was broken by her confession, rather than grateful for her selflessness. 'He adored me, I sacrificed myself to him, and we were miserable,' she wrote.

Roland wrote to his old friend Bosc d'Antic in January about his fear of death being worse than death itself, adding, 'and this is the least of my worries'. He asked Bosc to burn the letter, but if he had hoped to conceal his private heartbreak from his political enemies he was unsuccessful. Jérôme Pétion told Georges Danton who told Camille Desmoulins of Roland's *'chagrins domestiques'*.

The events of spring 1793 dealt a death blow to the political hopes not just of the Rolands, but of all the Girondins. After the king's death, even the most prominent of them seldom got to their feet in the Convention. Freedom of the press was suspended and Girondin printing presses were smashed. Although France had begun to make head-way against her foreign enemies, these enemies were multiplying as she invaded Holland and declared war against Britain. In March the French army chief General Dumouriez, to whom the Girondins had publicly pledged their support, tried to march on Paris and declare the dauphin king; his treachery was another nail in the Girondin coffin.

Long-anticipated civil war – what Manon Roland had once be-lieved would regenerate the nation – became a reality as the royalist region of the Vendée, on the central west coast of France, rose against the revolution. Food was scarce and everyone was afraid. In March, the Girondin Pierre Vergniaud spoke prophetically before the Conven-tion: 'it must be feared that the revolution, like Saturn, successively devouring its children, will engender, finally, only despotism'.

Extremism had become normal. In the popular newspaper *Père Duchesne* in February, Jacques Hébert had written that if a God existed, 'he is evidently a republican *sans-culotte*. If a [G]od does not exist, which is most probable, let us continue without interruption our pre-tended career of wickedness with renewed energy, and an increase of sacrilegious excesses; and within a short time, both the reigns of gods and kings will be at an end, and the universe will contain nothing but a regenerated and enlightened family of atheists and republicans.'

In late February, the women of the streets began protesting against the rising cost of necessities like soap, sugar, coffee and candles. Fights broke out outside bakers' doors. People were dying of starvation in the faubourg Saint-Antoine. Hostility towards shopkeepers and merchants who were accused of hoarding ran high, and a deputation of laundresses petitioned the Jacobin Club, the Commune and the Convention to try and get stringent measures passed against hoarders, and price maximums set on essential items. Their rallying cry was 'Bread and soap!'

The Jacobins refused to allow the women to use their meeting-rooms, arguing that 'repeated discussions about foodstuffs would alarm the republic'. If the women were allowed to use the room, argued one member, 'thirty thousand women might assemble together and incite in Paris a movement disastrous to liberty'. First tyranny must be vanquished, they said, then food would be affordable; their work on the constitution was far more important than a bread shortage. At the Convention, Jean-Lambert Tallien declared that rumours of an impending famine were unfounded and stirred up by aristocrats. Women were merely their tools. 'To provoke trouble, women are placed in the front ranks; they are pushed into crying out, then the men appear who instigate the uprising.' The laundresses were then admitted into the *manège*: apart from food, they said, bleach had become so expensive that the poor would soon be unable to afford white underwear. They demanded the death penalty for speculators and hoarders.

The next day a group of women overran several warehouses, seizing their goods and selling them at pre-revolutionary prices. Well dressed women were seen on the streets, 'influencing people and stirring up trouble'. Protesters claimed that the Girondins were responsible for the high prices.

Price-fixing became one of the most important issues of early 1793. The Girondins, arguing that it would be impossible to standardize prices, let alone enforce them, resisted any efforts at new legislation. Their opposition to the price maximum, to regulation of trade and to more radical demands like a special tax for the rich, made them seem unsympathetic to the needs of the people, and the Montagnards pressed their advantage. 'I believe that the people are never wrong,' said Robespierre. 'The people suffer . . . they are still persecuted by the rich, and the rich are what they always have been, that is to say hard and unpitying.'

In March 1793, the Convention decreed the formation of a revolutionary court, the Revolutionary Tribunal. Its public prosecutor, Antoine Fouquier-Tinville, was given permission a few weeks later to have any citizen arrested, charged and tried on the grounds of a single denunciation. Trials could be neither appealed against nor quashed.

The man who seemed to best capture the popular mood of savage, almost jubilant resentment of the spring and summer of 1793 was the tireless Montagnard deputy and journalist Jean-Paul Marat. Marat was a short, ugly, nervous man in a threadbare coat who took revolutionary disregard for his appearance so far that Danton had to remind him patriotism did not preclude a clean shirt. Because of his chronic herpes and psoriasis he did not shave; he scorned not merely stockings but socks and tied his shoes with string; he sometimes wore a collar of ratty ermine fur and carried a pistol in his belt, which he used as a dramatic prop in front of the Convention when he threatened (rhetorically) to kill himself for his principles.

Marat's newspaper (*L'Ami du Peuple*) was violent, crude and passionate. Desmoulins called him Cassandra Marat because he had predicted that Mirabeau would take the king's money, that the king would flee, that Lafayette would desert France and Dumouriez betray her. Marat's devotion to his work of exposing counterrevolutionaries was so great that he had lived in hiding for weeks at a time so as to avoid arrest and continue publishing. To the sans-culottes his radical patriotism was unimpeachable: 'he will always prevent the counter-revolution from masking itself in red cockades,' said Desmoulins. His political opponents, however, thought his conviction that he was the only patriot in France a delirium.

One of the most interesting aspects of the Marat cult was his appeal to women. Like Robespierre, he attracted an ardent following of female supporters who, far from being repulsed by his appearance and the stridency of his opinions, venerated him. In his private life, too, Marat was surrounded by women, and seems to have treated them as his equals. His much younger common-law wife – in true sans-culotte fashion Marat had no need for 'notary and *curé*' – Simone Évrard devoted her savings to *L'Ami du Peuple* and helped Marat bring out each issue. Marat's publisher was also a woman, Anne Colombe, one of those arrested alongside Pauline Léon and her mother following the massacre on the Champs de Mars in July 1791.

In April the Girondins, who had so often been a focus of Marat's fiery tirades, succeeded in indicting him for abuse of his position and forcing a trial in front of the National Convention. Marat took the stand on 24 April like a persecuted victim of Girondin paranoia. His supporters cheered so loudly that he himself had to ask them for silence. A sympathetic Revolutionary Tribunal acquitted him and, triumphant, he was wreathed in laurel and roses and carried round the Convention on the shoulders of the crowd.

Their failure to destroy Marat only hastened the Girondins' fall.

At the end of May a warrant was issued for Roland's arrest, and this time Danton neither could nor would recall it.

The Rolands had stayed on in Paris after he left office in January in an unhappy state of fear, resignation and despair. Roland, heartbroken at his wife's betrayal, became obsessed with publicly clearing his name. He published detailed accounts of his administration and vainly wrote to the Convention, eight times in four months, demanding that they examine his report, but 'the Jacobins and their supporters continued to scream that he was a traitor'.

By mid-May, Manon had decided to take Eudora back to Les Clos. In her memoirs she wrote that she had decided to leave Paris for many reasons, chief among them that it would be easier for Roland to avoid arrest if he were alone; for herself, innocent and courageous, she had no fear. She added in an oblique marginal note that another, 'entirely personal' reason had been the most important factor in her decision to go: her love for Buzot.

Illness delayed their departure. By the time Manon had recovered it was 31 May. Five days earlier at the Jacobin Club, Robespierre had called on the people to rise up against the 'corrupt deputies' of the National Convention. Paris was preparing for another crisis: the city gates were closed, several wards had armed themselves in readiness for any sign of trouble and fights were breaking out on the streets. The tocsin sounded continually, producing 'a confusion of sounds inexpressibly horrible'.

That morning, under pressure from a band of armed activists, the Commune's General Council agreed to a tax on the rich; to the arrest of the Girondin deputies and former ministers, including Roland; and to the creation of a paid sans-culotte army that would enforce revolutionary laws like the price maximum. When the demands were brought before the Convention later in the day, the Girondin deputies resisted them. The proposals were referred to the Committee of Public Safety.

Some friends came to the Rolands' rooms to wish them well, and advised Roland to go into hiding. At five that evening six armed guards arrived with an order from the Commune's revolutionary committee for Roland's arrest. Roland protested that the committee did not have the authority to arrest him, and the leader of the guard agreed to return to the Commune to investigate the matter. He left his men with Roland.

Manon 'saw at once that we must denounce this occurrence to the Convention with as much publicity as possible'. Still wearing her morning gown and seizing a black veil as she left, she ran downstairs, jumped into a hackney coach and ordered it to take her to the Tuileries. The Place du Carrousel was thronged with menacing sans-culottes bearing rifles and pikes. When she entered the Convention building (which had moved from the *manège* into the Tuileries palace itself) she found every door barred by armed guards and a 'fearful uproar' coming from the main chamber. Using language she imagined a follower of Robespierre might use, Manon handed an usher a letter begging for an audience, but received no response. 'There is nothing to be done at present,' she was told. 'The Assembly is in indescribable tumult.' Sans-culottes petitioners at the bar were calling for the arrest of the principal Girondins; some deputies had escaped, others were being threatened, 'and nobody knows what is coming next'.

Finally she managed to get a message through to Vergniaud, who appeared after a long time. Wearily, he said he might be able to get her admitted, 'but the Convention is no longer capable of doing any good'. Frustration and desperation made her argue. 'Boiling with indignation, void of all fear, passionate for my country whose ruin I could see before my eyes, conscious that all I loved in the world stood in mortal peril,' Manon felt herself 'at the height of my powers and in a unique situation'. 'If I am admitted I shall have the courage to say things which you cannot safely say,' she told Vergniaud, who knew there was no hope. 'I am afraid of nothing. Even if I cannot save Roland I shall proclaim truths which the Republic ought to hear.'

Vergniaud convinced Manon that she would not be seen for at least several hours, and she rushed off to the lodgings of Jean-Baptiste Louvet, the man who had accused Robespierre of setting himself up as a dictator the previous autumn. Not finding him at home, she jumped again into a carriage but found the 'wretched horses' too slow. She paid off the driver and ran across the river, through packs of armed men, arriving home sweating and out of breath. The guards who had come to arrest Roland had left; Roland was in hiding nearby. She saw him briefly – not knowing it would be for the last time – and set off again for the Tuileries. It was past ten and the lamps were being lit in the empty streets.

When she reached the Place du Carrousel she found the Convention had closed for the night. Outraged that they were not in permanent emergency session, she asked a group of sans-culottes loitering around beside a cannon, 'Did everything pass off well?' 'Marvellous well,' they replied. 'They were all embracing one another and singing "La Marseillaise", over there under the tree of liberty.' The 'sovereign' Parisian Commune would arrest the Girondins, they told her, 'sort out the fucking traitors and defend the republic'.

When Manon returned home, she found a man there who warned her that Roland would be arrested that night. As she sat down to write her husband a letter, a deputation from the Commune knocked at her door. It was past midnight. She told them that Roland was not there, and that she did not know where he was. Leaving a guard at the door, they withdrew. Manon ate some supper and went to bed; there was nothing else she could do.

An hour later the deputation returned, this time with a warrant for Manon herself. As with the mandate issued against Roland the previous afternoon, it came from the Commune but gave no grounds for the arrest. Although laws prohibited nocturnal arrests, and although no law had sanctioned the creation of the committee at whose authority she was to be taken, Manon knew resistance would be fruitless: 'a "law" was now little more than a word which was being used to deprive people of their most widely recognised rights'.

Dozens of men, their breath stinking of garlic and rough red wine, milled around the fifth-floor apartment's two rooms as Manon packed a night-case and some books for herself and took out the things Eudora would need; plans for her to stay with friends had already been made for just such an eventuality. The Justice of the Peace appeared and set about placing seals on the windows, drawers and cupboards. When the man trying to put a seal on her pianoforte was informed it was a musical instrument, not a cabinet, 'he pulled a foot rule from his pocket and measured it as if he had some fairly good idea of where it might go'.

At seven that morning Manon was taken downstairs and out to the waiting carriage through a double row of armed men. A crowd had gathered. 'One or two women cried, "to the guillotine".' Inside the coach, on the way to the prison, her guards asked her if she would like the windows closed to protect her from the mob's stares. Manon was defiant: 'Innocence, however sorely oppressed, will never adopt the posture of the guilty.'

The next day, the besieged Convention voted to indict twenty-nine of their number. As Vergniaud had predicted three months earlier, the revolution was beginning to devour its own children.

9

MARIÉE

Juliette Récamier

FEBRUARY–APRIL 1793

There is in her the seed of virtues and principles that one rarely finds so developed at such a young age . . . [Juliette is] tender, sensitive, loving, charitable and good, dear to everyone who knows her.

JACQUES-ROSE RÉCAMIER

Juliette Récamier

In February 1793, a middle-aged banker in Paris named Jacques-Rose Récamier wrote home to his brother-in-law Delphin in Lyon that he was planning to get married. Read carefully, it was a strange letter for a prospective bridegroom – Récamier took care not to reveal the girl's name, which would have been well known to his brother-in-law, until he was halfway through the letter – but, given the times, nothing was normal any more.

Récamier opened by saying that his decision had been made not out of blind passion, but with 'all the calm of reason and the discrimination of the wise'. The girl, he said, was 'unhappily, too young' (she was just fifteen, twenty-six years younger than him) but he had 'never seen anyone who answered better to my heart's desire'. Others might be more beautiful, but in her, 'candour, modesty and sweetness are joined to all the charms of youth' and, although he was not in love, he was convinced that she would make him happy. As well as all her advantages of education, accomplishments and temperament, she was an only child and an heiress. It would be difficult, he told Delphin, to find a girl 'more happily born'.

When he had asked the girl's parents for permission to marry their daughter, they seemed delighted with the idea, as long as she approved. The girl herself was moved to tears to discover the affection in which Récamier held her, and from his subsequent visits Récamier said he was sure that his feelings were reciprocated. 'My dear friend,' he wrote, 'have you already guessed the charming subject I must reveal to you? It is Mlle Bernard.'

Juliette Bernard had been born in Lyon on 3 December 1777. Her flirtatious mother was '*singulièrement jolie*' and had a sharp head for business. She had helped Juliette's weak, elegant father become a successful notary. Juliette was brought up by her mother to 'play some great part' in the world: Mme Bernard was very conscious of the power that came with beauty.

The Bernard household was an unusual one. Jean Bernard had an inseparable friend, Pierre Simonard. He and Bernard had known each other since childhood, married at the same time – Simonard was one of the witnesses at the Bernards' wedding in 1775 – and had their children at the same time. When Simonard's wife died, Simonard and his son came to live with the Bernards. Simonard was the brains and the leader in their relationship: occasionally Bernard rebelled against his tyranny, but they were always reconciled within a few days, 'to the great satisfaction of them both'. In 1786 the Simonards, *père et fils*, went with the Bernards to live in Paris.

Ambitious, pretty Marie Bernard had her own affairs to distract her from her husband's closeness to his friend. One of her lovers was probably Alexandre de Calonne, Comptroller-General to Louis XVI (and rival of Jacques Necker), who gave Jean Bernard the job of *receveur des finances* that brought them to Paris. Another may have been Jacques-Rose Récamier, who was about five years older than her, and who also moved to Paris in 1786.

For the first two years that her parents were in Paris, Juliette stayed in Lyon at the Benedictine Couvent de la Déserte. She left the innocent calm of the nunnery with regret, arriving in tumultuous Paris in about 1788. Her parents lived well in the opulent world of well-to-do merchants and financiers, taking a box at the theatre and giving lavish parties. Juliette, aged eleven, continued to read widely, in English and Italian as well as in French, and to study dancing, singing, the piano and the harp; she submitted to her mother's assiduous attention to her toilette.

Manon Roland, too, whose parents came from a similar background to Juliette's, remembered her own mother taking great pride in her appearance, dressing her 'little doll' in elegant, expensive clothes and curling her hair with hot tongs so that she would look her best when the family took their Sunday stroll through the gardens of the Tuileries.

In early 1789, Juliette visited Versailles, where the queen herself noticed her beauty. She was taken to the royal family's private apartments and measured against Madame Royale, who was about her age. Juliette was a little taller than the princess.

Throughout these years of Juliette's childhood and young adulthood, Jacques-Rose Récamier was a regular visitor to the Bernards' house on the rue des Saints-Pères on the left bank. Récamier was a tall, blond man with the classical learning, generosity and frivolous tastes of the ancien régime. Despite his legendary optimism, and despite his useful friendship with the respected revolutionary Bertrand Barère, the sight of Louis's execution shook Récamier. He forced himself to watch the blade of the guillotine fall on the royal neck, and on the necks of his acquaintances, to prepare himself for a possible similar fate. In the Paris of 1793 no one could avoid suspicion. He knew as well that Jean Bernard, who had been in the service of the king, would only be able to deflect attention for so long.

During the month after the king's death, just days before the Parisian market women rioted over rising prices and when a brutal programme of Jacobin repression was being instituted in Lyon, Récamier made his offer of marriage. He was accepted – according to his account – first by Marie Bernard, then by M. Bernard, then by the fifteen-year-old Juliette herself. 'It is just at this period of general upheaval that a man must look for happiness within his own home, and double his courage by gathering it together,' he wrote to his brother-in-law, as if to explain why he was giving up his carefree bachelor existence, and at such a time. 'The prevailing principles of liberty and equality allow more simplicity in life, and such simple habits bring one much closer to real and solid pleasures than the whirl and display of society.'

Récamier acknowledged that some might question the 'possibly somewhat warmer feelings' he had had for Mme Bernard in times gone by, but he did not think public opinion could reproach him with anything. He insisted to Delphin that he no longer felt anything more for Juliette's mother than friendship, and begged him to make sure the rest of the family joined him in welcoming Juliette into the family.

Reconstructing events, against a backdrop of increasing danger, it is hard not to agree with Juliette's most recent biographer (and the rumours throughout her life) that her fiancé was in fact her father. Her parents' relationship was distant. Récamier had been a close friend of the family since before Juliette's birth, and admitted that he had entertained tender feelings for Mme Bernard when they first met. 'One could say that my feelings for the daughter correspond with those I had for the mother,' he told his brother-in-law.

The hazards of daily life at the start of what would become the Reign of Terror prompted him to offer his daughter, if such she was, the best protection he could. As his wife, Juliette would bear his name and have access to his wealth and extensive contacts. She could also take with her most of her parents' money, as a dowry, and would receive Récamier's fortune if he died; in this way the assets of both Récamier and the Bernards were safeguarded in her blameless hands. Juliette's mother approved of his plans, he told Delphin. 'The varying circumstances of her life have taught her, better than most women, the value of one's own self-respect and of the respect of others.'

The marriage was chaste; the adjective used to describe Récamier's feelings for his bride was always 'paternal'. Juliette's niece and adopted daughter said that their marriage 'was never anything but a nominal tie': Récamier treated his innocent wife like nothing more than 'a daughter whose beauty charmed his eyes'. The purity of their relationship made observers at the time speculate that either he was her father or she had a physical disability which prevented lovemaking. Whatever the truth, Récamier made no physical demands on his wife. As he put it, he 'respected her sensibilities' and, being a man of his times, he found his pleasures elsewhere.

Whether Juliette guessed Récamier was her father when she married him, or whether she knew of his relationship with her mother, to whom she remained close all her life, is not known. She accepted him 'without the least worry about the future he offered her'. Later in life, she spoke of him 'as of a kind friend totally uncongenial to her'. Repugnance was the word Juliette's niece used to describe her attitude to the physical side of her marriage. While on the one hand Récamier may have been seeking to protect his illegitimate daughter by marrying her, on the other he was concerned with the practical neccessities of their new life together. They wanted to marry quickly, he wrote. 'There will be every household requisite to buy, from the first plate to the first tablecloth, stores of every kind, and so many other things,' he told Delphin. Setting up home would be no easy matter, in such times, 'when everything is so dear'.

Récamier's economic worries, at least, were unfounded. As a merchant and banker, with commerce in his blood – his father had been a successful Lyonnais hat manufacturer – he was ideally poised to exploit the revolutionary chaos by buying up abandoned or confiscated aristocratic property and manufacturing desirable items like ribbons, cloth, plates and buttons in patriotic designs. Nobody wanted anything associated with the ancien régime; quite apart from the desire to follow fashion, it might be incriminating. Although gambling in itself was considered 'aristocratic' by the most puritanical revolutionaries, even playing-cards, in 1793, had 'sages' like Brutus or Plato instead of kings, and 'virtues' like justice and prudence or the seasons for queens. For the canny (or unscrupulous), fortunes were waiting to be made.

Strange times call forth strange expedients. Despite the unusual nature of their union, Jacques-Rose and Juliette's marriage underlines the fact that, even as the Reign of Terror began, daily life carried on. Women married, bore children – giving them revolutionary names like Civilisation, Cérès or Phytogneâtrope, meaning 'mother of warriors' – looked after their families, and hoped to survive. As the historian Richard Cobb writes, 'we must not make too much of violence, at least in its crudest form: like Terror, like meat, it was a rare luxury, a weekend affair, or the accident of Feast Days and anniversaries'.

10

ACTIVISTE

Pauline Léon

May–August 1793

> Some women meet, undoubtedly excited by the Furies;
> they are armed with pistols and daggers; they make public
> declarations and rush to all the public places of the city,
> bearing before them the standard of licence.

Antoine-Joseph Gorsas

The Republic offering her bosom to all the French

ON 13 MAY 1793, the *Moniteur* reported that a group of *citoyennes* had gone to the Hôtel de Ville to register the first revolutionary society solely for women. The group, which was to be called the Société des Républicaines-Révolutionnaires, was formed by two women: twenty-nine-year-old Claire (nicknamed Rose) Lacombe, an actress from the south of France who had arrived in Paris in the summer of 1792, and the thirty-five-year-old *chocolatière* Pauline Léon. They hoped the society would, in Léon's words, hasten the revolution and bring on a 'glorious' new era.

Rose Lacombe had become something of a celebrity since arriving in Paris the previous summer. Like Théroigne de Méricourt she had a gift for self-dramatization, and like both Théroigne and Pauline she repeatedly demanded for women the right to bear arms in defence of the *patrie*. She shared Léon's loathing of Lafayette, demanding before the Legislative Assembly in July 1792 that he be replaced as head of the army. Alongside Théroigne, she was one of three women rewarded with a civic crown for her bravery during the storming of the Tuileries on 10 August 1792.

Her speech to the Assembly in July 1792 reveals a little about her motivation and philosophy. As an unemployed actress, Lacombe said she regretted being unable to donate money to the fatherland, but she was still able to 'pay it homage with my person. Born with the courage of a Roman and with the hatred of tyrants, I would consider myself fortunate to contribute to their destruction.' As a single woman she declared that she was in a position to play an active role in 'combating the enemies of the Fatherland', but would condemn mothers for abandoning their children to follow her example. They ought to do their duty by staying at home and instilling in their children 'a love of liberty and a horror of despots'. With their usual backhanded gallantry, the deputies congratulated one 'made more for softening tyrants than for struggle against them' for her patriotism, and awarded her the honours of the session.

By the time they registered their society, Lacombe, Léon and their associates were already familiar figures in the visitors' galleries of the Commune, the Jacobin Club and the National Convention. Léon later said that she spoke before huge crowds at the ward assemblies and in popular societies during this period: there, she 'manifested my love for the Fatherland, propagated the principles of a sweet equality, and supported the unity and indivisibility of the Republic'. The scholar Dominique Godineau estimates that in 1793 Paris there were only a few hard-core *militantes*, many with links to one another. They included Léon and her mother; their neighbour Constance Évrard; Jean-Paul Marat's publisher Anne Colombe; and a woman known in police reports as *la Mère Duchesne*, one Femme Dubouy, an ardent Robespierrist who was famous for shouting and making crude gestures in the tribunes of the Commune, the Jacobins and the Convention.

Common men active in Parisian political life were more numerous than women, but still formed only a modest proportion of the population. From August 1792, each of the city's forty-eight wards had an elected assembly which in turn elected the powerful municipal government, the Commune. (Pétion had become mayor of Paris with only 14,137 votes in a city of 550,000.) But on average only a tenth of the eligible voters turned out.

Paris's radicalization was thus engineered by a small percentage of committed activists, generally men with a little education – clerks, tradesmen or shopkeepers rather than true sans-culottes, who struggled to survive hand to mouth and lacked the time to devote to organized political protest. The activists packed sectional assemblies, persistently petitioned the Convention, intimidated voters at elections and took to the streets bearing arms when they saw trouble ahead. During the spring of 1793, the leaders of these militants – known as *enragés* – developed a radical programme of reform which the Société des Républicaines-Révolutionnaires supported wholeheartedly.

The républicaines-révolutionnaires met in the library of the Jacobin Club rather than the main chamber, which had been deemed off limits for women's meetings when the laundresses tried to use it in February. Their official regulations – one of the few extant documents concerning their activities – stated that the group's aim was 'to instruct themselves, to learn well the Constitution and laws of the Republic, to attend to public affairs, to succour suffering humanity, and to defend all human beings who become victims of any arbitrary acts whatever'; its purpose was 'to be armed to rush to the defence of the Fatherland'.

Each month, a new president, vice-president and four secretaries, whose responsibilities included taking minutes and dealing with club communications, were elected. An archivist, a treasurer and their respective assistants were chosen every three months. Three committees were formed: Administration, Relief and Correspondence. New members had to be introduced by an existing member and seconded by two others; their names were then inscribed on the register and they were given a membership card. All had to swear an oath on joining the Society: 'I swear to live for the Republic or die for it; I promise to be faithful to the Rule of the Society as long as it exists.'

During their sessions, the president was distinguished from the rest of the républicaines-révolutionnaires by her red Phrygian cap. This was a potent appropriation of masculine attire. Since the previous year, sans-culottes men had been wearing these *bonnets rouges* as demonstrations of their symbolic emancipation from the servitude of the ancien régime. Until this point, women had seldom worn them: the figure of Liberty on the Republic's seal had hers draped over the point of her pike, more as decoration than as a declaration of citizenship.

Pauline Léon – along with the rest of the members – 'vowed to execrate the scoundrels Roland and Brissot and the whole gang of federalists and . . . undertook the defence of all persecuted patriots such as Robespierre [and] Marat'. Part of what the républicaines-révolutionnaires called attending to public affairs involved stalking the streets of Paris in search of counterrevolutionaries, conspicuous in their *bonnets rouges* and the red and white striped trousers of the sans-culottes, with pistols or daggers tucked into their belts. Their tricolour cockades were always prominently displayed. They were the new bullies of the streets, replacing the *poissardes* as the city's most aggressive activists and 'exclusively' occupying the tribunes of the Convention and the political clubs. As Pauline Léon had hoped, they saw themselves as agents of liberty, hunting down the nation's internal enemies.

In their eyes, one of these enemies of the revolution was the unlucky Théroigne de Méricourt. A group of républicaines-révolutionnaires was patrolling the Tuileries gardens and the corridors of the Convention on 15 May, as the struggle between the Montagnards and the Girdondins was nearing its climax, when they encountered her on the Feuillants Terrace. They were checking that visitors to the Convention had entry cards, making sure passers-by were wearing the revolutionary cockade (not yet required by law) and stopping anyone whose politics they suspected; they seem not to have known or cared that their vigilance might be an 'arbitrary act' from which others might need protecting.

Very little survives of Théroigne's activities in the early months of 1793 except for an undated broadsheet she published at about this time which was posted around Paris on thick, blue-grey paper. It warned Parisians of the dangers facing them and the traps which had been so artfully deployed to waylay them. In stark contrast to the républicaines-révolutionnaires' robustly hands-on approach to the crisis, she pleaded for a calm, reasoned response: 'Fellow citizens, let us stop and think, or else we are lost.' Conspirers against democracy were inciting anarchy and civil war in order to demonstrate that the people were incapable of governing themselves, she said; both the rebels and France's invaders seemed more 'determined to defend despotism and religious prejudices than we are to defend liberty'.

But, concluded Théroigne, 'danger will unify us yet again, and we will show you what men who wish for liberty, and who are working for the cause of humankind, are capable of'. She proposed that six women be chosen from each ward every six months, 'the most virtuous and the most serious for their age', whose job would be to reconcile and unite the men of their area by reminding them of the dangers threatening liberty and the fatherland. These women would wear long scarves bearing the words *'Amitié et Fraternité'*, and they would supervise patriotic girls' schools and take part in national festivals.

Nothing could have been further from the tomboyish swagger of the républicaines-révolutionnaires.

On sighting Théroigne, whose political sympathies were well known, they shouted 'Brissotine!' and accused her of distributing Girondin propaganda. They had been hoping to run into her for weeks; now they turned on her with 'incredible fury' and gave her '*le fouet*' – a whipping. It was only when Jean-Paul Marat appeared, an unlikely hero, and shielded her under his arm that they let her go. Despite his fierce reputation, Marat seems to have disliked watching individuals suffer. Paul Barras recorded seeing him rescue a beleaguered aristocrat from a mob by giving him a kick; as with their encounter with Olympe de Gouges, the mob's anger turned to laughter and they lost interest. After this humiliating attack on Théroigne, a commemorative plate appeared for sale depicting her bare buttocks.

Four days later, a deputation from the Société des Républicaines-Révolutionnaires accompanied an *enragé* delegation of the Cordeliers to the Jacobin Club to demand the foundation of revolutionary courts all over France and the arrest of anyone suspected of being a counter-revolutionary. The Girondin deputies, who had hitherto been more sympathetic than the Montagnards to the idea of women having political rights, were horrified at the women's attacks on them. On 20 May, Manon Roland's lover François Buzot denounced what he called the impudent women from these 'depraved societies', calling them 'avid for death and blood'. They were, he said, 'monstrous women who have all the cruelty of weakness and all the vices of their sex'.

Another Girondin deputy, the journalist Antoine-Joseph Gorsas, described the women of the Society as Furies, 'intoxicated Bacchanalians', crazed by the revolution. 'What do they want?' he asked. 'What do they demand? They want to "put an end to it"; they want to purge the Convention, to make heads roll, and to get themselves drunk with blood.'

As the atmosphere of crisis intensified, the républicaines-révolutionnaires filled the streets shouting, '*Vive la Montagne! À la guillotine les brissotins! Vive Marat! Vive le Père Duchesne!*' They occupied the area around the Convention, checking people's permits and tickets, and when challenged replied, 'Equality? If we are all equal, I have as much right to enter as someone with a card.' One Citoyenne Lecointre addressed the Jacobins in the name of the Society on 27 May, saying that she and her companions were not 'domestic animals' and promising they would form a phalanx to annihilate all aristocrats.

Just before the end of May a police spy reported nervously that 'evil influences, under the mark of patriotism, have excited these revolutionary heroines to riot and to take up arms so as to dissolve the Convention and cause rivers of blood to flow in Paris'. Although Robespierre and the Montagnards were willing to harness the Société des Républicaines-Révolutionnaires' energy to the cause of ridding them of their political opponents, not everyone was convinced it would be easy to rein in the 'Maenads' afterwards. Between 31 May and 2 June, when the Parisian radicals pressed the National Convention to expel the Girondins, the républicaines-révolutionnaires played a critical role. 'Who rang the tocsin?' asked a desperate Girondin deputy. 'We did!' cried the women in the tribunes. A 'troupe de furies, avide de carnage' prevented Girondin deputies from fleeing the Convention. Helen Williams described Robespierre's female army standing 'in the passages of the Convention armed with poniards'.

Afterwards the Montagnards praised the républicaines-révolutionnaires for their contribution to the coup. 'Their zeal is indefatigable, their vigilance penetrates plots, their actions thwart them, their audacity exposes intrigues, their boldness prevents dangers, their courage surmounts them,' said Louis-Pierre Dufourny, a prominent Jacobin and Cordelier, at the end of June. 'Finally they are republicans and revolutionaries.' Buzot, fleeing to Caen to make a stand against the Jacobins, confirmed the role the 'hideous coquines of Paris' had played in the Girondins' fall.

Other women were inspired by the républicaines-révolutionnaires' example. A group of citoyennes from one of the Paris wards presented the Society with a martial standard, praising them for the 'firmness and intrepidity' of their actions on 31 May and 2 June and congratulating them on having broken 'that prejudice . . . which made passive and isolated beings out of half the population by relegating women to the confined sphere of their households . . . Why should women, gifted with the faculty of feeling and explaining their thoughts, see themselves excluded from public affairs?' A woman's first duty was still to her home, they said, but 'after they have attended to their indispensable occupations, there are still some moments of leisure, and *les femmes citoyennes* in the fraternal societies who consecrate them to surveillance and to instruction have the sweet satisfaction of seeing themselves doubly useful'.

On 24 June 1793 a new constitution was adopted by the Convention containing innovations such as the right to work and the right to resist one's own government if it became oppressive. Although the principal authors of the constitution (including Gilbert Romme, Bertrand Barère, Tom Paine and Condorcet) had included a carefully worked-out system of checks and balances, this had been largely disregarded by the Montagnards in their desire to make political concessions to the sans-culottes. Condorcet dared to protest; a warrant was issued for his arrest and, like the other Girondins, he went into hiding.

The constitution's authors had considered the issue of women's rights. Originally Condorcet had been the strongest advocate for enfranchising women, although, perhaps shocked by the radical new involvement of women in public life in the spring of 1793, latterly he had not pursued this objective with any vigour. The constitution denied women political rights for the time being. 'The vices of our education still oblige us to perpetuate this exclusion, at any rate for several years to come.' A woman from Beaurepaire complained to the Convention in July that 'women are far from being equal; they do not count in the political system. We demand from you primary assemblies, and, as the Constitution rests on the rights of man, we demand it all today.'

Women may not have been included in the liberties of the new constitution, but they were determined to participate in celebrating it. In Paris and across France they gathered alongside the men to send messages of support to the Convention, often participating in mock elections as demonstrations of their approval – acting out a privilege they had not been granted. They promised to marry only true patriots and to raise their children in the principles of liberty and equality. A police spy said of the women celebrating, 'It would seem that, born slaves of men, they have a greater interest in its [liberty's] prevailing.' As Dominique Godineau comments, the roles women played in these celebrations were 'ornamental' – as they were at all revolutionary festivals – but they reveal the potent ambiguity of women's importance to the revolution. Although they were excluded from the body politic, they were still determined to comment on and participate in public affairs, and their presence at and approval of significant events had become an essential part of revolutionary life.

As recognition of the part they had played in ousting the Girondins, the Société des Républicaines-Révolutionnaires was allowed to march in the Convention's official procession marking the adoption of the constitution. Pauline Léon expressed to the Convention the 'joy and satisfaction' of the *citoyennes* of her ward 'over the completion of the Constitution'.

In the midst of these celebrations, a twenty-five-year-old woman named Charlotte Corday left her home in the Norman town of Caen, where François Buzot and other Girondins were preparing for their final struggle against Robespierre and the Commune. A fervent supporter of the Girondins, she saw the coup of 2 June as a degradation of the revolution's purity. One of the anti-Jacobin tracts circulating in Caen in the spring of 1793 read, 'Let Marat's head fall and the Republic is saved! . . . Marat sees the Public Safety only in a river of blood; well then his own must flow, for his head must fall to save two hundred thousand others.' Mlle Corday saw Marat as perverting France, and became convinced that if he were removed, the revolution would be saved. Before setting out for Paris, she left her Bible lying open to the story of Judith, and wrote to her father apologizing for leaving home without his permission.

When Charlotte Corday arrived in Paris on 11 July she was disappointed to find that Marat's persistent arthritic psoriasis had confined him to his apartment near the Cordeliers' Club on the left bank: she had hoped to kill him in public, at the Convention. Two days later, in the already blazing sunshine of a summer morning, she got up early and walked the short distance from her rented room to the Palais

Royal. She made several purchases: a newspaper reporting the recent demand in the Convention that the death sentence be pronounced on the expelled Girondins; a tall black hat with black tassels and a green cockade to replace her provincial white bonnet; and a kitchen knife with a wooden handle and a five-inch blade.

A hackney coach dropped Corday off outside Marat and Simone Évrard's apartment in the rue des Cordeliers just before eleven thirty. Simone's sister told her that Marat was too ill to see anyone. Charlotte left him a letter saying that she had important information about the Girondins hiding in Caen, but forgot to leave her address. She returned to her lodgings. That afternoon, Corday summoned a hairdresser to her room and changed into a spotted muslin dress with a pink fichu; she tucked the knife, her birth certificate and a letter to the French people into her bodice. She put on her new black hat with its jaunty green rosette.

At seven in the evening, Charlotte took another cab to Marat's rooms. This time she was luckier: she arrived at the same time as a bread delivery, so she made it up the stairs before she was challenged by Simone. Marat heard her telling Simone about the escaped Girondins, and shouted out from the tiled bathroom next door that she should come in. In the summer heat, one of the only ways Marat could ease the itching, scaly sores on his body was to soak in cool kaolin baths. He kept an upturned wooden box beside his tin bath which he used as a desk; on one wall hung a map of France, on another a pair of crossed pistols beneath which was scrawled the word 'Death'.

Simone, still suspicious, showed the young woman in. Charlotte told Marat about the situation in Caen, and listed the names of the Girondin plotters there. 'Good,' he replied, 'in a few days I will have them all guillotined.'

When Simone left the room, Charlotte, who was sitting on a chair next to the bath, stood up and pulled the knife out of her bodice. She stabbed Marat once, at the top right of his chest, beneath his collar-bone, and pierced an artery. Her blow was fatal; as she later said, it was just luck. Marat shrieked, '*À moi, ma chère amie!*' and sank back into the rapidly staining water.

As Simone, one of Marat's newspaper distributors and various neighbours rushed into the room to try to save his life, Charlotte Corday sat quietly awaiting her fate. The news spread rapidly, and furious crowds soon thronged the street outside Marat's home, baying for the murderess's blood – one woman said she would like to cut her into pieces and eat her. But the officials called to the scene persuaded the mob that killing Corday would mean they would never discover what had really happened.

Corday was taken to the Abbaye prison (she was kept in the cell occupied by Manon Roland the month before) and the investigation into her crime began. People found it hard to believe that a woman had so premeditatedly killed Marat – his own brother and sister refused to accept it, holding that he had been 'assassinated by a scoundrel wearing women's clothes' – and that she had acted alone. Corday was fully aware of how much the fact of her femaleness changed the significance of her crime, writing, 'No one is satisfied to have a mere woman without consequence to offer to the spirit of that great man.'

Charlotte Corday was guillotined on 17 July. She went to her death remorseless and composed. 'Her beautiful face was so calm that one would have said she was a statue,' wrote one onlooker. 'Behind her, young girls held each other's hands as they danced. For eight days I was in love with Charlotte Corday.' The Girondin Pierre Vergniaud, in hiding, said of her, 'She has killed us, but she has taught us how to die.'

Threatened by her femininity, the Jacobins did all they could to besmirch Corday's myth. Four days after her death, a vilely misogynistic notice about her was posted throughout Paris. This woman being called pretty was not pretty at all, it thundered.

> She was a virago, chubby rather than fresh, slovenly, as female philosophers and sharp thinkers almost always are. Moreover, this remark would be pointless were it not generally true that any pretty woman who enjoys being pretty clings to life and fears death . . . Her head was stuffed with all sorts of books; she declared, or rather she confessed with an affectation bordering on the ridiculous, that she had read everything from Tacitus to the *Portier des Chartreux* [a book of pornography very popular in the eighteenth century] . . . All these things mean that this woman has hurled herself completely outside of her sex.

The discovery, at her autopsy, of the unmarried Corday's virginity added further fuel to Jacobin flames: her chastity was used – just as proof of sexual activity would have been used – to confirm their theories that she was an unnatural, unfeminine woman.

Marat became a revolutionary martyr. David's portraits of him and of Michel Lepeletier, murdered in January 1792, flanked the president's chair in the hall of the National Convention; his bones were interred in the Panthéon.

The Société des Républicaines-Révolutionnaires carried Marat's boot-shaped tin bath in his funeral procession on 16 July, and afterwards continued to parade it and his bloodstained shirt through the streets like relics or fetishes. On the following day, the day of Corday's death, they swore before the Convention 'that they will people the land of liberty with as many Marats as children borne by the Revolutionary Republican Women, that they will raise these children in the cult of Marat, and swear to put in their hands no gospel other than Marat's works, with verses in his memory, and curse the infernal fury brought forth by the race of Caen'.

Ten days after Corday was killed, with the enemy again at France's frontiers and half the country in open revolt against the revolutionary regime in Paris, Maximilien Robespierre took his place for the first time on the Committee of Public Safety, recently created by the National Convention as a means of centralizing and strengthening executive power. Twelve men sat on the Committee, which met around a large green-paper-covered table in the gilded Pavillon de Flora at the top of the queen's staircase in the Tuileries – the room which had once been Louis XVI's private office.

The consolidation of authority in the hands of the Committee of Public Safety ushered in a new revolutionary era. Having scrambled to power on the backs of the Parisian militants of the Commune, the Montagnards now turned sharply around to kick their makeshift ladder away. The path of the revolution had changed: from the summer of

1793 it was about not reform, but Terror. In the words of Antoine Saint-Just, one of the Committee's chief propagandists,

> There is no prosperity to be hoped for so long as the last enemy of liberty shall breathe. You have to punish not only the traitors, but even those who are indifferent; you have to punish whoever is passive within the Republic and does nothing for her; for, from the time that the people manifested its will, everything that is opposed to it is outside sovereignty; everything that is outside sovereignty is enemy.

In the same month, the Société des Républicaines-Révolutionnaires moved their meeting-place from the Jacobin Club to the former Church of Saint-Eustache, beside the central marketplace of Les Halles. This physical move reflected their ideological move away from the Montagnards and a personal veneration of Robespierre towards the anarchic philosophy of the *enragés*, who were pressing for stricter control of prices and trade and ever more direct democracy.

The *enragés* were led by a militant curé named Jacques Roux, 'the red priest of the *bon sans-culotte* Jesus Christ'. Roux was a sectional representative to the Commune for one of the poorest, most marginal and most desperate areas of Paris. He had accompanied Louis XVI to the scaffold and encouraged the laundresses to riot and pillage in February. In late June he issued an *enragé* manifesto calling for another September massacre, directed this time against hoarders and speculators, and demanding that the government force shopkeepers to trade without making any profit themselves.

At about the same time, the laundresses seized a boatload of soap on the Seine and distributed it amongst themselves, protesting again about high prices. The laundresses and market women were not *enragées*, although they shared many of the same concerns. They formed a distinct group separate from and increasingly hostile to the républicaines-révolutionnaires, who had further antagonized them by moving their headquarters to Saint-Eustache. These women were *poissardes*, the wives and daughters of sans-culottes, and by 1793, with their daily lives as hard as ever, they were beginning to question what the revolution had achieved. During the riots in February a drunkard among them was heard to say that in the old days there had been only one king; now there were thirty or forty.

Some républicaines-révolutionnaires were from less deprived backgrounds than the market women, but they were politically more extreme. For them, as for the *enragés*, the revolution would not be over until true equality had been established. As Théophile Leclerc, one of the *enragé* leaders, wrote in August, 'A state is on the verge of ruin when you find extreme poverty and abundant wealth existing side by side.' Society, he said, should take from the rich to give to the poor.

Twenty-two-year-old Leclerc was an engineer's son from near Montbrison. Inflamed with revolutionary ideas in 1789, when he was eighteen, he had tried to join the National Guard but was turned down because of his age and small size, joining the army instead and going to Martinique as a soldier. After a short but turbulent army career – during which, aged only twenty, he saved his companions by addressing the National Assembly on their behalf – he fought in Lyon alongside the most extreme revolutionaries. Arriving in Paris in the spring of 1793, he became a passionate disciple of Jacques Roux. The vehemence with which he attacked the Girondins in the days leading up to their fall led to his being expelled from the Jacobin Club.

The week after Marat's funeral, Leclerc began publishing *L'Ami du Peuple par Leclerc*, taking the name as homage to the *patrie*'s new martyr and attempting to step into Marat's shoes. Leclerc's causes were radical, protosocialist: he petitioned for utilitarian, egalitarian schools, arguing that every child should have the same education; he preached that true justice could only be exercised by the people; he claimed that 'food supplies belong to everyone' and proposed that the state buy food directly from the producers and distribute it evenly to all.

Leclerc moved into the rooms of Rose Lacombe, who was seven years his senior. His youthful radicalism energized the Société des Républicaines-Révolutionnaires. He and the other *enragés* were unique among revolutionary groups in that they valued women contributing to political life. 'Victory is assured when women join with the sansculottes,' wrote Roux that August. Another *enragé*, Jean Varlet, who wore a badge proclaiming himself an 'apostle of liberty', told the Convention earlier in 1793 that he wished the Jacobins' apathy would 'be replaced by the energy of the women of 5 and 6 October [1789]'.

'It is your special duty to warn of [hoarders and aristocrats], Republican Revolutionary Women, generous women truly above all praise for the courage and energy you have developed; your sex, gifted with a much greater sensibility than ours, will feel more vividly the misfortunes of our country,' wrote Théophile Leclerc in his newspaper on 4 August. 'Go – by your example and your speech awaken republican energy and reanimate patriotism in lukewarm hearts! Yours is the task of ringing the tocsin of liberty! Time is short, the peril extreme! You have deserved first place, fly, glory awaits you!'

Inspired by Leclerc, Rose Lacombe, Pauline Léon and the Society rose to the challenge. Throughout August, as the anniversary of the storming of the Tuileries drew closer and bread queues grew longer, the républicaines-révolutionnaires joined the *enragés* in ever more persistent demands for influence – or further insurrection.

The writer Pierre-Joseph-Alexis Roussel took Lord Bedford, a visiting Englishman, to witness one of their meetings in the crypt of the former Church of Saint-Eustache. They counted sixty-seven women sitting on two rows of benches on either side of the room, with the president and officers of the Society, in their red caps, opposite the entrance. Visitors watched from the rear of the room, separated from the members by a chest-high bar. Roussel and Bedford did not share the *enragés'* views on political women. They described the meeting as a ridiculous, grotesque spectacle – they could hardly stop themselves from laughing as they watched the proceedings, they commented.

Rose Lacombe was in the president's chair. She read the minutes and correspondence and invited one Femme Monic to give her address on the utility of women in government. According to Roussel's note, Monic kept a small haberdashery shop and was 'director of the knitters [*tricoteuses*] at the Jacobins' as well as an informer for the Committee of Public Safety. Roussel added that the radical deputy Claude Basire had told him that he wrote Monic's speech for her.

To ringing applause, Monic listed the great female heroines and warriors of history, from Judith to Joan of Arc, from the Amazons to the matrons of Sparta. But she had no need to search the 'dust of history' for inspirationally heroic women, she said, 'since we have them in our revolution and right before our eyes'. She gave the examples of 'Reine' Audu leading the king back to Paris in October 1789 and their own president, Rose Lacombe, who had led a corps of *fédérés* into the Tuileries the previous August and still bore the scars she received on that day. 'If women are suited for combat,' continued Monic, 'they are no less suited for government!' Catherine the Great of Russia proved it, but 'even when the reins of government are held by men, women alone move and direct them'. She cited Catherine de Medici and, more controversially, Mme de Pompadour and 'the courtesan Dubarry [just guillotined], who was herself a doll, [and] made a marionette out of Louis XV. Thus one can prove that women have always directed governments. Thus one can conclude that they deserve to govern. I would almost say, better than men.'

Roussel and Bedford found Monic's examples risible and her confidence in her rhetorical style utterly misplaced. Other républicaines-révolutionnaires rose to their feet to suggest even more 'ridiculous' proposals, such as admitting women to all branches of administration and the formation of a women's army into which prostitutes would be forced to enlist. The women finally agreed, after much debate, to send a petition to the Convention, demanding a decree that would require women, as well as men, to wear the tricolour cockade.

Olympe de Gouges then stood up and congratulated Monic on her speech. Not only did women govern empires, she added, but 'they are the force behind everything'. As such, women must use their power over men. 'Isolated, man is our slave; it is only when reunited in a mass that they overwhelm us in their pride.' She recommended that women should direct and regulate public festivals in which they would incite men to patriotism and virtue by refusing to bestow their favours on those who did not deserve them. 'Whoever hesitates to fight the enemy will hear her voice speaking these words to him: Stay, you cowardly soul; but never count on being united with your lover; she has sworn to reject the desires of a man who is useless to his country.'

Roussel and his guest left the meeting with much to discuss. Bedford confessed that 'the delirium of those women frightens me'. Roussel replied that women were 'the most active force in society, the common centre to which all the passions of men are attracted', and it was 'thus a manifest contradiction not to count them for anything in our code of laws'; still, the 'universal and consequently dangerous ascendancy' of women over men made it impossible to allow them rights. 'They are strong enough,' he concluded patronizingly. 'Let us leave them with the empire of grace and beauty.'

One of the ways in which the Jacobins sought to counteract the influence of the républicaines-révolutionnaires during the summer of 1793 was a campaign to exalt women as mothers, and especially breast-feeders, of future republicans. *Citoyennes* did not need to participate in public affairs, they argued, when the role they played at home was so vitally important.

Jacques-Louis David used four turning-points of the revolution as the explicitly Jacobin framework for the celebrations of the anniversary of 10 August. At the first stage, the site of the Bastille became the triumph of Nature; at the third, Liberty was enthroned at the Place de la Révolution, where Louis XVI had been guillotined; at the fourth, a gigantic Hercules represented the French people crushing federalism – a feat not yet accomplished.

The second station was a triumphal arch erected on the boulevard des Italiens to honour the heroines of October 1789. Although laurel-wreathed actresses sitting on cannons represented the market women, David's script for the pageant was not in keeping with the originals' militant spirit. 'O Women! Liberty attacked by the tyrants has need of heroes to defend it. It is for you to breed them,' they were pointedly reminded – the implication being that they were to be mothers to heroes, not heroines themselves. 'Let all the martial and the generous virtues flow together in your maternal milk and in the heart of the nursing women of France.'

This was a double-pronged attempt to identify the Republic with a nurturing mother and to restrict women to the domestic sphere by glorifying their activities there. It was not a new concept. In Rousseau's *Émile*, Sophie's fecundity and willingness to breast-feed her baby were proof of her modest virtue – in contrast to the unwomanly, barren, pleasure-seeking bodies of aristocratic women like Marie-Antoinette, who were typically portrayed as flat-chested. 'In making yourselves more motherly, you make all hearts more human,' wrote Mme Le Rebours in her 1775 *Advice to Mothers Who Wish to Nurse Their Infants*.

Despite their best intentions, not all mothers had such positive experiences of nursing their children. Manon Roland, devoted disciple of Rousseau, was disappointed to find that even though she had breast-fed Eudora, her daughter was 'cold and indolent', adding, 'her dulness and lack of spirit will never give me the joy for which I had hoped'. Germaine de Staël did not even bother to try to breast-feed her children; she always had more important affairs to attend to.

From 'the nectar of the age of reason' – natural and wholesome – breast-milk became the food of future republican heroes. Nursing one's own children, instead of handing them over to wet-nurses, was hailed as a patriotic duty. When the aristocratic Lucy de la Tour du Pin was in disguise in Bordeaux in 1793 and a group of uncouth red-bonneted clerks saw her breast-feeding her baby, she was called a '*charmante nourrice*' and given a loaf of white bread, an unheard-of luxury at the time.

'We are all your children,' were the words inscribed on contemporary statues of Liberty. One 1793 etching showed her bare-breasted, with a masonic level hung round her neck on a ribbon indicating that all Frenchmen had equal access to her nourishing milk. The female bosom became, instead of an erotic area, one of virtue and patriotism. A pamphlet described how the 'nipple does not flow freely until it feels the lips of a baby in need; in just the same way, those who are the guardians of the nation can give nothing without the kiss of the people; the incorruptible milk of the revolution then gives the people life'.

At a time when the debate over who controlled food sources and distribution was raging and long lines of disgruntled people waited daily outside bakeries for their quota of bread, identifying the Republic as a mother feeding her children/citizens was an astute move, emphasizing how dependent – rather than demanding – the Committee of Public Safety wanted the French people to be. But Pauline Léon and the members of the Société des Républicaines-Révolutionnaires had no intention of resigning themselves to domesticity when the principles of liberty and equality were under fire.

11

PRISONNIÈRE

Manon Roland

June–August 1793

I have never enjoyed greater calm than in this strange
situation.

Manon Roland

Manon Roland's miniature of
François Buzot

As soon as he heard the news of his wife's arrest, Jean-Marie Roland fled Paris. Wits quipped that although the body of Roland might have left the capital he had left his soul behind him.

When Manon arrived at the Abbaye prison near the Place Saint-Germain on the morning of 1 June, she was taken beneath the stone gates and through a dark waiting-room where the guards slept on camp beds; as she entered, 'men stood up in a flurry of agitation'. At the top of a filthy staircase was 'quite a clean little room', where she was offered breakfast and allowed to sit down while instructions were given for her care. Later, Manon learned that these orders had been brutally severe but the prison keeper, an honest, diligent man, was able to avoid following them to the letter because they had not been written down. The keeper's plump wife took her to her room, and said how sorry she always was to see women arrive at the prison, adding kindly, '"for they are not all serene and calm like Madame"', wrote Manon. 'I smiled and thanked her and she locked me in.'

Despite her cell's dirty walls, the double bars on the windows and the pallet-bed 'without curtains' upon which she was expected to sleep, Manon was resolved to meet her trials with the fortitude of her antique heroes. She reflected that at least the room was relatively large and she had been given a pillow and a coverlet. Her situation was a crisis she felt herself magnificently prepared to meet: 'although, listening to my innermost soul, I may have detected some excessive emotionalism, I found nothing there to make me ashamed, nothing which did not justify my courage or which I did not feel capable of mastering'.

Her first visitor was one Citoyen Grandpré, a man Roland himself, as Minister of the Interior, had appointed prison inspector. During the

September massacres the previous year, Grandpré had informed Danton of the atrocities being committed and been dismissed with an oath. He was horrified to see Manon behind bars, and advised her to write a letter to the National Convention, which he would deliver. Although he urged her to soften her accusatory tone of outraged innocence, the letter still went unread: Manon did not know it then, but the Convention was otherwise occupied, expelling the Girondins from their number.

On the evening of 3 June, a haggard, unkempt Bertrand Barère – a Montagnard who sat on the newly formed Committee of Public Safety, but who almost exclusively among the Robespierrist Jacobins had retained his personal independence and remained on good terms with his Girondin friends – arrived at Manon's friend Helen Williams's house with tears in his eyes. Over and over again he said that 'since the national representation was violated, liberty was lost; [he deplored] the fate of the Gironde [Barère came from the south-west], above all of Vergniaud, and execrat[ed] the Jacobins, and the Commune of Paris'. Soon after this visit he stopped coming to see Williams: political expediency had triumphed over goodwill. Later on that summer Williams was arrested and imprisoned. Despite her sincere and publicly avowed republicanism, with France at war with England, as an English-woman she was considered an enemy of the state.

Other visitors to the Abbaye came and went as Manon settled into her captivity, still without being formally questioned or charged. More prisoners arrived daily, and in order to avoid sharing she was moved into a smaller cell overlooking the gaol entrance. All night long, through the bars of her tiny window, she could hear the shouting and jostling of the sentries and new prisoners arriving. By the summer of 1793 almost three hundred people were held in the Abbaye alone.

Manon kept the damp room immaculate, eating her simple meals from the corner of the chimneypiece so that she did not disturb her makeshift desk, which she covered with a white cloth. She asked her maid to bring her books, including Plutarch's *Lives*, which she had not read since she used to take it to church instead of a prayer book as a child, and David Hume's *History of Great Britain*, to improve her English.

A few days after her arrival she was allowed a newspaper, and read of the warrants issued for the arrest of the twenty-two Girondin deputies. This news – which she would have known meant the almost certain deaths of Roland, many of their friends and, worst of all, of Buzot – made Manon despair for the first time. 'Folly and crime have triumphed,' she wrote. 'All that was notable for probity, force of character and talent is now proscribed ... Farewell, our sublime illusions, our generous sacrifices, our hopes, our happiness. Farewell, beloved country.' And farewell Buzot, she must have been thinking: farewell love, before she had truly tasted it.

The scurrilous *Père Duchesne*, ever hostile to the Rolands, pictured Manon in the Abbaye bemoaning her fate. 'The evil *sans-culottes* of Paris have messed up all my plans,' it imagined her saying. 'What will become of me if my dear Buzot, if my friend Gorsas, if my little Louvet, if the favourite of my heart, the divine Barbaroux, will not incite civil war in the provinces?' Buzot and a group of fugitive Girondins actually were trying to muster support, in Normandy, and Manon was indeed fervently hoping to hear news of a regional uprising. Brissot was one of several who refused to allow the Jacobins to make him into a criminal by going into hiding. He was arrested soon after Manon. 'My conscience,' he wrote, 'spoke to me with a louder voice than all these terrors from without.'

Manon spent her first weeks of imprisonment fending off incompetent functionaries and writing defiant, futile letters protesting her own and the Girondins' innocence. On 12 June – about the time that she heard the words of *Père Duchesne* shouted outside her window describing her as a toothless, lascivious hag and advising her to repent of her sins before she was executed – Manon was interrogated for the first time. She gave nothing away.

Her first precious letters from Buzot arrived at the Abbaye on the 22nd. 'How many times I've re-read them! I press them to my heart, I cover them with kisses,' she wrote back. 'I was no longer hoping to receive them.' Buzot had left Paris in secret on 2 June, the day before the warrants for his and the other Girondins' arrests were issued, bearing Manon's miniature and letters and locks of her hair. Along with Jean-Baptiste Louvet, Charles Barbaroux and Jérôme Pétion, he was trying to muster provincial resistance to Robespierre's Parisian regime. He had written to Manon from Caen on 15 and 17 June, and left the letters in his hometown of Évreux with a trusted friend who managed to get them to her in Paris.

Manon assured Buzot that she was being well treated and told him she spent her days rereading her favourite authors and writing. Her almost elated composure in prison, she said, was something only he could understand:

> If they attempt some sort of trial, I shall be able to defend him [Roland] in a way that will enhance his reputation. Thus I shall be able to acquit myself of a debt I owed him for his sorrows . . . Don't you see that by being alone, it is with you that I remain? It is through confinement that I sacrifice myself for my husband and save myself for my lover, and it is to my tormentors that I am indebted for this reconciliation of duty and love; don't pity me! Others may admire my courage, they do not know my joys; you who must share them, preserve all their wonder by the steadfastness of your valour.

Two days after Buzot's letters arrived, the gaoler's wife came to Manon's cell and told her that a prison administrator wanted to see her. Manon followed her down the corridor and found two men waiting for her. After confirming that she was Citoyenne Roland, they informed her that she was to be set free. All the papers were in order: she was to be permitted to return home, and the seals on her apartment were to be lifted. 'With a smooth smile', one of the men asked her if she knew where her husband was. Manon did not deign to answer. She excused herself and returned to her cell to gather together her few belongings.

Her maid, who had been allowed to visit her regularly, wept with joy as she packed Manon's bundle, but Manon felt weirdly impassive. The physical effects of being released from gaol could be inconceivably powerful. When another prisoner, Jacques-Claude Beugnot, was being moved between the Conciergerie prison and La Force, he did not understand why he and his guard, who had waited for hours for a carriage, could not walk the short distance. The guard told him that when he breathed fresh air he would find himself unable to walk. When Beugnot finally got outside his legs buckled beneath him and he had to sit down in the street, overwhelmed by his temporary liberty and the sweet air of freedom.

Leaving the Abbaye – her vacated cell to be inhabited that same day by Brissot and three weeks later by Charlotte Corday – Manon set out for the nearby rue de la Harpe in a hackney cab, flying out of the carriage and up the stairs of the house 'like a homing pigeon'. She had not taken four steps when she heard a voice behind her saying, 'Citoyenne Roland? ... We arrest you in the name of the law.' Her release had been a ruse: because she had been detained irregularly on 1 June, she had been set free only to be arrested again by indisputable order of the Committee of Public Safety, charged with conspiracy against the revolution and complicity with her husband and the rest of the wanted Girondins – her punishment for presuming to step away from the hearth.

The Rolands' landlord's son rushed to the local ward office and returned with two commissioners, who made a formal objection to Manon's new arrest. She wrote a few quick notes to her daughter and to friends who might pass the news on to her husband, and then the entire party crossed the river en route to the Hôtel de Ville, where the commissioners planned to register their protest against the arrest and argue Manon's case.

From behind closed doors, as she sat in a bustling anteroom, the distressed and frustrated Manon could hear the debate becoming increasingly heated. Eventually she opened the door and asked to be admitted, if not to participate in the discussion at least to be present during it. 'You would have thought the office was under siege simply because a well-behaved woman wanted to hear what they were saying about her,' wrote Manon. 'I had to withdraw for fear of being thrown out.' Finally a superintendent asked her to follow him. She threw open the office door again and shouted, 'Commissioners of the ward of Beaurepaire, I give you notice that I am being abducted.' They replied that they could do nothing about it except try to ensure she faced a proper trial. Manon was taken to her second prison, Sainte-Pélagie.

The good bourgeoise was 'not at all reassured by my new abode'.

Sainte-Pélagie was a former hospice for prostitutes, located, as Manon put it, 'in a very undesirable quarter', isolated and remote. Notable recent inhabitants had included the Scottish courtesan and mistress of the duc d'Orléans, Grace Dalrymple Elliott, and Louis XV's former mistress Mme du Barry. When Manon was being signed in, she made the mistake of protesting indignantly at a 'man of sinister appearance' poking around in her night-case with 'indecent curiosity'; he turned out to be her turnkey.

She was allocated a cell six feet by twelve containing two beds, two very small tables and two chairs, for which she was asked to pay 30 livres a month (she had it reduced by half for single occupancy), and she bought a writing-desk, paper, pens and a jug. Her neighbour was a procuress – 'one of those creatures who seduce the young and sell the innocent' – and the woman living above her was a forger and murderess. Every morning the women's doors were opened by the gaoler and they were allowed to spend the day moving freely through the prison's corridors, stairs and hall.

The windows of the men's section were so close that male and female prisoners were able to communicate unrestrainedly. 'Gesture supplies the want of contact and these windows become theatres for the enaction of the most lewd and shameful debauchery,' wrote Manon. The other prisoners' wanton behaviour provided a stark contrast to the purity of her feelings for Buzot, yet this atmosphere of frenzied lust-fulness – revolutionary prisoners were notorious for the passionate intensity of their love affairs, snatched beneath the shadow of the guillotine – was a sardonic reminder to her of 'animal' pleasures she had glimpsed but never enjoyed. In the section of her memoirs written in Sainte-Pélagie, where she described her looks and 'natural sensu-ality', she concluded feelingly, 'if my conscience would allow me today to make fuller use of the attractions which I still possess I should not be sorry'.

Appalled by the 'indescribable' conversations of 'these dregs of humanity', Manon spent her first days at Sainte-Pélagie in her cell. It is hard not to think that she was sent to Sainte-Pélagie – out of the multitude of prisons in Paris – deliberately, by men who knew how proud she was of her morality and who delighted in her fabricated reputation as a lascivious man-eater. 'This is where the respectable wife of a distinguished public figure is made to lodge! Such is my reward for a virtuous life!' she burst out, in one of her less controlled moments. 'It is not surprising that I am ready for death.'

Although she tried at first to eat the portion of beans and the pound and a half of rough stale bread provided to each prisoner daily by the state, Manon was forced to pay the keeper's wife to cook for her: 'a cutlet and some spoonfuls of vegetables for dinner, some greens in the evening; no dessert, nothing for breakfast but bread and water'. In this she was modest, as she was well aware. At the Luxembourg prison, formerly a royal palace, where *le tout* Saint-Germain were housed, aristocratic prisoners either sent out for tavern food or had their own chefs prepare their meals and bring them to the gaol.

The cruelty of being allowed to glimpse freedom only to have it snatched away upset her even more than the thought that she was still in prison, and when she first arrived at Sainte-Pélagie Manon could not sleep, spending her nights in a kind of wakeful nightmare. But her self-discipline and determination not to allow her enemies the satisfaction of seeing her defeated soon reasserted itself. 'All they had done, after all, was add to their own crimes,' she reflected. 'They had not substantially altered the conditions which I had already learned to endure.'

Strict routine helped soften the monotony of her days. In the mornings Manon studied English, reading the poetry of James Thomson and the philosophy of the Earl of Shaftesbury; in the afternoons she sketched. Her old friend Bosc d'Antic faithfully brought her flowers from the nearby Jardin des Plantes; Luc-Antoine de Champagneux, a friend from Lyon days, encouraged her to write; Grandpré brought Sophie Grandchamp to see her. One day when Helen Williams visited Manon she found her reading Plutarch, the sweetness in her dark eyes unchanged. The most notable absence was eleven-year-old Eudora, whom Manon did not dare to summon. 'These tyrants hate even the children of victims, and my poor girl ... can scarcely appear in the streets without despicable creatures pointing her out as the offspring of a conspirator!' When Helen asked her how Eudora was, she burst into tears.

Her cell, in the July heat, was so hot that after a few weeks the gaoler's wife began to allow Manon to use her room during the afternoons, and then moved her into a room beneath her own. Mme Bouchard treated her as a guest, allowing her to forget her incarceration. She planted jasmine outside Manon's windows so that the scented tendrils would curl around the bars; Manon sent for her pianoforte. Knowing that Roland and Eudora were safe, that her friends in Normandy were gathering their forces and that she was in contact with 'the man who was most dear to me', she began to feel a strange contentment.

In the Abbaye, and continuing in Sainte-Pélagie, Manon began to record her memories of the events of the past few years in a memoir that is a bold defence of her own and Roland's actions. She wrote on cream or pale green paper, in thin notebooks, with carefully numbered pages; her writing is swift, sure and elegant, with very few mistakes. Her thoughts raced on to the page.

She devoted much of her energy to character sketches, describing the men she saw as agents of her downfall, Danton and Robespierre, in particular detail. Manon had loathed Danton on sight, but she had been one of Robespierre's most ardent supporters when she first knew him, and she covered many pages analysing her early view of him. In 1791, she explained, she had attributed all his faults to excessive patriotism and love of liberty: she had thought him reserved, for example, because he was modest, not because he trusted no one and looked down on everyone. Time had shown her, however, that Robespierre spoke rarely and never gave a straight opinion because he was devious and secretive, and that he stole other people's ideas because he hoped to get the credit for them. Still she conceded that he had 'defended his principles with heat and obstinacy and had the courage to continue doing so when there were very few others still on the side of the people'.

Manon's handling of Robespierre is fascinating because their ideas and attitudes were so close: what she admired in him was often what she was proud of in herself. Both had rushed to participate in the revolution and championed it from its first days; both were inspired by Rousseau's egalitarianism and devoted to the classical republican ideal, in which the self is sacrificed to the state; both were spiritual but anticlerical, but believed in religion's social utility; both equated private morality with public happiness and exalted the role of virtue above all other traits. Both were egotistical, uncompromising and prone to dreams of martyrdom; both, in words the historian Alphonse Aulard used about Manon, at heart 'believed nothing good could come to the revolution save from' them. In 1793, what divided them were specific political issues more than general philosophical ones.

One crucial point where their ideas diverged was the issue of women in public life. Robespierre was a true Rousseauian segregationist. He never acknowledged women who stepped out of the domestic sphere. In the National Assembly's early debates on citizenship, although Robespierre was celebrated as a champion of the rights of previously passive male citizens like black men, Jews and servants, he did not even address the subject of women possessing natural and inalienable rights. When Olympe de Gouges or Théroigne de Méricourt challenged him publicly, he scorned to respond.

During the Rolands' time away from Paris in the autumn of 1791, when Manon had made overtures to Robespierre implying that their correspondence might be useful to him in formulating his political theory and decisions, he pointedly had not replied. Mme Roland, quietly sewing by her husband's hearth, had been no threat to him; Roland *née* Phlipon (as she proudly signed herself to him in these letters), running her husband's ministry, arguing with those who disagreed with her, beating on the doors of the National Convention and demanding to be heard, was quite another proposition.

Outwardly, she and Robespierre agreed on the issue of women. When Manon declared that women were valuable to society because of their virtues rather than their intelligence, it might have been Robespierre himself – or Rousseau – speaking. But, as with Germaine de Staël, another devotee of Rousseau's who insisted she did not want to play a part in public life and then strove with every fibre of her being to do so, Manon's words said one thing, her actions another.

Although as the wife of a minister Manon had lived as modest a life as possible, her obvious interest in and aptitude for politics escaped no one. It was as if she thought that without the powdered, scented flirtatiousness of ancien régime boudoir politics no one could suspect her of intrigue. Her scathing dismissal in her memoirs of the men with whom Roland had worked must have been daily evident on her face, exposing how thoroughly she believed she could do their jobs better than them: 'the thing that has struck me most has been their universal mediocrity . . . it is hardly surprising that we have fallen step by step under the dominion of crass ignorance and shameful incompetence'. She treated Danton – whom she misjudged with the most serious of consequences, preventing any kind of reconciliation between Girondins and Jacobins when a rapprochement was still possible – with a shameful mixture of arrogance and disdain. The Jacobins she opposed would have found it hard not to see her as another scheming salonnière in the mould of Germaine de Staël or the influential royal mistresses.

For Manon, too, admitting that she liked being near power and wanted to wield it herself would have been a confession of corruption. For her – as for Robespierre, Marat and many other revolutionaries – one of the defining characteristics of the ancien régime's immorality was its domination by women. As the historian Dorinda Outram observes, 'to the degree that power in the Old Regime was ascribed to women, that meant that the discourse of the Revolution was committed to anti-feminine rhetoric'. The revolution became a crusading instead of a destructive force: it would replace the unnatural world of boudoir politics with virtue – government by men alone, whose intrinsic qualities (so the argument went) made them the natural leaders of society.

Manon was thus caught between her commitment to virtue, which required her political passivity, and her desire to contribute to the creation of a new France. In her memoirs, as if to exonerate herself, she emphasized again and again her love of domestic life and her devotion to her husband and his interests. The fact that she often described this devotion in terms of martyrdom is just one indication that it was a struggle for her, although the idea of self-sacrifice was a peculiarly potent one for revolutionaries of her stamp; Robespierre was also in thrall to it. It may have been that stressing how hard she found it to be virtuous, as Rousseau did in the *Confessions*, the model for Manon's memoirs, made her count her success all the greater.

As the memoirs make clear, Manon would never have moved into the public sphere but for the extraordinary circumstances of her life. Her intellectual principles – that devotion to Rousseauian virtue – would have triumphed over the emotional needs she had confessed to Roland during their courtship: her love of drama, her desire to play the principal role in any situation, her yearning for circumstances that would force her on to centre stage. But when her chance came, it was as if she had been waiting for it. 'This seemed my moment,' she wrote of the May day she had rushed to the Convention on Roland's behalf, and pleaded so eloquently with Vergniaud to get her access to the rostrum.

Had it not been for the revolution, Manon might also have failed to fulfil her potential as a writer. Her passionate interest in the events of the day initially persuaded her to write, albeit anonymously, for friends like Champagneux's and Brissot's journals. More importantly, as Dorinda Outram points out, being in prison gave Manon a Woolfian 'room of her own': no longer a dutiful daughter, wife or mother, she had, for the first time, the space and opportunity to become a writer. A lifetime of repressed individualism and sensuality found its release in gaol in torrents of words.

In the first month of her imprisonment Manon had written enough of her 'Historical Notes' to fill a volume. Knowing that she was writing for posterity, and considering her work 'my moral and political testament', she smuggled her notebooks out of prison with various friends including Bosc d'Antic and Champagneux, the future editor of her memoirs. When, on the August night that she was arrested, Helen Williams destroyed the papers she had sneaked out of Manon's cell, terrified that possession of them would further incriminate her, Manon was devastated: 'I must admit that I would rather have been thrown on the fire myself.' Bravely, she started all over again.

Writing – justifying herself – was her consolation, the focus of her constrained energies. After the ferment and intensity of the past two years, being in prison suddenly gave her time to think. 'Here, behind bars and bolted doors, I enjoy the freedom of my thoughts, I summon objects that are dear to me, and I am at greater peace with my conscience than my oppressors are with their power.' She was poignantly aware of the irony of physical imprisonment granting her a new sense of imaginative and emotional liberty.

Prison also allowed her to luxuriate in her love for Buzot. As she wrote to him from Sainte-Pélagie on 3 July on receiving another letter from him, 'can I complain of my misfortune, when such delights are reserved for me?' Dignified in any situation, she would have been 'proud of being persecuted in a time when character and probity are proscribed', but the freedom to love Buzot without hiding her feelings from Roland – whom she referred to as '*le pauvre*' – made her treasure her 'sweet' imprisonment. 'I find it delightful to unite the means of being useful to him in a manner that allows me to be more yours,' Manon wrote, looking forward to the moment when sacrificing her life for Roland would earn her the right 'to give you alone my last sigh'. Her love letters – indeed, all her writing – became a substitute for physical experience, enabling her, as Outram writes, to 'overcome the contradiction between the unchastity of her desires and the self-portrait she cherished as chaste wife', all the while preserving for herself the dramatic heroine's role.

'How I cherish the bars where I am free to love you without feeling torn and to occupy myself with you without ceasing!' she wrote to Buzot. This new pleasure was so intense that she rejected the idea of escape: returning to freedom would mean exchanging 'chains that honour . . . for others that no-one can see'. Still she could not help herself hoping, as it became clear over the summer of 1793 that resistance to the Committee of Public Safety was doomed, that Buzot would flee France for the United States and that one day she would be able to join him there.

Out of superstition, Manon told Buzot, she had not wanted to bring his miniature into prison with her, but she could not bring herself to leave it behind. She wore it tucked into her bodice, hidden beside her heart where she could feel it at every moment, 'this sweet image, weak and precious consolation for the presence of the subject', and took it out to kiss it and weep over it. Her words recall the scene in *La Nouvelle Héloïse* when Saint-Preux unwraps Julie's portrait with trembling hands. 'How immediate, how powerful is the magic effect of these cherished features,' he tells her. 'Wherever you may be, whatever you may be doing at the moment when your portrait is receiving all the homage your idolatrous lover addresses to your person, do you not feel your charming face bathed with tears of love and sadness? Do you not feel your eyes, your cheeks, your bosom caressed, pressed, overwhelmed by my ardent kisses?'

Manon slipped a tiny piece of paper into the back of the locket, describing Buzot as 'a loving soul, a proud spirit and an elevated nature ... [who] cherished peace, private virtues and the pleasures of an obscure life'. Thrown into politics by circumstance, he had conducted himself 'with the ardour of hot-headed courage and the inflexibility of austere integrity', only to be declared traitor to the country to which he had sacrificed himself. One day, she predicted, posterity would honour him, and his portrait would be placed among 'those of the generous friends of liberty who believed in virtue, and dared to preach it as the sole basis for a republic, and who had the strength to practise it'.

Manon's stay in the 'pleasant little room' beneath Mme Bouchard's was cut short in early August when a prison administrator saw someone entering her room and asked to see inside it. The keeper's wife was making life too comfortable for Manon, he complained. 'She can do without it [the pianoforte],' he told Mme Bouchard. 'Send her back to the corridor at once. You must maintain equality.'

Mme Bouchard could not argue. Although she allowed her back to the room near hers during the day and permitted her to leave her books and papers there, Manon had to return to her damp cell, the fetid air of the dark corridor and the screeching of the great iron bolts in their sockets as her door was unlocked every morning and locked again each night. But a month away had brought unexpected new prisoners, reflecting political changes outside the prison walls. Manon's neighbours were no longer whores and murderesses, but other Girondin women: the wives of a Justice of the Peace denounced for 'unpatriotic talk' and of a president of the Revolutionary Tribunal.

An old friend, Mme Pétion, had even arrived – one of the few Girondin wives Manon had had time for. Pétion had eluded his guards in Paris and fled to Normandy with Buzot. 'I would hardly have believed when I was sharing your worries at the Hôtel de Ville last August 10, that we would be celebrating the anniversary together in Sainte-Pélagie,' Manon said to her when they met, 'and that the monarchy's fall would lead to our undoing.'

12

RÉVOLUTIONNAIRE

Pauline Léon

AUGUST–NOVEMBER 1793

Since when is it permitted to give up one's sex? Since
when is it decent to see women abandoning the pious
cares of their households, the cribs of their children, to
come to public places, to harangue in the galleries, at the
bar of the senate?

PIERRE-GASPARD CHAUMETTE

The invention of the *bonnet rouge*

RÉVOLUTIONNAIRE

Pauline Léon

August–November 1793

OUTSIDE ON THE STREETS, in September 1793, a police spy reported to the Committee of Public Safety that '*une petite crise à l'occasion des cocardes*' – a little trouble over cockades – had broken out in Pauline Léon's neighbourhood, the faubourg Saint-Germain.

Since July the previous year, all men had been required by law to wear a tricolour cockade as a symbol of their devotion to the Republic. Although women's fashions also reflected the fervid patriotism of the era, women, as passive citizens, had no such public obligation. But throughout the hot, delirious summer of 1793, the Société des Ré-publicaines-Révolutionnaires, led by Léon and Lacombe, had taken to roaming through the capital and accosting women who were not wearing tricolour rosettes – women who, they claimed, were implicitly counterrevolutionary because they did not sport their politics on their shoulders. During the Society's meeting observed by Pierre-Joseph-Alexis Roussel and Lord Bedford, the only decision the républicaines-révolutionnaires actually made was to send a petition to the Convention requesting that a law be passed forcing all women to wear them.

Their aggressive tactics simply scared most women – bands of ferocious women dressed as sans-culottes were just another reason to stay off the streets in 1793 – but the républicaines-révolutionnaires' antagonists, the *poissardes* of Les Halles, were enraged by their bullying as well as by the fact that by transferring their headquarters to Saint-Eustache they had moved on to their territory. According to the police report, the républicaines-révolutionnaires were stopping female passers-by, demanding to see their cockades and threatening them with a whipping – like the one they had administered to Théroigne de Méricourt four months earlier – if they were not wearing one. The market women retorted that they would slaughter the républicaines-révolutionnaires if they continued to accost them, and accused the women who wore the cockade of being *putains*, or sluts. They had no money to spend on such things, they said, when bread was so dear. Screamed insults were exchanged and blows were not always avoided; one woman in Les Halles was stabbed for venturing out unadorned.

A police observer was confused and suspicious about the way that on one day, in one area of the city, women would be beaten for wearing a cockade, while another day, in another place, they would be beaten for not wearing one. 'The cockade is the veil behind which evil-doers hide their perfidious plans,' he reported. 'One cannot spy on their [the women's] movements too much.' As ever, the fear of conspiracy hung heavy in the air.

Paris had always been an alert, inquisitive, observant city. People watched each other, as Richard Cobb comments, not necessarily – or not always – out of malice, but often simply out of curiosity. 'Two citizens cannot whisper without a third craning his neck to hear what the conference is about!' wrote Louis-Sébastien Mercier in 1781. The revolutionary government knew exactly how they had come to power – with a speech at the Palais Royal and the women of Les Halles demanding bread – and they were determined to monitor what the people on the streets were saying and thinking. Spies whose remit was to report back to the Committee of Public Safety haunted the city's alleys and arcades, stood in the long lines for bread, eavesdropped on *poissardes* and prostitutes, followed the prices of sugar and soap and noticed which plays sold out.

In mid-1793, the tension on the streets, as reported by the *observateurs*, was aggravated by another severe bread shortage. Long queues formed overnight outside bakers' shops. In Bordeaux, Lucy de la Tour du Pin remembered that the terror of daily life was so great that people were afraid to exchange a word on the street, 'and the queue represented, as it were, a lawful assembly where the timid could talk to their neighbours or learn the latest news without exposing themselves to the imprudence of asking a question'. But the mood could turn in a moment from friendly neighbourhood chatter to menace or fury, and some women preferred to wait in men's clothes to avoid being hassled.

Bread riots – at their most dramatic, like the women's march on Versailles in the autumn of 1789 – were traditionally dominated by women. The fact that the demonstrators' actions stemmed from frustration at not being able to feed their families made them somehow palatable to the men in power: protest caused by maternal love was seen as natural, even commendable, however inconvenient it might be. But the bread disturbances of the second half of 1793, from the revolutionary government's point of view, had troubling political undertones. Hungry, angry women in the faubourg Saint-Antoine were crying, 'Our husbands made the revolution; if necessary, we will make the counter-revolution.' Spies thought the name of the king – since Louis XVI's execution, his young son, still imprisoned – was, if not yet on people's lips, already in their hearts.

Although some women remained passionate supporters of the revolution, by 1793 others had begun to turn back to their traditional ways of thinking, frustrated by the new regime's inability to serve their needs any better than the king had. In the provinces peasant women showed their discontent by harbouring seditious local priests and pointedly keeping religious holidays and dressing up in their best clothes on Sundays.

Opponents to the revolutionary regime had been in open and brutal revolt in the Vendée region since the spring of 1793. Here, as in Paris, the mood of desperation inspired several women to step out of the domestic arena and on to the battlefield. The peasant Renée Bordereau, who fought in the royalist army disguised as a man, would become known as the Joan of Arc of the Vendée. The revolutionary army had massacred forty-two members of her family including her father, who was killed before her eyes. Filled with 'rage and despair', she 'resolved to sacrifice my body to the King, to offer my soul to God, and I swore to fight until death or victory'.

Across the country in Lyon, the once prosperous hometown of the young bride Juliette Récamier, another civil war was raging. Here, too, counterrevolutionary women were proud to contribute to the cause in which they so ardently believed. 'A single heart beat in every breast, a unique sentiment inspired the men and the women: to resist tyranny,' wrote Alexandrine des Écherolles, the teenaged daughter of a retired army officer, in her diary. In May the people of the town had stormed the *mairie*, seizing Joseph Chalier, the despised agent of the revolutionary government, whom they executed on the same day the counter-revolutionary heroine Charlotte Corday was guillotined in Paris.

Expecting repercussions, the men and women of Lyon began to prepare for attack. 'The most delicate women participated in armed exercises, the testing of cannons,' recorded Alexandrine. 'Nothing seemed to frighten or surprise them.' The new Republic's forces reached Lyon in August and trained their guns on the city walls. Alexandrine joined other women in helping to put out fires caused by the bombardment, and assisted the local priest in collecting donations to feed the hungry and homeless and the children orphaned by the conflict. 'I joyfully saw myself called to play an active role in our history, which gave me a great importance in my own eyes,' she wrote. Despite the determined lightness of her tone, her words make clear that like so many other women during this period, in the midst of disaster and destruction Alexandrine was discovering a new sense of self and a new pride in her sex.

The foreign war effort had also seen, in 1793, a series of catastrophic surrenders and defeats for the revolutionary regime. Austrian and Prussian armies had advanced deep into French territory, heading for Paris, and at the end of August the British – who had declared war on France after Louis XVI's execution – took the port of Toulon. Ironically, the war – which the Jacobins had opposed, and so effectively used to destroy the Girondins – had become a means by which the Committee of Public Safety was able to consolidate its grip on power. 'Who dares to speak of peace?' demanded Bertrand Barère, answering his own question. 'The aristocrats, the moderates, the rich, the conspirators, the pretended patriots.'

War made brutal centralization and repression necessary in the name of the public interest, and provided the government with excuses for mass conscription (decreed in August), requisitioning, plunder and murder. In September Robespierre could look out of the windows of the Tuileries, where the Committee of Public Safety met, and see the new workshops erected in the palace's gardens. All the workmen of Paris had been ordered to manufacture muskets and cannon out of metal melted down from church bells, altars and objects confiscated from houses abandoned by émigrés; nuns' habits were made into bandages. The detritus of the old regime would provide the new with the instruments of its triumph.

In Paris, the disputes over the cockade were worsening, stimulated by what was, to the revolutionary government, a terrifying impulse: the desire of common women to participate in public life. Even at the time, it was obvious that '*la guerre des cocardes*' (as the historian Alfred Soboul called it) was about far more than bunches of ribbon.

The Committee of Public Safety was trying to marginalize the républicaines-révolutionnaires' radical allies the *enragés* by appropriating their ideas where they could, undermining the sectional societies that were the source of their influence and attacking their leaders. One of the most serious complaints against them was that they 'flattered the women's pride, seeking to persuade them they should have the rights of men, citing examples through history in science and government, saying that affairs would be better conducted by *bonnes républicaines*'.

Throughout the summer, Pauline Léon and Rose Lacombe and their followers in the Société des Républicaines-Révolutionnaires became progressively more outspoken in their opposition to the Jacobins in general and to Robespierre in particular. Proud of the role they had played in expelling the Girondins in June and emboldened by the faith the *enragés* placed in them, they began to speak scornfully of the 'coward' Robespierre, calling him 'Monsieur' – rather than the patriotic, republican 'Citoyen' – and wondering aloud how he dared treat them as counterrevolutionaries. Other members of the Society, still passionate Robespierrists, were angry at their attacks; divisions crystallized.

As autumn began, a group of mutineer républicaines-révolutionnaires confronted Léon and Lacombe about their outspokenness. Lacombe, they said, belittled Robespierre, telling them, 'You are infatuated with and enthusiastic about Robespierre, whom I regard only as an ordinary citizen.' She publicly criticized his measures, denouncing the bloody harshness of the government's efforts to crush the counterrevolution in Lyon and, in October, calling the Convention's decree declaring the Republic revolutionary until peace had been achieved a measure that would only to drive the people to incessant revolt and further carnage. In stirring Rousseauesque language, Pauline Léon was calling for the dissolution and re-election of the Convention, on the grounds that its members had been lagging in their seats long enough. 'The prolongation of power,' she declared, 'was often the tomb of liberty.'

When the Committee of Public Safety questioned Rose Lacombe about how many *citoyennes* belonged to her Society, she replied three or four thousand. One of the newer républicaines-révolutionnaires – who said she was the hundred and seventieth member of the Society – asked her why she had lied so barefacedly. 'We must make those white beaks grow pale and tremble,' answered Lacombe defiantly.

The républicaines-révolutionnaires also confronted Lacombe about her relationship with Théophile Leclerc. It was alleged that the 'immoral' Leclerc had shared Lacombe's lodgings for some months. This charge reveals a personal rupture between Lacombe and Pauline Léon, simmering away beneath their intimate political alliance, and perhaps explains why Léon, previously so conspicuous on the stage of Parisian radical politics, had allowed herself to fade into the background beside her swaggering, exhibitionist friend.

In November 1793 – three months after Lacombe and Leclerc's liaison was scrutinized first by the républicaines-révolutionnaires and then by the Jacobins – Théophile Leclerc married not Rose Lacombe, his established mistress, but her associate Pauline Léon, a woman thirteen years older than him. Their unexpected union followed an angry scene in front of the society, in which Léon accused Lacombe of sleeping with Leclerc. Although Lacombe had previously denied living with Leclerc, face to face with Léon, she had no choice but to admit it.

Leclerc's mentor Jacques Roux, the red priest, had been arrested for the first time in August, released and then arrested again on 5 September, the day Terror was declared the order of the day. Bertrand

Barère had denounced *enragés* he described as counterrevolutionaries stirring up the women of the streets. Roux was sent to prison not by order of the government, but by the 'unanimous judgement' of the Jacobin Club. Among his confiscated papers was a letter praising militant women who had 'the doubly advantageous attribute of conquering through charm and through fearlessness', and declaring that the moment when the *enragé* 'mass of republicans' would be ready 'to crush tyranny' was approaching.

In early September Leclerc was denounced as a counterrevolutionary by one of the rebel républicaines-révolutionnaires, Citoyenne Govin (the testimony of only one person being enough by this time to secure a warrant). Rose Lacombe sprang to Leclerc's defence. She demanded an explanation from Govin and ordered her expulsion from the Society if she could not prove her allegations; she accused the Committee of Public Safety of arresting all the best patriots.

Lacombe was present in her usual place in the tribunes of the Jacobin Club on 16 September when they debated the issue of Govin's denunciation of Leclerc and her subsequent removal from the Society. A Citoyen Chabot took the floor to describe how Lacombe had become a counterrevolutionary menace, demanding the release of political prisoners being held without trial and threatening him with the wrath of her army of women.

A few days earlier, Lacombe had gone to Chabot's house to argue the case of the former mayor of Toulouse, held for some months without charge because he was rich, popular, of noble blood – and had offended Chabot's vanity when the latter was commissioner to his region. 'She claimed that one didn't keep men in prison like that; that Revolution or no Revolution, they had to be questioned within twenty-four hours, released if they were innocent, and sent to the guillotine at once if they were guilty – in short, all the remarks that you hear aristocrats mouthing all the time when we arrest one of their friends,' Chabot said. His views on guilt were very much in line with his leaders': the day after this speech, the Law of Suspects was passed, ordering the arrest of all those who by their own or their associates' words or behaviour showed themselves to be 'advocates of tyranny or federalism and enemies of liberty'.

Lacombe's brave defence of a victim of injustice was enough to incriminate her in Chabot's 'cockroach eyes' (as she described them). 'I told him that we didn't get rid of the tyrant [Louis XVI] in order to replace him with others,' Lacombe reported. She accused Chabot himself of being an enemy of the revolution and insisted that she had not insulted Robespierre, but merely tried to warn him against his evil associates.

Chabot's distrust of Lacombe in particular was aggravated by a more general misogyny. 'It's because I like women that I don't want them to be forming a body apart and calumniating even virtue,' he protested to the Jacobins. He had taunted Lacombe by insisting he could never refuse anything to a woman; she retorted that she pitied her 'country because the counterrevolutionaries also had women, and it wouldn't be difficult for them to obtain pardons by sending [their] women to him'.

'It is these counter-revolutionary sluts who cause all the riotous outbreaks, above all over bread,' stormed Chabot. 'They made a revolution over coffee and sugar, and they will make others if we do not watch out.' Others confirmed that Lacombe meddled everywhere and encouraged her followers to speak scornfully about 'Monsieur Robespierre'. Her liaison with Leclerc was raised, of note as much because of Leclerc's supposedly aristocratic background as for any depravity implicit in their living together: 'Citoyenne Lacombe, or Madame Lacombe, who likes nobles so much, is sheltering a noble in her house.'

Just as the Club turned its attention to the case of Leclerc – who had declared in his newspaper that 'if they wanted to arrest him, he would stab both the person who issued the arrest warrant and the person who executed it' – Lacombe stood up and demanded the chance to speak. Cries of 'À bas la nouvelle Corday!' greeted her request; the women in the galleries nearby hissed, 'Intriguer!' and 'Get out, miserable woman, or we will tear you to pieces!' Lacombe stood her ground, loudly protesting that she would speak or perish. 'The first one of you who dares to come forward, I am going to show you what a free woman can do!'

'The tumult and disorder became so great that the president donned his hat [to call for order],' recorded the minute-taker. 'It was only at the end of a considerable period that calm returned.' The president pointed out to Lacombe that causing turmoil in a group of people trying calmly to debate a point concerning the interests of the people was counterrevolutionary in and of itself.

At the Jacobins' orders, Lacombe was prevented from speaking in her own defence and seized by guards, who took her to the Tuileries to be questioned by the Committee of Public Safety. After two hours waiting in the Committee's antechamber, one of her guards took pity on her and escorted her back to her lodgings near the Palais Royal. When they got there they found the *commissaires* of the local sectional committee had placed seals on all her belongings and on the doors, so she could not enter. As it was late at night and the streets were dangerous, her kindly guard offered her a bed for the night. Just then appeared two members of the Société des Républicaines-Révolutionnaires, who had ventured out into the dark streets to find word of Lacombe, and took her home with them. Meanwhile the Jacobins had voted to order the Society to expel her and to recommend that all female agitators be arrested as counterrevolutionaries.

The following day, at Lacombe's request, the *commissaires* returned to inspect her papers. 'We found nothing suspect,' they reported. 'On the contrary, we found nothing but correspondence of fraternal societies, which breathes the purest patriotism, and different personal letters where the public good and patriotism were beautifully expressed.' The seals were lifted and, for the moment, Rose Lacombe was safe.

Soon afterwards a furious, defiant Lacombe gave the Société des Républicaines-Révolutionnaires her own account of the Jacobins' session and her argument with Chabot. 'All the ills that are befalling Paris are attributed to us,' she lamented, decrying 'these monsters, who are strong only when they oppress the weak'.

One of the most important elements of the threat that Lacombe posed to the Jacobin elite was her eloquence. They accused her of using 'hypocritical and Feuillant [by extension, aristocratic] language' and seeking to undermine the constitution. For her part, Lacombe understood that controlling the language of the revolution was the essence of the Jacobins' political mastery. A large part of her rage at their treatment of her stemmed from frustration at the way they distorted the meanings of potent words and twisted the charges of their accusers back at them. 'Be careful, Robespierre,' she had warned on 16 September. 'I noticed that those accused of having lied believe they can side-step the denunciation by accusing those who denounce them of having spoken ill of you.'

Within days the undaunted Lacombe was petitioning the Convention once more, this time demanding the arrest of the wives of émigrés and urging the rehabilitation of prostitutes. As an actress – actresses were viewed by most people as little more than whores – Lacombe empathized with the plight of prostitutes. She saw them as victims rather than criminals and recommended that they be given honest employment and state housing, and made to listen to patriotic lectures intended to save them from the error of their ways.

The robustly respectable market women of Les Halles, like the austere revolutionary government, viewed 'public women' as agents of counterrevolution whose corrupted morality would contaminate the Republic. Like gambling, fancy dress and pornography, prostitutes represented an aristocratic libertinism that was thought to ruin virtuous citizens. It was even rumoured that they were paid agents of the British prime minister, William Pitt. Several times in September police spies reported that women working in the Palais Royal were speaking out against the revolution and, 'by their rudeness [*incivisme*] and other vices', were contributing to the atmosphere of unrest and dissatisfaction that continued to prevail there. To the *marchandes*, if women who wore cockades defended and protected prostitutes, then women who wore cockades were little more than prostitutes themselves. Lacombe's petitions on their behalf only underlined her personal immorality and political deviance.

Despite Lacombe's brush with the Jacobins, on 21 September the républicaines-révolutionnaires succeeded in persuading the Convention to pass a law compelling women as well as men to wear cockades. The first failure to display one would result in eight days in prison; the second would provoke an enquiry into the offender's politics.

A police report described how the issue of the *cocarde* inspired women with the disquieting 'desire to share the political rights of men. They say, when women have the cockade, they will demand civic cards, they will want to vote in our assemblies, to share our administrative offices, and from this conflict of interests and opinions will result a disorder favourable to their projects.' Wearing the cockade would be a statement of active citizenship. However, the report added, despite their ambitions the militant women did not appear to be counter-revolutionaries: in general, they showed the deepest respect for the nation and the government.

The market women were furious. Although they were vitally interested in politics when it affected their ability to make a living or to feed their children, they saw the political world as an exclusively masculine domain and the women trying to enter it as perverse and unnatural. Their energies were concentrated on survival; having time to fight for new rights would have been an unimaginable luxury. Wearing the cockade, they argued, would bring with it the responsibilities of full citizenship, including the obligation to bear arms in defence of the *patrie*. These they stoutly rejected.

Consternation greeted the new edict. 'One can put it on the right, the left, in front, behind,' wrote one government spy. 'This frivolous question, which has already excited violent brawls, is not yet decided.' On its first day the law caused a fracas on the rue des Petits Champs, around the corner from Lacombe's lodgings and not far from Les Halles, in which a group of dandies were seen encouraging some market women as they attacked a group of '*citoyennes patriotes*'. Elsewhere fishwives snatched rosettes from breasts, and trod them into the mud.

Marchandes and républicaines-révolutionnaires were not the only people embroiled in the drama. One middle-class woman who was accosted for refusing to wear the cockade was defiantly anti-revolutionary. A man appeared before the Committee of Public Safety to testify that he had stopped a Citoyenne Guérin for not wearing one, asking her if she was a republican. She replied that on the contrary, she was 'very much an aristocrat' and, though she finally gave in and bought one from a street seller, she said as she fastened it to her hat that 'she would never betray her own way of thinking'. Called up before the Committee to explain her words, Guérin said that she understood 'being an aristocrat' to mean 'not doing evil to anyone, living off her revenue, doing good when she was able to, and bearing everything they might want her to bear'. Two of her neighbours were summoned, who declared that Guérin had been acting oddly for some weeks; after three days in custody she was released on grounds of mental instability. Only madness could have explained such a reckless disregard for revolutionary dress and vocabulary.

Their triumph over the cockade inspired the républicaines-révolutionnaires to press for their rights to bear arms and to hope to force women to wear the *bonnet rouge* as well. Hitherto only sansculottes and the républicaines-révolutionnaires themselves, as they patrolled the capital's streets, had worn the red Phrygian cap, ancient symbol of freedom. For these latter women, the *cocarde* was a simple badge of patriotism, but the *bonnet rouge* was laden with more potent meaning. Militant women who donned the cap, an explicitly masculine item of clothing, were implicitly claiming the rights and responsibilities of active revolutionary citizenship – they were claiming the rights of men.

Almost everyone except the républicaines-révolutionnaires viewed women wearing red caps as a terrifying threat to masculine authority and an augury of more violence and upheaval on the city's streets. The républicaines-révolutionnaires insisted they were as free to wear the *bonnet rouge* as a cockade, and openly paraded in their bonnets, provoking angry retaliation – they were snatched off their heads and trampled underfoot, and the women were called bitches and whores. 'Pull off their *bonnets*,' people cried, 'because the only people who have them are prostitutes and women paid off by the aristocracy to wear them.'

At the end of October, after almost a month of unrest and escalating scuffles on the streets, a group of drunken market women stormed a meeting of the Société des Républicaines-Révolutionnaires in the crypt of Saint-Eustache. Crying, 'Down with red bonnets! Down with Jacobin women! Down with Jacobin women and cockades! They are all scoundrels who have brought misfortune upon France!', they attacked the group's members, beating them up and knocking several unconscious, and tried to destroy the Society's symbols, an *oeil de vigilance,* a tricolour flag and four pikes. A man who tried to intervene on behalf of one *citoyenne,* who was being battered senseless with a wooden clog, was stabbed.

It did not take the revolutionary government long to realize that this violence – even though the républicaines-révolutionnaires were its victims – provided them with an excuse to disempower these tiresome women for good. The following day, a deputation of *poissardes* petitioned a sympathetic National Convention with their complaints against the républicaines-révolutionnaires and demanded the right to wear what they pleased. Fabre d'Églantine, Jacobin deputy and member of the Committee of Public Safety, stood up to attack female societies, declaring that if women were allowed to wear the red cap, they would soon demand the right to carry pistols. He argued that the groups were composed not of mothers, daughters or sisters, 'but adventurers, knights errant, emancipated girls [meaning whores] and female grenadiers'. Women must be defined by their relation to men; their autonomy would threaten the very foundations of the Republic. At the end of the session, possibly prompted, the market women returned to the bar of the Convention to request that all female clubs be abolished.

A day later, on behalf of the Committee of Public Safety, the lawyer André Amar delivered a theatrical report on the disturbances at the National Convention that revealed the depth of the Jacobins' fears of women involving themselves in public life. On 28 October, he said, six thousand women had gathered in Les Halles to protest against the 'violence and threats' of a group of women wearing pantaloons and red bonnets whom they accused of trying to force them to wear an outfit intended for men. The riots that ensued, he said, were believed by the local ward to have been fermented by 'malevolent persons [who] have put on the mask of exaggerated patriotism' hoping to bring about counterrevolution in Paris. The ward requested that female societies be banned and freedom of dress be re-established.

Amar said that the Committee's investigation of these events had prompted it to ask itself some basic questions: 'Can women exercise political rights and take an active part in affairs of government?' and 'Can they deliberate together in political associations or popular societies?' To both questions, the Committee had decided the answer was no.

Participating in government, declared Amar, required 'extensive knowledge, unlimited attention and devotion, a strict immovability, and self-abnegation' – qualities most women did not possess. Nor did they have the physical and moral strength necessary to debate, to deliberate, or to resist oppression. Even meeting in popular societies was wrong, since doing so would require women 'to sacrifice the more important cares to which nature calls them' as well as their 'natural' modesty and timidity. Nature and morality had granted women certain immutable functions: looking after the home and family, educating their children in republican ideals and elevating the souls of those close to them through their softness and moderation. 'We must say that this question is related essentially to morals, and without morals, [there is] no republic,' said Amar, making explicit the link in Jacobin patriarchal, bourgeois philosophy between women leading a purely domestic life and greater civic virtue. He recommended that women's groups should be banned.

Only one deputy dared to question Amar's conclusions. 'Unless you are going to question whether women are part of the human species,' asked Citoyen Chalier, 'can you take away from them this right [to assemble peaceably] which is common to every thinking being?'

'Here is how the suspension of these societies can be justified,' responded Deputy Basire, with typically Jacobin disregard for the rights of the individual when they conflicted with his party's power. 'You declared yourselves a revolutionary government; in this capacity you can take all measures dictated by the public safety.'

The measure was passed.

A jubilant article in the *Révolutions de Paris* reported that women were no longer permitted 'to organise in clubs; they will be tolerated as spectators, silent and modest, in the patriotic societies; in effect women can no more go searching for news outside their homes; there they will wait and receive it from the mouths of their fathers or their children or from their brothers or husbands'. Women could and still did observe the proceedings of all-male public associations – continuing to heckle the speakers, cheer their favourites, clatter their knitting-needles, eat and drink, scream insults across the floor and refuse to leave when asked to. But they could no longer comment independently on public affairs.

At first, some former républicaines-révolutionnaires vainly tried to challenge the law that had dissolved their society. A group of them reached the bar of the Convention a few days later and tried to protest against the law 'occasioned by a false report [which] forbids us to assemble', but their voices were drowned out by the scornful hooting and laughter of the deputies, and they left the hall 'precipitously'.

On 17 November, in front of the General Council of Paris, the last defiant républicaines-révolutionnaires made a final bid to be heard. The galleries erupted when the women appeared in their red caps, and the president of the Commune, Pierre-Gaspard Chaumette, launched a furious attack. 'Impudent women who want to become men, aren't you well enough provided for?' he thundered, to warm applause. 'What else do you need? Your despotism is the only one our strength cannot conquer, because it is [the despotism] of love, and consequently the work of nature. In the name of this very nature, remain what you are, and far from envying us the perils of a stormy life, be content to make us forget them in the heart of our families, in resting our eyes on the enchanting spectacle of our children made happy by your cares.'

His emotive appeal clearly touched the women, because apparently they immediately removed their red caps and replaced them with head-dresses 'suitable to their sex'. One of them may have been Pauline Léon, whose marriage to Théophile Leclerc would take place two days later. Despite the bombast of her earlier speeches and petitions, by the end of 1793 Léon seems to have been almost relieved to slip into obscurity as a loving wife to a 'poor and persecuted patriot', as she described Leclerc.

It is unlikely that she kept in touch with her co-founder of the Société. Rose Lacombe drifted around France for a year or two, odd prison spells alternating with occasional acting work, before sinking out of the official records.

'I devoted myself altogether to the care of my household, and I set an example of the conjugal love and domestic virtues which are the foundation for love of the Fatherland', Pauline Léon wrote later. One of the revolution's most ardent campaigners for women's rights had finally surrendered to republican segregationist rhetoric – or, perhaps, simply, to love.

13

VICTIME

Manon Roland

AUGUST–NOVEMBER 1793

> One can no longer hope for any good or be surprised at
> any evil.
>
> MANON ROLAND

Mme Guillotine

WHILE CHAOS RAGED on the streets of Paris in the autumn of 1793, inside the prison of Sainte-Pélagie Manon Roland sat serenely finishing her memoirs. But her proud show of calmness was a front, designed to confound her enemies, reassure her friends and shore up her own shaky courage. To visitors, she presented a face of persecuted but tranquil innocence; alone, she spent hours staring out of her barred windows, weeping. 'I can feel my resolve weakening,' she wrote on 28 August. 'I am agonised by the suffering of my country and the loss of my friends.'

Since July, Manon had received no further letters from Buzot, though he remained the focus of all her fondest dreams. She still allowed herself to imagine he had escaped to the United States, 'sole asylum of liberty', but she no longer hoped to join him there to help him find the 'domestic happiness' she felt certain he deserved. 'But I myself, alas, am done for; I shall never see you again.' Tears flowed down her cheeks as she wrote those words, and, to distract herself, she turned once again to her memoirs.

Having finished her account of the revolution, her own and Roland's part in it and her observations of the men with whom she had been thrown into contact, Manon began to recall happier times, using the memories of her childhood to block out the desperate reality of her present situation. Following Rousseau, she resolved to 'paint the good and the bad with equal freedom'. She had been hardened by adversity, she wrote, and aspired to nothing more than candour.

Her account of her youth is a remarkable document, passionate and fiercely self-aware. The events she had endured over the past three years had done nothing to lessen her innate sense of drama or self-worth. As she contemplated martyrdom, Manon did not under-estimate the importance of her story. 'Perhaps one day these artless pages may lighten the darkness of some other unfortunate captive, helping him to forget his own misery in thinking of mine,' she wrote. 'Possibly, too, those who seek to understand the human heart through a novel or a play may find something worth studying in my story.' Steeped as she was in the works of Rousseau and the sentimental novels of her youth, suffering all the tortures of doomed, unfulfilled love, she sought to understand and come to terms with her own intensely lived emotional life, the 'sensibility of the heart' and the 'soul that was too great to be confined' but which had so often been curbed and frustrated.

Eventually, as news from outside filtered into Sainte-Pélagie, Manon grew impatient with her work. On 3 October the National Convention outlawed the fugitive Girondins (who included Roland and Buzot), charged forty-one more and ordered the arrest of another seventy-six. The newspapers reported that the government believed it was closing in on the wanted men. 'How Robespierre loves blood!' Manon burst out. 'I cannot go on writing in the midst of all these horrors which are tearing my country apart,' she wrote, rushing her account of her life before the revolution to its conclusion. 'I cannot live among its ruins. I prefer to be buried beneath them.'

Hearing the news, Manon decided that she could best defeat her enemies not by waiting for release or for the chance to speak from the scaffold, but by refusing to allow them to make an example of her. 'Every hour that I remain alive gives tyranny new scope for boasting,' she wrote. 'I cannot beat them, but I can at least defraud them.' Before she began to starve herself to death, Manon wrote a series of letters in which she apologized to her husband and daughter for abandoning them, gave instructions for her small assets and various possessions to be given to Eudora, and expressed her hopes for her daughter's future. Her last thought was of Buzot. 'Farewell, dear——,' she began. 'No, I am not saying farewell to you. Leaving this world brings me nearer to you.'

On the 14th, Manon was taken to the prison hospital, where she wrote a letter to Robespierre that she did not send. It was not a plea for mercy – her innocence was, she said, its own witness – nor an appeal to the man she had once valued and believed to be a 'sincere and ardent friend of liberty'. Instead she asked him why it was that as a woman, and thus necessarily a passive citizen, she was to be exposed to the same fate as active citizens. She was not asking for her own sake, she wrote, but for the future well-being of France: how could the Republic mete out the same treatment to her, a loyal woman who had made all the sacrifices of which she was capable for her country, as to selfish, perfidious enemies of the state? 'Assuredly,' she concluded, 'justice and liberty no longer reign here.'

Two days later, Marie-Antoinette was executed. Despite the fabricated and humiliating charges against her, at her trial on 12 October the queen had 'made no defence, and called no witnesses, alleging that no positive fact had been produced against her', wrote Helen Williams. The guillotine democratized death. Meeting her end, her white hair roughly cropped for the blade and her hands bound, Marie-Antoinette was no more and no less than any of the machine's other victims, although her dignity in death elevated her more than her status in life ever had.

That August, Germaine de Staël had braved public opinion once more to issue from her exile in Switzerland a heartfelt *Reflections on the Trial of the Queen, by a Woman*. Staël portrayed Marie-Antoinette as a despised and vulnerable widow torn from her young son and facing her own death, and urged the women of France to rise to the defence of one of their own. Perhaps because of the heartbreak caused by Narbonne leaving her, Germaine was sympathetic to Marie-Antoinette's suffering; all women, she argued, could understand each other's tragedies and ought to extend to each other mercy and humanity.

But Staël's emotive appeal could not compete with the feverish anti-monarchism that was electrifying Paris, distracting the people from their hunger and fear. During the same month as Marie-Antoinette's execution, the bodies of all the French kings since St Louis were exhumed from their resting-places in Saint-Denis, thrown into common burial grounds and covered with quicklime. The bestselling play of the moment was Sylvain Maréchal's melodramatic *The Last Judgement of the Kings*, showing at the Théâtre de la République.

Despite the desperate shortage of gunpowder due to the war effort, the government granted the producers twenty pounds each of saltpetre and powder for the explosive climax, in which all the monarchs of Europe were killed. The play's theme was considered so stirringly patriotic that copies of the script were sent to the troops fighting on the frontiers.

Although Manon's first suicide attempt failed, like many of her imprisoned Girondin friends she continued to consider it an option. Their veneration of the ancients, who were bound by no Christian taboos, led them to see suicide as heroic, a completely free act that expressed supreme courage and stoicism in the face of death and the unknown. Contemporaries spoke of suicides as being made 'Romans again'. Closely allied to that other revolutionary fantasy, martyrdom, suicide was also a public, political act – an expression of defiance to the regime that had destroyed their hopes for France. In addition, it was explicitly masculine; Manon was determined to show that women could die as boldly as men. In death at least she would be their equal.

But her old friends Bosc d'Antic and Sophie Grandchamp refused her requests for poison, and, when she heard that the trial of the Girondins was set for 24 October, Manon steeled herself to stand witness for her friends, convincing herself that their cause could be better served by her courage in court. On the 24th she was taken from Sainte-Pélagie to the Palais de Justice, where she waited all day, only to be returned to prison that night without having been called. It was not until 30 October that the Revolutionary Tribunal announced that no witnesses would be called in the Girondins' defence.

'We are accused of doing nothing, but has our position been realised?' asked Robespierre, from the tribune of the National Convention, on the 25th.

> Eleven armies to direct, the weight of all Europe to carry, everywhere traitors to unmask, agents paid by the gold of foreign powers to confound, faithless officials to watch over, everywhere obstacles and difficulties in the execution of wise measures to smooth away, all tyrants to combat, all conspirators to intimidate, almost all of them of that caste once so powerful by its riches, and still strong in its intrigues – these are our functions.

In prison, awaiting execution, Jacques-Pierre Brissot and his associates were, according to Helen Williams, 'in such a state of elevation, that no one could approach them with the common-place and ordinary topics of consolation'. Pierre Vergniaud told her 'that he would rather die than live a witness to his country's shame'. Manon was living on a similarly intense plane of impassioned rectitude and nervous energy. Like her friends, she almost welcomed her impending martyrdom because it brought her closer to the historical vindication she felt sure would one day be hers. When Sophie Grandchamp visited her, she saw shining in Manon's eyes a strange '*sorte de joie*'.

For Manon, there was a secret joy in the knowledge that in death, unlike in life, she would be treated as the peer of the men whose political hopes and dreams she had shared. The fact that, despite her sex, she was considered dangerous enough to be executed alongside her one-time associates was something to be proud of; the possibility of being a martyr to the cause of freedom and justice, like the Romans she had worshipped as a child, made death hold fewer terrors.

During their trial one of the Girondins, Charles Éléonor Dufriche-Valazé, hid a knife in his papers and killed himself when the predictable verdict of guilty was declared, just as the Robespierrist Camille Desmoulins is said to have cried out, 'My God I am sorry for this!' Vergniaud had gone into prison bearing a phial of poison but, on finding that two of his friends, whom he had hoped would escape the guillotine, were to be executed with him, he gave the poison away, 'resolving to wait the appointed moment, and to perish with them'. The following March, Condorcet was one of the few Girondins who successfully committed suicide in prison, taking poison on the night he was arrested.

Those Girondins who chose the scaffold over suicide went to their deaths on 31 October in a spirit of proud defiance. The twenty-two men, who included Brissot and Vergniaud, were said to have 'displayed a villainous courage'. As they climbed into the tumbrel, they sang the 'Marseillaise'; many laughed as they mounted the scaffold. The executioner Charles-Henri Sanson gave a remarkable demonstration of revolutionary efficiency, dispatching them all in about half an hour, but the effect of the deaths was not all that the Committee of Public Safety had hoped for. A police report described many onlookers walking away from the spectacle 'with sad expressions and in the greatest consternation'.

On the same day, Manon Roland was transferred from Sainte-Pélagie to the Conciergerie, the fourteenth-century round-towered fortress on the Île de la Cité in which the Revolutionary Tribunal was held, and from which her friends had departed on their last journey that very morning. The Conciergerie was a normal prison, but it also served as the final stop for prisoners on their way to the scaffold across the Seine in the Place de la Révolution; in the two years leading up to July 1794, 2,700 condemned people would spend their last moments there.

Accused of 'conspiring against the unity and the indivisibility of the Republic and attempting to introduce civil war', Manon knew with grim certainty that when she arrived at the Conciergerie there would be no going back. 'As for me . . . it is all over. You know the malady that the English call "heartbroken"? I have it without remedy, and I have no wish to delay its effects; the fever grows and develops,' she had written to a friend before leaving Sainte-Pélagie. 'It is as well. My liberty will never be returned to me; heaven is my witness that I was loyal to my unhappy husband!' Buzot she believed captured; she had nothing else to live for.

On 1 November, Manon was questioned for the first time. Although her cook Lecocq and her maid Fleury refused to testify against her – for which disturbing personal loyalty they were imprisoned – they had confirmed that many of the executed and fugitive Girondins had regularly dined with the Rolands. Mlle Mignon, Eudora's fifty-five-year-old clavichord teacher, had been persuaded to denounce the Rolands, but her evidence was largely inconsequential. Manon was forced to answer questions about her relationship with Buzot, but she insisted on referring to him solely in association with Pétion and Brissot as particular friends of both her and her husband.

Further interrogated, she said only that she had for each of them the degree of estimation and attachment that each merited.

Returning to her cell, Manon spent the next few days reading, writing letters and speaking words of comfort to her fellow-prisoners. She 'seemed absorbed in profound meditations', her soul calm as she awaited death. Beugnot, a moderate Girondin who had expected to find her vain, intolerant and probably cruel was surprised to discover that although they disagreed politically, she was a sensitive, gentle woman. Her serenity and generosity transformed even her prison cell, where she dispensed money, advice and hope to other prisoners.

Beugnot described Manon as being not beautiful but agreeable-looking, with an expressive face. Another prisoner noticed that 'misfortunes and a long confinement had left upon it [her face] traces of melancholy which tempered its natural vivacity'. Beugnot found her voice rather than her looks the most striking thing about her. 'No woman could speak so purely, gracefully and elegantly,' he remembered, praising the harmony and rhythm of her speech, the grace of her gestures and the noble expression in her eyes. Despite himself, he was captivated by her words, as well as how she spoke them. Her broad education and natural intellect made her a stimulating conversationalist, even if she did express views to which he was ardently opposed. When Beugnot tried to make her admit that the king 'had met death with true magnanimity,' Manon responded, 'Very well, he was fine enough on the scaffold; but there is no reason for giving him credit for it. Kings are reared from childhood to act a part.' Her own suffering had not diluted her political radicalism.

Manon's unfaltering republicanism did not shake Beugnot, though. 'The tender and delicate foot of woman is unfitted to tread these paths bristling with iron and stained with blood,' he reflected, pondering the issue of feminine emancipation. 'In order to walk there steadily she must make herself a man, and a masculine woman is a monster.'

Beugnot was impressed to find that despite her outspokenness she was a devoted wife and mother. When they discussed the ideal of virtuous marriage and what it entailed, she declared proudly, 'The coldness of the French astonishes me. If I had been at liberty and my husband led to execution, I should have stabbed myself at the foot of the scaffold; and I am convinced that when Roland learns of my death he will pierce his own heart.'

When Manon saw Sophie Grandchamp for the last time, she gave her a small packet of letters and embraced her warmly. Just over a week earlier, in Sainte-Pélagie, Manon had wept as they shared a miserable supper together. 'It is for my country that I spill these tears; my friends are dying martyrs to liberty,' she had said. 'These are not the marks of weakness their memory demands. Now my fate is fixed; I have no more uncertainty. I will join them soon and I will summon the dignity to follow them.'

She asked Sophie whose death had had the strongest impact on her. Sophie replied, Charlotte Corday's. Manon managed to choke down some food, and asked if Sophie would stand witness to her final moments. Her hands shaking, Sophie answered that she would. 'It's awful, my request horrifies me,' cried Manon. Then, more calmly: 'Promise me only that you will see me pass.' Knowing Sophie would be there, she said, would assuage her terror during her dreadful journey to the Place de la Révolution; one person at least would ensure that she was not abandoned alone to her ordeal, would render her homage at the moment of her death.

On 8 November, Manon was called before the Revolutionary Tribunal to hear her sentence. She dressed carefully, in a white muslin dress with a black velvet sash and a simple hat resting on her loose chestnut hair. Beugnot noticed that her expression, though still calm, was more animated than usual as she prepared to mount the stairs to the vaulted medieval hall, above the Conciergerie's cells, in which the court met.

When Manon rose to begin her own carefully prepared defence, she opened by pleading the Girondin cause. The judge immediately interrupted: the accused, he said, could not abuse her right to defend herself by glorifying condemned traitors. Manon turned to the onlookers to witness this injustice, but her appeal was met with cries of 'Long live the Republic! Down with traitors!'

Manon Roland was convicted of being an accomplice, if not an author, of a conspiracy against the Republic, and sentenced to death that same day. It was less than four months before her fortieth birthday. 'You find me worthy to share the fate of the great men whom you have assassinated,' she said. 'I will do my best to mount the scaffold with the same courage they have shown.'

Descending on to the level of the cells, Manon gave the prisoners waiting to learn her fate a rueful thumbs down signal. Honoré-Jean Riouffe thought he detected 'a certain joyfulness in her swift steps', perhaps because she believed that in death she would finally be united with Buzot. She ate her last meal with Lamarche, a forger with whom she was to go to the scaffold, and tried to make him smile. Afterwards a guard cut their hair in readiness for the guillotine's blade. 'It suits you admirably,' she told Lamarche. 'You have the head of an ancient Roman.'

She was surprised when her hands were tied behind her back before she was helped into the tumbrel; she was not used to it, she said. Lamarche climbed into the cart ahead of her, not thinking to allow her to go first. '*Tu n'es pas galant*,' scolded Manon, gently. 'You're not a gentleman.'

It was a cold, grey afternoon. Manon had asked Sophie Grandchamp to stand at the Pont-Neuf, where the red-painted tumbrel, drawn by two horses and accompanied by five or six gendarmes, would cross the Seine on to the right bank. The spot she had chosen was less than a hundred yards from the house on the quai de l'Horloge in which she had grown up. As they reached the bridge, Sophie could see Manon scanning the crowd for her face. 'She was fresh, calm, smiling,' wrote Sophie; the pleasure that her presence gave Manon was evident on her friend's face. As she watched, the cart turned off the bridge and trundled at walking pace over the cobbles towards the Place de la Révolution. The journey could take as long as two agonizing hours, through jeering or impassive crowds.

At the scaffold, Manon insisted that Lamarche go before her. To wait and watch your companions die was seen as more difficult to bear and women were usually accorded precedence. Perhaps Manon felt that she could stand the wait better than the frightened Lamarche; perhaps she just wanted to feel the breath in her chest and the air on her skin a few moments longer.

An immense statue of Liberty stood on a plinth in the Place de la Révolution where Louis XV had once reigned in bronze majesty. She wore the *bonnet rouge* – unlike the républicaines-révolutionnaires, her intentions were not suspect – and leaned on a pike. On mounting the scaffold, before placing her neck calmly on the block, Manon looked up at her and said, 'Oh, Liberty, what crimes they commit in your name!' In her friend Helen Williams's eyes, she had triumphantly achieved her hopes of dying nobly, proving that feminine sensibility could be as heroic as masculine stoicism: 'What more than Roman fortitude dignified the last moments of Mme Roland?'

As Manon had predicted, when Roland heard about her death he left his hiding-place in Rouen and, somewhere on the Paris road – ensuring his body would be found – leaned forcefully forward on to his swordstick. He left two notes. One said that 'he had died as he had lived, in honesty and virtue'. The other said he was committing suicide 'not out of fear but out of indignation. I left my refuge as soon as I learned that they had murdered my wife. I no longer wish to live in a world so covered with crimes.'

Buzot heard the news of Manon's execution in Bordeaux, where he was living in a cellar belonging to a wigmaker of Saint-Émilion with Barbaroux and Pétion. '*She* is no more, *she* is no more,' he wrote to a friend in Évreux. 'The scoundrels have murdered her. Consider if there is anything left for me to regret on earth!' The following June their hiding-place was discovered and the fugitives decided to commit suicide. In her last letter to Buzot, Manon had urged him, if he was in danger of being apprehended, to 'die a free man as you have lived'. Barbaroux's shot misfired and he was captured and guillotined; Buzot's and Pétion's corpses, half-eaten by wolves, were found in a wheatfield a week later.

Women tended to form the majority of the spectators in the Place de la Révolution. The infamous *tricoteuses*, or Furies of the guillotine, knitted stockings for their husbands and sons away fighting the nation's external enemies while they monitored the elimination of the nation's internal enemies on the scaffold.

Officially, the guillotine was known as 'the sword of liberty'. To the ruling Jacobins it represented impartial justice, as merciless and incorruptible as they themselves hoped to be. Something of a cult of the guillotine developed during the Terror. Hymns were composed to 'Sainte Guillotine,' addressing the 'admirable machine' and 'proud device'; a play called *La guillotine d'amour* was playing at the Théâtre du Lycée in 1793. As the historian Andrea Stuart comments, the guillotine was 'familiarized, domesticated and commodified: miniature guillotines were made into paperweights, children's toys and even hair ornaments and earrings'.

The main reason for watching the enemies of the state go to their deaths was not support for the new regime, but a macabre fascination with the ultimate exercise of power. 'It was not the love of the republic that each day drew so many to the place de la Révolution,' wrote Camille Desmoulins, 'but curiosity, and the new play that could have but a single performance.' Although the crowds lining the streets to watch the tumbrels go by were often boisterous, the onlookers in the Place de la Révolution were more usually apathetic and bemused than bloodthirsty. The scaffold was raised and surrounded by policemen or soldiers, usually on horseback, so from ground level it was hard to get a clear view, even when Sanson held up a victim's head. The quick competence with which the executioner worked made the spectacle more like watching a professional butcher than a theatre of propaganda.

Most victims made an effort to be dignified, and many royalists uttered a last defiant cry of *'Vive le roi!'*, but there were a few notable exceptions. Some victims composed songs that would raise their spirits on the *trajet*, the long route to the Place de la Révolution, which were known as *chansons de guillotine*. Many became well-known hymns, like 'Mourir pour la patrie', first sung by a Girondin newspaper editor on his way to the scaffold. '*C'est le sort le plus beau, le plus digne d'envie,*' went the chorus: it is the most desirable, the finest fate. Others laughed and danced in the tumbrels, or poked fun at the onlookers.

When Louis XV's former mistress, the ageing courtesan Jeanne du Barry, was killed in the spring of 1793, 'she showed very little courage on the scaffold,' wrote Grace Dalrymple Elliott, who had been held alongside her in Sainte-Pélagie. Elliott thought that if everyone protested like Barry, 'Robespierre would not have dared to put as many to death as he did, for Mme du Barry's screams, they told me, frightened and alarmed the mob'.

Manon Roland was one of several prominent women, including Marie-Antoinette and Olympe de Gouges, who were executed in the autumn of 1793 at the same time as the Jacobins crushed the Société des Républicaines-Révolutionnaires. The Jacobin regime may not have been prepared to admit that women were capable of exercising the same political rights as men, but they saw no contradiction in imprisoning and executing them for political crimes – for many, like the wives of émigrés, simply crimes of association.

Olympe de Gouges had been arrested nearly two months after Manon, on 20 July. At first she tried to avoid the guillotine by pretending she was pregnant, but since she was forty-five her claims were greeted with derisive scorn. During her trial, which took place on the second day of Manon's hearing, 2 November, she boldly outlined her federalist ideas, criticized Marat and described Robespierre as 'ambitious, without genius or soul . . . ready to sacrifice a whole nation to become dictator'. She was killed two days later. Different versions of her last words survive. One has her shouting, 'Children of the Fatherland, you will avenge my death!' to which the onlookers responded, *'Vive le République!'*. The other, more poetic account sees her lamenting her destiny with improbable perspective: 'Oh fatal aspiration to fame! I wanted to be a somebody!'

In 1904, Olympe de Gouges's 'case' was analysed by a Dr Guillois as an instance of revolutionary hysteria. Her symptoms were 'abnormal sexuality', or having fallen into prostitution, which he speculated was caused by hormonal irregularity; 'narcissism', shown by her whore's habit of bathing daily; and a defective moral sense, as demonstrated by her refusal to remarry. Even at the start of the twentieth century, women who claimed equal rights were seen not as campaigners for justice, but as sexually depraved madwomen.

The revolutionary press delighted in making connections between Gouges, Marie-Antoinette, Charlotte Corday and Manon Roland. Their shared fate was a warning to other women who dared hope to have an independent voice. 'Marie-Antoinette was a bad mother, a debauched wife, and she died under the curses of those she wished to destroy,' declared the *Moniteur Universel* on 19 November. 'Olympe de Gouges, born with an exalted imagination, took her delirium for an inspiration of nature', while 'the Roland woman, a fine mind for great plans, a philosopher on notepaper, the queen of a moment' was worst of all: 'a monster however you look at her ... Even though she was a mother, she sacrificed nature by trying to raise herself above it; the desire to be learned led her to forget the virtues of her sex.'

Fabricating an 'unnatural' sexuality – painting Corday as a tortured virgin, Marie-Antoinette and Manon as depraved adulteresses swapping sexual favours for influence, and belittling Gouges for believing that in her forties she was still attractive enough to have lovers – which they could then attack was the means by which the Jacobin regime sought to prevent other women from following their example. If women who spoke out lost their reputations and society's respect, then very few others would be willing to speak out.

Spurious reports about Manon's life and last moments leaked out in the years following her death. It was said that on her last night in prison she had played on the harpsichord 'in *so strange, so shocking,* and *so frightful* a manner that the sounds will never escape her [a fellow-prisoner's] memory'. *The Female Revolutionary*, published pseudonymously by 'Plutarch' in England in 1806, contained an entirely false description of Manon, 'the faithless subject, and the malignant conspirator'. 'She evinced an early inclination for literature and gallantry,' it began, as if unsure which crime were graver. 'Before she was fifteen she had lovers, and before she was sixteen she was an author.' But her memoirs and letters have confounded her enemies and guaranteed her immortality. In the spring of 1795 Manon's friends Bosc d'Antic and Luc Antoine de Champagneux published her memoirs under the title *Appel à l'impartiale postérité*.

Mary Wollstonecraft's biographer Claire Tomalin suspects Wollstonecraft may have edited the first English edition of Roland's memoirs while she was in Scandinavia in 1794. Certainly the two women had moved in overlapping circles during the 1790s, sharing friends in London and Paris, most notably Helen Williams, one of those to whom Manon had entrusted her precious notebooks from prison. Williams had burned hers when she was arrested in August

1793, but it is quite possible Wollstonecraft received the remainder from another source.

Over the next decades, influenced by her writing, a new generation of romantic historians like Michelet and Lamartine held Manon up as their revolutionary muse – the embodiment of the passion, faith and purity of true republicanism.

Only one mystery remained. Manon's veiled references to a lover in her memoirs had piqued the curiosity of readers since the publication of her *Appel*, but the deaths of some and the loyalty of others who knew the secret ensured that Buzot's identity remained hidden for seventy years after her death. It was not until 1863, when a package of manuscripts taken to a Paris bookseller on the banks of the Seine was found to contain the five letters written by Manon to Buzot from prison, that his name and their hopeless passion were finally revealed.

On 10 November – the day that a broken-hearted Roland committed suicide on an empty provincial road – the first Festival of Reason was held in Paris. This was the high point of revolutionary dechristianiz-ation. The Republic's secular calendar had been introduced the previous month, with its months and holidays renamed using nature and agricul-ture as inspiration. According to the new system the festival was held on 20 Brumaire Year II: the second *décadi*, or twentieth day, of the month of mists, in the second year of the Republic. The day itself was called Herse, or 'harrow', after the farm implement used to till the fields at that time of year.

In several venues across Paris, living women embodied Liberty in public tableaux. The most important of the festival sites was the recently deconsecrated cathedral of Notre Dame, renamed the Temple of Reason. Statues believed to be French kings (in fact they were Old Testament kings) on its façade were beheaded; its sacred treasures were looted and destroyed. The role of Liberty in the former Notre Dame was played by Sophie Momoro, the beautiful wife of a radical Parisian printer who had been the first, in 1789, to publish the writings of Camille Desmoulins. She had been chosen by the Jacobin and Cordeliers' Clubs as a woman whose 'character renders beauty respectable and whose severity of morals and manners repulses licence', although political opponents claimed that she was a former prostitute, forced on to the streets when her convent was sacked and closed in 1791, who had been the mistress of Jérôme Pétion before being handed over to Antoine Momoro.

Accounts vary, but anything from fifty to two hundred young girls dressed in white and wreathed with oak leaves, singing republican hymns, preceded Liberty into the flower-decked 'Temple'. Sophie Momoro was wearing a white dress, a long blue cloak, like the Virgin, and a *bonnet rouge*. There was apparently no danger that she would try to usurp the rights of man. It was perhaps to her that the poet Pierre Jean de Béranger addressed his poem 'The Goddess: on a person whom the author saw representing Liberty at one of the festivals of the revolution':

> Is it really you, so beautiful when I saw you,
> With a whole people thronging round your chariot
> Saluting you and calling you immortal . . . ?

Four men carried Mme Momoro on her throne up the aisle towards a flame representing 'the torch of truth' that burned alongside busts of revered philosophers. An embroidery depicting a tree of liberty, equality and reason spreading its roots over the globe hung above the altar. The tree was surmounted by the red cap, and beneath it were scattered the remnants of religion and royalty: a torn-up Bible and fragments of crowns and sceptres.

The Commune's president, Pierre-Gaspard Chaumette, who seven days later would turn the remaining républicaines-Révolutionnaires away from the city's council, gave an impassioned speech decrying fanaticism. Cries of '*Vive la Montagne!*', '*Vive la République!*' and '*Vive la liberté!*' greeted his words. Chaumette imagined, wrote Mercier bitterly, 'that he had expelled the Deity from the Universe'.

A Feast of Reason was held in the *poissardes*' Church of Saint-Eustache, former meeting-place of the Société des Républicaines-Révolutionnaires. The choir was decorated like a pastoral landscape, with rickety paths winding between faux-rock precipices made of wood, clumps of trees and miniature cottages. Tables laden with hams, sausages and bottles of rough red wine – the only vice allowed to the sans-culottes – stood around the church. A drunken dance was held in the chapel of the Virgin at Saint-Gervais.

Similar celebrations were held across France, but *citoyennes* were not always accorded so prominent a place in them. In Pau, the women of the town applied to the commune for permission to take part in the procession, but were refused. Undaunted they turned up at the *mairie* ready to march all the same. In Lyon, the ruthless Jacobin Joseph Fouché enforced the revolutionary regime's recapture and subjugation of the city with a rigorous programme of dechristianization during which all Christian iconography was removed from the churches and an ass, dressed in the robes of Lyon's bishop and with a Bible and a missal tied to its tail, paraded through the streets. A Festival of Reason was held in the former Cathedral of Saint-Jean in which the city's new officials prostrated themselves before a statue of Liberty and sang an 'anti-hymn' composed by Fouché praising 'Reason as the Supreme Being'.

This official anticlericalism, to which Robespierre was violently opposed, was short-lived. In December an order of the National Convention reaffirmed the principle of freedom of worship.

It was perhaps not a surprise, given the turbulent political atmosphere of the Terror in Paris, that both Chaumette and Momoro would meet their ends on the scaffold only months after the Festival of Reason. Momoro left a letter for his wife, who was imprisoned two weeks after his death. 'Republican woman, preserve your character. You know the purity of my patriotism. I shall preserve the same character until death,' he wrote, unaware that his political guilt would implicate her. 'Raise my son in republican principles. You cannot manage the printing press alone, so dismiss the workers. Hail to the Marat citizenesses! Hail to the Republicans! I'll leave you my memories and my virtues. Marat has taught me to suffer.'

Afterwards, much was made of the fact that the women who embodied variously Liberty, Equality, Nature, Victory and Reason at these festivities had not had spotless reputations. Several were actresses, always viewed askance by the general public. The costume of one Liberty, Mlle Maillard, a singer – considered little better than an actress – scrupulously adhered to contemporary engravings of Liberty, complete with a red ribbon tied around her hair and bare breasts.

This was one explanation for why no second Festival of Reason was observed. Women of dubious character were thought to besmirch the pure ideals they were representing, and anyway women, who did not possess the qualities of reason or liberty, could not very well act their part. Nor could a regime that had made the exclusion of women from public life one of the foundations of its authority venerate women as personifications of its ideal virtues. The gap between theory – in which women were exalted – and practice – in which they were disparaged and denigrated – had become too great.

A week after the Festival, the Convention voted to replace the female figure of Liberty on the new Republic's seal with a colossus representing the French people. Designed by Jacques-Louis David, this figure of a giant crushing federalism with a club succinctly expressed the two overriding concerns of the Montagnard Jacobins in the late autumn of 1793: destroying the federalism that threatened their control of the provinces, and removing women once and for all from the public sphere.

Manon Roland, who had appealed to Liberty at the moment of her death, would perhaps have seen in Liberty's demotion the essence of the brutal injustices perpetrated by the regime that had destroyed her.

14

MAÎTRESSE

Thérésia Cabarrus Fontenay

April 1793–April 1794

As for Thérésia, she is always an enchantress.
PIERRE-ÉTIENNE CABARRUS

Jean-Lambert Tallien

As THE TERROR INTENSIFIED in the late spring of 1793, Thérésia Cabarrus, former marquise de Fontenay, travelled south from Paris with her ex-husband, four-year-old son Théodore and three servants, heading for Bordeaux. Fontenay planned to leave France for Martinique, and the port of Bordeaux – not yet controlled by radical Jacobins – was his best hope for escape. Thérésia had no immediate plans to leave France. Her family, rich merchants, came from the south-west, so she was sure of a safe haven there. When they reached Bordeaux in early May, the newly divorced couple went their separate ways. At nineteen, for the first time in her life, Thérésia was free – her own woman, neither a daughter nor a wife.

Her brothers Domingo and Francisco and her uncles Dominique and Galabert were waiting to welcome her to Bordeaux, and a circle of admirers soon gathered at her shapely feet. Two young friends, Édouard de Colbert and Étienne de Lamothe, vied for Thérésia's attentions, angrily stalked by her possessive brother Francisco. In the heat of the early summer, Thérésia, Francisco, her uncle Galabert and her two swains visited the spa-town of Bagnères in the Pyrenees. On the way their rivalry spilled over into open antagonism. Lamothe, who had declared his love to Thérésia and been smiled upon, was challenged to a duel by the disappointed Colbert.

Lamothe described the *coup d'épée* he received at Colbert's hands as a blessing, because it meant that Thérésia, touched by his gallantry, sent her brother, uncle and Colbert away and nursed him back to health. Lamothe later told a friend that he had never 'met a woman so endowed with such power to seduce and arouse the sexual passions'. He was mad with lust, he said, and when Thérésia willingly surrendered to him he experienced unparalleled ecstasy. 'Thérésia and I, happy as one is when one loves and one is free, spent the period of my convalescence in the most beautiful countryside, feeling ourselves in the bosom of a joy that has never in my life been equalled.' Their pleasure may have been deeply felt, but it was also fleeting: when he had recovered, Lamothe rejoined his regiment of hussars in the revolutionary army and Thérésia returned to Bordeaux.

Thérésia, little Théodore, her man-servants William Bidos and Joseph and her lady's-maid-cum-secretary, the pretty Frenelle, moved into a spacious apartment on the first floor of the Hôtel Franklin, overlooking the city's public gardens. Its contents attested to its mistress's accomplishments: a piano stood open by the flower-covered balcony, near a harp and a guitar lying on a sofa; books, pages of music and an abandoned piece of embroidery were scattered over the parquet-floored room; a half-sketched miniature leaned on an easel beside an ivory palette and a box of oil-paints. In her airy rooms, scented with orange-blossom, Thérésia was both artist and muse. Her languid, graceful presence made the horrors of the revolution seem far away.

But much of Bordeaux, capital of the Gironde region after which Manon Roland's moderate friends had been named, openly opposed the radical regime in Paris. Virtual anarchy raged on the streets beneath Thérésia's window. In August 1793, the National Convention appointed Jean-Lambert Tallien and Claude Ysabeau *représentants en mission* to Bordeaux, charged with bringing the area under central control. Although Ysabeau had arrived in Bordeaux in August, it was not until 16 October that the *représentants* made their formal entrance into the city, wearing their official blue redingotes, tricolour sashes and plumed hats, and accompanied by three battalions of infantry. Richard Cobb describes 'the roving *représentant*' coming into town 'in a clatter of majesty, with the dust of an escort and to the sound of trumpets, that left the villager gaping and made the urban tailor anxious to be seen at the table of the great man'.

They made their headquarters at the former Grand Séminaire and erected a guillotine beneath their windows in the Place Nationale. Price maximums were imposed on foodstuffs so grocers refused to sell what goods they did have, bringing further hardship to an already hungry population; rationing was introduced, granting each adult a pound of meat and a pound of rough black bread (two pounds for breast-feeding mothers) a day. Every household was required to post by the door an official notice, on paper headed with the words 'Liberty, Equality, Fraternity or Death' and edged with red, white and blue, listing the names of everyone who lived inside. People tried to make these forms as hard to read as possible – in pale ink, posted as high up as they could reach. Between October and December Tallien and Ysabeau condemned 126 opponents of the revolutionary regime, executing forty-two and acquitting a further forty-three.

Tallien had spent five months on mission in Tours in the spring and summer of 1793, where his energy, charm and organizational flair won him local approval and respect. *Représentants*, or 'people's representatives', were as often homicidal monsters as reasonable administrators – the most notably power-crazed being Joseph Fouché and Jean-Marie Collot d'Herbois in Lyon – so for the inhabitants of Tours to consider Tallien the best of a bad lot was high praise. No ambitious republican could afford to avoid the militant language of the times, and Tallien was not immune to the muscle of phrases like 'Bleed the purses and level the heads'; but when one Mercier du Rocher met Tallien in Tours in May he found him 'severe and sweet at the same time'.

One of Tallien's early reports back to Paris from the Gironde confirms Rocher's observation. A few days before their official entry into the town, Tallien wrote that there was much work to be done there. 'You think that Bordeaux is subject to the law,' he wrote. 'Well, you fool yourselves, none of the revolutionary laws decreed by the Convention are executed in Bordeaux.' Enemies of the state were concealed throughout the population, he said. The letter concluded with a fond salutation – incongruous after his fighting words – '*Ysabeau et moi vous embrassons.*'

Lucy de la Tour du Pin said that Thérésia and the dashing *représentant* met – or renewed their acquaintance, after exchanging glances in Paris – at a spa, probably Bagnères, before Tallien arrived in Bordeaux in October. Since Tallien was in the Pyrenees in September this is highly likely, although Tour du Pin's extra detail, that the smitten Thérésia followed Tallien to Bordeaux, is less probable because she was already established there. 'He had rendered her some service or other which she repaid with an unbounded devotion she made no effort to conceal.'

The bond between the privileged young divorcée and the up-and-coming republican may have seemed strange to their contemporaries – their friends on both sides of the social divide found the match hard to comprehend – but, apart from the obvious chemistry between them, there were some significant points of contact, or gaps in one into which the other fitted. Both, in one way or another, were outsiders, longing for approval and recognition. Thérésia may have been rich, beautiful and well connected, but she was a foreigner and a parvenu. Even by eighteenth-century standards, she had been brought up without affection, shunted from place to place and used as a pawn by her ambitious parents.

Tallien was the only child of elderly parents, but he had no ancestors and no fortune – not even a baptism record or a birth certificate – and he was assumed by many to be a bastard. Although he had benefited from his upbringing in an aristocratic household he had never been considered part of the family; he was both too well educated to feel himself one of the people and too poor to believe his dreams were within his grasp. That he was sympathetic to the caste in whose milieu he had grown up was evident from his actions during the September massacres, when he protected Germaine de Staël's friends and saved the king's former valet from execution; but, equally, the zeal with which he embraced the revolution suggests that he recognized he could fulfil his potential only under a new regime.

Thérésia, fifteen when the Bastille was stormed and nineteen in 1793, was also a child of the revolution. She had absorbed its democratic ideas at the Convention and in popular societies; she had watched Mirabeau, Danton and probably even Tallien himself expound the policies and philosophies that were transforming her world. The influence of her aristocratic but dedicated Montagnard ex-lover, Félix Lepeletier, had helped her see herself as a revolutionary and a republican. She was impressionable enough to regard Tallien the *représentant* not as a printer's apprentice thrust by circumstance into a position of power but as a genuinely important man whose greatness would be enhanced by her presence at his side. Equally, the vicissitudes of the revolution had given her a matchless instinct for survival; at some level, she loved Tallien because she believed he could protect her.

For his part, Tallien was enthralled by the glamour Thérésia represented. He had grown up close to but excluded from the glittering aristocratic world that meant everything in ancien régime France. Bold, sophisticated, seductive Thérésia was his chance to breathe that rarefied air, and he could not resist her. The intensity of their affair was fostered by the crisis atmosphere of heightened reality in which they were living. Throughout the revolution lovers like Thérésia and Tallien, like Manon Roland and Buzot, thrived on a potent combination of fear and exhilaration, idealism and desperation. Emotions were much closer to the surface when death was so near and life was so precious.

As early as 18 November, agents for the Committee of Public Safety were writing back to Paris denouncing Tallien 'for having intimate relations with the Cabarrus woman, wife of the ex-aristocrat Fontenay, who has so much influence over him that she has become the *protectrice* of her caste, nobles, bankers and hoarders'. Even though the revolution had legitimized divorce, the fact that Thérésia was no longer married to an aristocrat did not absolve her from suspicion. 'If this woman stays close to Tallien any longer,' the spies continued, 'the regime's reputation will fall into discredit.'

They were right to suspect that Tallien's liaison with Thérésia would diminish his effectiveness as a revolutionary enforcer. From the very start of their relationship, Thérésia had no scruples about using her influence over Tallien to save her friends. Emboldened by her hold over him, she had already appeared before the newly established revolutionary committee to plead the case of the widow of an executed Girondin, even though a decree of 25 October made anyone who pleaded mercy for a detainee themselves subject to arrest. It would not take long for desperate fugitives to discover that the way to the *représentant* was through his mistress's soft heart.

Soon after Thérésia returned to Bordeaux in October from Bagnères, she received a note from an unnamed woman asking for an interview, who said she had met 'Mme de Fontenay' in Paris and knew that she was 'as good as she is beautiful'. Thérésia replied that she could come whenever she liked. Half an hour later, Lucy de la Tour du Pin, a former lady-in-waiting to Marie-Antoinette who had met Thérésia in Paris at the opera with their mutual friend Dondon de Lameth, walked into the Hôtel Franklin disguised as a good bourgeoise in a skirt and fitted waistcoat with a red kerchief around her hair.

The former marquise was living in hiding in Bordeaux, hoping to have the sequestration on her father-in-law's property lifted so that she and her young family could return to live there. She begged Thérésia for advice, and Thérésia told her she would arrange a meeting with Tallien. 'You will be safe as soon as he knows that you are my main interest here,' she assured her. Mme de la Tour du Pin left, 'encouraged by the interest she had shown and wondering why she should have shown it'. The following night at ten o'clock, as directed, she returned to the Hôtel Franklin. Thérésia was there, and her candlelit rooms were full of people, but Tallien had not yet arrived. Eventually the rumbling of his carriage – one of the few remaining in the city – was heard on the cobblestones outside. Thérésia sent the trembling Lucy in to see him.

At first, she did not dare to look directly at Tallien, who was waiting for her, leaning against the wall. He questioned her, gently at first and then closely, about what she wanted and why. When she replied to questions about her family with the names of well known courtiers and royalists, he said brusquely, 'All these enemies of the Republic will have to go', making a 'beheading gesture' with his hand. Indignation made Mme de la Tour du Pin bold: she raised her eyes to 'the monster' and saw in front of her a young man of about twenty-six – just a few years older than her – whose pretty face, which he tried to make look stern, was surrounded by a mass of unruly blond curls escaping from a shiny military hat with a tricolour plume.

'I have not come here, citizen,' she said, 'to hear the death warrant of my relatives, and since you cannot grant my request, I will not importune you further.' She left him – smiling slightly, as if bemused by her impudence – and went home convinced that all hope was lost. Thérésia was less easily discouraged. She accused Tallien of not being kind to her friend, and he promised she would not be arrested; but for the moment there was little more he could do.

Towards the end of November Tallien heard news from Paris that his father had died. He applied for leave to visit his mother – he was her only child – but did not go. It appears that the Parisian spies had secretly obtained a warrant for Thérésia's arrest and, without Tallien's knowledge, had her imprisoned in late November or early December. Thérésia stayed in the forbidding Fort du Hâ just long enough to receive lasting scars on her feet and legs from the rats who nibbled at prisoners foolish enough to fall asleep, before Tallien engineered her release and saved her from the guillotine. It was said that Thérésia's first-hand account of the barbarity with which prisoners were treated prompted Tallien to tour the dungeon himself. He banned uselessly harsh measures forbidding visitors, and ordered the gaolers to allow the inmates to walk on the terrace each day. A grateful prisoner composed a carmagnole in Thérésia's honour.

Thérésia was free in time to attend Bordeaux's own Festival of Reason on the cold, clear morning of 10 December, a month after the Parisian celebrations. An actress representing Reason led the procession of carts bearing the local churches' treasures and the usual white-clad girls through the city, to the accompaniment of military bands playing revolutionary songs. The riches plundered from the churches were burned on an enormous pyre. *Représentant* Ysabeau, a former priest, gave a speech in praise of the reign of Reason.

'Consider my terror that same evening,' wrote Mme de la Tour du Pin, when Thérésia casually told her that Tallien had said that he thought Lucy 'would make a beautiful Goddess of Reason'. Horrified, Lucy replied that she would prefer to die, but the pragmatic Thérésia, 'surprised', simply shrugged her shoulders'.

Three days later, at seven forty-five on a dark winter's evening, five men attacked Tallien in the street, but did not manage to kill him. Thérésia may have been softening Tallien's heart in individual cases, and resistance to the revolution was still fierce, as this attack showed, but the *représentants'* work of subduing the seditious Gironde region was gradually bearing fruit. By Christmas Tallien and Ysabeau were close to establishing control over the exhausted, hungry inhabitants of Bordeaux. Tallien wrote to tell his mother of the attempt on his life but dismissed her fears for his safety. 'Such is the fate of those who fight for liberty. We must forget ourselves and think of nothing but the well-being of the twenty-five million men we are charged with protecting.'

On 22 December, Ysabeau wrote to inform the Committee of Public Safety that Tallien appeared to be married to '*une étrangère*' and added, 'for the falseness of the pretended marriage, consult General Brune, who has a stronger connection with the lady in question than Tallien'. Guillaume Brune was a talented young general stationed in Bordeaux with whom Thérésia had also been flirting; at Tallien's suggestion, he had just been recalled to Paris. Ysabeau's impassioned denunciation of Tallien's rival suggests that he too may have harboured contradictory feelings for Thérésia, at once desirous and censorious; or perhaps that, despite his disapproval of his friend's liaison, he wanted him to be happy.

After Brune's departure, no serious rivals for Thérésia's affections remained. By the end of December, she and Tallien were an established couple. Nearly every day they could be seen driving around Bordeaux in an open carriage, with Thérésia in the guise of Liberty, holding a pike and wearing the provocative *bonnet rouge*, leaning her exquisite head on her lover's shoulder. Although fashion magazines had been recommending since 1792 (and until they stopped being published the next spring) that women should wear muted colours like brown and grey instead of patriotic but inflammatory red, white and blue, Thérésia was quite unafraid that her highly politicized costumes would attract the wrong kind of attention, and probably unaware of the fate that had befallen the républicaines-révolutionnaires earlier that autumn in Paris.

A *fête triomphale* was held on 30 December to celebrate the revolutionary army's recapture of Toulon from the British. Ships with all their pennants flying were anchored in the harbour, salvos were fired, hymns to liberty sung and a procession of town officials and girls in white dresses made its way once again to the new Temple of Reason. Thérésia had been invited to write a *Discours sur l'Éducation* for the occasion, which Tallien read out for her. 'His heavy and monotonous style', as one observer described it, did not distract the audience from the sermon's author, sitting beside the *représentants* in a dark blue cashmere *amazone* of military cut, with yellow buttons, scarlet cuffs and a fur-trimmed scarlet velvet hat perched on her dark curls cut *à la Titus*.

Thérésia had a special interest in the education of children, because her former lover Félix Lepeletier's brother Michel had been working on a scheme for national state schools at the time of his murder in January 1793. Her speech showed her dedication to the ideas of Rousseau and John Locke, her devotion to liberty and to the Republic, as well as her own tender, unconstrained nature. Pedantry and dry scholasticism should be removed from children's schooling; courage, grace and virtue should be instilled in their hearts; and luxurious clothes, she added, were 'enemies to moral and republican dignity'. Her heartfelt appeal to *mères de familles* – 'remember that a careless, negligent mother is a public catastrophe that society should treat with all possible contempt' – can be read as a reproach to her own ambitious, unfeeling mother. 'Sacred liberty, stir up their [children's] hearts,' she concluded. 'Already everybody wants to bow down before you; as at the dawn of a beautiful day, the shade and the sun still clash over our blue fields, but the dim part of this enchanted scene will soon disappear . . .' The discourse was greeted with such acclaim that she was urged to have it published as a pamphlet; as author, she signed herself 'citoyenne Cabarrus Fontenay'.

Ten days later the speech was read out again, this time by Thérésia herself. The duchesse d'Abrantes, who did not think Tallien had done justice to his mistress's words, speculated that the change came about because Thérésia had been irritated by his original delivery. 'At intervals the expression of her countenance showed that she was a little out of humour at the manner in which the discourse was read, and on the following *décadi* she read it herself in the church of the Franciscans.'

Although Thérésia's address reflected received republican wisdom about a woman's most important role being that of mother to future

republicans, her own irrepressible independence and self-respect set
the tone for her arguments. While applauding the idea of state education, she did not distinguish between the education boys and girls
should receive – something the radical Jacobin, Saint-Just, was recommending. Crucially, the confidence she demonstrated in expressing
her opinion in such testing times reveals her as a woman unwilling to
confine herself to a private, domestic sphere.

While Lucy de la Tour du Pin waited for news on her application to
Tallien, she saw Thérésia regularly during the winter of 1793–4. She
echoed the feelings of many Bordeaux residents about Thérésia when
she said that despite her unconventional private life and intimacy with
a man many saw as a murderer, the evidence of her goodness was so
abundant that it was impossible not to warm to her. Her rooms in the
Hôtel Franklin were nicknamed the Bureau des Grâces – a pun on the
French word *grâce*, which means both elegance and favour or mercy.
When she complained that the guillotine occupied too intimidating a
position in the town, directly outside Tallien's office and rooms in the
Place Nationale – the roll of the drum notifying all Bordeaux's citizens
when the next death was imminent – it was moved away and placed
inside the prison walls.

The dangers to which she exposed herself only intensified the
pleasure she received from imperilling her life for others. As she wrote
to her son, many years later, she felt an elation and an abnegation of
the self at sharing the fears of those more unfortunate than herself.
'I risked my life with joy, again and again: if I died, I would go to
heaven, if I was saved I would live blessed by those who owed me their
existence.'

Lucy was with Thérésia one day as she waited for news of the fate
of a man for whom she had pleaded with Tallien. When Tallien's
secretary, Alexandre (by coincidence, the former secretary of Louis de
Narbonne, Germaine de Staël's one-time lover), arrived at the Hôtel
Franklin and informed them that the man had been acquitted, Thérésia

and Lucy ran breathlessly through the streets to his house, 'stopping for neither hat nor shawl', to tell his wife and daughters that he had been saved. 'She rushed in like a mad thing, crying, "He's acquitted" . . . [the wife] threw herself to the floor at Mme de Fontenay's knees, kissing her feet. The girls kissed her dress. I have never seen such a pathetic scene,' Lucy wrote later. Numerous stories survive recounting the lengths to which Thérésia went to save the lives not just of her friends but of anyone whose story moved her to pity. A Mme de Gage was provided with false passports by Thérésia, enabling her to leave the country. 'You are an aristocrat, Madame,' said Mme de Gage, thankful but perplexed. 'I confess it,' replied Thérésia. 'Alas! But I love Tallien.'

Detractors accused Thérésia of accepting money and jewels for the pardons and passports she extracted from Tallien, but no proof supporting these allegations exists and Thérésia was rich enough in her own right not to want to be paid for her generosity. Hungry for attention and adulation, the satisfaction she felt in her own achievements and the praise she received from the grateful beneficiaries of her goodness, who called her 'divine, heavenly *libératrice*' and offered her 'admiration, adoration and devotion until death', were thanks enough.

Lucy de la Tour du Pin exonerated Thérésia from any kind of avarice, but related a story in which *représentant* Ysabeau told a young woman that he would free her husband for the enormous sum of 25,000 francs in gold – a currency strictly prohibited by the revolutionary regime. He took payment of the money that she had scraped together and told the woman that her husband had already left prison; what he did not mention was that he was on his way to the scaffold. Thérésia confirmed that Ysabeau 'loved gold', while she made Tallien give passports away for nothing; like a child with arguing parents, she learned to exploit their differences to obtain the papers she wanted.

Both Ysabeau and Tallien were criticized for greed and for relishing the spoils of their rank while the common people starved. The winter of 1793–4 was a harsh one, and famine gripped France again. By the end of 1793, sugar had gone up five times in price since the start of the revolution, candles seven times and the cost of wine and brandy had doubled. Bordeaux was reduced to misery, remembered one of Tallien's political enemies, Louis Prudhomme, in 1797, while the tables of 'these new Luculluses' groaned beneath the weight of the finest wines and the most exquisite delicacies.*

The people of Bordeaux called fine white bread – the kind that they could no longer obtain from the bakeries – '*pain des représentants*' and Lucy de la Tour du Pin remembered that the butchers saved the best cuts of meats for the *représentants*' table. However, when they were recalled to Paris in the spring of 1794, accused of moderation and clemency, Ysabeau and Tallien swore that they had not appropriated government funds. Tallien declared that he had eaten bread made from grass while he was in Bordeaux. 'Luxury suits neither my principles nor my tastes,' he wrote. The fact that he left Bordeaux as poor as when he arrived suggests at the very least that he was not selling pardons to enrich himself; love – for Thérésia – seems to have been his only motivation.

When rumours of high-living reached Paris and the Committee of Public Safety, Ysabeau and Tallien were forced to write back defending themselves. They lived like '*vrai sans-culottes*', they said, in the modest cells of the former seminary, on the Convention's prescribed amount of six livres a day. In view of the recent attempt on Tallien's life, their bodyguards were necessary, if only to maintain order in their permanently crowded offices.

Late in January, fearful of where these rumours would lead, Thérésia sent a copy of her *Discours sur l'Education* to a member of the Committee of Public Safety, whom she knew well, she said, through a mutual friend. Her speech was a pretext: she was hoping for his support, should she ever need it. The letter concluded, 'believe in the esteem and fraternal sentiments of Thérésia Cabarrus Fontenay'.

It may have done more harm than good. Her letter was received eight days after she sent it, in early February. On the 8th the Committee of Public Safety wrote directly to Tallien and Ysabeau, chastising them

---

* Similar feelings of resentment arose in German-occupied Paris during the Second World War. 'In years when an egg was a magnificent luxury,' writes Miranda Seymour in *The Bugatti Queen* (London, 2004), p. 217, 'food was increasingly associated with the idea of power. The German alone had regular access to good food in Paris; while their hosts starved, they ate like victors.'

for forming relationships in Bordeaux that might affect their duties. Tallien responded five days later with another dignified defence: he and Ysabeau were scrupulously observing every edict and the Committee would find nothing with which to reproach them. They were combining, he said, the inflexible severity of the law with justice and humanity.

That same month Thérésia made another attempt to win over the Committee by donating 9,000 livres to the desperately empty coffers of the Convention. A decree of August 1793 allowed people to donate – or required them to donate – large sums of money to help repay the vast national debt.

But Parisian scrutiny did not deter Thérésia's efforts to save lives. In February, by threatening to leave Tallien if he did not help her friend, she managed to get passports for Lucy de la Tour du Pin and her family to leave France for Martinique, their hopes of remaining in France having been dashed. She and Tallien arrived unexpectedly one day when Lucy was sitting down to lunch in the small house in the middle of a vineyard where she was staying just outside Bordeaux. Tallien approached Lucy 'with all the grace of manner which had characterised the great gentlemen of the former court and said in the kindest possible way, "I understand, Madame, that I can today make amends for the wrongs I have done to you, and I wish to do so."'

The figures show that during the five months between December 1793 and May 1794, when Thérésia left Bordeaux, only seventy-six people were executed by order of the city's revolutionary committee. In the two months thereafter those numbers nearly tripled, coming into line with other rebellious regions like Toulon, Nantes and Lyon, on which the central government was trying to impose its rule.

Thérésia's role as an effective petitioner for mercy was one of the few sanctioned for women by the Jacobin regime, though little heed was paid to their entreaties elsewhere. In Lyon in December 1793, which had been renamed Ville-Affranchie, or Liberated City, after it fell to the revolutionary army in October, ten thousand women signed a petition begging the authorities to spare the city's inhabitants from further bloodshed. Their pleas fell on deaf ears. Nearly two thousand people were executed there during the winter and spring of 1794 – including more than two hundred on a single bloody day.

In mid-February, as the atmosphere of suspicion and fear in Bordeaux escalated, Thérésia suspected that she might be pregnant and sent for a midwife. The woman who came to see her was hiding an aristocrat in her house, disguised as a patient. Mme Lage de Volude had escaped France in 1789 but returned to Bordeaux to see her family on a false passport, on which she was no longer able to travel. When the midwife saw the piles of passports lying on Thérésia's desk, she asked Frenelle who they belonged to. Frenelle replied that her mistress had much influence over Tallien, and helped brave people in distress – especially émigrés. A short while later, using a false name, Mme Lage de Volude gave Frenelle a diamond necklace to ask her mistress to help her.

When the woman came to see Thérésia a few days later she was still ill in bed, but no malady could detract from her dazzling beauty. Thérésia greeted her like a long-lost friend, saying she thought she recognized her from a meeting at a masonic lodge a few years earlier. Her openness and candour surprised her visitor. Laughingly, she began telling Mme Lage de Volude how she had sent a portrait of herself, painted for Tallien, to her former lover Félix Lepeletier. Although Lepeletier had treated her badly, she said, nothing could break their attachment. The members of the Surveillance Committee, who hated her, had ordered the packet opened and sent to Tallien. He had come to see her the day before in a fury, she continued, 'spitting blood' and threatening to send her to the guillotine. She had received him in a state of perfect calm, convinced him of the innocence of her note and the stupidity of the Committee, and persuaded him to return the portrait to her. Recklessly, Thérésia told Mme Lage de Volude that Tallien 'was paying dear and long for the wickedness he had committed'.

On subsequent visits, Thérésia continued to open up to Mme Lage de Volude. She confided 'that she had always wanted to be the mistress of a king [and] that she needed occupation with affairs of state and great power'. Charles IV of Spain had taken a fancy to her, she claimed,

and she had had to leave the country. Mme Lage de Volude added
here that Thérésia was deceiving herself: she had heard of no woman
for whom Charles IV had shown a preference.

Tallien was desperate to marry her, but Thérésia had told him that
she could not marry without the consent of her father, who was being
held in prison in Madrid (imprisoned by the king she claimed desired
her) and to whom she could not get a letter. 'Hand me your letter,'
said Tallien, 'and I give you my word that in fifteen days or three weeks
you will have an answer.' Thérésia protested: it was impossible. 'Believe
that nothing is impossible for us,' he declared.

Thérésia told her new friend that she had written to her father but
told him nothing about the 'pretended marriage'. A few weeks later,
full of impatience and excitement, Tallien brought her the response.
When she calmly put the letter in her pocket he demanded to know
what the answer had been. 'He did not speak of that which you are
looking for,' she told him. 'I have never seen a more foolish face than
his,' she gloated to Mme Lage de Volude.

Despite the contradictions of her feelings for Tallien, Thérésia was
seriously considering marrying him. During one of their last meetings,
she asked Mme Lage de Volude for her advice. Predictably, her friend
questioned the legitimacy of a marriage made by a municipal act,
instead of in a church. 'Believe me: you will make your life a public
scandal and you will make yourself dependent on a man whom you do
not respect.' She urged Thérésia to reunite with Fontenay so that when
the émigrés – and morality – returned to France they would welcome
her back into their sweet and consoling society. Tallien was a *régicide*
who had 'committed all possible crimes'; marrying him would only
bring her dishonour and social ostracization, despite all the good she
had done.

Thérésia replied that she wished she had known no one except
people as worthy as Mme Lage de Volude, but confessed she had been
alternately alienated by the decorum of her husband's family and led
into waywardness by her friends. Women like Dondon de Lameth,
Germaine de Staël and Félicité de Genlis had, with their wild parties
and misbehaviour, led her into temptation, and she had lost her moral
compass. It was not passion that attached her to Tallien, she continued,

but 'a sort of honour and duty', since she was responsible for the dangers to which he was exposed. 'No,' she said. 'I will not abandon him.' If Tallien defeated his enemies and rose to power, she said, Mme Lage de Volude and her friends could count on her friendship.

Despite her ingrained disapproval of Thérésia, Mme Lage de Volude admitted she could not help liking and even respecting her. One night at dinner – after Thérésia had cried over the women's predicament and made Tallien sign a passport for her as he climbed into his carriage on his way out of Bordeaux – she burst out, 'You women of feeling and grand principles, you have a very bad opinion of me; but I hold, and I will prove to anyone, that I have done much more good than you because for many months, I have not slept without having saved someone's life; while you others, with your royalism and all your romantic sentiments, I beg you to tell me how you have been useful?'

Tallien left Bordeaux for Paris on 22 February; Mme Lage de Volude's passport was the last he signed for Thérésia. He had realized that he could only defend himself against his enemies in person, in Paris – before it was too late.

Lucy de la Tour du Pin arrived at the Hôtel Franklin two hours after his departure to find Thérésia in tears. The faithful Alexandre, Tallien's secretary, who had been left behind in Ysabeau's service, rushed off to obtain for Lucy the last signatures she needed. He assured her that Ysabeau signed papers without really looking at them as he left the theatre, because he was in such a hurry to get to his supper. Sure enough, Alexandre returned near midnight with the visas, 'so out of breath that he fell into an armchair, unable to say more than: "Here it is." Mme de Fontenay embraced him most warmly, and so did I, for it was really he who saved us,' wrote Lucy later. 'I have never seen him since; he may have paid with his life for the services he rendered to so many people who have forgotten all about them.'

One other person was waiting with Lucy and Thérésia for Alexandre's return: a sullen, silent M. de Fontenay. Lucy turned to leave, but Thérésia held her back, saying she would send someone home with her later, but 'first she wanted to show me something pretty'. She opened a jewel box and emptied it on to a handkerchief she had spread on a table. Magnificent diamond necklaces of the finest quality tumbled out over one another. Thérésia showed them to Lucy and then tied the corners of the handkerchief together and handed it to her ex-husband. He took the bundle and left, still without a word. 'He gave me some of them; the remainder came from my mother,' Thérésia told the amazed Lucy. 'He, too, is leaving tomorrow for America.'

When Lucy de la Tour du Pin, her husband and her two young children finally boarded their ship in Bordeaux harbour, Thérésia came to bid them farewell, 'her lovely face wet with tears of joy'.

Tallien returned to Paris to find the city tense and cowering beneath Robespierre's rule. 'Anarchy from within, invasion from without. A country cracking from outside pressure, disintegrating from internal strain. Revolution at its height. War. Inflation. Hunger. Fear. Hate. Sabotage. Fantastic hopes. Boundless idealism,' writes the historian Robert Palmer of this period. 'And the horrible knowledge, for the men in power, that if they failed they would die as criminals, murderers of their king. And that dread that all the gains of the Revolution would be lost. And the faith that if they won they would bring Liberty, Equality and Fraternity into the world.'

Three weeks before Tallien's arrival, on 5 February, Robespierre addressed the National Convention on behalf of the Committee of Public Safety. 'If the mainspring of popular government in peacetime is virtue, . . . during revolution [it] is both virtue and terror – virtue, without which terror is disastrous, and terror, without which virtue is powerless,' he declared. 'Terror is nothing more nor less than prompt, severe and inflexible justice.' He denounced tyrannies as if unaware that his own regime was becoming one. 'We seek an order of things in which all the base and cruel passions are enchained,' he said, while hundreds of people were going to their deaths each day. Individuals' freedom and even their lives did not seem such precious commodities when the future of the French Republic, which he believed it was his mission to establish, was at stake.

Outside the Convention hall, half of Paris was going hungry. The prices of meat and vegetables were at record highs. 'The grocers continue to give the citizens garbage,' reported a police spy. 'Their brandy is abominable, the vinegar is as worthless as the oil; the best of it is not fit to be eaten on salad.' Women on the streets were not only taking their own children with them to beg, but kidnapping other people's so as to incite greater generosity from passers-by.

'Do you believe that if this committee restrained their audacity, there would be so many unjust imprisonments?' an old man asked a government agent. 'No – you would see 3000 or 4000 or 5000 fathers returned to their children; for I do not let the small number given in the newspapers fool me; and the republic which seems to be covered with mourning cloth would become the haven of happiness.'

Popular discontent only strengthened the resolve of the Committee of Public Safety. 'Some wish to moderate the revolutionary movement,' said Collot d'Herbois, one of the most bloodthirsty of the Committee members, at the Jacobin Club. 'What! Can a tempest be steered?' Later, before the Convention, he declared that indulgence was a 'dangerous weakness': 'we are hardened against the tears of repentance'. His colleague Saint-Just agreed. 'A revolution like ours is not a trial, but a thunderbolt called down on the wicked.'

In the face of sentiments like these, Helen Williams was right in saying that Terror required 'the most daring courage to be humane'. Tallien, his revolutionary ardour softened by love, would need courage to defend his humanity against his critics. Although the reception he received at the Committee's meeting-room in the Tuileries was icy, his first address to the Convention was as successful as he could have hoped. After outlining his and Ysabeau's successes in Bordeaux, he made an appeal for accusations to cease and for trust and respect to be restored among France's rulers. Echoing Camille Desmoulins's new journal, the *Vieux Cordelier*, he called for the true patriots – those who had been present at the first days of the revolution, 'who were not hiding in their caves while we were at the Bastille' – to steer its course faithfully.

'We will go home later to our gabled cottages, and there we will savour the pleasure of having fulfilled our noble responsibilities, of having responded to the needs of the nation, of having justified the trust placed in us,' he concluded, appealing to his listeners' pastoral fantasies. 'There we will enjoy in peace the happiness of having brought the people happiness: it is a boon that we prefer to all the treasures on earth.' Although Tallien was elected president of the Convention (they rotated every fifteen days), Robespierre was unmoved by his arguments. 'I cannot look at that Tallien without shivering,' he said.

Robespierre's fear of his political rivals was not restricted to Tallien. Anyone who did not accept his vision for France was viewed as a traitor; personal loyalty never clouded his resolve. Having eliminated the radical *hébertistes* (the supporters of the journalist Jacques Hébert, publisher of *Père Duchesne*, including Antoine Momoro and Pierre-Gaspard Chaumette) who dominated the Commune of Paris, at the end of March he turned his attentions to Georges Danton and his followers, who drew their strength from the Convention. By this stage, the *dantonistes* were 'indulgents', moderates, who were calling for Terror to be contained, for patriotism to be brought back into line with humanity.

The *dantonistes* went to their deaths with dignity and remorse for the excesses to which they had been witness. In prison, Helen Williams reported Danton as saying that he had instituted the Revolutionary Tribunal 'not to become the scourge of humanity' but 'to prevent the renewal of the massacres of September [1792]'. 'In revolutions the power always remains in the hands of villains,' he said. 'It is better to be a poor fisherman than to govern men. Those fools! They will cry "Long live the Republic!" on seeing me pass to the scaffold.' Robespierre had offered him the chance to betray his friends in return for his life, but he had refused it.

Even Camille Desmoulins's childhood closeness to Robespierre could not protect him. He went to the scaffold alongside Danton, just as the two men had gone together to the Tuileries on the night of 9 August 1792. His wife had come each day with their baby to gaze up at his window, much like the little boy described by Helen Williams who came every day to the Luxembourg and asked the guard, with his hat in his hands, '*Citoyen, vous me permettrez de saluer mon papa?*' – 'Citizen, will you allow me to wave to my father?' – and stood beneath the prison walls, blowing kisses up to his father's window while his father inside wept.

'Adieu Loulou, adieu my life, my soul, my divinity on earth,' wrote Camille to his wife from prison, in a turmoil of romanticism, desperation and grief. 'I feel the river banks of my life receding before me, I see you again Lucile, I see my arms locked about you, my tied hands embracing you, my severed head resting on you. I am going to die . . .'

Lucile Desmoulins perished a week after her beloved husband. At the Luxembourg, Camille had made friends with another prisoner, Arthur Dillon – Lucy de la Tour du Pin's father. After Camille's death Dillon tried to smuggle a letter of sympathy and some money out to Lucile, but it was intercepted and used as evidence of a conspiracy between them. She was executed, wearing white, on the same day as Dillon. 'Among the victims of the tyrants, the women have been particularly distinguished for their admirable firmness in death,' wrote Helen Williams. 'Perhaps this arose from the superior sensibility which belongs to the female mind, and which made it feel that it was less terrible to die, than to survive the objects of its tenderness.'

'One can no longer go out, some said, without seeing the guillotine or those being taken to it,' a police spy reported. 'Our children are getting cruel and it is to be feared that pregnant women will bring forth children with marks on their necks or still as statues because of the distressing sights they are subjected to in the streets.' Another spy heard some apprentices talking as the tumbrels rumbled past them. 'Good Lord, when will we have had enough of shedding blood?' said one. 'When we've no longer any guilty left,' replied another. A third said, 'A man's death doesn't cost much.' 'If they guillotined people for thinking, how many people would have to die?' asked a fourth, and then added, 'Don't let's talk so loud . . .'

Tallien survived the purge of the *dantonistes*; while he shared some of their views he was not close enough to their leaders to be condemned alongside them. Although a Montagnard radical, Marc-Antoine Jullien, had been dispatched to Bordeaux to continue the Committee of Public Safety's revolutionary work there, and the investigation against Tallien and Ysabeau was ongoing, for the moment Tallien was free – waiting and planning for the day when his enemies would be vanquished and his mistress back in his arms.

15

LIBÉRATRICE

Thérésia Cabarrus Fontenay

MAY–JULY 1794

A general deliverance, a universal resurrection.

CHARLES DE LACRETELLE

The entrance to the women's side of
La Force prison

EVEN WITHOUT TALLIEN in Bordeaux to protect her, Thérésia continued to help all those who appealed to her tender heart. She persuaded the 'fierce' Ysabeau to pardon a few more souls, including the Girondin Jean-Baptiste Louvet, whose newspaper Roland had once funded, and helped set up the Hospice de Sainte-Croix for the aged indigents of Bordeaux.

She knew she could threaten or tease Ysabeau into complying with her demands, but when nineteen-year-old Marc-Antoine Jullien (son of Rosalie Jullien), an ardent Robespierrist charged with purifying and regenerating the revolutionary regime in Bordeaux, arrived there on 10 April it was clear that her reign of mercy was over. Thérésia's emollient beauty would not melt his glacial revolutionary virtue.

Jullien wrote to inform Robespierre that 'Bordeaux seems to have been until now a labyrinth of intrigues and waste. Revolutionary justice here is hungrier for money than blood. One woman has captivated the authorities of the entire town. The favourite is called Thérésia Cabarrus. It is she who forced the Committee of Surveillance to give free rein to her corruptions,' he wrote, his tone rising to shrill hysteria. 'I denounce the free union between Tallien and this foreign woman. I accuse Tallien of softness and moderation.'

Thérésia made a final attempt to demonstrate her unimpeachable republicanism four days after Jullien's arrival, when she delivered a second sermon, this time to Bordeaux's National Club. Her subject was women, that 'portion of the human race which exercises such a great influence on morals'. Despite the lack of humanity Robespierre and his followers had recently shown women as varied as Marie-Antoinette, Manon Roland and the members of the Société des

Républicaines-Révolutionnaires, Thérésia hoped that her eloquence would soften their hearts towards her, but she could hardly have chosen a less auspicious subject.

She opened conventionally, insisting that she did not want women to develop 'the absurd ambition of appropriating men's rights, and thus lose the virtues of their own sex'. But, she continued, in a republic, 'everything must be republican': everyone must serve their country. How could women instil modesty and morality into their children, if they were not first taught them? How could they acquire the character, sentiment and goodwill necessary to be wives and mothers if they were not educated and respected? In particular, Thérésia requested for women a role as nurses of the unfortunate, the sick and the dying, for which their quality of compassion especially fitted them. Compassion – which she had shown so fearlessly in Bordeaux – she described as 'the germ inherent in all virtues . . . not a sterile, fleeting emotion but a profound and bravely active sentiment'. She urged her listeners to allow women to take the name of *citoyenne*, 'the veritable title of their public-spiritedness', not as an empty description but with pride and faith, and concluded by expressing her own hope of being 'one of the first to carry out these sweet, these delightful duties'.

Thérésia's discourse was published and distributed, as her last one had been, and delivered to the National Convention. On 24 April it was read out in front of the deputies there, who applauded it and gave it an honourable mention in their minutes. But Robespierre, who had lost his own mother's love (he was orphaned as a child) and was incapable of forming an intimate, adult relationship with a woman, was hardly likely to be moved by her appeal. Impulsive, spoiled, untroubled by conventional morality, easily swayed by her emotions, Thérésia represented all that Robespierre despised politically and distrusted personally – a warm-hearted, flesh-and-blood symbol (to a man who was wary of the flesh above all else) of all he hoped to eradicate from France. If, as Thérésia said, they had met in the early years of the revolution, the motives behind his almost obsessive interest in destroying her become even clearer.

On 4 May, in Bordeaux, Thérésia received a passport permitting her to travel to Orléans (in these times passports were necessary for domestic as well as international travel) where she said she planned to live in retirement. '*Signalement: taille cinq pieds 2 pouces, visage blanc et joli, cheveux noirs, front bien fait, sourcils clairs, yeux bruns, nez bien fait, bouche petite, menton rond*' – 'Description: height five feet 2 inches, face pale and pretty, hair black, forehead well made, light eyebrows, brown eyes, nose well made, small mouth, round chin.' Leaving Théodore behind with an uncle and the faithful Joseph, she set out for Paris via Orléans. Along the way, her carriage made a stop near Blois where she met another young fugitive, Joseph de Camaran, comte de Chimay. Her distress and her beauty would stay in his mind.

Just after her arrival in the capital, on 20 May, Robespierre personally signed the warrant for Thérésia's arrest, his tiny writing isolated at the bottom of the page. Also in his hand was the order that when she was arrested, she was to be held in solitary confinement and forbidden any privileges, like exercise, that might allow her to communicate with anyone. His interest was unusual: in the month of Prairial, Robespierre wrote only fourteen of the 608 documents issued by the Committee of Public Safety for which an author can be ascertained, and his cramped signature on their decrees was equally rare. 'All the papers relating to the Cabarrus woman must be gathered together,' he wrote, assigning two men to her case. 'Never did Robespierre pursue a victim more remorselessly,' remembered one of his associates.

Since Tallien was under investigation, the lovers did not dare to meet openly, although one spy reported seeing them dining together in a restaurant in the Palais Royal. Like so many at this time, Thérésia could not risk spending too many nights in one place, moving between the houses of friends willing to take the risk of harbouring her.

Paris in the spring of 1794 was a city of 'silent streets and barricaded doors'. 'Everyone seemed to slip through the shadows'; people wore their hats drawn down over their faces and dared give no sign of recognizing one another on the streets. 'Women did not go out at all, men rarely,' remembered the marquis de Frénilly. 'The whole of people's lives was centred in their homes where they spoke little, in a low voice, and with the doors securely closed.' Servants were encouraged to inform on their masters, children to inform on their teachers; no one could be trusted.

Blood literally flowed in the drains, and the city stank like a charnel-house. Dogs drank from the thick red pools beneath the scaffold in the Place de la Révolution, while alongside it hordes of listless prostitutes of all ages and both sexes grimly solicited custom. The executioners complained that they had to replace their clothes all the time because they were so stained and sodden with blood. One of the only concessions made by the Commune to the palpable fears of Parisians was to maintain the street lights at night.

Even – or perhaps especially – the deputies of the Convention were loath to walk the streets unprotected. Many carried pistols or sword-sticks, or paid guards to accompany them. Tallien had a Spanish dagger that Thérésia had given him. One night in June, according to one of the spies directly accountable to Robespierre, he walked home from the Jacobins with a man with a 'heavy stick'. The spy, Guérin, complained that the street in which Tallien lived – the rue de la Perle in the Marais – was so straight and short that it was hard to keep watch on him; there was nowhere for an observer to conceal himself.

Robespierre too needed bodyguards. The president of the Committee of Public Safety, Marc Guillaume Vadier, posted his own spy, one Paul Auguste Taschereau-Fargues, to watch over Robespierre; but Taschereau double-crossed him, spying on Vadier for Robespierre instead. Their world was claustrophobically intimate, overstretched loyalties criss-crossing in a complex web of treachery and allegiance, given then withdrawn: Taschereau was also a friend of Tallien's, and through him Thérésia's, advising them about how she could avoid arrest.

Three days after Robespierre signed Thérésia's arrest warrant, a nineteen-year-old girl called Cécile Renault went to his lodgings in the rue Saint Honoré. When she was told that he was not at home, and asked what her business was, she replied that she had just come 'to see what sort of a thing was a tyrant'. Although she was only carrying two unconvincing-looking knives, she was accused of attempting to murder Robespierre. When questioned by the Committee of Public Safety, she said that she deserved to die – not because she had wanted to kill Robespierre but because of her anti-republican sentiments. Renault and her entire family – except for two brothers fighting at the front, whom they could not be bothered to wait to recall – were guillotined.

Robespierre's response to this assassination attempt, if such it was, and another two days earlier on his colleague Collot d'Herbois, was to introduce the laws of 22 Prairial (10 June) which were designed to expedite revolutionary justice. Henceforth people could be arrested simply for 'impairing the purity of the revolutionary government' – a crime of which Thérésia was certainly guilty. When suspects were tried, no proof was needed to convict them and they were not allowed either a defence counsel or to call witnesses. 'Arbitrary power against which the revolution ought to have been directed,' as Germaine de Staël observed, 'had acquired a new strength from the revolution itself.'

Towards the end of May, Thérésia and Tallien were reunited at her ex-husband's country house, Fontenay-aux-Roses, near Versailles. Robespierre's spies reported that Tallien had spent several nights at the house of the Cabarrus-Fontenay woman, former noble, whom they had thought was in Paris. The net was closing in on her.

Thérésia was arrested in a Versailles hotel on the night of 30 May and taken straight to a revolutionary committee in the capital where she was interrogated. Helen Williams, arrested with her sister the previous summer, described the committee rooms and their ante-chambers at night as 'crowded with commissaries and soldiers, some sleeping, some writing, and others amusing themselves with pleas-antries of a revolutionary nature, to which we listened trembling'. Pikes and guns were leant casually against the walls, tobacco smoke filled the air and the red-capped guards were usually drunk. As Richard Cobb writes, inebriation was 'an important component in a certain type of revolutionary excitability'. Wine stains smear the minute books of popular societies and gaolers' records.

By 1794 Paris had about fifty makeshift prisons, but they were so full that it took some time to persuade one to admit Thérésia. She and her escort spent a day and most of a night driving around Paris looking for a gaol with space for her, passing the bloody guillotine in the Place de la Révolution several times, to the delight of her guards. Finally the women's side of La Force, originally a debtors' prison, in the Marais, agreed to take her.

Rat-infested, damp and filthy, La Force was one of the most feared of the revolutionary gaols; the princesse de Lamballe, Marie-Antoinette's friend, had been taken from there, killed, disembowelled and mutilated in September 1792. Its only equal in notoriety was Sainte-Pélagie, where Manon Roland had been held. Eight guards watched greedily as Thérésia was strip-searched and given a rough, sleeveless shift to put on. Her clammy stone-walled cell contained a straw pallet instead of a bed. For twenty-five days she was held there alone, not allowed to see the sky, not allowed to wash or to change her clothes. When Robespierre was informed about how dreadful the conditions were in which the celebrated beauty was being held, he is said to have said, 'Let her look in a mirror once a day.'

On 8 June, Robespierre presided over the Festival of the Supreme Being, his rebuttal of the moves towards dechristianization and official atheism made at the end of 1793 by his political enemies, several of whom were already dead. Robespierre disapproved of violence against religion almost as strongly as he disapproved of the Catholic Church's former abuses, and he passionately believed that republican morality was incompatible with godlessness. 'The true priest of the Supreme Being is Nature itself; its temple is the universe; its religion virtue,' he had declared a month earlier, when he announced that the *fête* would take place. 'Its festivals [are] the joy of a great people assembled under its eyes to tie the sweet knot of universal fraternity and to present before it the homage of pure and feeling hearts.'

It was rumoured on the streets of Paris that Robespierre was planning to use the festival to 'proclaim himself king, open the prisons and re-establish order and religion', but in the event he contented himself with leading the procession of white-clad girls and deputies carrying

Thérésia Cabarrus in La Force, holding her shorn hair in her hand as she waits to be called to the guillotine. She is dreaming of her lover, Jean-Lambert Tallien, whose portrait is on the wall behind her.

Tallien, brandishing the dagger Thérésia gave him, challenges Robespierre before the National Convention on 9 Thermidor.

The closure of the Jacobin Club in November 1794. Although Thérésia is not shown she was said to have locked the Club's doors.

The women of the people storming the National Convention in May (Prairial) 1795, calling for 'Bread and the Constitution of 1793'.

La Chaumière, the rustic cottage Thérésia made into a masterpiece of Directory style.

Left Thérésia in about 1805, as exquisite and statuesque as ever despite her exclusion from imperial society.

La Belle Espagnole ... ou ... la Doublure de Madame Tallien

How the British viewed the Directory: the caricaturist James Gillray's depictions of Thérésia in 1795 (*above*) and (*right*) dancing with Joséphine in front of her lover Barras and Napoléon, 1799.

Below Joséphine and her ladies in Italy, 1797.

Thérésia's lovers: Gabriel Ouvrard (*left*) and Paul Barras.

Right Germaine de Staël, wearing her trademark turban and holding one of the twigs she habitually played with as she spoke.

Top The most visited bedroom in Paris: Juliette Récamier was so proud of her bedchamber she invited all her guests to admire it.

Left Juliette Récamier in 1805, just before her husband went bankrupt and (*above right*) a typically louche Directory salon.

Théroigne de Méricourt at La Salpêtrière in 1816, the year before she died.

bouquets (handy for masking the stench of blood and rotting flesh that permeated the city) and playing a central role in the symbolic tableaux devised by David. Like the king on his last official public appearance in July 1792, Robespierre was conspicuous in a sea of unpowdered heads by the old-fashioned formality of his hairstyle.

David's decorative scheme for the celebrations re-emphasized the exclusively domestic, maternal role that Robespierre expected of female republicans. Women taking part in the festival were explicitly defined as mothers. Pregnant women and breast-feeding mothers with their babies were specifically invited to walk in the procession supported by their husbands, and unmarried girls wore ribbons embroidered with the motto, 'When we are mothers'. In Le Puy, at a similar celebration in honour of the Supreme Being, when an old woman gave a signal during the ceremony in the deconsecrated church every woman in the congregation turned round and lifted their skirts at the altar as a raucous mark of disrespect for the new idol.

Liberty herself had been officially demoted by David, for here she was represented not by a statue of an idealized female figure or a red-capped actress, as in previous festivals, but by an oak tree. The figure of Hercules, cipher for the French people, held a tiny statuette of Liberty in his mighty fist. She was no longer a goddess before whom the French nation bowed down: Liberty had become its plaything.

After Thérésia's arrest, Paul Auguste Taschereau-Fargues saw a devastated Tallien on the Champs-Élysées. He did not need to ask why he looked so sad. Tallien's mother rented an attic room opposite La Force so that her lovesick son could sit close to where Thérésia was being held, and breathe the air she breathed.

Robespierre's agents visited Thérésia at La Force and tried to persuade her to betray Tallien, promising her her freedom and a passport, but she replied that she would prefer to die. Only Taschereau's intervention kept her from being brought before the Revolutionary Tribunal. Finally, hoping that she might incriminate herself or Tallien if she was placed in less severe conditions, Robespierre ordered Thérésia put into the common cells.

Prisoners, expecting every day to die, tried to live as normal a life as possible in their confinement. About fifteen gaols – called *maisons de santé* – were, until the high point of the Terror, reserved for the richest inmates, who were held without locks on their doors or bars on their windows and guarded, in the Luxembourg, by a famously kind turnkey. Men and women ate together at large, communal tables; people sang and formed musical groups; games of cards, charades and epigrams were played, as they had once been played in gilded salons. Conversation was still highly prized. 'You may kill us when you please,' was the philosophy, 'but you cannot prevent us from being civilised.'

Gossip and flirtation were the pleasures of prison life, and lasting attachments were often formed. At the Luxembourg, in particular, there were so many aristocratic detainees that the atmosphere was that of a house-party. Some inmates could not resist using their forbidden titles, continuing to address one another in whispers as 'Madame la duchesse' or 'Monsieur le comte' – increasingly often with fatal repercussions.

Women who had once changed their clothes three times a day with the help of several maids preserved these habits as a matter of pride, despite having to do their laundry themselves and having been allowed to bring with them to prison when they arrived only as much clean linen as they could tie up into a handkerchief. In the morning these ladies came down in a 'coquettish demi-toilette ... arranged with a freshness and grace that by no means suggested they had spent the night on a pallet, and oftener still on fetid straw'. At midday for exercise they reappeared in full dress, with their hair elegantly done and their manners 'more decided and dignified' than earlier. The yard of the Conciergerie at noon was, according to Jacques-Claude Beugnot, like a garden 'adorned with flowers, but fenced round with iron'. At night they changed once again into relaxed 'undress'.

The spirit of camaraderie was pervasive. 'United by the strong bond of common calamity, the prisoners considered themselves as bound to soften the general evil by mutual kind offices.' Gallows humour also helped cut the tension. At the Conciergerie prisoners play-acted the Revolutionary Tribunal and the execution, adding a final scene in hell attended by ghosts swathed in sheets and the Devil tugging at the victim's feet.

Each evening, the list of the names of the following day's victims arrived, and summonses from the Revolutionary Tribunal. To be called to the Conciergerie was to receive a death sentence: no one left there except in a tumbrel. After the laws of Prairial were passed the pace of the killings increased dramatically. One hundred and fifty-five people had been guillotined in the month of Germinal (March–April); 354 died in Floréal (April–May); 509 in Prairial (May–June); and 796 in Messidor (June–July).

Great *fournées*, or batches, of prisoners were taken off at once to the guillotine. At the height of these events, known as the Great Terror, 149 people left the Luxembourg in a single night. Some went mad. One girl whose entire family had been killed remained in prison motionless, refusing to eat, clutching her pet parrot to her bosom. When her friends tried to persuade her to eat, telling her that her parrot was hungry, she would say only, 'No, he wants nothing – my parrot is like me, he wants nothing.' Others were inspired to extraordinary acts of courage, selflessness and dignity. When a fifty-year-old prisoner heard the guards shout out his twenty-one-year-old son's name, which was almost the same as his, he answered the call 'with uncommon alacrity' and went in his son's place 'with a look of exultation to the scaffold'.

There were so many headless bodies to dispose of, and so little time, that the corpses were simply stripped, thrown into a mass grave-pit and covered with quicklime to staunch the sickly smell of rotting flesh and prevent the dogs and rats from feasting on the bodies.

It was not just the rich who were imprisoned during this period, but anyone associated with the former ruling class; they seldom had access to advice on their cases or money to ease their time in prison. The female gardener employed at Lucy de la Tour du Pin's house in Paris was arrested in the autumn of 1793 for making remarks 'unworthy of a citizen' and held in the Abbaye for eight months. When she was interrogated the following May, she insisted that she had never 'allowed herself to be dragged into involvement in any political matter', and later supplied the ward officials with letters detailing her honesty signed by thirty-three known patriots. Her case was far from unique.

Rose de Beauharnais, the future Empress Joséphine and a friend of Tallien's, was held in Les Carmes, a former convent whose walls were still stained with the blood from the September massacres eighteen months earlier. Most of the women there, packed as many as eighteen to a cell, wore short shift dresses called *pierrots*, saving their best clothes for the journey to the scaffold. They might be called to the guillotine at any moment, and they wanted to be ready; they also kept their hair short to avoid having it cut by the executioner. Rose had been arrested on April 20. Her twelve-year-old son Eugène rushed to ask Tallien to come to their aid. But 'he who would have been willing to help us was already powerless to do so,' remembered her daughter, Hortense.

Eugène and Hortense, unable to visit their mother in Les Carmes, used to send her irascible pug, Fortuné, past the gaoler with notes for Rose tucked into his collar. Letters were smuggled into the cells hidden in pies or roast chickens, sewn into coat linings or scrunched around fruit and vegetables. One day towards the end of June, after she had been moved out of solitary confinement, a stone wrapped in paper fell at Thérésia's feet. She picked it up and kissed it, knowing at once that it was from Tallien.

Théroigne de Méricourt and Pauline Léon were further victims of the atmosphere of intensifying crisis. Léon was arrested on 3 April 1794, less than six months after her marriage to Théophile Leclerc and the dissolution of the Société des Républicaines-Révolutionnaires. 'A natural sentiment and an irresistible one for young married persons' had led her to visit Leclerc at the front in March, where they were both arrested without charge and taken to the Luxembourg.

It is possible that Léon had gone to the front to fight alongside her husband, as she had always hoped to do. In 1793 the patriotic

Élisabeth Dubois, wife of Pierre Favre, was one of several women who testified to having joined the army where their husbands were serving. Her husband's regiment of gunners granted her the rank and uniform of *capitaine en second*, the same as her husband, and she fought and was taken prisoner alongside him. When the Austrians discovered she was a woman her life was spared, although all her companions were slaughtered.

Also in the spring of 1794, Théroigne de Méricourt's brother Joseph had written to his local ward informing them that she was in a 'state of madness' and requesting judicial intervention in her case. Since her beating at the hands of the républicaines-révolutionnaires in May 1793, Théroigne had slipped from the official gaze but had been gradually descending into madness. Joseph's attempts to forestall her arrest were unsuccessful, and, having been heard making 'suspect remarks', she was taken into custody on 27 June.

During her confinement in early July she wrote to Antoine Saint-Just, though she had apparently not met him, begging for his help. Her letter reveals her encroaching psychosis. 'If you are unable to visit me where I am now, if you simply do not have the time, could I not arrange to be accompanied to your house?' she wrote. 'We must establish union.' She needed money, light and paper, she told him, so that she could carry on her work. 'I have great things to say ... [but] I must be free in order to write.' If she remained in prison, patriotism would be degraded, but if she were released she 'could still put everything to rights, if you would second me'.

Young, handsome and famously chaste, Saint-Just was the perfect focus for Théroigne's fantasies: powerful enough to help her and austere enough not to frighten her. But although her letter reached him, in the chaos of the first days of Thermidor, he did not even have time to open it. It was found among his papers, still sealed, after his death.

Saint-Just was Robespierre's henchman in the fight to defend his vision of the revolution against an ever increasing party of opponents who knew that his triumph would mean their certain deaths. Robespierre's enemies – many of whom had once been his friends and allies – were made up of several disparate groups, united by their resentment of his dictatorial pretensions and their concern about the direction in which the revolution was heading: the few surviving *dantonistes*; members of the Committee of General Security, whose power Robespierre was seeking to undermine (he had stopped referring business to the Committee of General Security in June); rebel members of the Committee of Public Safety itself; and former *représentants en mission* who had been chastised by the Committee of Public Safety either for the repressive severity of their measures (like the atheist Joseph Fouché in Lyon) or for suspected corruption (like Tallien himself). According to Paul Barras, a former *représentant* accused of embezzlement and bribery, Robespierre had said he wanted to rid the revolution of men who were full of plunder and blood.

Several of his opponents approached Robespierre during this period, hoping to come to terms with him. Barras and Stanislas Fréron, two ex-*représentants*, paid him a surprise visit at his rooms in the rue Saint-Honoré, while he was undergoing his morning toilette. White with hair-powder, his lips tight-clamped together, Robespierre ignored his visitors; then brushed his teeth, washed his face and hands in a basin and finished dressing. He neither looked at Barras or Fréron nor addressed a word to them before they eventually left. As Barras commented, it could hardly be called an interview.

On 11 June, a week and a half after Thérésia's arrest, Tallien had written to Robespierre, swearing that he had altered 'neither in his principles nor in his conduct. Not for a moment have I ceased to be a true friend of justice, truth and liberty.' He knew that the Committees saw him as an 'immoral man', he said, but if they could see him at home, with his aged, respectable mother, they would find that there luxury was banned. Tallien insisted that he had never profited from the revolution; everyone in Bordeaux would confirm that his actions there had been governed by energy, wisdom and justice. 'These are my sentiments, Robespierre,' he concluded, echoing the tone of virtuous self-justification that Robespierre himself employed. 'They will never change. Living alone, I have few friends, but I will always be one of the true defenders of the rights of the people.' Robespierre responded by banning Tallien from the Jacobin Club.

As the realization that he was the focus of an amorphous conspiracy grew upon him throughout June and July, Robespierre became more paranoid, more controlling and more isolated. Robespierre 'was the Terror itself', Barras wrote later. As Germaine de Staël pointed out, the people had respected him because they believed him 'incapable of personal views': the 'Incorruptible' was their mouthpiece, the embodiment of their revolutionary will. But as soon as his impartiality was called into question, wrote Staël, 'his power was at an end'.

Afterwards, Robespierre's challengers would each try to claim the distinction of having formed the plot that brought him down. Fouché wrote: 'Tallien contended for two lives, of which one was far dearer to him than his own: he therefore resolved upon assassinating the future dictator, even in the Convention itself'; he added that it was he who had persuaded Tallien to abandon this foolhardy idea and stand united with the others. Barras also claimed credit for telling his allies that they would all perish if Robespierre did not.

Thérésia believed that it was for her sake that Robespierre fell. On 25 July (7 Thermidor) she claimed to have smuggled a letter out of La Force to Tallien, with whom she had been in communication since her release from solitary confinement. She had just been told that she was to be brought before the Revolutionary Tribunal the following morning, 'that is to say to the scaffold'. It was so unlike the dream she had just had, she continued, in which Robespierre did not exist and the prison doors had been opened. 'But, thanks to your great cowardice, there is no longer anyone capable of making my dream a reality.' Tallien is said to have replied, 'Madame, rest assured that I will have the courage; calm yourself.' Another version has Thérésia sending her letter wrapped around a knife destined either for Robespierre's heart or for Tallien's, and ending dramatically, 'I will go to my death despairing that I belonged to a coward like you.'

It is unlikely that either of these versions is scrupulously accurate. None of Thérésia's correspondence to Tallien while she was in prison survives, and she was always happy to embroider the truth if it would make a better story. But it seems clear that she knew Tallien was the only person who could save her and that Tallien had, as Fouché observed, a double reason for desiring Robespierre's end.

On 8 Thermidor Robespierre appeared at the National Convention, immaculate in the same sky-blue silk coat and daffodil-yellow breeches he had worn at the Festival of the Supreme Being. He warned the deputies against tyrants and the enemies of the revolution, many of whom, he declared, were hidden among their number. The men he accused, whom he refused to name, knew exactly who they were. Jean Dyzez said two days later that on 9 Thermidor Tallien's head was 'almost touching the guillotine'.

Next day, Saint-Just took the tribune at the Convention and began to speak – 'I am from no faction. I will fight against them all' – but after only a few sentences he was interrupted by Tallien, who stood up to condemn Robespierre for making a speech in his own name the day before, rather than on behalf of the government. Others followed behind him. Robespierre tried to speak in his own defence, but was prevented from doing so by the session's president Collot d'Herbois, one of the discontented members of the Committee of Public Safety, who rang his bell to drown out Robespierre's voice. 'À bas le tyran!' shouted the deputies. One described him as the leader of a cult; another was heard to call, 'It's the blood of Danton that chokes him!'

'Until now I have kept silent because I knew that the man who was close to becoming the tyrant of France had formed a list of proscribed persons . . . [but yesterday] I trembled for my country; I saw the army of the new Cromwell forming, and I armed myself with a dagger to pierce his breast if the National Convention should not have the courage to accuse him,' cried Tallien, brandishing a knife, perhaps the one given to him by Thérésia. 'I demand that we stay in session until the sword of the law has safeguarded the Revolution, and that we order the arrest of the traitors.'

Although the Commune made a half-hearted attempt to mobilize the wards in Robespierre's defence, sounding the tocsin and marching a small force of National Guards to the Convention, for the first time since August 1792 they lacked momentum and support. Late that night, Barras led the troops under his control to the Hôtel de Ville, where Robespierre and his associates had fled earlier that afternoon.

As Barras and his men approached, it seems Robespierre and his friends resolved to kill themselves rather than be captured. Robespierre's younger brother, Augustin, jumped from one of the hall's windows, landing in front of the approaching force. Inside, the crippled

Georges Couthon was lying paralysed and bloody on the staircase; he had apparently thrown himself out of his wheelchair and down the stairs, but had not died. Joseph Lebas had been more successful – he had blown his brains out – but Robespierre had only managed to shatter his jaw. He was lying in agony on a council table. 'Do you suffer, your majesty?' asked the sans-culotte guards sardonically when they arrived. Saint-Just alone was unscathed, standing cool and defiant as he waited to be taken.

The next day, after a brief appearance before the Revolutionary Tribunal where they were formally identified (but not tried), Couthon, Saint-Just, Robespierre and nineteen others were bundled roughly into tumbrels and driven through the city to the Place de la Révolution. The route to the scaffold took them along the rue Saint-Honoré, past Robespierre's lodgings, where the carts stopped. Dancing, clapping, singing, taunting crowds encircled them; strangers who the day before would not have dared look at one another in the streets kissed and embraced; oxblood was splattered on to the walls of Robespierre's house.

Marxist historians believe that 'when the Thermidorians killed Robespierre, they killed the revolution', and even today many historians end their analysis of the revolution with Robespierre's death. A more measured view is that held by François Furet, who views 9 Thermidor as the end of the revolution because it was the 'victory of representative over revolutionary legitimacy', but thinks we must neither detest Robespierre nor exalt him. He was as much victim as manipulator of his times. 'Robespierre is an immortal figure not because he reigned supreme over the revolution for a few months,' writes Furet, 'but because he was the mouthpiece of its purest and most tragic discourse.'

He echoes Joseph Fouché, years after the fact, who said that although at the time he was 'too near a spectator of events' to appreciate them fully, he had since come to believe that seeing Robespierre as a dictator was doing him 'too much honour; he had neither plan, nor design; far from disposing of futurity, he was drawn along, and did but obey an impulse he could neither oppose nor govern'.

Robespierre's contemporaries were generally less equivocal, removing from themselves any blame for their own complicity in the Terror by painting him as personally responsible for all its horrors. Very few regretted his demise, even those most closely associated with him. On 11 Thermidor, the day after Robespierre's death, one theatre was playing *La Mort de César* and another *L'Hypocrite en révolution*. Newspaper editors informed their readers that 'at last, France is free'; grisly prints depicting Robespierre squeezing blood from a heart into a cup from which he was about to drink went on sale in the stalls of the Palais Royal. All Paris erupted in a delirious outpouring of relief and joy. 'To finish the revolution was an idea of all others the most soothing to the public mind,' wrote Helen Williams.

Louis-Sébastien Mercier, whose political sympathies were Girondin, excoriated Tallien for not taking his victory further. 'Tallien!' he exclaimed. 'Thou raised thyself as a cowardly sluggard rises at length when the fire reaches the mattress of his bed.' But many more viewed Tallien as their saviour from the stench of death and daily fear that had become their lives. Mary Wollstonecraft, in Le Havre in August, wrote that she was 'still pleased with the dignity of his conduct', admiring his talents, his humanity and his 'openness of heart'.

Tallien revelled in his triumph. In the days after 9 Thermidor he let it be known that he had acted from the purest and most impartial political motives as well as from the most ardently subjective ones. 'I would prefer to save twenty aristocrats accidentally than to expose one patriot to unjust oppression,' he declared before the Convention, saying that 'Terror is the weapon of tyranny' and arguing for liberties curtailed under the Jacobin regime such as freedom of the press and freedom of speech – even for former aristocrats – to be restored. 'Terror is a pervasive involuntary trembling, an exterior tremor that affects the most hidden fibres, that degrades man and assimilates him to beast,' he declared, undermining Robespierre's concept of Terror as an instrument of social regeneration and justice. 'It is a collapse of all physical strength, a concussion of all moral faculties; a disturbance of all ideas, an overthrow of all affections; it is a veritable disorganisation of the soul.'

On the day after Robespierre's fall news of their salvation began filtering through the gaol walls to the prisoners inside, still awaiting their deaths. One man's wife had permission to write just '*Je me porte bien*' – 'I am well' – on the packet of clean laundry she brought him each day. On the day Robespierre went to the guillotine, she wrote, '*Ah, que je me porte bien!*' – 'Oh, how well I am!'

At Les Carmes, where Rose de Beauharnais was held, a woman stopped on the streets outside and began gesticulating up at the barred windows. She shook out her dress, and then picked up a stone, and repeated these actions again and again. Finally the prisoners grasped what she was doing – miming '*Robe*' and '*pierre*' – dress and stone – and shouted his name down to her. The woman nodded and drew her finger across her throat, and then began dancing and applauding.

Prisoners – including Rose de Beauharnais and Pauline Léon, but not Théroigne de Méricourt, who would shortly be placed in an asylum – were swarming out of Paris's gaols throughout August. The mad elation they felt at their release was tempered in almost every case by grief for those they had lost.

Thérésia rejoiced when she heard the news of Robespierre's death, years afterwards calling 9 Thermidor 'the most beautiful day of my life, since it was in part by my little hand that the guillotine was overturned'. She was released from La Force three days after Tallien had stood up in the Convention, waving the dagger she had given him, and called for Robespierre's arrest. Tallien later declared that the warrant for her execution was found among Robespierre's papers; for the second time, he had saved her life.

16

ÉPOUSE

Thérésia Tallien

AUGUST 1794–OCTOBER 1795

Beautiful women are everywhere in Paris ... Here alone
of all places on earth they deserve to hold the reins of
government; men make fools of themselves over them,
think only of them, and live only for them. A woman need
come to Paris for just six months to discover what is her
due and what is her empire.

NAPOLÉON BONAPARTE

Thérésia Tallien in one of
the blonde wigs she popularized

THÉRÉSIA EMERGED from La Force to find herself a celebrity, hailed as '*Notre Dame de Thermidor*' by an adoring public. 'No-one was unaware of the part I had played on 9 Thermidor,' she told one of her children, many years later. 'The letter which had provoked and accelerated that day was on everybody's lips, known by heart to everyone.' 'She seemed to us at that time humanity incarnate in the most ravishing of forms,' wrote Charles de Lacretelle, a Thermidorian journalist who believed Thérésia had had more influence for good than he and all his peers combined. Newspapers described her every movement in hungry, rapturous prose. Wherever she went she was followed by grateful crowds and guarded by a band of devoted *muscadins*, dandies, who had seized control of the streets from the sans-culottes.

The *muscadins*, or *jeunesse dorée*, were a group of idle young men with anti-revolutionary sentiments, a mixture of liberated prisoners, deserters from the revolutionary army, clerks and actors. With the tacit support of the new regime, they patrolled the streets, intimidating and insulting people they suspected of Jacobinism. Their ringleader was Stanislas Fréron, an ally of Tallien's during Thermidor, who had been his friend since the early days of the revolution. Both were Parisian, both had been journalists before entering the Convention in September 1792 and both had been *représentants* accused by Robespierre of corruption. René Levasseur, a defiant Jacobin, called Fréron an 'evil genius'.

Just as the sans-culottes had been immediately recognizable by their red caps, striped trousers and wooden clogs, so too did the scented *muscadins* wear what amounted to a uniform. Theirs, however, instead of being deliberately populist was exaggeratedly mannered. They favoured oversized grey or brown coats, high, stiff cravats, very tight breeches and long white stockings wrinkling around the ankles. It was an imaginary version of the clothes English country gentlemen were thought to wear, and a mockery of the republican plainness of dress that had dominated the first years of the revolution. Monocles were fashionable accessories, as were leaded canes or knotty wooden cudgels with which they harassed passers-by. Their pomaded, powdered hairstyles were extraordinarily elaborate: cut *à la victime*, very short at the back, and either falling over the eyes at the front or in *oreilles de chien* – 'dogs' ears' – long, ear-covering ringlets. *Muscadins* also spoke with a distinctive drawl, dropping their r's. '*C'est ho'ible*,' they would lisp.

Determinedly frivolous, vain and affected, they prided themselves on their amorous adventures – which was perhaps part of the reason they worshipped Thérésia. Their fingers were heavy with rings, each apparently the souvenir of an *affaire du coeur*. Both men and women, released from the fear of death, now abandoned themselves to a post-apocalyptic pursuit of physical gratification as a way of reminding themselves that they were alive. People's affections, as Helen Williams put it, 'burst forth with uncontrollable energy'. Everyone understood the need to test boundaries, to escape limitations, to feel free.

'Life began again,' wrote Lacretelle of this heady period, describing strangers embracing on the streets and at the theatres, astonished to find themselves survivors. 'Men's hearts and minds, which had a brief while since been so hideously transformed, seemed now to have grown more exalted, to have been purged of all their dross . . . Faults were forgotten, generosity was the order of the day . . . All were bent on pleasure.' Williams agreed: 'The theatres, the public walks, the streets, resounded with the songs of rejoicing; the people indulged themselves in all the frolic and gaiety which belongs to their character; and all the world knows that joy is nowhere so joyous as at Paris.' But the inverse of this wild jubilation was a listless sense of cynicism and ennui. People who had lived through the Terror had looked into the depths of hell; nothing could restore their lost innocence.

One of Thérésia's first free acts, at Tallien's request, was to visit the children of his friend Rose de Beauharnais and reassure them that their mother would shortly be released. Sweet-natured, pleasure-loving Rose, ten years Thérésia's senior, was universally adored. When the two women met soon afterwards, they instantly became inseparable friends, united by their desire to drown out their memories of prison and deprivation with a surfeit of hedonism and luxury.

In mid-August Thérésia wrote to a friend in Bordeaux with whom she had entrusted her things asking her to sell her guitars, her mahogany paper-holder, her orange trees, a walnut casket, her horse and her open carriage. She regretted that she was not there to sell some of her dresses, as her time in prison had been so expensive and Fontenay had diminished her fortune by selling houses and land that were not his to dispose of. With the money made, she asked for wine, sugar, coffee, tea, candles and soap to be bought and sent to her, along with some bottles of oil. These were 'absolutely indispensable', she said. Paris lacked all basic necessities. Guests invited to dinner parties at this time committed 'an unheard-of impoliteness' if they did not bring with them their own bread and candles.

'Tallien loves you and embraces you with all his heart,' Thérésia concluded; although they were not living together, their affair continued. 'Happiness is on every face. Long live the Republic for ever! As one of their victims, I say perish the factions, the intriguers. My writing is messy, but I am moving house and very busy.'

Despite supplying the list of instructions to her friend in Bordeaux, Thérésia returned briefly the following month to collect Théodore and close her affairs there.

Back in Paris, she took a house in the rue Saint-Georges, in the up-and-coming *quartier* of Chaussée d'Antin on the right bank, a quiet, exclusive area. 'The greatest of all miracles,' wrote Mercier, 'is that this superb city still exists.' Thérésia and Fréron had the words '*L'Égalitie, la Fraternité, la République ou la Mort*' erased from the walls near her new house.

On 3 September, the on-going relationship between Thérésia and Tallien excited comment at the Jacobin Club, still open despite the triumph of its political opponents. 'We demand from Tallien an exact account of his liaisons,' said Réné Levasseur, a Jacobin deputy, 'that he tell us where he stands with an émigré's wife, who turns out to be the daughter of [one of] the king of Spain's bankers.' Less than a week later, an attempt was made to assassinate Tallien as he returned to his mother's home in the rue de la Perle one night. 'Villain, I have been waiting for you for a long time!' shouted his assailant, shooting him in the left shoulder and then running away. The injury was a serious one which went septic; a newspaper reported that 'one of the purest and most intrepid defenders of the people' had had to be bled three times.

When Tallien had recovered from his bullet wound, he and Thérésia went to see a play at the Odéon, arriving in her distinctive ox-blood coloured carriage. Having made their entrance through a crush of fans, they walked into the theatre itself to find 'the entire audience was standing on chairs and benches, where the ovation was prolonged into more applause and cries of love'. For the moment, each shared in the other's triumph; it was a parity that would not last for long.

People worked hard to forget the horrors of the Terror, but as the ramifications of Robespierre's fall filtered down through the political classes, Tallien became an object of hatred among displaced Jacobins and disappointed sans-culottes. Many suspected his political integrity, along with that of his fellow-Thermidorians Fréron, Barras and Fouché. Levasseur said that when he heard that Robespierre had been defeated his first emotion was joy, but on finding out who had risen in his place he feared for France. 'The men who had taken control were, for the most part, men without principles, ambitious mercenaries.'

Even those favourably inclined towards Tallien and his friends, like Germaine de Staël (who had been escorted out of Paris by Tallien in September 1792), questioned their intentions. 'The new revolution which has just occurred has put the villains-for-the-love-of-profit in place of the villains-for-the-love-of-crime,' she wrote. In just a few months, the tenor and direction of the revolution had been transformed. Individualism was no longer viewed as a crime against the state; rigid, austere virtue was no longer its governing sentiment.

In their efforts to allow some kind of normality to reimpose itself on society, the Thermidorians relaxed the Jacobins' stringent economic controls and limited the executive arm of the government. Freedom of religion was reinstated and price maximums lifted, but political clubs lost the rights of affiliation, correspondence with each other and petitioning. The result of these confused policies was political compromise, dramatic inflation, corruption and lawlessness. The upheaval was rendered less dangerous than two years earlier because the threat of invasion had diminished – the republican armies, winning victory after victory on the French frontiers, were becoming a formidably victorious force. Nonetheless, it threw a dislocated and traumatized populus into near-anarchy. Visitors arriving in Paris, where the once mighty Commune had been dismantled and the wards' powers limited, commented on the city's 'strange character of uncertainty, of displacement. Nothing seemed to be in its place.'

Throughout the autumn the debate over what should happen to the Jacobin Club raged on the streets of the capital. In November Thérésia, accompanied by Stanislas Fréron and a band of *muscadins*, ceremoniously locked its doors, shutting the Club down for good, and presented the keys to the National Convention. 'That woman is capable of closing the gates of hell,' commented the British prime minister, William Pitt.

Despite the new sense of political freedom on the streets, daily life after Thermidor was as hard as ever. The harvest in 1794 was one of the worst recorded in Western Europe. Even in August people had been complaining that they could only buy rough black bread; by December of the coldest winter since 1709, they were starving. It was not unusual to see households keeping a thin goat for its milk, or fattening a family of rabbits. Queues for the coarse, expensive bread might last all day. The government printed more paper money, but merchants refused to sell their goods for debased currency.

'Subsistence is always the subject of conversations,' reported a police spy. The Seine froze over, and barges carrying firewood could not get through. People began foraging for fuel in the Bois de Boulogne and the Bois de Vincennes, decimating the ancient forests there. Exquisite panelling, furniture and picture-frames from abandoned *hôtels* were torn apart and thrown on fires. Hungry wolves prowled the city boundaries. On the streets, desperate for money, people were selling whatever they could lay their hands on: beds, marble statues, books, paintings, used clothes, china. The whole city looked like an enormous junk shop, its streets jostling with gangs of *muscadins* and a 'universal *brocantage* [buying and selling]'. Most essential items were available only on the black market. 'Nothing was either bought or sold except in secret,' remembered Frénilly. 'Every purchase was a conspiracy.'

In the republican Year III (September 1794–September 1795), mortality rates in Paris reached a record high for the second year running. But in 1794–5 the culprit was dearth, famine and freezing temperatures, rather than Madame Guillotine. Suicide rates soared, especially among young, poor, single women.

One household seemed oblivious to these hardships that winter. On 26 December Jean-Lambert Tallien finally married Thérésia Cabarrus-Fontenay, who was four months pregnant. Their principal witness was Stanislas Fréron; Rose de Beauharnais attended Thérésia.

Almost as soon as their relationship had begun, Thérésia had expressed doubts about her feelings for Tallien and in several cases been openly disloyal to him. To some, she declared that she loved him, but it seems more likely that she saw their destinies as intertwined and irrevocable – an alliance of mutual dependency from which she neither could nor should extricate herself. 'When one comes through a storm, one cannot always choose one's lifeline,' she wrote to a friend, years later. In Bordeaux she had said that she could not leave Tallien because she was responsible for his political difficulties; in Paris, perhaps, she felt she could not leave him because she was responsible for his success. Then, too, she longed to play a great part on the world's stage. Tallien, the hero of the hour, looked as if he had a brilliant career ahead of him. In late 1794, even despite the first rumbles of criticism, there were few more promising men to whom to be attached. Her pregnancy was the deciding factor. As contemptuous as Thérésia was of convention, she did not want to have a baby out of wedlock.

Tallien had no such scruples about their union. When soon after his wedding a deputy at the Convention asked him to define his relationship to the fabulously rich Cabarrus woman, he responded with pride. He had never wanted to bring her into the public eye, he began, but he could remain silent no longer; the calumnies heaped upon her forced him to speak. 'We speak of Cabarrus's daughter,' he said. 'I have known her for a long time; I saved her life in Bordeaux; her unhappiness and her virtues inspired me with affection and respect.' In La Force, pressed by Robespierre's men to betray him, she had responded with indignation. 'This, citizens, this is the woman who is my wife.' This semi-official announcement of their marriage only made his enemies despise him more.

Thérésia's reservations about marrying Tallien were made clear by the prenuptial agreement they drew up. Wary after her experiences with Fontenay, she was leaving nothing to chance. The contract specified that their goods were to be owned separately and that Thérésia was to remain in control of her own money. Any children were to be brought up by their parents each according to their respective fortunes.

After the civil ceremony, statuesque and glowing, Thérésia defied the icy temperatures outside to welcome the guests to her wedding feast wearing a short white muslin tunic, draped like a Greek statue's and caught up at the shoulders with antique cameos. Her finely modelled arms and hands were exposed and on her bare feet she wore thin cothurni, or sandals strapped around her ankles. The party was held at La Chaumière, the thatched cottage that had formed part of Thérésia's dowry when she married Fontenay. It was set in what were then the outskirts of Paris, near the modern avenue Montaigne. The area was rural in feel, populated by cowherds, milkmaids, laundresses, and gardeners attending their lettuce beds and vineyards. La Chaumière itself was theatrically rustic, a rose-covered, weather-stained brick cottage with a mossy thatched roof, set in a secluded grove of poplars, fruit trees and lilacs.

People coming out of prison, their eyes accustomed to the darkness of crowded, damp cells, found solace in the light and greenery of rural idylls like La Chaumière. Harking back to the fashion for the pastoral which had marked the early revolution – and of which Thérésia had been an enthusiastic proponent, with her *fête champêtre* at Fontenay-aux-Roses in 1789 – this desire for nature was both escapist and therapeutic. 'I would like so much to live in the woods and the forests,' wrote one disenchanted political wife in 1793, echoing Manon Roland's longing for her serene way of life at the Rolands' farm near Lyon. When the artist Jacques-Louis David was in prison in 1794 (guilty of supporting Robespierre), he painted a lyrically restorative landscape of the Luxembourg gardens from his cell window. La Chaumière served this purpose for Thérésia; it was the ideal 'gabled cottage' Tallien had rhapsodized about before the Convention in the spring of 1794.

The cottage's deliberately humble exterior gave no indication of the opulence of its neoclassical interiors. Etruscan vases stood in the Pompeian-style hall. A large fountain, dominated by a statue of Neptune holding a trident,* formed the centrepiece of the main salon. In an age of scarcity, the rooms were extravagantly heated and lit; hot-house jonquils, hyacinths and heliotropes scented the air; rich dishes like lobster Thermidor were served up by Thérésia's chefs. Upstairs her huge bed, draped in yellow, was set into a mirrored alcove, with gilded bronze cupids guarding each corner. Standing nearby was a nude statue of the goddess Diana, bearing an unmistakable resemblance to Thérésia herself.

Although the newlyweds remained in the rue Saint-Georges until the winter of 1795 (and it remained Tallien's official address on the Convention's registry until 1796), from this period La Chaumière became the focal point of Thermidorian social life. Thérésia's charm and beauty, Tallien's political position and their joint fame attracted the most glittering characters of the new society, all meeting on equal ground. Republican manners were still the fashion. Lapdogs – Thérésia's little Minerve ate out of a gold bowl studded with emeralds – were trained to bark at the word 'aristocrat', and the title *citoyen* sufficed for everybody. But the new mores were tempered by the old-fashioned etiquette

---

* In 1785 Sir Joshua Reynolds bought Bernini's fountain of Neptune holding a trident with a Triton at his feet, originally made for the Villa Negroni; he considered it the finest work of its type.

of the returning exiles, and to have been in prison during the Terror was 'a necessary introduction to good society'. Gradually *vous* replaced *tu* in polite conversation; tricolour cockades, though still theoretically obligatory, were less and less prominently displayed.

In this oddly meritocratic atmosphere, energy and money replaced birth and breeding or revolutionary fervour as the sole currencies of social status. Thérésia's guests were mostly young, ambitious, charismatic and full of passion. Their experiences over the past few years had taught them that they could rely only upon themselves, and they were determined to suck all they could from life. 'People speak of patriotism and liberty,' wrote a German visitor to Paris at this time, 'but it is power and riches that they want; it is glory and vanity that intoxicate them.'

One found at La Chaumière in 1795 deputies to the Convention of all political stripes, including Théroigne de Méricourt's hero Emmanuel Joseph Sieyès, the Girondin journalist whom Thérésia had saved in Bordeaux, Jean-Baptiste Louvet, and Tallien's friends Paul Barras and Stanislas Fréron; foreign grandees, like the US envoy James Munroe; the playwright Marie-Joseph Chénier, responsible alongside David for most of the revolutionary *fêtes*, the actor Talma and his actress wife Julie; contractors, speculators and profiteers, including Jacques-Rose Récamier and the dashing young Gabriel Ouvrard, for whom the phrase *nouveau riche* was invented; and soldiers like Lazare Hoche, who had been the lover of Rose de Beauharnais while they were both held in the Luxembourg and whom she still adored.

Their lust for excitement and experience was mirrored in the exotically beautiful women who surrounded them. Aimée de Coigny – whom Gouverneur Morris had ogled in 1789 – was a returned émigrée who had been imprisoned in Paris during the Great Terror. The poet André Chénier, Marie-Joseph's brother, had known Aimée in Saint-Lazare prison and immortalized her as *La Jeune Captive*, describing her 'enchanting face, her figure like a Venus'. Citoyenne de Coigny's husband's mistress was Fortunée Hamelin, a Creole heiress so dark-skinned people doubted the 'purity' of her blood. She doused herself in attar of roses and was renowned for her kindness, her sparkling wit and the uninhibited lasciviousness of her dancing.

Rose de Beauharnais, another languid Creole, was Thérésia's closest, most constant companion. When Tallien and Thérésia's daughter was born in May (conceived on her release in August 1794), Rose was asked to be her godmother and the little girl was given the names Thermidor-Rose-Thérésia. The two women were partners in crime, co-conspirators, far more than Thérésia and her new husband ever were. Rose wrote to Thérésia in the spring of 1795 about a ball they were to attend together, asking her to wear 'that peach-blossom dress you are so fond of' and a red handkerchief on her head with three kiss-curls on each side of her face. Rose planned to wear the same thing, she wrote, and she predicted the effect of their paired beauty would be 'wondrous', driving the other female guests to despair.

Thérésia, 'l'idole du jour', revelled in her role as uncrowned queen of Thermidorian society and ordainer of its fashions. Her daring costumes were worlds apart from the modest styles of previous years, mocking expressions of disdain for the bourgeois morality so earnestly preached by Robespierre and which suddenly seemed so outdated. Profligacy and cynicism as well as wantonness were the hallmarks of the new era, extreme reactions to the deprivation and loss of hope engendered during the dark years of the Terror. 'Never had fashion exercised an empire more extravagant and more fickle,' wrote Alexis de Tocqueville. 'A strange thing, despair had made all the frivolity of the old *mores* reappear. Only frivolity had taken on new characteristics: it had become bizarre, chaotic, and so to speak, revolutionary; like serious things, pleasure had lost its rules and boundaries.'

Just as the early revolutionaries had been inspired by the philosophies and personalities of Greece and Rome, Thérésia was inspired by their aesthetics, modelling her outfits on the sparse costumes worn by antique statues, many of which, to Mercier's disapproval, were on public display in the gardens of Paris. She appeared in the finest unstarched Indian muslin dresses caught up under the bosom and trimmed with lace – styles called by dressmakers *robes à la Vestale* or *à la Minerve* – which left her magnificent arms and legs bare. People whispered that she dipped them in scented oil or misted them with water so that they would cling even more closely to her body. Underwear might be a tunic or body-stocking of flesh-coloured silk, or nothing at all. Thérésia was fond of enumerating the drawbacks of corsets, 'adding that it was not when a woman was dressed that it mattered so much whether she was beautiful'. It was joked that the *sans-chemises* had replaced the *sans-culottes*.

The *merveilleuses*, as Thérésia and her friends were known, even dared to appear in public bare-breasted, perhaps subconsciously modelling themselves on the bare-breasted figures of Liberty that had dominated the iconography of the early years of the revolution. Thérésia was painted by Jean-Baptiste Isabey wearing a blond wig and with one breast exposed; Fortunée Hamelin appeared at the theatre with her breasts covered only by a *rivière* of diamonds, and was said, for a bet, to have walked the length of the Champs Élysées in her languorous Creole gait, with her breasts bare. On another occasion, Thérésia bet a guest at one of her parties that her entire outfit, including sandals and bracelets (she favoured gold armlets in the shape of serpents with engraved emerald heads), did not weigh more than two six-franc coins; to prove it, in front of everyone, she stripped and placed her clothes on a scale, winning the wager.

Women's bodies, which before the revolution had been unrecognizable beneath their carapaces of whalebone and horsehair, then during the revolution had been either unnoticeable in drab, shapeless dresses or disguised as men's in *amazones* or striped trousers, were suddenly very prominent. Through their daring, fantastical experiments with fashion, the *merveilleuses* renegotiated women's cultural visibility, making themselves at once defiantly feminine and unignorable. Thérésia, with her fancy-dress classicism, was at the forefront of this social movement. She went to the Opéra in the guise of Diana, wearing a leopard-skin draped over one shoulder and carrying a jewelled quiver.

Although hairstyles seemed simple they required lengthy sessions with Messieurs Bertrand or Hippolyte, the celebrity coiffeurs of the day. Thérésia usually wore her dark hair cut short but she also owned fifty wigs, said to be made from the hair of guillotine victims, in a rainbow of colours including red, blue and violet. She popularized the cropped blonde wig *à la Titus* which, in November 1794, had become so fashionable that a newspaper expressed the vain wish that ladies would return to their natural hair colour.

Hats were of vital importance: huge velvet jockey caps, oriental turbans, plumed bandeaux and simple straw bonnets raced in and out of fashion. Their flimsy dresses had no pockets, so women started carrying tiny morocco leather handbags, known as ridicules or *réticules*. An admirer was always on hand to carry anything bigger than a handkerchief or a pot of rouge, a *merveilleuse* essential. Every woman of fashion prided herself on wearing her Indian cashmere shawl in a distinctive way. Thérésia draped her wraps 'with inimitable grace and infinite coquetry'. On their feet the *merveilleuses* wore light silk slippers or sandals tied with tassels or jewelled straps around the ankle.

Thérésia loved jewellery, wearing diamond toe rings and anklets to hide – or perhaps to draw attention to – the scars on her feet and legs from the rat bites she had received in prison. Hoops of diamonds set in gold around her thighs glittered through her muslin dresses. 'One could not be more richly undressed,' commented Talleyrand.

Even though they no longer bore their owners' coats of arms on the doors, in post-Thermidor Paris carriages, like jewels, were rare marks of wealth and status, expensive, aspirational objects of desire. A German visitor reported that Parisians were obsessed with carriages of all types: curricles, phaetons, *wiskis*, diligences, gigs, buggies, berlines, rattle-traps, chariots, *dormeuses*, *demi-fortunes*. One courtesan at this time had rose diamonds set into her horses' harnesses; Paul Barras's harness was silver. Thérésia's dark-red cabriolet was instantly recognizable on the streets of Paris after Thermidor, because so few people could afford such vehicles.

Permissiveness in fashion was reflected in familiar, licentious manners. People spoke freely, slangily, with abandon. Ladies used words that ten years earlier would have caused duels if they had been uttered in their presence. Old-fashioned scruples had disappeared: men appeared in drawing-rooms in their boots; they did not scruple to compliment women to their faces (something that was seen before the revolution as an insult to their modesty); friends addressed one another by their first names. Women sat on sofas with their legs tucked up under them, displaying their feet and ankles, and went out in public unaccompanied.

Good health had become fashionable. Fresh air was all the rage. A cult of the physical, derived from the ancients, inspired men and women to take vigorous exercise, walking, riding and swimming. Chariot races were held in the Champs de Mars. For women, though, the appearance of delicate health was still considered attractive; powder was a valuable tool in producing this effect.

Released from their corsets, ladies ceased to swoon and ate and drank in public for the first time, despite the consternation this caused in some masculine hearts. 'The beloved is always pictured to the fancy like some airy spirit,' wrote a German visiting Paris in 1795, 'and it really grieves one to see her eat with a *great appetite*.' Restaurants serving luxuries unaffordable to nine-tenths of the population opened up all over Paris, run by formerly private chefs made redundant by the revolution.

Another German visitor was shocked to see pregnant women out in public. These 'fecund belles' had lost all their delicacy and reserve, he said, and he attributed it not to an innate desire to begin again after the devastation of the Terror, nor to the new fashions for unrestrictive clothing which revealed swelling bellies, but to loose women indulging in light liaisons. He might have been thinking of Thérésia.

The showplace for the *merveilleuses'* insouciant beauty was the immensely popular public balls which began during the freezing winter of 1794–5; it was to one of these that Rose and Thérésia planned to wear their matching outfits. Anyone who could pay could buy a ticket for these frenzied events, when men and women forgot their troubles, singing wildly as they danced, 'intoxicated by the speed and the voluptuous music', while outside on the frosty streets emaciated children were begging for bread.

'Despairing of escape from their hardships,' wrote Alexis de Tocqueville, Parisians 'tried not to think of them.' Dancing was not just the pursuit of pleasure but a way to escape, almost to protest against grief. The poor had their own riotous dances, held on both Sundays and *décadis* (after Thermidor they kept both of these days as holidays) in smoky cellars dimly lit by cheap tallow candles or earthen oil-lamps, where they drank rough brandy and danced jigs in their wooden clogs to the tune of a single fiddle. Other balls were held in the ruins of empty hotels and churches, in cemeteries, in the yards of former prisons and on the very boulevards themselves.

The most notorious of these ticketed parties was the *bal des victimes*, held on the first floor of the Hôtel Richelieu, to which only those who had lost a near relative during the Terror were invited. The room was draped in black: black ribbons tied on to the musicians' violins, black hangings on the walls, black crêpe on the chandeliers. Dancers of both sexes had their hair cut short at the back, *à la victime*; women wore thin shifts like the ones in which their mothers and sisters had gone to the scaffold, and narrow red ribbons around their necks, as if to show where the guillotine's blade had missed. They greeted each other with sharp, awkward nods in imitation of the motion made by severed heads as they dropped into the basket below.

These extraordinary, macabre balls were for the survivors one way of making sense of the devastating events through which they had lived, of coming to terms with their shared trauma. In the words of the historian Ewa Lajer-Burcharth, they were a form of 'collective cultural mourning'. But they were seen by disapproving contemporaries as evidence of a worrying moral decline. The insolent extravagance, the cynicism and lack of conscience or inhibition in their quest for pleasure that marked Thérésia and her set were seen either as an insult to the memories of those who had died during the Terror or as the destruction of the revolution's legacy.

La Chaumière was at the heart of this corruption. It became known as a salon in which business was done. 'What do they do at Mme Tallien's?' asked the journal *Le Thé*. 'They negotiate.' For Thérésia, used since her spell in Bordeaux to asking and granting favours, it was a small step to the lobbying culture endemic to these post-Thermidor times. She 'enjoyed the only role fitting to her sex,' remembered Antoine Thibaudeau. 'She took over the department of favours.' Nothing was too much trouble: 'the beautiful Mme Tallien always loved to please her friends'.

Thérésia dispensed kisses to Jacobins who promised they would convert, and to journalists like Lacretelle who wrote flattering things about her. People sought protectors for new business ideas and help in recovering confiscated fortunes or obtaining official pardons for émigré friends and relatives. 'Contracts might be for anything, from oats to cavalry sabres, and as likely as not carried off by a woman wearing flesh-coloured tights and diamonds on her bare toes.' Paul Barras said that Thérésia did happily accept money for favours, but it was 'not the main object . . . [rather] the means of obtaining the pleasures she was fond of which she procured for others'.

Perhaps because he felt emasculated by his rich wife, Tallien increasingly became known for his avarice. Although he saved nothing, his enemies claimed that he made fortunes several times over through stock-jobbing, speculating and trafficking in black-market necessities like candles and soap. Journalists (he had reopened his newspaper, *L'Ami des Citoyens*) and deputies to the Convention earned very modest wages; Tallien may have felt obliged to resort to these schemes just to keep up with Thérésia and her profligate friends.

Voices of opposition to the new regime and to those who were seen to be profiting from it had been heard towards the end of 1794, and by early the next year the complaints were growing louder. The ostentatious wealth of the new rich only served to highlight the destitution of the rest of society. Tallien's willingness to surrender to the luxuries bought by his wife's wealth was seen as moral weakness; his devotion to a woman who embodied such unrepublican virtues as opulence and sexual liberation undermined his political reputation. 'It is impossible, no matter how much strength of character one has, not to be influenced by the society one frequents,' wrote one former Jacobin, Antoine Thibaudeau, commenting on how easily members of the Convention were seduced, mocked and used in the new salons of Thermidorian Paris.

The similarity between La Chaumière and Marie-Antoinette's toy farm at Versailles was not lost on Tallien's opponents. As early as January 1795, newspapers that obsessed over Thérésia's every appearance were calling her '*une nouvelle Antoinette*' as often as they described her as a goddess. Boudoir politics was thought to have returned, and Thérésia, who exemplified this new corruption, was condemned. 'The airs of a courtesan suffice to make her a sensation,' commented one journalist sniffily in January 1795.

That same January women waiting in bread lines were saying that the counterrevolution was not far away and that the market women who had started the revolution would bring it to an end. The contrast between rich and poor, between the sated and the starving, had become too great to bear. By March the women were protesting on the streets and calling for a king who would give them bread; others were heard to say that at least under Robespierre their bellies had been full. Bread was limited to four ounces per person per day and the price of a loaf was soaring. An insurrectionary poster was pasted on to the city walls, calling for the wives of sans-culottes to occupy the tribunes of the Convention to prevent the counterrevolution taking place.

In early April hungry, angry men and women surged into the Convention hall and scuffled with guards and *muscadins*, calling for bread. When calm was restored, the Thermidorians used the disturbance to expel the remaining Jacobins from their number. The most prominent of them, Barère, Collot d'Herbois and Billaud-Varenne, who had been arrested the previous month, were deported to Guiana. Marat, patron saint of the Jacobins, had been officially de-Pantheonized two months earlier.

Counterrevolutionary reaction, known as the White Terror, was spreading across France. Jacobin prisoners were massacred and 'aristocrats' released from gaol. National conscription meant that deserters from the army were officially viewed as traitors, but in many conservative areas of the country they were welcomed home. Royalists – constitutional monarchists rather than agitators for a return to the ancien régime – gathered beneath their banners a whole variety of followers with new grievances and resentments. In Amiens they cried, '*Du pain et un roi!*'

In Paris the people's demands for bread had not been satisfied, and in early May women were observed taunting and provoking their men 'to rebellion and to pillage', calling them cowards and haranguing them for allowing their families to starve. By then a baguette from the baker's cost 16 livres; they had been 8 or 9 sous in 1789. Women were goading their husbands – in the words of a police spy, 'firing them up with their seditious propositions and stimulating the most violent excitement', communicating all their rage to them. 'If you go to present a petition about it [the lack of affordable bread] to the National Convention, you are arrested,' one woman was heard to say to a friend on 18 April. 'The popular societies have been closed. That was in order to plunge us back into slavery. We are all suckers.'

On 1 Prairial (20 May) women occupied the tribunes of the Convention while their husbands and sons outside armed themselves with pikes and cannon. The crowd cried, 'Bread or death!' and *Du pain et la constitution de 1793!'*, storming the hall in defiance of the guards, who tried to herd the women out of the galleries with whips and the butt ends of their bayonets. When the deputy who had been charged with provisioning Paris confronted the mob he was shot and his head stuck on to a pike. The protesters forced the Convention to pass a series of Jacobin measures that would have bolstered the dwindling power of the wards, and of the revolutionary committees, before being expelled from the hall by the National Guard late that night; the measures taken were repealed then and there.

The Convention responded to the violence – of the same kind that two or three years earlier had been coordinated and manipulated by men like Danton, Hébert and Tallien himself – by disarming the faubourgs. The women of faubourg Saint-Antoine at first resisted handing over their cannon, but without success. From this point onwards, it would no longer be possible for the people of the streets to generate political change through protest and uprising.

Common women, described as bloodthirsty Furies, were seen as instigators of this violence. One hundred and forty-eight were arrested for inciting the revolt. Most had previous records as militants; most were wage-earners whose brothers, husbands or sons were fighting in the republican army; none were young mothers. Pauline Léon, so recently released from prison, was not among them.

Women were barred from attending the Convention without a male companion, and from participating in political meetings. Gathering in public in groups of five or more was forbidden. The Société Fraternelle des Deux Sexes was denounced as a 'hotbed of insurrection' but its female members resisted attempts to close it down.

Even the national spinning workshops set up in 1790 were dismantled; women were officially encouraged to work at home. In this way, said the official report to the Convention, the unfortunate classes would avoid long and miserable journeys to work, thus saving time they could devote to their families. The manufacturers' expenses would be lessened and quality improved. Working at home would also prevent 'inconveniences that might result – for morals or for public tranquillity – from numerous gatherings of simple people who are credulous and easily led astray by perfidious suggestions of malevolence and seduction'.

For these women of the Parisian streets, whom the revolution in all its incarnations had failed to provide with food for their children, the response to the riots of Prairial was one betrayal too many. How else could the working woman 'assess the revolution except by examining her wrecked household', asks the historian Olwen Hufton, 'by reference to her children aborted or born dead, by her own sterility, by the disappearance of her few sticks of furniture, by the crumbling of years of effort to hold the frail family economy together, and what could her conclusion be except that the price paid for putative liberty had been far too high?'

From 1795 many returned to the old ways, once again finding the support and succour they needed in the Church. The Thermidorians had re-established religious tolerance, and on 11 Prairial the Convention was persuaded to authorize worship in former churches. A few days later mass was celebrated in fifteen churches in Paris for the first time in three years.

In late June, encouraged by the change in the political atmosphere since the events of Thermidor, royalist forces landed at Quiberon in Brittany. By July Rose de Beauharnais's ex-lover, General Hoche, had defeated them and taken nine thousand men prisoner. As émigrés returning to France in arms, they were all automatically subject to the death penalty. Hoche and Tallien, there as a *réprésentant*, hesitated to carry out the sentences, and told the prisoners they would sue for acquittal. Tallien returned to Paris to present their case to the Convention.

But in Paris Tallien had been accused of corresponding with royalists, and, desperate to prove himself a true republican, he argued instead that rigour rather than clemency be shown to the rebels. About 750 men were executed. Thérésia was devastated by the deaths. Weeping, she told Charles de Lacretelle afterwards that if she had been there, she believed she could have prevented the killings. On a political level, Tallien had endeared himself neither to the increasingly powerful constitutional monarchist faction nor to the remaining radicals.

Quiberon, said Thérésia, gave people an excuse to tear down the hero of Thermidor, although in truth that process of re-evaluation had already begun. Tallien's political enemies had remembered his role during the September massacres as secretary to the Commune, and accused him of colluding in the atrocities committed then. Later that autumn Antoine Thibaudeau publicly reminded Tallien that he had defended the bloody events of September 1792. The windows of La Chaumière were smashed. 'But for me, I could not abandon my duties,' Thérésia lamented. 'I could not accuse him who had brought such glory to my name; I would have had to bid farewell to that glory which so intoxicated me.'

Tallien failed to plead for the Quiberon prisoners on the anniversary of 9 Thermidor. Thérésia remembered giving a dinner that night at which she raised a toast: 'To forget mistakes, to forgive injuries, to the reconciliation of all the French.' Her guests then raised their glasses, in return, to '*Notre Dame de Thermidor*'. But although she was still adored by Parisian society, the backlash had begun. Her enemies had started calling Thérésia '*Notre Dame de Septembre*'.

Even a great love would have trembled beneath the pressures imposed on Thérésia and Tallien's marriage, and theirs was an alliance born of desire, fear and ambition. Tallien had betrayed his revolutionary principles for Thérésia and she had abandoned her caste for him. In Paris, the common ground they had shared in Bordeaux had slipped away from beneath their feet. 'Tallien's company repels me, but I cannot pull myself away from it,' she said to a friend. 'It is the only way of satisfying my thirst for celebrity.'

Tallien resented the adulation still showered upon his wife; Thérésia could not learn to respect her husband. Watching them together, said one observer, was like seeing 'a lion sharing a cell with a pet dog'. Tallien was a man 'with nothing in the way of merit', said one of his fellow-deputies. Even Thermidor, wrote his accomplice on that day Paul Barras, showed 'Tallien incapable of rising above the commonplace'. His eloquence was contrived, his conversation laborious, his manner vulgar. Barras nicknamed him Robinet d'Eau – 'water tap' – because of the relentless stream of his insipid monologues.

'Too much blood [stained] the hands of that man,' Thérésia told a friend later. 'I was always repelled by him.' But she never reproached herself for her association with Tallien, considering herself not an accomplice to his crimes, but rather the only thing that had restrained him.

Sensing that he had lost her love, Tallien responded with rage, violence and jealousy. By late 1795 the husband of the most desired woman in Paris was said to be boasting of his encounters with prostitutes. And as Tallien's marriage turned sour his political career waned; his personal and public fortunes were inextricably linked.

On 22 August, the Convention approved a new constitution which returned control of France to men of property – a return, as some had it, to the state of affairs in 1789. It was, as Furet writes, 'another attempt to realise the eighteenth-century ideal of enlightened bourgeois liberalism': happiness was seen as an end to be pursued, not a right to be seized; equality meant equality of opportunity, not equality of rank or wealth. Avoiding tyranny and promoting stability were its twin aims. Former radicals accepted this retreat from their ideals because the Terror's excesses had been so appalling.

A French citizen was defined at this time as a male taxpayer, born and resident in France and over twenty-one years of age; he had the right to vote for 'electors', men of twenty-five and over who possessed disposable incomes equivalent to two hundred days' ordinary labour. These perhaps three hundred thousand electors chose the governing houses, made up of the Council of Five Hundred and the Council of the Elders. The Elders would select five Directors (who formed the government's executive branch) from a list of ten names nominated by the Council of Five Hundred. Tallien was elected to this Council, but given no more prominent role in the new government.

One of the first five Directors was Paul Barras, who assumed office in October 1795. Barras, like Tallien, was a former deputy to the National Convention who had been a *représentant en mission* in 1793, then recalled by the Committee of Public Safety in early 1794. Like Tallien, he had been hailed as one of the architects of Robespierre's fall. The similarities between them ended there.

Barras was forty when he moved into his official apartments at the Luxembourg, the former palace and revolutionary prison renamed the Palais Égalité. He was an elegant, self-assured *ci-devant* viscount from Provence whose ancient lineage had not hampered his republican ambitions. Tall, dark, unscrupulous and inscrutable, Barras was a dissolute, dandified roué who loved pleasure as much as his mistress, Rose de Beauharnais, and Thérésia. At parties, accosted by colleagues, he would say, '*À demain les affaires!*' – 'Leave business till tomorrow!'

At the round of balls, concerts, dinners and card parties of the hedonistic summer of 1795, Barras's constant companion was a swarthy Corsican soldier, Napoléon Bonaparte, whose career seemed paralysed by his previous support for Robespierre. Barras and Napoléon had met at the siege of Toulon in the autumn of 1793, where Napoléon showed the first signs of the military genius that would propel him to greatness. With his stringy, unwashed hair, bony face and ill-fitting greatcoat, the young general possessed none of the looks, influence or wealth that distinguished the men of Thérésia's circle; compliments froze in his mouth and he laughed at the wrong moments. But what Bonaparte lacked in polish he made up for in drive and self-belief.

When Barras brought him to La Chaumière, the inexperienced young soldier was captivated by Thérésia: by her fame, her dazzling looks, her casual friendliness. Writing to his young sweetheart in Marseille, he callously described the women he was meeting in Paris in words that vividly evoked Thérésia. They were, he said, as beautiful as in old romances ... as learned as scholars ... their *toilette*, the arts and pleasure occupy all their time. They are philosophers, lovers, courtesans and artists. But what all these frivolous women have in common is an astonishing love of bravery and glory. Truly, they inspire the nation with the courage to conquer Europe ... their work and their delight is to win brave men to their cause.

Misinterpreting Thérésia's open informality – when he appeared in a brand-new uniform made of rationed fabric she had requested for him she called out, 'So, my friend, you have your trousers!' – he dared try to make love to her, declaring his 'unconquerable passion'. Thérésia responded with an incredulous laugh that Napoléon would not forget.

Barras had a solution to his protégé's disappointment – his own mistress, Rose de Beauharnais, of whom he had tired. Placed next to her at dinner *chez* Barras, the ambitious Napoléon was intoxicated by Rose's sweetness, her graceful elegance and practised admiration. As for Thérésia, '*roi Barras*', as he was becoming known, had plans for her too.

RETOURNÉE

Germaine de Staël

MAY 1795–JANUARY 1798

The universe is in France; outside it, there is nothing.

GERMAINE DE STAËL

Benjamin Constant

IN MAY 1795, Germaine de Staël wrote to a friend that she was *'joyeuse, sur la route de Paris'*. After nearly three years of exile, she was returning to the city she loved more than anywhere else in the world, the place that consoled her for the happiness that continued to elude her in her private life. Heavily pregnant, she had left blood-soaked Paris in September 1792, as the massacres spread across the city. She spent three months at her father's house, Coppet, in Switzerland, waiting for her second son to be born, and five weeks later rushed to England to be with his father, her lover of four years, Louis de Narbonne.

Narbonne had not been waiting for her. Devastated by the news of Louis XVI's execution, he believed that he had betrayed the royalist cause by not dying at the king's side; he had little emotional energy left to devote to the woman who had persuaded him to change his political allegiances when they fell in love. The path of their affair, conceived at the start of the revolution, had followed its course from exhilarated optimism through passion and betrayal to resigned futility.

Germaine returned to Switzerland and to Monsieur de Staël in the early summer of 1793, each brought back to their marriage by necessity rather than affection. Germaine, her reputation destroyed by her public devotion to Narbonne, needed the respectability of a husband; Éric Magnus, ruinously bankrupt and incapable of economy, needed his father-in-law's millions.

Reluctantly reconciled to their rapprochement and excruciatingly aware that Narbonne no longer loved her, Germaine comforted herself by gathering together a group of friends at the house she rented near Coppet. 'Talking seemed everybody's first duty,' observed a visitor, describing the way Germaine and her endless stream of house-guests followed no daily routine, instead meeting at meals to discuss, argue, debate and be dazzled by their hostess. 'The only thing she feared was solitude, and boredom was the scourge of her life.'

For a long time she mourned Narbonne, her first adult love, and poured the pain she felt at the failure of their relationship into her work. *On the Influence of Passions on the Happiness of Individuals and of Nations*, begun in 1792 and published four years later, meditates with agonizing poignancy on the connection between passion and suffering and the impossibility for women – especially exceptional women – of achieving true happiness in both love and work. After Narbonne, as she put it, she had 'to begin life anew, but minus hope'.

Throughout the autumn and winter of 1793 Germaine embarked on an expensive programme of expatriation, helping more than twenty friends and friends of friends escape from Terror-struck France. She paid Swiss men and women, specially selected to resemble the people they were rescuing, to travel to Paris, where they would hand their passports over to the person waiting for them who would then cross the border into Switzerland with legitimate, but wrong, papers. The rescuers would leave France either on forged passports or claiming that they had lost their papers. If there was a problem the Swiss border guard could confirm their identities. 'There is, in the short span of existence, no greater chance of happiness than to save the life of an innocent man,' wrote Germaine at this time. It was a sentiment with which Thérésia Tallien would have whole-heartedly agreed.

Mathieu de Montmorency, one of the most distinguished liberals of Germaine's 1789 salon, was just one of the friends she rescued in this way. In the spring of 1794 he heard news from Paris that his brother had been guillotined; his wife and mother were still in prison. Gradually, Montmorency's views changed. The former duke who had fought under Lafayette in the United States and demanded the abolition of aristocratic distinctions in France had become a committed monarchist, finding refuge from his political regrets in devout Catholicism. Montmorency's wife and mother, saved by Robespierre's fall, joined Germaine's colony after their release from prison, soon after Narbonne's long-awaited arrival there. Her heartbreak healing,

Germaine had recently embarked on a liaison with a dashing Swedish count. Narbonne's pique did not prevent him resuming his former affair with Mathieu de Montmorency's mother. And so, notwithstanding the unusual circumstances, a strange harmony was restored to Germaine's unconventional household.

This harmony was upset with the arrival on the scene of the gangling, red-haired Swiss Benjamin Constant, who called at Coppet late one autumn evening in 1794 hoping to meet the celebrated Germaine. On hearing that she had just left, he galloped after her carriage. When he caught up with her, she invited him to continue his journey inside. Thus began a conversation that would last for fifteen years.

Brilliant, precocious, eccentric and unstable, Constant found in Germaine his intellectual match and fell in love with her at once. In his unfinished *roman à clef*, *Cécile*, he described her when they met – she was twenty-eight, he a year younger – as being neither tall nor slender, with an unattractive complexion and strong, irregular features, but 'the most beautiful eyes in the world, very beautiful arms, her hands a little too big but dazzlingly white, a superb bosom'. Despite her physical flaws, in animation she became 'irresistibly seductive', her 'very sweet voice' breaking endearingly when she was moved. 'Her gaiety had an indefinable charm, a kind of childlike goodwill which captivated the heart, establishing between her and those she was talking to a complete intimacy, which broke down all reserve, all mistrust, all those secret restrictions, those invisible barriers which nature puts up between all people'.

Disinclined to relinquish her Swedish count, Germaine admired Constant but was unimpressed by his efforts to make her love him. Benjamin, she wrote to her lover, was dying of love for her 'and inflicts his unhappiness on me in a way which removes his only charm – a very superior intelligence – and makes me in turn pity him, which in turn tires me'. If Count Ribbing heard that Constant

> had killed himself in the woods of Cèry, which he has just rented
> so that he can spend his life in my garden and in my courtyard, do
> not in truth think it to be my fault [she continued]. I have praised
> him sincerely for his work entitled *L'Esprit des religions*, in which
> he shows a talent like Montesquieu's, but [he] forgets that his looks

are an invincible obstacle, even for a heart that did not belong
to you.

This was harsh from a woman who was so insecure about her own
looks that she could not bear to hear other women described as ugly.

When Constant was not tormenting Germaine with staged suicide
bids (much as she herself had pushed Narbonne away with letters
declaring her own desire to die two years earlier), their extended,
impassioned conversations led to a productive working partnership.
She and Constant, by this stage both convinced republicans, influenced
and edited one another's thoughts as they debated France's future.

His influence on her thinking is evident in her December 1794
Reflections on Peace Addressed to Mr Pitt and to the French, in which she
argued for an acceptance of the Republic as a fait accompli and urged
its new rulers to create a constitution which would unite 'the possible
with the desirable'. Above all, she declared, peace must be achieved so
that France – and Europe – could be saved. 'If France crumbles, Europe
must crumble,' she wrote. 'As long as one persists in pitting foreigners
against them [the French] they will fight, they will win', and French
victories would spread revolution and unrest across the globe. She was
delighted to discover that Pitt's opponent, Charles Fox, twice quoted
from her pamphlet in the House of Commons in March 1795 when he
called for peace with France and stressed the need for morality in
international relations.

Given her obsession with French politics, and the changed situation
in Paris since 9 Thermidor, it is perhaps surprising that Germaine had
not rushed back to re-establish her salon there. Certainly she had
hopes of playing what her father worriedly called an 'honourable and
unexpected role' in public life, and had 'a secret plan to make yourself
talked about'. But in May 1794 her mother had died, unregretted by
Germaine but profoundly mourned by her father, and she was reluctant
to leave him behind alone and grieving.

Instructed by the Swedish government to open communications
with the new French regime, M. de Staël returned to Paris in January
1795. Against all his advice his wife, accompanied by her elder son
Auguste and Benjamin Constant, finally joined him there five months

later. On hearing the news that she had crossed the French border, Staël staggered into his secretary's room, gasping, 'Damnation! My wife is arriving!'

Germaine and Benjamin arrived in Paris five days after the Prairial risings to find the streets full of troops and the people sullen, resentful and starving. It was a strange, dislocated time. The fervour and focus of the Terror had been replaced by a strange lassitude, in which idealism had been replaced by bitter cynicism.

With both of their assets safely held abroad, for Germaine and Constant as for Thérésia, living was cheap. 'What things a man could do here with 200,000 francs in cash!' marvelled Benjamin. He took a large suite of rooms near the rue du Bac on the rue du Colombier, for which he paid one silver écu a month, while Germaine reinstalled herself at the Swedish embassy. They were the lucky ones. The once desirable neighbourhood of Saint-Germain was desolate and empty, its grand *hôtels* vacant, vandalized, pillaged, boarded up, posted with signs reading '*propriété nationale*' and daubed with revolutionary slogans.

Almost immediately Germaine's salon became a meeting-place for moderate political opinion, attracting many of the same people as La Chaumière but there to talk politics rather than do business. 'What do they do at Mme de Staël's?' asked a newspaper. '*On s'arrange*'– they place themselves, they improve themselves, they sort things out. Without disowning the friends of her caste, the royalist aristocracy, said Antoine Thibaudeau, Germaine was 'frankly republican'. Her salon in the rue du Bac was 'open to all parties' and its hostess was forgiven this impartiality 'by virtue of her sex, her wit, her talent, her principles'.

Germaine threw herself back into the social whirl. 'Like the muse of history beside a dancing-girl of Herculaneum', she visited her old friend Thérésia Tallien at La Chaumière, thanking her husband for escorting her out of Paris in September 1792. She was horrified by the *bals des victimes*, but enthusiastically embraced the *merveilleuses*' fashions: the following winter, having returned ahead of the new styles to Lausanne, she appeared in front of astonished guests at a ball in her honour clad in 'flesh-coloured pantaloons that clung very tightly to her skin, and covered only with gauze, like the ballerinas at the opera'. The Grecian look Thérésia had popularized did not suit everyone as well as it did her.

'We hear about nothing but Mme de Staël's dinners,' noted the *Gazette de France*. 'We have even noticed that as a result of those charming evenings some of the men of the day are better turned out.' Germaine had been compared to Circe, it continued, but unfairly. 'Circe transformed Ulysses's courtiers into bears [in fact pigs], whereas here Mme de Staël has almost managed to do the opposite.'

Bears had indeed changed into courtiers and courtiers into bears in her absence; Germaine found society much changed. Impoverished former aristocrats and returned exiles stood out despite the new plainness of their dress because of their innate elegance. Many of them were trying to recover lost fortunes, confiscated by the revolutionary government during the Terror. Germaine had her own case to pursue. Not only was Necker on the government's proscribed list of émigrés, but when he had resigned from the ministry and left France in 1790, as a gesture of confidence he left behind the two million francs – more than half his own fortune – that he had personally deposited in the state treasury; this she hoped to recover.

Surviving Jacobins, over-sensitive to the nuances of polite society and unsuccessfully emulating the manners of the old regime, were often surrounded by aristocratic women hoping to obtain their help on behalf of ruined sons, brothers and husbands, pouring 'graceful flattery' into their 'rough ears'. Those implicated in the Terror – like Tallien and Barras – excused themselves with inconceivable sophistry, arguing that they had sacrificed themselves for the public good or somehow been compelled to act as they did. Many admitted that they had failed to stand up against the horrors of the time simply out of fear. Little by little the new leaders of Thermidorian society were recreating a court with all its abuses, 'only taking great care to appropriate them [the abuses] to themselves'.

The new constitution was submitted to the Convention in June 1795, the month after Germaine's return; it was discussed as much in her drawing-room as in the halls of the Convention. All anybody on the streets wanted was a fresh start, free from the cursed legacies of both the ancien régime and the Terror, but the Convention decreed that two-thirds of the new Councils of Five Hundred and of the Elders would be chosen from among their number, rather than by general election. As Thibaudeau explained to Germaine, 'the principles of the revolution must be abandoned, but power must stay in the hands of the men who made it'. Their hopes of succeeding to government by legitimate channels dashed, the constitutional monarchists began to consider seizing power by force.

As the remaining Jacobin deputies mustered their opposition to the proposed Directory which they feared would be dominated by counterrevolutionaries, Tallien (by this time openly associated with the right wing but distrusted by them for his revolutionary past) was publicly called a Septembrist and Germaine was accused of politicking and royalism as well as cuckolding her husband, and asked to leave Paris. Although she agreed to leave the capital, she did not go far, staying at Mathieu de Montmorency's nearby château and continuing to involve herself in politics.

Knowing that the Jacobins would respond with brutal savagery to a monarchist rising, she warned her aristocratic friends to be careful. 'They hate you more [than the Convention] and have hated you for a longer time . . . I foresee only bloodshed and the blood of my friends shed in vain.' She counselled them not to try to force political change, but to wait until they could use legitimate channels to promote their interests. 'To speak of the sovereignty of the people is something quite new for you,' she told Thérésia's friend, the royalist journalist Charles de Lacretelle. 'You are fumbling with a language which they know better than you and which they created for their own use.'

Some listened to her advice, but others did not. In early October, after the election's unpopular results had been announced, with the incoming councillors heavily weighted to former deputies of the Convention, several moderate Paris wards declared themselves in a state of insurrection and sounded the call to arms. On 4 October, as the rain poured down outside, the Convention granted Paul Barras emergency command of the army, making him responsible for turning back the *muscadin*-dominated insurgents preparing to march on the Tuileries.

Barras's young protégé, Napoléon, was at the theatre when the note arrived commanding him to report for duty at once. According to Napoleonic legend, the unemployed general took his time to decide whether to join Barras or the forces opposing him. The day before he had told his friend Jean-Andoche Junot that if the rebels would make him their chief, he 'would see to it that the Tuileries would be invaded within two hours, and we would chase those miserable deputies out of there'.

By the next afternoon (13 Vendémiaire Year III), when the rain had finally stopped and the fair-weather rebels prepared themselves to attack, Bonaparte was ready for them. For the first time in revolutionary experience, a popular offensive was met with gunfire – Napoléon's celebrated 'whiff of grapeshot' that killed about three hundred rebels, dispersed the rest within a matter of minutes and confirmed the imminent ascendancy of Barras and the Directory.

Benjamin Constant and François de Pange, an old friend of Germaine's with whom she was at this time unrequitedly in love, were arrested on the day of the attempted coup and only released after Germaine appealed directly to Barras. Despite her efforts to warn her royalist friends against challenging the Convention and despite her avowedly republican opinions, so many of Germaine's friends were implicated in the Vendémiaire rising that she was labelled dangerous, 'a corrupter of all those deputies she invites to dinner' and ordered to leave France.

M. de Staël managed to obtain a suspension of the decree on condition he could persuade his wife to leave Paris voluntarily. She spent the autumn at a spa in Normandy and in early 1796, once her exile had been officially confirmed – M. de Staël may not have been entirely assiduous in his efforts to have it overturned – she went back to Switzerland after less than six months in her beloved Paris. She would not return for over a year.

On 3 November 1795 the Directory officially began and Paul Barras – the Don Juan of Jacobinism, as one of his many enemies dubbed him – became the most powerful man in France. He had informed the Convention before it dissolved that the man responsible for their deliverance was Napoléon Bonaparte, and requested that the young officer popularly known as General Vendémiaire replace him as Commander in Chief of the Army of the Interior.

The love affair engineered by Barras between Bonaparte and his mistress Rose de Beauharnais began at about the time of Vendémiaire. Rejected by Thérésia, Barras wrote, Napoléon began to pursue her friend, sending her cashmere shawls and diamonds purchased with his generous new salary as head of the French army. Each believed the other to have expectations of a fortune – expectations Barras, as confidant to both, did nothing to quell. Thirty-two-year-old Rose's past did not deter Napoléon; as he said to Barras, he preferred love 'ready-made'.

Napoléon had his own brusque methods of courtship. During the winter of 1795–6, magicians and fortune-tellers were all the rage. Thérésia and Rose both loved having their fortunes told, and Thérésia read the cards. One night at La Chaumière, Napoléon pretended to be a palm-reader. He took first Thérésia's and then several other people's hands, 'inventing a thousand follies'. When he came to Lazare Hoche, an ex-lover of Rose's and a military rival, his mood changed and he said curtly, 'General, you will die in your bed.' Less than two years later, his prediction had come true: Hoche, at only twenty-nine and one of the most talented and charismatic soldiers of his generation, had died of pneumonia.

Rose allowed Napoléon to seduce her, but, not in love, she was more wary about marriage. Eventually, counselled by Barras, she consented. The Scottish courtesan Grace Dalrymple Elliott, who also claimed to have rejected Napoléon, visited Rose while she was engaged, admiring an expensive blue and silver dress from England lying on her bed. 'How could you marry a man with such a horrid name?' asked Grace. 'Why, I thought that he might be of service to my children,' replied Rose. 'I am going to dine at the Directory by-and-by, and shall go part of the way with Bonaparte.'

Barras wanted to use Rose – or Joséphine, as Napoléon called her, and as she would become known to history – to manage his impetuous, besotted friend. He waited until they were engaged before arranging for the French army in Italy to be handed over to Napoléon's control. As Frénilly observed, Barras 'got rid of her by giving her the Italian army as a dowry'.

Joséphine would disappoint her former protector, her extravagance forcing her to greater and greater follies of debt, scandal and pleas for intercession on her behalf. Despite their past relationship and his continued closeness to her during this period, in his memoirs Barras savaged Joséphine, describing her as a money-crazed nymphomaniac who deceived all her lovers with other men and never loved 'except from motives of interest . . . the lewd Creole never lost sight of business'. Her charms, he said, were derived from artifice and cunning, and she was so jealous of Thérésia's beauty that 'they seemed, so to speak, to be waging a mutual war, even when they were actually sharing each other's triumphs'.

Joséphine married Napoléon on 9 March 1796. The bride, wearing a white muslin dress with a tricolour sash tied beneath her breasts, and a medallion Napoléon had given her engraved with the words, 'To Destiny', arrived at the dingy *mairie* on time at 8 p.m. The groom, distracted by his invasion plans for Italy, was three hours late. Jean-Lambert Tallien and Paul Barras, Thérésia's husband and her new lover, served as witnesses to the ceremony. Thérésia attended Joséphine; their bond was as close as ever. The complicated nature of their inter-twined relationships bothered neither of them. For the moment, their friendship ran deeper than love affairs could touch.

By early 1796 Thérésia was established as Barras's mistress. Although he was reticent about the exact nature of their relationship in his memoirs – and far more loyal to her than he was to Joséphine – they were frequently seen in public arm in arm. Thérésia made no secret of her disdain for Tallien and acted as Barras's hostess at lavish receptions in his official apartments in the Luxembourg and at the house parties he gave at his country house, Grosbois (once the property of one of Louis XVI's brothers), just outside Paris.

Thérésia was probably also taking other lovers, a circumstance which seems to have left the amoral Barras unmoved. 'It was a known fact that Mme Tallien braved her husband to a certain extent, when she wished to love another than him,' he wrote, commending her for preserving her decorum. Her liaisons, said Barras – and who knew better? – 'were for her genuine enjoyments to which she brought all the ardour and passion of her temperament'. In London, Georgiana Duchess of Devonshire's sister Lady Bessborough heard that Thérésia 'has not taken vows of chastity, but is not by any means as much the reverse as is pretended'.

Despite Barras's detachment, or perhaps because of her passionate temperament, theirs was still a tempestuous relationship. Barras also took other lovers – men as well as women, it was rumoured, though no evidence of his homosexuality survives. Observers reported frequent arguments and reconciliations. But their mutual dedication was unshakeable, utterly different in nature from Thérésia's relationship with her husband. She always concluded her letters to Barras with sentiments like, 'I love you and will love you all my life, with a devotion nothing can touch', and she meant it.

The intimacy of the little coterie at the heart of Directory life, centred on Thérésia, is revealed in the letters written to Joséphine by Napoléon from Italy in the spring of 1796. In the midst of white-hot protestations of adoration, in which Napoléon declared that he could not live without his Joséphine, he tortured himself by picturing her not thinking of him, imagining her with Thérésia, dining with Barras or playing with her bad-tempered pug. At the bottom of every letter were messages for her friends: remembrances to Barras, Thérésia, Tallien and often to their children. When seven-year-old Théodore de Fontenay started at boarding school Thérésia requested that he be allowed to share a room with Eugène de Beauharnais, Joséphine's son, and Jérôme Bonaparte, Napoléon's brother, so that he would feel at home.

Finally Napoléon persuaded Joséphine to join him on campaign. Thérésia invited her teenaged daughter, Hortense, to stay at La Chaumière while her mother was away, but Hortense was less malleable than her brother Eugène. As she put it, she 'stubbornly' refused, preferring to stay on at school for the holidays. Thérésia may not have realized it, but staying at La Chaumière would have ruined Hortense's reputation.

Joséphine's letters from Milan betray her homesickness. Despite the round of splendid parties held in her honour, she was bored to death, she told Thérésia; all she could do to cheer herself up was talk to other people about her '*chère Thérésita*' for whom she was busy hunting out the antiquities that she loved. 'Ah, if she were here, I would be more happy,' she continued, asking for news of home, of Tallien, of Barras and of the children, especially her two-year-old god-daughter Rose-Thermidor, and lamenting her foolishness in marrying Napoléon. If it were not for him, she would still be Thérésia's 'dear little mother', Joséphine wrote, referring to their ten-year age gap, and sending her '*mille baisers bien tendres*'. She sent a bolt of crêpe and a couple of straw hats back to Thérésia, some coral for Rose-Thermidor and cheeses for Tallien's breakfast; she told Thérésia how happy she was to have received a letter from Barras, whom she adored.

To outside eyes, the almost incestuous nature of this dense web of relationships at the centre of the new government was evidence of its fundamental corruption, and Thérésia became the focus of a swelling tide of censure. Napoléon's friend Junot described leaving Barras's apartments in the Luxembourg, while Napoléon was away winning battle after battle in Italy, with Joséphine on one arm and Thérésia on the other. Hordes of people pressed in to stare, pointing Joséphine out as 'Notre Dame des Victoires' – 'and see who is on the other side of the officer; – that is Notre Dame de Septembre!'

The press, too, for so long her champions, began to turn against Thérésia. In the spring of 1796 the *Tableau de Paris*, sarcastically listing her accomplishments, marvelled at how 'a woman of so many talents has found the secret of boring all the world!' At the same time, across the Channel, Thérésia's exotic beauty was transformed beneath James Gillray's biting pen into something altogether more coarse, reflecting the racism of the day, with thick frizzy hair and African features. Some years later, satirizing Napoléon's rise to power, Gillray portrayed Thérésia and Joséphine dancing naked and bejewelled for a sozzled Barras while Napoléon peeped hungrily out from behind a curtain.

Thérésia's evident adultery and her suspected promiscuity gave the press and the public ample scope for criticism. Early one morning, returning home alone from a ball, her dark red coach was attacked by thieves. An admirer who was following her chased them away. 'Moved to tears at this proof of the young man's solicitude for her welfare,' Thérésia 'insisted on his driving home with her', reported the *Petite Poste*, adding that her cavalier did not leave La Chaumière until the next afternoon. 'Her humanity is so general that she is now as unwilling that any man shd pine away in an hopeless passion for her, as she was anxious to save those persons who under Robespierre's reign were destined for the guillotine,' wrote one visitor to Paris. When she walked out in public, people stuck signs to her back reading '*Propriété Nationale*' or '*Res Publica*' [literally, 'public thing']. 'They begin to make so many jokes about her that she is quite to be pitied.' Confronted by rude and staring crowds, Thérésia maintained an extraordinarily dignified imperturbability.

Without naming her friend, even Germaine – one of the women to whom Thérésia attributed her initial fall from virtue before the revolution, and herself a notorious adulteress – bemoaned the erosion of manners and respect in Directory society. 'How shall a pure and proud model of woman be found in a country where social relations are not guarded by the most vigorous propriety?' she asked. In a republic, where distinctions between people are based solely on personal qualities, she argued, both men and women ought to be doubly scrupulous about their behaviour.

But despite the general denigration of her actions, Thérésia remained the most celebrated woman in Paris. She exemplified her age. When Lord Granville Leveson Gower arrived from London as part of a peace mission in October 1796 he told his mistress, Lady Bessborough, that Paris was 'by far the most profligate place I ever set my foot in; there does not appear to be a remnant of any thing like virtue or principle'. All Lady Bessborough wanted to hear about was Thérésia Tallien: what she looked like, what she wore, how she behaved. Gower confirmed that she and Joséphine were 'the only women much admired at Paris', and added that his best chance of seeing them was at one of the public balls. Thérésia's dresses all came from London, Gower reported, and he ordered a wig for his beloved from her wigmaker.

Thérésia's perceived depravity mirrored the lavish dissolution of the society that both reviled and adored her. The Directory was a period of corruption and lassitude, its rule, in Tocqueville's words, 'nothing but anarchy tempered by violence'. The men who controlled its administration were 'second-rate revolutionaries' who occupied the government, but did not govern. Helen Williams said that some of them were former Jacobins who had sacrificed their principles for power, others were simply speculators and gamblers, while most were 'indifferents, who, from a sort of benevolence of temperament generally voted with the moderate side of the house' but who, when their stomachs started rumbling, would abandon the debates on which the salvation of their country hung, throw off their official robes, 'and the first sound they utter is *soupe à la tartare*'.

Only the army (and the men who supplied it), sweeping to victory under Napoléon's command, was thriving. Clumsy, inept laws were decreed and ignored by people who lacked the strength either to obey or to resist them. In February 1796 the *assignats*, the paper money on which the economy officially depended, were worth no more than they cost to print. The Directory government spent more time debating what its official costumes should be than in seeking to engage the exhausted, cynical public with their regime.

It was not until 1798 that the councillors and deputies began wearing their long-awaited uniforms, flowing red toga-style capes, 'like tragedy heroes', over blue coats, tricolour sashes and dramatically plumed hats. Since a man's politics were thought to be revealed in his dress and demeanour, it was hoped that fitting out the nation's leaders in classical dress would mould them into ideal classical rulers. But inspired by the same impulse to fancy dress that motivated Thérésia and the *merveilleuses*, the gilt-trimmed costumes' very theatricality, according to one onlooker, prevented them from being 'seriously dignified and truly imposing'. Barras, tall, elegant and deadpan, was one of the few men it suited – but he preferred to wear his own clothes.

Germaine de Staël, who had spent most of 1796 with her father at Coppet in Switzerland, talking, writing, finally falling in love with Benjamin Constant, and trying in vain to persuade the French government that she was a French citizen and thus could not be prevented from returning to the country of her birth – they countered that she was the daughter of one foreigner and the wife of another – arrived back in Paris in May 1797. She was eight months pregnant.

Although her husband was no longer Swedish ambassador, Germaine set up house once again in the rue du Bac, where she gave birth to a daughter with Benjamin's flame-red hair. Within a week of her accouchement she was sending out invitations to dinner.

'I still love this country,' she had written to a cousin, when she crossed the border into France; she felt she had come home. 'We have hardly any security, no money at all, and much discomfort. But there is meaning in the very air one breathes, there is energy, there is a kind of welcome from people known and unknown which one feels in one's own country.' Germaine found in France, she said, 'more space to live in, less limited thinking even among common people; a sweeter air, what can I say?'

Recent elections had brought into the Directory, for the first time, a majority of constitutional monarchists. People began to parade their royalist sympathies openly, wearing black collars on their coats as coded mourning for Louis XVI or clothes embroidered with fleurs-de-lis or white plumes; ladies' fans bore the spangled motto *'Vive le roi!'* Returned émigrés made a point of speaking English to show that they had spent the revolutionary years across the Channel, even though most had not bothered to learn the language while they were there. 'When in public we even made a rather amusing pretence of poverty, eating for instance, out of *culs noirs*, as though china were too costly. It was the height of good manners to be ruined, to have been suspected, persecuted, and above all, imprisoned,' remembered Auguste François de Frénilly. 'People greatly regretted that they had not been guillotined, but said they were to have been the day after or two days after the 9th of Thermidor.' Even Barras was said to be prouder of his pre-revolutionary title of viscount than of being a Director of the new Republic.

In late 1796 another former aristocrat, Talleyrand, had returned to France from the United States, where he had spent some time with Lucy de la Tour du Pin and her family on their homestead in upstate

New York. Germaine, who had been instrumental in having his name struck off the list of émigrés barred from returning to France, was delighted to be reunited with her old friend. She and Thérésia Tallien set about introducing him to Directory society, recommending him to Barras as a man – a republican – of talent and diplomacy. 'No man,' said Talleyrand, 'could equal a woman in serving the interests of a friend or lover.' Barras appointed him Minister for Foreign Affairs the following July, allowing Benjamin Constant (as a compliment to Germaine) to tell him of his new post. While they drove to the Luxembourg, so that Talleyrand could thank Barras for the appointment, Talleyrand could talk of nothing but the vast fortune he hoped to make.

Germaine continued what Joseph Fouché, once Barras and Tallien's accomplice in Robespierre's fall and soon to become Napoléon's chief of police, called her 'intriguing' throughout the spring and summer of 1797. She was trusted by neither side. 'Who has asked you to meddle in matters that are of no concern to you?' demanded a royalist newspaper. 'Miserable hermaphrodite that you are, your sole ambition in uniting the two sexes in your person is to dishonour them both at once!'

Despite the prominent social and cultural role seized by women like Thérésia during the Directory, as this attack on Germaine shows the misogyny that had characterized the early revolutionaries was still very much alive; it was one of the few attitudes shared by the Robespierrists of 1793–4 and the Directory government. In 1795, echoing Antoine Saint-Just's views on female education, the Committee of State Education was hearing suggestions that schoolgirls should spend their time washing their brothers' shirts. A report the following year confirmed that women's principal role was that of mother. Female sexual desire was thus not only useless but dangerous, since it interfered with the fulfilment of their sole obligation to society.

Although Barras had praised Thérésia's easy, uninhibited sexual nature he did not want to see women stepping out of a purely domestic role; part of his criticism of Joséphine stemmed from his disapproval of her using sex for gain. 'Far from contesting the superior merit women may have displayed in the various ranks of society,' he wrote in his memoirs, describing how he had pointedly declined an invitation from Manon Roland to dine at the Ministry of the Interior in 1792, 'I have rarely found that their happiness or that of others was in any way bettered by their unsexing themselves and taking upon themselves men's duties.'

During the Directory, as with the dissolute Barras, women were viewed merely as sensual creatures of emotion and superficiality. Only a few lonely voices dared contradict the prevailing view. Louis Theremin argued in 1798 that women had been 'entirely neglected' by the revolution, either because their indifference had been assumed or because they were thought to be unworthy of participating in it. Since the revolution, lamented Germaine, 'men had found it politically and morally useful to reduce women to the most absurd mediocrity'. Theremin suggested that if women were given a stake in the new regime they might have an interest in its survival.

Louis-Sébastien Mercier condescendingly held that the reason women were supporting the counterrevolution was because, loving baubles like magpies, they had been distressed to see their lovers' epaulettes, ribbons and robes swept away by the political changes. When 'they perceived that there was something severe and serious in a revolution,' he concluded, 'they turned away from it'.

One female figure had quite literally turned away. In September 1792, the figure of Liberty chosen for the new national seal had stood proud and direct, facing towards the viewer with her pike at the ready in her hand. The Directory's seal, by contrast, showed her turned away from the viewer, seated and pensive, a figure not of youth, courage and vigour but of matronly contemplation, even remorse.

Thérésia, Joséphine and the *merveilleuses* all personified the Directory view of femininity – indeed, they surpassed it. Despite their tender hearts and determined frivolity, their awareness of their beauty and its worth, of the power of public interest in their private lives, was astonishingly modern. Through their creative patronage of art, architecture and design they shaped the image of the Directory that survives to this day, moulding an entire aesthetic movement. The column inches devoted to the ever-changing extremes of fashion during this time were just one indication of the contemporary obsession with women and their place in society.

Some onlookers saw this as a positive development – 'Never have women occupied public opinion in a similar fashion; never have they influenced affairs in so apparent a manner,' wrote one journalist – but others disagreed. 'The Pompadours, the Dubarris [sic], the Antoinettes return to life, and they are the ones who govern,' raged the *Tribun du Peuple*, 'and who kill your revolution.'

Cultured, exclusive courtesans in the tradition of Mme de Pompadour and Mme du Barry had returned to high society; indeed many saw Thérésia herself as no more than a high-class prostitute. She played on these assumptions, dressing for parties as Aspasia, the Greek courtesan who became Pericles' consort. Barras also compared his mistress to the hetaerae of ancient Greece. When he saw Thérésia and Talleyrand tête-à-tête at the Luxembourg, he called her his 'beautiful Athenian' and asked her if she wanted to govern like a second Aspasia.

Such comparisons were not always complimentary. A pamphlet addressed 'to the greatest whore in Paris' reviled Thérésia for her 'revolting' voluptuousness, her impudence and her decadence. 'Your whims and your tastes are more closely observed than the decrees of the government,' stormed the anonymous author, who signed himself Beelzebub, demanding to know who paid for her jewels and accusing her of corrupting innocent young men. The prostitutes on the streets were angels compared to her, he continued, and Thérésia set them their example. Lower-class whores flooded Paris's streets in the late 1790s. They teemed beneath the arcades of the Palais Royal among the ice-sellers, pickpockets and lottery-ticket vendors – looking like cheap versions of Thérésia and her friends with their 'breasts uncovered, heads tossing, colour high on their cheeks, and eyes as bold as their hands' – whispering obscenities to male passers-by.

The prostitutes interrogated by the police were on average in their early twenties and came mostly from the provinces. They had had no one to fall back on in Paris when they lost their position in a household or were left pregnant by a lover who failed to marry them as he had promised. Driven on to the streets because they could not afford to buy food or had a baby to feed, they lived desperate, itinerant lives, sleeping where they could find a bed, stealing handkerchiefs or a loaf of bread if an opportunity arose, and always hungry. Their experiences underlined the vulnerability of women in revolutionary France and the hazards and insecurity facing them in a society that valued them so little.

It was these frightened, lonely young women who drove up the suicide rates. Richard Cobb gives the example of Louise-Émilie-Charlotte Harmond, aged fourteen, whose body was fished out of the Seine at Sèvres in July 1799. The description of the clothes she was wearing when she died survives in poignant detail: the embroidered muslin dress over a toile slip stitched with her initials, a pair of dirty cotton stockings and shoes, a scarf of blue and white striped silk around her neck, and a tiny piece of soap wrapped in chiffon.

All through the spring and summer of 1797, émigrés streamed back into Paris and the royalists mustered their strength. Lucy de la Tour du Pin and her husband came back from their farm in the United States hoping to recover some of their lost fortune. One new way of making money was surprising and unwelcome to her: when she landed in France Lucy sent for a hairdresser, who astonished her by offering her 200 francs for her long fair hair. The blond wigs popularized by Thérésia were still the height of fashion.

One of Lucy's first calls was to La Chaumière to thank Thérésia, to whom she owed her escape from Bordeaux. Thérésia, who was just pregnant (probably with Barras's child), wept as she told Lucy how unhappy she was with Tallien, describing what she called his unreasonable suspicions, the speed with which he took offence and how he threatened to kill her when he was jealous. The scenes she had enjoyed provoking in Bordeaux had acquired a dark new import; on one occasion, when she arrived home late after a party, she had been forced to flee the house as he loaded his pistol. That March, she had instituted divorce proceedings against him on the grounds of irreconcilable differences but, persuaded out of it by her friends and hoping they might still make peace, she abandoned them soon afterwards.

Other observers confirm that Thérésia was, during this period, trying in vain to justify why she had felt obliged to marry Tallien in the first place, saying that she had never loved him but had sacrificed herself 'to his wishes in order to spare the blood of many who were likely to be victims of the then established tyranny'. As Lucy was leaving La Chaumière, Tallien arrived. Frostily, she thanked him for the favour he had performed for her in Bordeaux and he replied that she could always count on him.

The elections had brought a majority of moderate royalists into the two houses of the Directory in April 1797, and only the Directors themselves (three of the five, Barras, Louis La Révellière and Jean-François Reubell, were committed republicans) stood between them and control of a France longing for a new regime of peace and stability. Lucy was amazed to see how indiscreetly confident her former friends were, loudly discussing their hopes and plans in front of servants and republican deputies. When she told them she was sure Talleyrand knew of every plot they were hatching, they laughed at her. Nearly every day she saw Germaine, whom she described at this time as 'all powerful'.

Over the summer Barras, supported by his two fellow-Directors, Talleyrand, the republican deputies and the army, decided that military action was the only means by which he could safeguard the Republic and his own power. In early September, as the streets filled with soldiers and the air of crisis intensified, Barras advised Thérésia, who was seven months pregnant with his child, to leave Paris for a few days. On the night of 3 September, Barras dined with Talleyrand, Germaine and Benjamin Constant, while outside the army, commanded by one of Napoléon's officers, peacefully occupied the city. Paris awoke the next day (18 Fructidor Year V) to discover its walls plastered with justifications of the coup and the news that anyone wishing to restore the monarchy or the 1793 constitution would be shot without trial.

About midday Lucy de la Tour du Pin and a friend, dressed inconspicuously, set out through streets full of soldiers to call on Germaine and find out what was happening. They were forced to take a circuitous route, as so many roads were blocked, and as they walked they were terrified by a 'number of those horrible women who appear only during revolutions or disorders, [and who] began insulting us, shouting "Down with the royalists"'. Much shaken, they arrived at the rue du Bac to find Germaine and Constant arguing about the inevitability of the coup and its possible repercussions.

Germaine's fears about the consequences of the coup were realized the following day when Barras and the Directors re-established their control over the dispirited and passive deputies. Prominent royalists were deported; press censorship was re-imposed; the spring elections were proclaimed invalid; and, on pain of death, refractory priests and returned émigrés were ordered to leave Paris within twenty-four hours and France within a week. The Republic's triumph had come at a price. Individual liberties and the principles of liberalism had been sacrificed, and Napoléon's support for the coup had left the government dangerously in his debt. As Barras had predicted earlier in 1797, 'we will all perish by the generals'.

Lucy de la Tour du Pin and her family were once again trapped without passports in a France hostile to their cause. Her husband approached Talleyrand who, despite the fact that he had spent the day of the coup playing whist, was too preoccupied by his own future to help anyone else. Remembering his previous helpfulness, Lucy went to see Tallien, who drew up a statement outlining their circumstances and delivered it by hand to the Minister of Police, returning it with his signature and recommendation to her after several anxious hours and with a note apologizing for not having been able to do more. 'The end of the letter,' she wrote, 'might have been construed to mean: "I wish you a good journey."'

Given the state of his marriage and the damage that helping royalists would have done to his shattered political career, it is surprising that Tallien was so ready once again to help his wife's aristocratic friends, but he seldom refused an appeal to his heart. Victorine de Chastenay was another desperate young woman who asked for Tallien's assurance after Fructidor and found him a gentle, obliging, trustworthy man – a far cry from the violent, gun-brandishing monster depicted by his unhappy wife or the self-serving hypocrite painted by his political enemies.

After Fructidor, Germaine fell once again under official suspicion. Extremists of both sides portrayed her as an intriguer and a threat to political stability. Despite her republicanism, her closeness to Talleyrand

and Barras and the fact that her salon had been at the centre of the government's plans to crush the counterrevolution, she continued to make every effort to help and protect her royalist friends, calling it a woman's duty to come to the aid of her friends whatever their opinions, and even enlisting Thérésia's help in obtaining the release of Charles de Lacretelle and a friend of his. Talleyrand observed with his customary cynicism that Germaine enjoyed throwing people overboard simply to have the pleasure of fishing them out of the water again. Only Barras's generous arguments on her behalf prevented her arrest.

Fresh from his victorious campaign in Italy, three months after Fructidor Napoléon returned to Paris a conquering hero, clothed like a wolf in the guise of a man of peace and humility. He pretended to be prouder of honours such as his election to the newly created academic Institute of France than of his military triumphs. Affectedly republican, he made a point, at a time when using '*Citoyen*' as a form of address had fallen into disuse, of continuing to address people thus. The general rejected the ostentatious fancy dress so beloved of the period, wearing austere, modest clothes, appearing on even the grandest of occasions in a plain grey greatcoat. His carriage, drawn by just two horses, was conspicuously unadorned.

Germaine was as enthralled by Bonaparte as was the rest of France. She spoke the words on everyone's lips when she told a friend in July that he was 'the best republican in France, the most-freedom loving of Frenchmen' – the man who could save France from itself. His 'tone of noble moderation', she said, inspired confidence: 'in those days, the warrior spoke like a judge, while the judges used the language of military violence'. Having received no reply to the letters of admiration with which she had already bombarded Napoléon, apparently urging him to discard his 'insignificant' wife in her favour, she begged Talleyrand to allow her to be present when her hero made his first official call at his ministry on 6 December.

Still exhausted from his campaign and the journey back to Paris, a sallow Napoléon arrived at Talleyrand's offices punctually at 11 o'clock. Germaine had been waiting there for an hour. For once, she was overwhelmed: the 'confusion of admiration' made her uncharacteristically speechless at first, and she found she had difficulty breathing when faced with those cold, marble eyes. But Napoléon 'bestowed very little attention upon her', as Talleyrand noted; he was more interested in meeting Talleyrand himself, to whose flattering letters he *had* been replying.

Subsequent encounters did not lessen Napoléon's fearsomeness. Germaine, admitting that he 'constantly' intimidated her, sensed he was impervious to her charms. 'I had a confused feeling that no emotion of the heart' – by extension, Germaine herself, the embodiment of passion – 'could act upon him'. He was, she felt, 'not like a creature of our species': 'his face expressed a sort of casual curiosity about all those human shapes he planned to bring into subjection as soon as he had the power to do so'.

Still she persevered in the belief that he would one day recognize her worth, continuing to send him letters that he did not read and attempting to engage him in debate. One day, calling on him unannounced, she was told that the general was in the bath. To Napoléon's horror, she tried to push her way upstairs, exclaiming, 'Genius has no sex!' Joséphine's daughter Hortense said that Germaine pestered Napoléon so much during this period 'that he did not, and perhaps could not, sufficiently try to hide his annoyance'.

On 10 December a reception was held for Napoléon in the courtyard of the Luxembourg palace. When his distinctively simple carriage drew up, the crowds outside cried, *'Vive la République!'* and *'Vive Napoléon!'* Talleyrand introduced the victor of Austria and Italy to the audience of dignitaries gathered in the courtyard as the 'son and hero of the Revolution … Far from fearing what some would call his ambition, I feel that the time will come perhaps when we must tear him away from his studious retreat.' After Talleyrand's hymn of praise, Napoléon allowed himself to be persuaded, with a great show of modesty, to speak a few terse words.

Talleyrand also gave a magnificent, old-fashioned ball in Joséphine's honour on 3 January that heralded the return to Parisian society of the spirit of the ancien régime. As at Versailles, only the ladies were seated at dinner; they were personally served by the male guests, who stood behind their chairs. The treasures Napoléon had looted in Italy were on prominent display. A daring, delicious new dance imported from Germany, the waltz, was danced in Paris for the first time that night.

After dinner Germaine, undeterred as ever, accosted Napoléon and asked him which woman he loved most. 'Madame, I love my own,' he replied stiffly. But which did he most admire? she persisted. 'The one best able to look after her household,' he said. Well, who was the greatest woman in history? 'The one, Madame, who has had the greatest number of children,' he replied, turning on his heel and leaving her, taken aback, to gasp, 'Extraordinary man!' at the small crowd of onlookers who had gathered to gape at the encounter.

It is unlikely that Thérésia attended Talleyrand's ball because she had recently given birth to a stillborn baby, probably Barras's, and had retreated at his suggestion to Grosbois to recuperate. An English visitor saw her at another party later in the month, looking, despite the pearls and diamonds in her hair, embattled, tired and preoccupied. Even republican wives disdained to visit her, he reported, and she was frequently exposed to unpleasant scenes and confrontations.

Recognizing that the time was not yet ripe for a seizure of power, Napoléon kicked his heels in Paris in the early months of 1798. When Talleyrand suggested that he invade Egypt, cutting off British routes to India and establishing a base from which to harry them in the Mediterranean, he adopted the idea enthusiastically. Between them, in March, they convinced a reluctant Directory to approve their notion, and secret plans were put in place for the campaign. The ambitious expedition was to be funded by annexing Switzerland and its rich resources of gold. Germaine managed to get an appointment with Napoléon to try to dissuade him from invading, but as ever with him her impassioned appeals fell on deaf ears. He would only repeat to her that the Swiss – who had been the happy citizens of a thriving republic for centuries – needed 'political rights'.

Germaine returned to Coppet in time to be by her father's side as they watched the French troops marching into Switzerland, listening to the army's drums sounding out along the tranquil shores of Lake Geneva. By special order of the Directory, Necker was left undisturbed. For Germaine, the only positive consequence of the invasion was that Swiss citizens were automatically granted French citizenship. Against her better judgement, her dreams of officially belonging to France had finally been realized.

Napoléon left France in May, mystery swirling around him like dust. Jean-Lambert Tallien followed a few weeks later. Tallien had lost his seat in the Council of Five Hundred and hoped, on foreign fields, to rebuild his career. The night before his departure, Victorine de Chastenay saw him at Barras's, where he still came, she said, 'with an appearance of friendship – but bitterness in his soul'. She had few hopes for her friend's future; life in a camp *'sans épaulettes'* would not be easy.

Tallien wanted a fresh start. The six years he had spent in the service of his country, he told his mother before leaving, had brought him nothing but ingratitude. Intriguers and rogues were the only people who flourished in times such as theirs, but he would never be either. He assured her that he would find friends among Napoléon's companions; he intended to establish himself in the world not only for his own sake but also for his children's. Circumstances demanded this heart-breaking separation from all he held dear, he said, but he was resolved to bear it and return to the bosom of his family a changed man in two years' time.

As his letter to his mother showed, Tallien still hoped that he and Thérésia had a future together. After the catastrophic French defeat by the British under Nelson at the battle of the Nile on 1 August, which he watched from the shore, Tallien wrote to his wife. He did not know, he said, whether she had yet received his previous four letters. Life in Egypt was hard, he told her: far from home, deprived of water, food and sleep, tormented by insects of all descriptions, of the forty thousand Frenchmen there were not four who did not wish themselves elsewhere. As for him, he wrote, although he had their little dog Minerve with him, he missed *'notre charmante Chaumière'* twenty times a day. 'Farewell, my good Thérésia, the tears drench my letter,' he concluded. 'The memories of your goodness, of your love, the hopes of finding you again still affectionate and faithful, of embracing my dear daughter, are the only things that sustain the unfortunate Tallien.'

The letter never reached Thérésia; it was intercepted by the British fleet. The following spring she began an affair with the young banker Gabriel Ouvrard, who had made his fortune in paper and then in supplying the French army and navy. They had known each other since the first careless days at La Chaumière. Barras stood aside with no ill-will, having them to stay at Grosbois together. In Feburary 1799, according to Thérésia, Ouvrard took her to a beautifully fitted house on the rue de Babylone and handed her the keys; she said that he had bought it for her because she had helped him so much in his work. In fact it was Barras who had paid for the house. Apparently unaware of his wife's new domestic arrangements, Tallien would remain in Egypt for three years.

He was away almost as long as Germaine, who stayed at Coppet with her father throughout the spring of 1798, to the delight of the republican press. 'The baroness among baronesses, the pearl of her sex, the divinity of oligarchs, the favourite of the God of Constancy, the protectress of the *émigrés*, in a word, the universal woman has at last left France,' hissed the journal *Amis des Lois*. 'Hapless Frenchmen, you will not see her again.'

Over the next eighteen months Germaine made regular experimental forays back to Paris, retreating at hints from the police or warnings from friends, and never able to re-establish herself securely in France because the government made it clear to her that she was not welcome there. Her 'intriguing' was seen as perfidious and her writings incendiary. Hell, she wrote, began to appear to her 'in the shape of exile'.

ICÔNE

Juliette Récamier

A serene light on a stormy scene.
FRANÇOIS-RENÉ DE CHATEAUBRIAND

A masked ball

In June 1796, Benjamin Constant's cousin Charles met Thérésia Tallien for the first time. Excitedly, he reported back that the most celebrated woman in Paris was 'brilliant with youth and health'. She was wearing a dress tied beneath the breasts with a green and orange ribbon, and her necklace of enormous amber beads made it look as if she really had 'a huge heart of gold'. In a clear voice vibrating with emotion, she regaled the gathering with what had clearly become her party piece, recounting her dreadful experiences during the Terror: her arrest at Versailles, being held for a day with nothing to eat or drink, forced to strip in front of eight Guardsmen and locked for twenty-five days in solitary confinement.

Two months later, as their friendship deepened, Thérésia showed Charles the letters she had written Tallien from prison. Constant, who found her beautiful and charming in person, was amazed to discover, on reading the letters, that they were vulgar, written in bad style and taste: 'she speaks of her *caboche* [thick skull, noddle], her *carcasse*, she says *gibier de guillotine* [guillotine fodder], she describes her guards, she remembers so crudely the moments spent in Tallien's arms.' Seductive but unestimable, Constant said, Thérésia reminded him of Mme du Barry; but asked how she could have been otherwise, given the course her life had taken and the adulation that had been lavished upon her since her teens. He reported that she had been supplanted as the uncrowned queen of Directory society by the eighteen-year-old Juliette Récamier. Thérésia had, he said in November 1796, 'reigned in peace until Juliette appeared'.

Thérésia's successor was the chaste beauty who had been married at fifteen, at the height of the Terror, to the forty-one-year-old financier

Jacques-Rose Récamier. Nothing in their conduct towards one another indicated that their relationship was anything but filial. While Juliette and her mother lived just outside Paris in the château de Clichy and her husband dined with them every day, he spent every night in town; his morals were said to be old-fashioned, probably a euphemism for keeping a mistress. Their classical hunting-lodge at Clichy, on the banks of the Seine near Neuilly, was said to have been built by Louis XV for one of his mistresses.

From the moment she emerged on to the Parisian scene, Juliette was adored. Joséphine, in particular, seems to have made a point of including her in the round of parties and gossip that fuelled Directory society. Writing to Talleyrand in the spring of 1796 about the dashing hussar Hippolyte Charles, with whom she was falling in love, Joséphine declared that Thérésia, Fortunée Hamelin and Juliette had all lost heir heads over him. The following month Juliette formed part of a tableau alongside Joséphine and Thérésia at a reception at the Luxembourg celebrating Napoléon's victories in Italy. She was seen during this period going up to Barras's apartments with Joséphine and Thérésia.

Afterwards, Juliette and Thérésia both played down their friendship but a portrait of the two women, Juliette leaning her head on Thérésia's shoulder, reveals their early intimacy. Certainly in 1796 and 1797 they moved in the same circles, attended the same balls, watched the same plays, were dressed by the same couturiers and admired by the same men.

Their subsequent rift, if rift there was, may have been caused by Thérésia's resentment of her younger rival's success. Charles Constant describes her on one occasion, threatened by Juliette's presence, throwing off her cashmere shawl and standing up to display 'her fine figure, her bare arms, her grace, the beauties of every kind which so few other women possess in so perfect a degree'. Juliette, 'with her quiet dress and simple grace', praised Thérésia and made no attempt to cast her 'splendours in the shade' – a response potentially more galling than any other.

Gossip columns pictured Thérésia criticizing the young woman. 'Are not her shoulders very large, her head too long, and her neck too short? Who does not remark that her lips are too thin, her teeth uneven, her fingers too small, and her feet too broad? Does not she walk as if she were running errands? And does she not still look like a mantua-maker?' she was imagined to have said. 'Her eyelids are surely painted, and the colour of her cheeks artificial; and when she speaks, what a disagreeable accent, what antiquated words, and what common and ridiculous expressions!'

Thérésia's defenders held that the fault was Juliette's. Many years later, when both women had died, Juliette's niece Amélie Lenormant published a memoir of her life. Soon afterwards, a friend of Thérésia's sent some of her letters to the author Arsène Houssaye, proposing her as a suitable subject with the words: 'Avenge thus the arrogance of this scornful beauty'. Apparently Juliette had lorded it over Thérésia and, when Thérésia was rejected by imperial society, pretended that they had never known one another. No record of Juliette's behaviour elsewhere makes this self-serving meanness sound likely, although her niece, in an effort to erase any hint of scandal from Juliette's life – not that there was much – insisted that she had never been a *merveilleuse* and specifically denied any acquaintance with Mme Tallien and her friends.

By late 1797, the careless gaiety that had characterized the first years following Robespierre's fall – and characterized Thérésia herself, the symbol of that period – had faded, although its mood of decadent extravagance was more pervasive than ever. The French needed a new idol, free from any taint of revolutionary violence, cynicism or exploitation. The virginal Juliette Récamier, whose burgeoning celebrity was almost a reproach to Thérésia, seemed created to fill this role.

Where Juliette differentiated herself from the *merveilleuses* was her real but deliberately nurtured image of modest chastity. She may have formed part of Thérésia's circle, but she remained untouched by the air of corruption and debauchery that clung to her friends. She was, said Mme de Boigne, 'the perfect woman', with all the charms, virtues and frailties that implied. Sweet-natured and high-minded, her appeal lay more in the passive qualities of reflecting her friends' interests and talents than in demonstrating her own. Her detractors thought her coquettish, indolent and proud, with the air of a convent girl; her admirers praised her quiet piety, her charitable works, her loyalty to her friends, her generosity and flair as a hostess and her overwhelming desire to please, which grew not out of the wish to be admired (perhaps another tacit reproach to Thérésia) but out of the wish to be loved.

Juliette's beauty, according to Récamier's nephew, 'was the least of her gifts' but it was no insignificant thing. Having heard of this paragon, Mme de Boigne was surprised that she hardly noticed her when she first saw her; then she looked again and found that she was 'wholly beautiful', with looks that appeared 'to greater and greater advantage every time she was seen'.

Tall and slim, radiantly pale, Juliette had a delicate, open face bare of makeup. Her looks were enhanced by her self-consciously austere style, an intentional reflection of her gentle serenity. She wore only white dresses – adding fuel to the rumours of her virginity – gathered beneath the bosom with plain blue, black or gold belts, no jewels except pearls – more symbols of purity – and her hair was simply drawn up with a thin ribbon in a tumble of chestnut curls.

One visitor, arriving in Paris at the height of Juliette's fame, expected to encounter 'a vain coquet, enveloped in clouds of incense, hardened by wealth, seeing and loving nothing in the world but herself; receiving homage as a duty with chilling pride'. Instead, he found her, in her unembellished white dress, 'like a violet in the grass': 'she seemed to blush at being so beauteous'. Other observers confirm that she 'seemed anxious to conceal her own attractions to enhance those of others'.

Despite her undoubted modesty, Juliette was very conscious of her powers of seduction. 'You intoxicate yourself with the perfumes that are burnt at your feet,' said one disconsolate devotee. Admirer after admirer, excited rather than discouraged by her notorious chastity, pursued her, and all were rejected with such warmth and graceful tact that they continued to adore her even when they knew there was no hope. She was made, said another, 'to electrify the world'.

Juliette both enjoyed and despised her celebrity, accepting the adulation with which she was showered as her due, somehow managing to encourage it without seeming to. She was fully aware of the effect she created, of 'the enthusiasm that I excited, the approval that my face obtained, the murmur of praise to be heard through the crowd' when she appeared. Her niece described Juliette standing up to get a better view of Napoléon as he finished his speech at the reception given in his honour at the Luxembourg in December 1797. Every head turned to look back at her; a rumble of appreciation swelled through the audience. For a moment it was she and not Napoléon on whom all eyes rested. He 'threw her a look of intolerable harshness' and Juliette sat back down.

Mme Lenormant makes out that this was the innocent Juliette's first foray into society, that no one in the audience would have known who she was; in fact, given the intimacy of Directory high society, she would have been familiar to most people there. Her standing up at such a crucial moment can only have been designed to draw attention to herself. This tension between reserve and display, between chastity and sensuality, was the essence of her appeal.

One of Juliette's first conquests was the ambitious, arrogant Lucien Bonaparte, six years Napoléon's junior. Tall and lanky, not handsome but appealing because of his classical republican idealism and his passion for government, Lucien had arrived in Paris on Napoléon's coat-tails, hoping to build a career and a fortune on the foundation of his brother's. Meeting Juliette in the summer of 1797, he fell deeply in love with her.

He began writing her poetic letters from 'Romeo', describing her arrival at a party with everyone clustering round her exclaiming at her beauty. All glances, he said, were her property when she appeared. 'At each of your movements, with each fold of your gown, it seemed as though flowers were opening.' Outwardly, Juliette met his passion with her usual cool serenity. Lucien told her that her immovable tranquillity was killing him, complaining that she could even make indifference charming. Inside, the sheltered girl was stirred. The 'idea of a man, entirely engrossed with me' had touched her; his agitation and despair had stimulated her imagination and excited her compassion.

Unmoved by her superficial life and her relationship with her husband, Juliette felt that her 'heart was made to love and to suffer ... As I loved nothing and only suffered from indifference, I considered that I was forgoing my destiny'. The ardent, romantic Lucien seemed to offer her a chance, for the first time, to feel. But when she discovered the scale of his ambition and the way he consoled himself for her lack with 'vulgar pleasures' – actresses and whores – she closed her heart to him and returned to her usual state of dreamy melancholy.

Juliette dealt with Lucien's unrequited adoration as she would deal with so many men in the coming years, with a combination of sympathy and negligence. 'Touched by the pain she had caused, sorry for the man's emotion,' she restored 'hope without being aware of it, merely by her pity, and [destroyed] it by her carelessness as soon as she had calmed the grief which had called forth this fleeting pity'. According to the critic Charles-Augustin de Sainte-Beuve, a friend, Juliette was a sorceress whose great talent lay in converting love into friendship, while leaving in the new association all the 'perfume' of the old.

It would take a woman, rather than a man, to raise her out of her apathy. In the autumn of 1798, Récamier arrived at Clichy with a woman unknown to Juliette and left them alone without introducing them, saying only that she had come to talk about the sale of a house. Her guest was eccentrically dressed, in a morning gown and a tiny hat laden with flowers; Juliette was 'struck by the beauty of her eyes and her expression'. When she began talking, saying how delighted she was finally to meet Juliette and mentioning her father, Necker, Juliette realized that the visitor was Germaine de Staël, who, despite her fear of exile, had ventured as close to Paris as her father's house at Saint-Ouen. Récamier had contacted her about buying one of Necker's properties, a house on the rue du Mont Blanc (now the rue de la Chaussée d'Antin) near where Thérésia had lived when she first came out of prison in the summer of 1794.

Juliette had read Germaine's *Letters on Jean-Jacques Rousseau*, and blushed to find herself in the presence of an author she admired so passionately. She was both intimidated and attracted by her, and shyly stammered out some compliments. Germaine, looking at her with friendly curiosity in her large eyes, began showering her with frank praise that Juliette confessed she found irresistible, and asked her to come often to see her before she left France for Coppet the following month.

This was the start of a friendship that would define both women and endure for the rest of their lives. Germaine, who had few female friends, saw Juliette as a vision of perfection, the embodiment of all the exquisitely feminine qualities of reserve, serenity and physical delicacy she was so conscious of lacking. 'An expression at one and the same time naïve and passionate gave her person an indescribable voluptuousness and a singularly likeable innocence,' Germaine wrote of her in her novel *Delphine* (interestingly, she called the character based on Juliette 'Thérèse'). If she wanted 'to portray a celestial being', she told Juliette, 'it would be your expressions I should use'.

It was fashionable for women of the eighteenth and nineteenth centuries to develop intense, almost romantic friendships like those between Germaine and Juliette and between Thérésia and Joséphine. Inspired by the intimacy between fictional heroines like Julie and Claire in *La Nouvelle Héloïse*, women looked to each other to provide them with companionship and emotional (and perhaps physical) solace and comfort, especially when the men in their lives were remote or unloving. Germaine cast herself in the role of adoring and sometimes jealous swain in her letters to Juliette. 'Do not have a greater friendship for any other woman than you have for me,' she pleaded in one. 'Say to me *I love you*,' she wrote in another, addressing Juliette as her angel. 'The emotion I will feel at those words will make me believe I am holding you to my heart.'

Juliette, timid and more used to receiving affection than giving it, was less forthcoming, earning frequent reproaches from Germaine. 'Why, whether in love or in friendship, is one never necessary to you?' she complained. But Juliette, rescued by Germaine from her life of banal frivolity, was equally committed to her. After their meeting, she wrote, 'I thought of nothing but Mme de Staël'.

Their friendship gave Juliette the chance to become something more than a simpering, affected *merveilleuse*. Through Germaine she was introduced to a sparkling circle of intellectuals where her own intuitive intelligence and interests could shine. Nothing was more engaging than watching Germaine and Juliette converse, wrote an enthralled Benjamin Constant, who saw them as beautifully complementary forces.

> The speed with which one was able to express a thousand new thoughts, the speed with which the other was able to grasp and judge them; there was that strong male intelligence which unveiled everything, and the delicate feminine one which understood everything; all this was united in a way impossible to describe if one had not had the happiness of witnessing it for oneself.

Imposing without being large, elegant without being ostentatious, the house Jacques Récamier bought from Necker at 7 rue du Mont Blanc became one of the most celebrated in Paris. The interior was a masterpiece of Directory style, designed by Louis Berthaut and assembled by the Jacob brothers, who had fitted out the newly-wed Bonapartes' house the previous year. Its bold modernity did not appeal to everyone. Laure d'Abrantes's old-fashioned mother thought it looked empty and uncomfortable.

Funded by her immensely rich and generous husband, Juliette entertained lavishly. This was the era of the nouveaux riches, before, as Hortense de Beauharnais noted, 'good society' had been revived: 'The wealth of France had passed into the pockets of the tradespeople, and it was they who entertained, and who squandered in a single night's entertainment a fortune they had acquired too easily.' Juliette's guests would arrive to find all the doors thrown open and the house blazing with expensive candlelight. Lamps illuminated the courtyard and rare shrubs stood in pots on the steps, which were covered with Turkish carpets. Like Joséphine Bonaparte, Juliette loved flowers. Her garden at Clichy was exquisite and her houses overflowed with blooms.

Dancing carried on through the night; supper was served at two in the morning. All the new dances were introduced at Juliette's balls, where Fortunée Hamelin's dancing was outshone only by her hostess's. Sometimes, with a show of reluctance, Juliette would allow herself to be persuaded to perform a solo shawl dance. In *Corinne*, Germaine ascribed Juliette's dancing to her heroine, a fictionalized, idealized self-portrait. She described her as a poet in her dancing, imaginative and emotional. 'In all her movements there was a graceful litheness, a modesty mingled with sensual delight,' she wrote. 'She appeared animated by an enthusiasm for life, youth and beauty which seemed to give an assurance that to be happy she needed no one else.' Crowds massed to watch Juliette; men kicked off their shoes and stood on the Jacob chairs to get a better view.

Juliette would invite her female guests to come and look at her gold and violet bedroom, reckoned to be the most beautiful in Paris; the men would rush to follow. Echoing the boudoirs of both Thérésia and Joséphine, the walls of her bedroom and bathroom were panelled in mirrors, recalling the legend of Psyche as told by La Fontaine, a story very much in vogue during the Directory. La Fontaine's Psyche lived in an enchanted palace filled with portraits of herself, before which she wallowed in ecstasies of narcissism while her invisible lover looked on.

The mahogany and ormolu bed was raised as if on an altar, with large gilded bronze swans at either end. It was draped in muslin edged with gold lace and canopied with gold damask. The mirror at its head was framed in violet damask; on the ceiling violet gryphons clutched gold garlands. Like Thérésia, Juliette was rumoured to have posed for the statue in her bedroom, but, typically, hers represented Silence. On one occasion she retired to bed during a party, while her room was still full of people. With her 'beautiful white shoulders expos'd perfectly uncover'd to view', wrote the shocked Lady Bessborough, visiting Paris at the time, Juliette was 'completely undress'd and in bed. The room was full of men.'

Her adjoining dressing-room was tented in eau-de-nil silk and had a recessed red leather sofa which turned into a bath. A day-bed standing in the dressing-room was very similar to the one on which Juliette was painted by Jacques-Louis David in 1800. Juliette had commissioned the painting, but she disliked it; perhaps she did not like to think of herself, as David's biographer Anita Brookner describes the image, as a child-bride, 'bewildered by her isolation' in an austere room tense with sexual fear and inhibition. David portrayed a bare-foot Juliette reclining seductively, but turned away from the viewer, her gaze opaque; he encapsulated the uneasy balance she maintained between passivity and provocation. She asked him to change it but he refused, telling her how hard he was finding it to do her justice. He kept the unfinished canvas in his studio. François Gérard's 1805 portrait was more to Juliette's taste, showing her rosy-cheeked and limpid-eyed, demure but approachable.

Juliette also frequented the subscription balls that continued to inflame Paris. In 1797, 644 public balls were held there. At the Jardins de Bagatelle in the Bois de Boulogne, hundreds of coloured lamps, suspended from trees and bushes, turned the gardens 'into a palace of rubies, emeralds, topazes and diamonds'. Tivoli, with its gilded and mirrored ballrooms and its landscaped gardens, was a 'perpetual circle of pleasures', wrote Henry Fox, staying in Paris in 1802. Entrance was three francs for a man and one for his female companion. Tivoli's gardens were illuminated apparently 'by the hands of fairies'; music played; fireworks exploded overhead; exotic fruit, ices of every colour, cake, lemonade and liqueurs were served.

Fox noticed 'dangerously fascinating' female figures gliding about. Women dressed as nymphs, oriental princesses or savages waltzed wildly with morose, expressionless men. Costumes were still daringly transgressive: there were men who came dressed as women, and women as men. Most ladies at 'these enchanting places' resembled goddesses in their Athenian robes, crowned with flowers, but many other styles were also popular. Egyptomania hit Paris, courtesy of Napoléon's expedition; the Turkish ambassador's arrival there in 1797 stimulated a craze for all things oriental, such as the turbans favoured by Germaine; Joséphine's admiration for the arts of the medieval period inspired *le style troubadour*.

At Frascati, another of these houses and gardens open to the public, Fox saw Juliette Récamier 'surrounded and almost overpowered by a multitude of persons admiring her'. Her mere presence drove people to distraction: one admirer was seen 'kissing and chewing the train of her dress like a lunatic'. Amongst her papers held by the Bibliothèque Nationale in Paris numerous poems written to her by anguished worshippers survive, comparing her to spring breezes or informing her that butterflies follow in her footsteps. '*Chère Juliette, je vous aime,*' reads one scrap.

The old crowd still gathered in Barras's apartments in the Luxembourg in the spring of 1799, but the mood outside was changing. In one room, people pressed round to watch Thérésia and Barras, their friendship unchanged by her established relationship with the banker Gabriel Ouvrard, playing cards with huge piles of gold in front of them. In another, Germaine – recently arrived from Switzerland – was praising Juliette Récamier to an enraptured Lucien Bonaparte. 'If one is happy to be Mme Tallien,' she was saying, 'I believe that one would be even more so to be the friend of Mme Récamier.'

Germaine and Benjamin had returned to Paris in April as, abroad, the French army began to suffer serious reverses against the British, newly rejoined by the Austrians and Russians. The Directory was now derided by all as a failure; political apathy and contempt for the government reigned supreme. Talleyrand later wrote that 'the Directory fell by the fault of its own members'; but in fact it was more that the leaders of the Directory, having built their administration upon the ruins of revolutionary idealism while denying their own complicity in the excesses that idealism had brought about, could never command the respect of the French people. Even its own leaders had never believed in its authority.

Blasé and beleaguered, the French people were ready for the man who would rescue them from the spectres of terror and anarchy. As Manon Roland had predicted from prison in 1793 (although she was thinking of Robespierre), France was 'waiting for the first master who will come along and subdue her'. Napoléon Bonaparte, campaigning in Egypt, was determined to be that master. 'I do not understand either the spirit or the supposed patriotism of those people [the French],' wrote an English friend of Germaine's visiting Paris that spring. 'They love public affairs, rather than the public good. Love of the public good does not often lead to places, pensions, business interests; only intrigue leads to all of those.'

That summer, Lucien Bonaparte wrote to his brother urging him to return to France, and began mustering potential allies at Juliette's house on the outskirts of Paris. Later he would claim that he engineered the coup of Brumaire with her in mind. Joseph Fouché said Lucien was animated at this time by 'two powerful passions' – love and ambition. Juliette's carefully maintained neutrality makes her own involvement in the plotting unlikely, but, given her closeness to Germaine (ordered to leave France yet again in July), it is more than probable that she knew of the plans afoot to overthrow the Directory.

By August, an uneasy alliance between Barras, Talleyrand and Emmanuel Joseph Sieyès awaited only a 'sword' – a military leader, in the parlance of the day – to command the army in their name. News of French victories in Egypt and on the French borders was announced in Paris by thundering cannon. Napoléon abandoned his post in Cairo and left for France at the end of August, landing in Fréjus on the south coast in early October. He raced to Paris through cheering crowds, the fulfilment of his dreams becoming more possible with each mile his horses covered.

After three weeks of plotting and double-crossing, Napoléon's plans were set. He had an appointment with Barras at eleven o'clock on the night of 8 November. Instead of going personally, he sent his friend Louis-Antoine Bourrienne to tell Barras that he had a headache 'but that he need not fear'. Barras listened until Bourrienne had finished his excuses, and said, 'I see Bonaparte has tricked me. He will not come back. It is finished. And yet he owes me everything.' He was right. Bonaparte had tricked everyone, but perhaps Barras – once his friend and patron, and himself no stranger to betrayal – most of all.

The following morning Napoléon was appointed Commander-in-Chief of the army of the Paris region. Thérésia, heavily pregnant with her first baby by Ouvrard but as loyal to Barras as ever, came up to his Luxembourg apartments while he was in his bath. She and Ouvrard had tried to alert him to Napoléon's machinations, but he had not listened. 'What can be done?' cried Barras, 'that man (designating Bonaparte by a coarse epithet) has taken us all in.' It was probably

Joséphine's failure to warn him of the coup (of the details of which, in fact, she seems to have been largely ignorant) that earned her such a hostile description in Barras's memoirs.

As he sat down to dinner that night Talleyrand and Admiral Bruix, another of Barras's former protégés, entered the dining-room. They told Barras, falsely, that the other four Directors had resigned and that they had come to receive his resignation. Without comment, Barras signed their papers. Talleyrand, who had two million francs in his pocket with which to buy Barras's compliance, kept the bribe himself. Afterwards, 'with charming vivacity', Thérésia told Barras that he should look upon his removal from office as a release, not a defeat. Away from power, she said, he 'would once more be worthy of' himself. He left Paris immediately and was barred from returning to the capital the following year. Neither Napoléon nor Joséphine ever answered his reproachful letters.

Early on the morning of 19 Brumaire (10 November) the Assembly of Elders and the Council of Five Hundred gathered at Saint-Cloud, just outside Paris, as instructed by Napoléon's men. Troops encircled the tumbledown château, which had not been used since Louis XVI and his family had spent their last free summer there in 1790. Napoléon hoped that, away from their usual meeting place, the councillors and deputies would be more receptive to his demands, but his success was by no means assured: most people in the know, including Talleyrand (who was lunching nearby with Fortunée Hamelin, among others) and Sieyès, had their carriages at the ready in case they needed to flee. Bullied by a furious Napoléon, eventually marched upon by their own Guardsmen under Lucien Bonaparte's command, at 2 a.m. a small group of reluctant deputies and Elders finally recognized the end of the Directory and swore in as provisional consuls Napoléon and the former Directors Sieyès and Roger Ducos, who had betrayed Barras to back Sieyès's bid for power.

Her timing unerring, Germaine de Staël had returned to Paris the previous day. Waiting to find out whether she should prepare to leave again, she received messengers from Saint-Cloud every hour. On hearing the news of Napoléon's success, her father wrote to congratulate her 'on the happiness you find in his glory'. In his letters he would continue to refer to Germaine's admiration for Napoléon but, as her biographer points out, these comments may have been inserted for the benefit of Napoléon's spies who were certainly reading Germaine's correspondence. For the moment, she considered Napoléon's rise the least bad of the options available to France.

Napoléon and Joséphine moved into the Luxembourg the day after the coup, and Napoléon spent the following weeks fine-tuning his seizure of power. The new constitution, in the words of one historian, was 'drafted by Sieyès and emasculated by Bonaparte', who removed the system of balances devised by Sieyès to prevent tyranny. There were to be four assemblies, but no elections. Napoléon proposed that one of the consuls – himself, unsurprisingly – should be named First Consul, with full executive powers, the term to be renewed after ten years. The other two consuls would have solely consultative roles; Napoléon nominated the republican-leaning Régis de Cambacérès and the moderate royalist Charles Lebrun. Sieyès, who had been taking riding lessons to prepare himself for life as a leader, was compensated for his many disappointments with grants of land which, as Germaine observed, finally compromised the former priest who had survived every stage of the revolution. Even before work on the new constitution was complete, Napoléon issued a public proclamation announcing that the revolution was over at last.

On 1 January 1800 the Tribunate, which debated laws before sending them to the legislature, met for the first time. Having assured Napoléon that he would be 'positive', Benjamin Constant had been appointed a tribune. Germaine gave a dinner the night before his maiden speech, which he had written with her and which was a bold defence of liberty and liberalism and an attack on the new regime. 'Tonight, your drawing room is filled with people whom you like,' Benjamin said to her. 'If I make my speech, it will be deserted tomorrow.' 'One must follow one's convictions,' Germaine replied.

The next day ten of her guests – including Talleyrand – wrote to say that they could not come to dinner that night. Talleyrand, who called treason 'merely a question of dates', had decided that his alliance with Napoléon meant more to him than his friendship with Germaine. His loss was a bitter blow – one she would expiate in her portrayal of him as the cynical, seductive Madame de Vernon in *Delphine* – and it would be followed by another. Having repudiated Germaine, several years later Louis de Narbonne gained access to Napoléon's circle of intimates and became one of his most valued diplomats.

As her romance with Constant faded, Germaine was left, at thirty-four, to ponder the elusiveness of love. 'I live with a wound in my heart as others live with a physical ailment. Do you think that after these experiences a new beginning is possible?' she asked the philosopher Joseph-Marie de Gérando.

> The three men I have loved most since I was nineteen or twenty are Narbonne, Talleyrand, and Mathieu [de Montmorency; probably only platonically]. The first is only a graceful husk, the second has not even salvaged the husk, and the third has lost his grace, although he has retained his adorable qualities. New friends have become dear to me, but it is the past which stirs my soul and imagination.

Benjamin, 'tired of being swept away in her whirlwind', was making vain attempts to leave Germaine (including marrying someone else) but they were too closely bound together intellectually and temperamentally to stay apart for long.

His speech at the Tribunate prompted a flurry of hateful articles directed more personally at Germaine than at Benjamin. 'It is not your fault that you are ugly, but it is your fault that you are an intriguer,' said one newspaper, urging her to return to Switzerland, taking Constant with her. 'She writes on metaphysics, which she does not understand; on morality, which she does not practise; on the virtues of her sex, which she lacks,' wrote another, imagining her saying, 'Benjamin will be consul; I'll give the Treasury to Papa; my uncle will be Minister of Justice; and my husband will be given a distant embassy. As for me, I shall have the supervision of everything.' After a tense interview with Joseph Fouché, the new Minister of Police, Germaine retired, for tactical reasons, to Saint-Ouen for a few weeks. When she returned to Paris she found herself ostracized by society.

Germaine was not the only woman to fall into disfavour at the start of the new regime. Joséphine was banned from seeing Thérésia, her best friend and most intimate companion for the past five years. Napoléon was determined to eradicate any hint of scandal from his wife's past in particular and from his rule in general. Thérésia, with her four children by three fathers – and whose humiliating rejection Napoléon had not forgotten – was considered a bad influence: Napoléon insisted that her dangerous friendship with his wife come to an end. His spies kept close watch over her. As once under Robespierre, all of Thérésia's correspondence was scrutinized by the police.

Thérésia was devastated at Joséphine's betrayal. In October she took the opportunity of having been asked for an introduction to Joséphine to write to the woman who 'was once my friend' on behalf of a man who had lost everything as a result of the revolution. She no longer indulged herself with the illusion of their friendship, she wrote; 'time, events and your own heart have undeceived me.' However, she could not resist reminding Joséphine 'that my friendship for you is proof against everything, and that it will end only with my life'. Her words would have hurt the First Consul's wife, who six years later was still begging him to allow her to see her old friend. Napoléon was obdurate about the woman he said was branded 'with horror and infamy'. 'If you value my esteem and wish to please me, never transgress this injunction,' he told her in 1806. 'If she tries to gain access to you, if she comes to you under the cover of night, tell your porters to keep her out.'

At first, Joséphine hoped that if Thérésia would sever her connection with Gabriel Ouvrard, the father of her baby daughter Clémence, Napoléon would relent. But despite Joséphine's pleas, Thérésia refused to leave him. Napoléon may have despised Ouvrard for winning the woman who had once turned him down, but he was happy to do business with him. His regime was funded with millions borrowed – and frequently left unpaid – from Ouvrard.

Aimée de Coigny and Fortunée Hamelin were also unwelcome at Napoléon's court. Fortunée, an admirer of Napoléon's, remained loyal despite his treatment of her, but Aimée de Coigny was a confirmed liberal who was outraged by his authoritarianism and prudery. Napoléon saw her at a party in about 1802. 'Do you still like men as much as ever?' he asked spitefully. 'Yes, Sire,' she replied. 'When they are polite.'

The *merveilleuses'* exclusion from consular society was part of a broader change, instituted from the top down, in France's moral climate. Napoléon wanted clothes to be less revealing and manners more decorous. Arms and bosoms were covered up; starch and stiff silks returned to fashion. His motivation was partly political – because France was at war with Britain, he forbad Joséphine from wearing her trademark diaphanous muslin, which was imported from India via London – but principally moral. Gradually the ease and informality of Directory society vanished, to be replaced with what Germaine described as an 'oriental etiquette'. Knee-breeches, which had not been worn since 1792, soon became required court wear once again.

Even Talleyrand, notoriously unprincipled, was persuaded to marry his mistress, Catherine Grand, a former courtesan. When she was presented at the Tuileries, Napoléon said to her, 'I hope that the good conduct of the Citoyenne Talleyrand will soon cause the indiscretions of Madame Grand to be forgotten.' She replied innocently, 'In that respect, I cannot do better than follow the example of Citoyenne Bonaparte.'

Despite the wit of this response, Talleyrand's wife was popularly considered a little stupid. Germaine declared that she could not understand why he had married such a silly woman. 'To have once loved Mme de Staël is all that is needed to understand the satisfaction of loving an idiot,' Talleyrand responded gallantly.

Bloodstains in the corridors of the Tuileries dating back to the day the former royal palace was stormed in August 1792 and faded red bonnets and revolutionary slogans painted on to its façade had to be erased before Napoléon and Joséphine moved into their new consular apartments there in February. On the day of their ceremonial arrival, Napoléon wore a gold-laced red coat and his carriage was drawn by six magnificent horses. He had come a long way from the sober, modest general rapturously greeted at the Luxembourg three years earlier. Joséphine hated their new home. She had been given Marie-Antoinette's former apartments and could not rid herself of the thought that they were haunted.

In another return to ancien régime life, the first masked ball since 1793 was held at the Opéra in the same month as the Bonapartes moved into the Tuileries. Female guests wore dominoes over their gowns; the men, in evening dress, were unmasked. Juliette Récamier, 'who was so timid without a mask, became entirely self-possessed under this disguise, and was able to converse much more freely'. When he saw Thérésia, scantily dressed as Diana in diamonds and a leopardskin, Napoléon stiffly had her informed that fancy dress was no longer in fashion.

Rather like Germaine bemoaning the dissolution of post-revolutionary society, Napoléon had no plans to observe his new code of morality himself. Deeply distrustful of women, especially after being informed of Joséphine's unfaithfulness, he was determined not to take an official mistress but dallied, as men of his class did, with actresses and opera singers. Only one woman, whom he had met just once, seemed worthy of him: the beautiful Juliette Récamier, so virtuous that she would not even sleep with her own husband.

Germaine's friendship with Juliette was one of her few consolations during her lonely period of exclusion from Parisian society; another was work. *On Literature* was published in April 1800. Although ostensibly not about politics, it was a passionate declaration of its author's liberal principles. Its themes were progress and the perfectibility of mankind – in which tenet, despite her own experiences, Germaine de Staël never lost her faith. 'It was often repeated during the Revolution in France that a certain amount of despotism was necessary to establish liberty,' she wrote. 'This is a contradiction in terms ... Institutions based upon force may simulate everything about liberty, except its workings.'

Napoléon tried to rise above *On Literature*'s popularity; another book, published soon afterwards, was harder to ignore. The satire *Zoloé*, possibly written by the marquis de Sade, came out in the summer of 1800. Sade, a distant cousin of Paul Barras's, was imprisoned before the revolution for his immorality and had been released from the Bastille when it fell in 1789. The eponymous Zoloé was clearly modelled on Joséphine; other characters were unmistakably Barras, Thérésia and Napoléon himself, thinly disguised as d'Orsec – an anagram of Corse, or Corsica.

Zoloé's world was one of feasting, intoxication, orgies and wanton debauchery led by Joséphine and Thérésia, portrayed as Maenads frenzied by lust, fame and gold. Echoing Barras's memoirs, Zoloé herself was described as having 'every quality of seduction . . . [and] a mad desire for pleasure' as well as 'the greed of a moneylender'; she spent 'with a gambler's fervour'. Thérésia, or Laureda, was 'all fire and love'. Her fortune allowed her to indulge her taste for depravity. 'Enamoured of the lubricities of Ovid and the furies of Sappho, she has exhausted all the combinations of voluptuousness.' Laureda's only regret was having married a pompous flunkey who mistakenly congratulated himself on serving the people and whose jealousy of her was always in vain.

Sade never admitted authorship, but Napoléon had him arrested in March the following year, ostensibly because of his novel *Juliette* which had been published five years earlier. He died in prison in April 1803.

Zoloé came out while Napoléon was in the north of Italy, dramatically defeating the Austrian army at the battle of Marengo. His forces had been financed by Gabriel Ouvrard. Marengo was, as one contemporary said, 'the baptism of the personal power of Napoléon'. From this point onwards, Bonaparte's dominance was unquestioned.

Germaine recognized that victory would confirm his grip on France. She was at Coppet, with the news of his campaign relayed to her by courier every hour, and she confessed later that she had hoped he would lose. Napoléon stopped in Geneva on his way back to Paris, where he met Necker for the first time. Necker pleaded his daughter's case, and Napoléon agreed to allow her to return to Paris. But although Germaine went back to Paris and guests flooded back to her salon, she was never invited to the Tuileries. Napoléon's dislike for her was well known. He sent his brother Joseph, who defied his wishes so as to remain friends with Germaine, to ask her what it would take to stop her criticism of his rule. He said he would be willing to return Necker's millions and overturn the 1795 decree of exile against her.

'In short,' Napoléon said to Joseph, 'what does she want?' 'My God,' replied Germaine, when this question was put to her, 'it is not a matter of what I want but of what I think.'

'Advise her not to block my path, no matter what it is, no matter where I choose to go,' Napoléon said to Lucien and Joseph, from his bath, as fresh instances of her defiance were relayed to him. 'Or else, I shall break her, I shall crush her. Let her keep quiet,' he concluded. 'It's the wisest course she can take.' There was, said Germaine, when she was told of Napoléon's words, 'a kind of physical pleasure in resisting an iniquitous power'.

It was during this period that they met face to face for the last time. At a reception at General Berthier's house, Napoléon stopped in front of Germaine and inspected her ample, generously displayed bosom critically. 'No doubt you have nursed your children yourself?' Germaine, frozen, for once could think of no reply. 'You see,' Napoléon turned to Lucien triumphantly, 'she doesn't even want to say yes or no.'

Germaine, who represented all the qualities Napoléon feared in women, may have been the most obvious recipient of his misogyny, but he did not reserve his venom for her alone. Literary women were a particular focus of his suspicion. 'A woman distinguished by qualities other than those proper to her sex,' wrote the government-controlled *Gazette de France* a few years later on the subject of women writers, 'is contrary to the laws of nature.' When he saw Condorcet's spirited widow Sophie, an old friend of Germaine's, at about this time, Napoléon informed her that he disliked seeing women meddling in politics. 'You are right,' she replied, 'but in a country where they lose their heads, it is natural for them to desire to know the reason.'

Some women of letters were more amenable to Napoléon's blandishments. The novelist Félicité de Genlis, who had returned from exile after the coup of Brumaire, demonstrated the same ideological dextrousness that had marked her behaviour during the early years of the revolution. In return for spying on her friends, she received a large pension and the use of apartments and a library.

Napoléon's control of government was so firmly entrenched by the spring of 1802 that he was able to expel Benjamin Constant from the Tribunate, deal with rumours of a coup with surprising leniency and make a very satisfactory peace with Britain. English visitors, deprived for a decade of French art, culture and fashion, rushed across the Channel and appeared in droves in the drawing-rooms of Thérésia, Germaine and Juliette.

That same spring Thérésia was finally divorced from Tallien. He had returned to Paris the previous year, after a brief stay in London (where the Duchess of Devonshire gave him her portrait set in diamonds) because his ship had been captured by the British fleet. Thérésia, who was about to have her second baby with Ouvrard when Tallien came back, destroyed his hopes of a reconciliation. Tallien wrote lovingly and forgivingly to her the day after their first meeting telling her that he believed the immorality with which society had charged her was more to do with the corruption of society and the world than with her heart, 'which is and always has been good'. His own feelings for her, he said, were those of pure and unalterable affection.

Many still braved Napoléon's disapproval to visit Thérésia. The prevailing view of her was that despite her indiscretions – the result more of the turmoil of the times than innate sinfulness – she was a genuinely kind woman whose current treatment was unfair. 'Few women had had it in their power to do so much good or seized so eagerly every opportunity of doing it as she had,' Germaine's friend General Moreau told Lady Bessborough, and 'none almost of men and women had met with more ingratitude.'

She was still stunning. When the painter Élisabeth Vigée-Lebrun returned to Paris the previous year she saw Thérésia at the theatre in all her 'glittering, radiant beauty'. Henry Fox was a regular guest at her house in the rue de Babylone in 1802 and found her a fascinating, elegant and infinitely thoughtful hostess. Despite the ambivalence with which her revolutionary past was viewed, she was still using it to her advantage: one evening's entertainment consisted of a ventriloquist imitating a revolutionary committee during the Terror.

When on 2 August 1802 an overwhelming plebiscite voted Napoléon consul for life, Germaine's salon became the focus of open opposition to his regime. 'They say she talks about neither politics nor myself,' he complained, 'but somehow it happens that everyone comes away liking me that much less.'

Napoléon used the pretext of Germaine's novel *Delphine*, based on her affair with Narbonne and set in the early years of the revolution, to let it be known that Paris was no longer open to her. She was in Geneva in December 1802 when *Delphine* was published, to enormous critical and popular acclaim. When it came out all Paris was closeted away reading it and delightedly working out who was who. Although professedly apolitical, Germaine's powerful attack on the hypocrisy of society, 'the tyranny of public opinion' as Constant put it, and her arguments for the rights of women could only enrage Napoléon, whose every concept of passive womanhood it challenged. 'Women,' as one character put it, are 'the victims of all social institutions.'

'He fears me. Therein lies my joy and my pride; therein my terror,' Germaine told François-René de Chateaubriand, preparing herself again for the ordeal of exile. 'I must admit to you that I am bound to be proscribed and I am ill prepared to bear the boredom of a long exile; my courage fails but not my will.'

A year later, her will had failed her too. In the autumn of 1803, 'like an Irishman who kept coming back until he was thrown out of a fourth-floor window', as she put it, Germaine tried to re-enter Paris but was formally exiled and escorted from France. Friends tried to intervene on her behalf, but Napoléon would have none of it. 'No, no, there is no truce nor peace possible between us; she asked for it, let her suffer the consequences.' Juliette declared that the man who could banish such a woman 'could never appear to me except as a despot'.

Germaine was never reconciled to exile. 'Anyone born on the

blessed soil of France cannot bear life elsewhere,' she wrote. When, some years later, her seventeen-year-old son Auguste (Narbonne's son) went to plead her case before the emperor, he was not unkind but unflinching. 'What I want is submission,' he told Auguste. 'Tell your mother my mind is made up. She will never set foot in Paris again, as long as I live. Besides,' he added, 'you can make politics by talking literature, morality, art, anything in the world. Women should stick to knitting.'

Napoléon's Civil Code became law in March 1804, two months before he was declared emperor. Unsurprisingly, the laws concerning women were designed to restrict their independence. Women were viewed as legal minors all their lives, passing from the custody of their fathers into that of their husbands. Submission and fidelity were the essence of their marriage vows. 'We need the notion of obedience, in Paris especially,' said Napoléon, 'where women think they have the right to do as they like.' Adulterous women (not their equally married lovers) were culpable in the eyes of the law; children's custody favoured the father. Illegitimate children, who had been recognized by the constitution of 1793, were no longer recognized. Secondary state education was to be provided only for boys. 'Public education is not suitable for them [girls], because they are never called upon to act in public.' Divorce was severely restricted but not forbidden – which was just as well, since five years later Napoléon's desire for an heir would bring him and Joséphine to the divorce courts.

After his divorce, it had taken Tallien over a year to find a job, even having petitioned Bonaparte. Proudly, he had refused Ouvrard's offer of La Chaumière and a generous annual allowance. In November 1804 he was sent to Alicante as consul. Ouvrard also went to Spain early the following year, cementing the end of his six-year relationship with Thérésia. At thirty-one, twice divorced and the mother of six children by three men, Thérésia was on her own for the first time in over ten years, but she would not be single for long.

She married for the third time in August 1805. Her husband – who had fallen in love with her at first sight when he caught a glimpse of her rushing back to Paris from Bordeaux in the bloody spring of 1794 – was the young comte de Caraman, son of a lady-in-waiting to

Marie-Antoinette. Thérésia had sought the blessing of the Pope when he came to Paris the previous December to crown Napoléon emperor; she made a point of stating her desire to regain the reputation she would not have lost, she said, 'had not her first husband been a fool and her second a rogue'. When in 1806 Camaran's father died and he and Thérésia became the prince and princesse de Chimay, Tallien said, 'It is all very well for her to call herself the Princesse de Chimères [a pun on Chimay, *chimère* meaning wild dream or illusion], but she will be Mme Tallien to the end.'

Juliette Récamier was idolized by consular society but gradually, under Germaine's provocative influence, she came to view Napoléon as a tyrant. In the spring of 1802, after an abortive plan by the generals Moreau and Bernadotte to unseat him, Juliette made a hastily arranged visit to England. Some said that she was advised to leave because of her public friendship with the plot's leaders; others that her departure was on account of the unwelcome admiration the First Consul had developed for her.

London worshipped Juliette as ardently as did Paris. She became friends with Georgiana Duchess of Devonshire and Lady Bess Foster, and flirted with the Prince of Wales. On the first Sunday in May, her visit to Kensington Gardens with the Duke of Hamilton and the Duchess of Somerset was recorded in the newspapers. Juliette looked like a goddess in a hat draped with a white veil that swept the ground, a fashion that had not been seen before in London; in the rush to try and touch her, she was almost stifled by the crowd.

Back in Paris, prints and engravings bearing her image multiplied on the stalls at the Palais Royal. A German friend described Juliette, on seeing a caricature of herself on a stand, asking the seller if it was a picture of a lady of ill-fame. 'Nay, God forbid,' he replied. 'It is a lady of the most spotless reputation.' He then praised her so highly – not realizing who she was – that she was consoled 'for the bitterness of the libel she held in her hand'.

Two years later, Napoléon, an admirer of Juliette since his brother's infatuation with her, began a pursuit in earnest. He sent Fouché to her country house at Clichy to present his suit. Fouché told Juliette how highly the emperor thought of her, and said that if she were to apply for a position at Joséphine's court he knew her request would be granted. She immediately declined the offer, arguing that her shyness, her love of independence and the simplicity of her tastes made her unfit for such a position; furthermore, her responsibilities towards her husband would preclude serving at court. Her real reason was Napoléon's treatment of Germaine. Fouché smiled – one can imagine how wolfishly – and said how useful she might be at court in arguing on behalf of the poor and oppressed, adding that a woman as noble and charming as she might exert a powerful influence over the emperor. 'He has not yet met a woman worthy of him,' he added significantly, 'and no one knows what the love of Napoleon might be, if he attached himself to a pure person.'

Soon afterwards, Napoléon's sister Caroline Murat invited Juliette to visit her. She spent the morning with Caroline, already a friend, and her husband, who tried to convince her to accept a position as Caroline's lady-in-waiting. A role in her establishment would protect Juliette from the empress's jealousy, they said, and would allow Caroline always to have Juliette near her.

As Juliette left, Caroline recalled her friend's admiration for Talma, and offered her her box at the Théâtre Français. This box happened to be opposite Napoléon's own, and both times Juliette used it she found him seated across from her, his opera-glass trained not on the stage but on her. Her surrender began to be spoken of as a certainty, though Juliette had avoided responding to Fouché's offer.

Finally Fouché visited her again, this time offering her the position of lady-in-waiting in Napoléon's own name. 'You can no longer refuse,' he said. But, knowing her husband supported her decision, refuse she did, incurring (as Thérésia Tallien had done) Napoléon's lasting rancour. On hearing, soon afterwards, that three of his ministers had met at her house Napoléon irritably enquired when his council had last convened there. He declared that any foreigner who frequented the Récamiers' house would be considered his personal enemy. Metternich, then secretary at the Austrian embassy, was obliged to visit Juliette in secret to avoid the notice of Napoléon's spies.

In late 1805 Jacques Récamier went catastrophically bankrupt. When Napoléon was asked to authorize the Bank of France to bail him out (Récamier, along with Gabriel Ouvrard, had been one of the few bankers upon whom Napoléon relied) he refused with the words, 'I am not Mme Récamier's lover, and I do not come to the aid of merchants who maintain a house that costs 600,000 francs a year.'

Juliette met her husband's reversal of fortune with serene dignity and courage. Knowledge of her good works, hitherto accomplished in secret, began to leak out; the society beauty was revealed as an angel. Out of respect for her, and partly out of contempt for Napoléon, whose treatment of Récamier had been broadcast around Paris, Parisian society made a point of calling at the house in the rue du Mont Blanc (already on the market) to express their sympathy.

Over the next few years, Juliette's life consisted of close friends and visits to Germaine at Coppet. Other regulars there included Constant, Mathieu and Adrien de Montmorency, Prosper de Barante, the German scholar August Wilhelm von Schlegel, the Swiss writer Charles-Victor de Bonstetten, Chateaubriand and various German princes. Most fell in love with Juliette and were gently guided towards devoted friendship. Only Chateaubriand succeeded in breaking down her defences and their love would endure till their deaths, his in 1848 and hers, from cholera, the following year.

In 1811, after the publication of Germaine's *On Germany*, Napoléon took advantage of one of Juliette's many absences to forbid her returning to Paris. The innocent Juliette's intimacy with Germaine, her independence of mind, had finally become a political issue.

19

FEMMES

Resist, keep resisting, and find the centre of your support
in yourself.

GERMAINE DE STAËL

Napoléon

UNDER NAPOLÉON'S RULE women were granted fewer rights than before the revolution and their voices were relentlessly suppressed. All the passion and optimism of the women of the early revolutionary period, exemplified by Germaine de Staël, by Manon Roland, Pauline Léon and Théroigne de Méricourt, and all the influence enjoyed during the Directory by Germaine, Thérésia Tallien and Juliette Récamier, had apparently come to nothing.

Manon Roland's bones lay in a common grave beside hundreds of others guillotined under Robespierre. Pauline Léon, released from prison after Robespierre's fall, does not reappear in the official records. After her turbulent years of political activism, she seems to have decided that a quiet life was worth more than the rights for which she had once fought. She was not alone. After the riots of Prairial in the spring of 1795 common women no longer involved themselves with political protest. It would take the upheavals of 1848 to bring them back on to the streets – with the Société des Républicaines-Révolutionnaires as their inspiration.

Thérésia Cabarrus, formerly marquise de Fontenay and Mme Tallien, died as princesse de Chimay in 1835, having spent the last years of her life in seclusion at her husband's estates doting on her many children and grandchildren and indulging her love for music and painting. The fact that despite her respectable third marriage she was never welcomed back into European high society (although her husband and children were) was a continual source of regret. 'If I should deign to defend myself, I should say to you,' she wrote to a friend in 1826, with her extraordinary ability to view the facts of her life as she wished them to be, 'is it my fault if M. de Fontenay betrayed and abandoned me, if

M. Tallien left for Egypt when his responsibilities required him in Paris?' In fact much of the blame for her exclusion from the world she had once almost reigned over can be attributed to Napoléon's inability to forget a slight or forgive a rejection – especially if it came from a woman.

When the unreliable memoirs of a revolutionary government agent called Sénart, which were overwhelmingly hostile to Tallien, were published in 1824 (four years after Tallien's lonely death) Thérésia declared herself heart-broken – especially on behalf of their daughter. Rose-Thermidor Tallien, called Joséphine during her childhood (Joséphine continued to pay for her god-daughter's education even after her break from Thérésia), took the name of Laure after her marriage to Félix de Narbonne-Pelet as a final rejection of the controversial circumstances of her birth which had so coloured the lives of her parents.

Although Napoléon had been able to ensure that Thérésia lost her best friend and was ostracized from her husband's world, he could not control his children. Thérésia's son by Chimay, Joseph, married one of Napoléon's illegitimate daughters; their four children could claim both Napoléon and Thérésia as their grandparents.

Juliette Récamier, who better conformed to the new ideal of a virtuous, modest woman, became one of the great literary muses of the nineteenth century through her long-standing friendships with Benjamin Constant, Pierre-Simon Ballanche, François-René de Chateaubriand – her only real love – and Germaine de Staël. She returned to Paris in 1814 after Napoléon's fall. In the 1830s, when she was in her fifties, she was described as still possessing an irresistible 'velvetiness' of manner.

The Duke of Wellington, who met Juliette in Paris in 1815 after the final defeat of Napoléon at Waterloo, was another of her admirers. 'I own, madame, that I do not greatly regret that urgent business will prevent me from calling on you this afternoon, since each time after seeing you I quit your person more than ever penetrated by your attractions, and less disposed to give my attention to politics,' he wrote. 'I will, however, wait upon you tomorrow . . . if you should be at home, notwithstanding the effect which these dangerous visits produce on me.'

Théroigne de Méricourt, officially declared insane in September 1794, was transferred from one grim asylum to another over the next thirteen years. Pierre Villiers, once Robespierre's secretary, visited her in 1797. He described her as a 'revolutionary Fury' still obsessed with the ideas of equality and liberty – as if those deluded hopes were proof of her madness. It is more than likely that Théroigne was treated during this period by Philippe Pinel, an early specialist in mental disorders. He believed that revolution 'expanded the soul' but he also argued that it caused a greater incidence of mental disorders and insanity because it acted as a powerful emotional stimulant. Revolutions, according to his theory, drove people to such extremes of emotion that many simply went mad.

Théroigne was finally placed in La Salpêtrière in 1807; here she would spend the last decade of her life ministered to by keepers who were little more than gaolers, clothed in filthy rags, fettered to the walls and fed like an animal through the bars of her damp, dirty, airless cell. Abandoned by her family to these inhumane conditions, the desperate Théroigne degenerated rapidly. If someone approached her she would threaten them, swear, accuse them of royalism and speak wildly of liberty and the Committee of Public Safety. Her world was still that of 1794.

By 1810, the asylum's records describe her as completely dislocated from reality, speaking to herself for hours on end, muttering ritualized incantations about committees, decrees, villains, liberty and the revolution, at times smiling at an imaginary audience. Often naked, even in the coldest weather, she punctuated her monologues with purifying baths of freezing water or self-abasement in muddy excrement.

Since her death in 1817 Théroigne's case has been seized upon by generation after generation of historians who have used her as a metaphor for the ruined idealism of the first years of the revolution. In the mid-nineteenth century Jules Michelet (basing his analysis on distorted reports of her life, since discredited) saw her as the fatal personification of revolutionary fury, savage, bloodthirsty and anarchic. In fact she seems to have been more victim than aggressor, a tragic casualty of her own exalted hopes for freedom.

It was Michelet who first attributed to women a prominent role in the revolution. He argued that the daily deprivations suffered by ordinary women – hunger, disease, the sight of their husbands and sons going off to war – made them overcome their traditional political passivity to become bold instigators of change. 'What is most *people* in the people, I mean what is most instinctive and inspired,' he wrote, 'is assuredly the women.'

Later historians, like the socialist Albert Mathiez at the start of the twentieth century, looked at women more sceptically, generally viewing their counterrevolutionary activity – their calls for a return to king and Church – as their most important contribution to the history of the period. To Mathiez, such women were political and religious fanatics who undermined the achievements of true (male) revolutionaries like Robespierre. On the other hand his contemporary, Jean Jaurès, commended the role women played in bringing the king to Paris in 1789 and forcing him to sign the Declaration of the Rights of Man. It was female hands, Jaurès wrote, 'that received for humanity its new, glorious title'.

But humanity's new, glorious title contained nothing within it for women. As Olympe de Gouges had pointed out, France still needed a declaration of the rights of women. Modern feminist historians have turned their focus to this central inconsistency in revolutionary history: the fact that when women became politically active, either from behind the scenes, like Germaine de Staël and Manon Roland, or on the streets, like Pauline Léon and Théroigne de Méricourt, they were agitating for rights from which they, as women, were actively excluded. A female figure might have represented Liberty, but for real women she remained an unattainable ideal.

Although women were silenced by the revolution, their role as republican mothers had been politicized. Remaining in the domestic sphere had become their essential contribution to the virtuous new republic. The message was that female independence, especially sexual independence, threatened the stability and security of the French nation. Thus the revolution, as Dorinda Outram suggests, 'succeeded perfectly in carrying out its "hidden agenda" of the exclusion of women from a public role'.

Helen Williams, the British writer living in Paris throughout this period, observed in 1801 that women only enjoyed the benefits of the new regime second-hand. The real question, she said, was not 'whether they [women] have gained by the revolution, but whether they have gained as much as they ought'. Her answer was an unequivocal no. Despite revolutionary champions of female rights like the marquis de Condorcet and Emmanuel Joseph Sieyès, she wrote, women were still woefully ill-educated and lacked basic political and civil rights:

> When Republican lawgivers shall have established public institutions where woman may receive the blessings of a liberal education, when they shall have allotted for her whose mind is enlightened by study, and refined by nature, some dignified employments, which, if she is destitute of fortune, may shield her from the cruel alternative of penury . . . or of uniting herself to a man whom her heart despises or rejects, then will she kneel, with that glowing enthusiasm, that instinctive impulse of admiration for what is great and generous which the female heart wants no lesson to feel, and bless the tutelary sway of the Republic!

With Napoléon's ascent to power, despotism, as so many observed, had merely changed hands. Women who had scrambled to unofficial positions of influence during the chaos after Robespierre's fall were systematically excluded from social life – especially those who had personally rejected Napoléon, like Thérésia, dared to disagree with him, like Germaine, or both, like Juliette.

But even Napoléon could not ensure that their voices were silenced completely. In the short term his political objectives may have been achieved by their removal from the public stage, but in the long term it would ensure that he would be remembered for injustice and tyranny.

Her ten years of exile only gave Germaine de Staël more reason to develop her ideas on the urgent necessity for liberty – especially for women. She declared that a society's treatment of its female citizens was the measure of its civilization. The old regime may have ridiculed feminine emotions but it had granted women influence, she argued, while the new order despised, belittled and excluded them. It was a measure of how much attitudes had changed since 1789 that she and others were no longer prepared to accept this state of affairs. Although the revolution had been more concerned with the rights of men than with the rights of humanity, it had shown women that their opinions were important and their contribution to society vital.

Germaine spent the early 1810s writing and travelling in continental Europe, Russia, Sweden and England, retreating as Napoléon's empire expanded towards her. Perhaps her greatest work, *On Germany*, was suppressed by Napoléon in 1810 but published in London three years later. In 1811, in secret, she married a dashing but not very intellectual army officer twenty-one years her junior; with him she finally achieved the personal contentment she had sought for so long. Their son, born when Germaine was forty-six, would marry Louis de Narbonne's granddaughter.

Napoléon was defeated by an alliance of British, Russian, Austrian and Prussian troops in 1814 and Germaine returned to Paris in triumph after a decade-long exile. Once again, her salon was the most important in Paris; once again, the circle she dominated drew up France's constitution, this time restoring Louis XVIII, Louis XVI's brother, the former comte de Provence, to the French throne. Although she fled when Napoléon escaped from Elba the following year, she need not have bothered. To regain power in France Napoléon needed a constitution – and the endorsement of Madame de Staël, the 'empress of thought'. His brother Joseph was sent to persuade her to return to support his new liberal rule, promising the return of Necker's money (still unpaid), a peerage for her son-in-law and the establishment of the liberal principles of government for which she had fought and suffered so long.

But while Germaine feared for France's independence if Napoléon's final bid for power failed, she could not conceive of supporting the man she saw as the enemy of liberty. 'The Emperor has done without a constitution and without me for twelve years,' she said to her cousin. 'He does not love one any more than the other.' She returned to Paris in the autumn of 1816, when Louis XVIII was restored to the throne for a second time. Her influence and advice were eagerly sought by France's new ruling caste. Some of these, like the Duke of Wellington, were new friends; many others, like Lafayette and Mathieu de Montmorency, had been close to her since those heady, idealistic days of their youth in the rue du Bac.

Germaine de Staël died in Paris on 14 July 1817 – twenty-eight years to the day after the Bastille had fallen and the revolution she had so longed for had begun.

NOTES

ABBREVIATIONS

BHÉSRF   *Bulletin d'Histoire Économique et Sociale de la Révolution Française*
CG   Germaine de Staël, *Correspondance générale*
HMW 1790   Helen Maria Williams, *Letters Written in France . . . to a Friend in England*
HMW 1794   ——, *Letters from France*
HMW 1796   ——, *Letters Containing a Sketch of the Politics of France*
HMW 1801   ——, *Sketches of the State of Manners and Opinions in the French Republic*
WRP   Applewhite et al., *Women in Revolutionary Paris*

For full information on the publications cited in the Notes, see the Bibliography on p. 417.

INTRODUCTION

I know of no woman: Herriot I, 33
manifesting my love for: Document reproduced in full in *WRP* 158
women, amidst their petty household: Tocqueville 31
had the deepest craving for: Schama 545

Chapter 1 · SALONNIÈRE

Go hence to Mme de Staël's: Morris II, 102
furnace of politics . . . some great revolution: The next quotations, Adams 266, 265
the noblest pleasure . . . and without foresight: The next quotations, Staël *Considérations* I, 386, 378–9 [French version, 1818]
To arms, to arms: Schama 382
The Revolution must be attributed: Staël *Considérations* I, 89 [English version, 1818]
touched the extreme limits: Herold 86
mille et mille . . . I do today: Staël *CG* I, 315, 21 July 1789
the governing principle, the directing: Goncourt 243
the social developments of the times . . .: For modern discussions of salons and their importance, see Gutwirth, *The Twilight of the Goddesses*, and Landes, *Women and the Public Sphere in . . . the French Revolution*
a short petticoat: Herold 124
impersonal and abstract convention: Sennett *Flesh and Stone* 73

A man who placed his: Boigne 32

the duchess, and her femme: Byrne 207

Do not people talk in: Sennett *Flesh and Stone* 110

Ah, Madame, you must be: Gronow 50; Ducrest I, 151, the other woman referred
    to was not Talleyrand's current mistress but his future wife, Catherine
    Grand.

intellectual melody: Staël *Corinne* 26

a certain way in which: Herold 71

If I was queen: Gay III, 23, quoting Mme Tessé

the arbiters of all things: Tocqueville 403

is to denature . . . the robust one: The next quotations, Gutwirth 138, 117

bid defiance to laws: Adams 234

The influence of women: Staël *Considerations* II, 148

were involved in . . . and natural intelligence: Melzer and Rabine 125

all its vigour: Gutwirth 86

the paradise of . . . scorned and mistreated: Melzer and Rabine 200

injustice of men . . . most perfect integrity: The next quotations, from 'On
    Literature' in Berger 186, 184

The feelings to . . . changed into spectators: Herold 104

in admiration . . . pleased with oneself: Boigne 189

to dazzle rather than to: Ducrest I, 85

of all the men I: Bruce 19

If it had depended: Faderman 101

the most courtly refinement: Burney 235

the inexhaustible treasures of grace: Herriot I, 76, quoting Sainte-Beuve

He is a . . . let alone gunpowder: Staël *Lettres à Narbonne* 48

stop your famous . . . be your fault: The next quotations, Staël *CG* I, 403, 256,
    both undated

her intellectual endowments . . . more obviously undesigning: Burney 236

the friend of Mme de Staël: Morris, I, 144

le comte Louis . . . changed his destiny: Staël *CG* I, 355, to Stanislas de
    Clermont-Tonnerre

of no duty . . . the strongest side: Morris I, 144

the great business . . . of all that: The next quotations, Rousseau *La Nouvelle
    Héloïse* 90, 61

maternal love became as much: Berry 404

There are no . . . seeking among men: Landes 72, and Gutwirth 126; both quoting
    Rousseau's *Letter to M. d'Alembert on Spectacle*

A taller stature, a stronger: Rousseau *La Nouvelle Héloïse* 108

Rousseau has endeavoured . . . over their happiness: Staël *Letters on . . . Rousseau* 15

always been half in love: Wollstonecraft 263

sought a man: Rousseau *Émile* 439

a passion of virtue: Staël *Letters on . . . Rousseau* iv

can only be read with: Brooks 33
It laughs at . . . hope of youth: Herold 196
too civilised in . . . of uniting them: From 'On Literature' in Berger 179
preferred the generous principles: Staël *Considérations* I, 353
not the provincial gentry: Hampson 53
It was the . . . classes of society: La Tour du Pin 75
a kind of school for: Mercier *New Picture* I, 30
decided every action: Staël *Considerations* I, 269
All Frenchmen shall wear: Herriot I, 67
We have some little compliments: Morris II, 246
of the first . . . for that company: Morris I, 6
Everyone tells us . . . will be happy: Adams 5
Either no individual . . . to Rousseauist views: The next quotations, Gutwirth 224, 204
Men whom the . . . maintain in silence: Moore *Roots* 65
mad about the English: HMW 1790 69
Everything had to be copied: La Tour du Pin 98
of privilege and liberty: May 128
attained the perfection of: Staël *Considerations* I, 14
seemed as criminal as if: Hampson, 48, quoting Chastenay
young, brilliant . . . thought they held: Chastenay 81
a demagogue by calculation: Staël *Considerations* I, 256
drunk with hope and joy: Talleyrand I, 47
You are wrong . . . air of conviction: The next quotations, Staël *Considerations* I, 188, and II, 140
La patrie est . . . to its aid: Shulim 268
my speaker . . . on the veto: Staël *CG* I, 33
As political affairs were still: Staël *Considerations* I, 379
Men of the . . . equality, but liberty: The next quotations, Staël *Considérations* I, 383, 386, 350

Chapter 2 · FILLE SANS-CULOTTE

Next year, you'll be behind: Vigée-Lebrun 71
There go some more: La Tour du Pin 145
no riotous scene . . . groundswell of menace: Ozouf 39
comic and abusive verse: Hufton 21
The women of . . . when everyone is trying . . . if we are left . . . We ask to be enlightened . . . the . . . fatherland in danger: The next quotations, WRP 53, 18, 19, 20, 158
and, with a spirit worthy: HMW 1790 27
for the happy revolution: Kelly 19, quoting *Le Moniteur* for 9 Aug. 1789
more from duty . . . obliged to resist: Staël *Considerations* I, 271
men didn't understand anything about: WRP 35

sweep away the . . . the fine one: The next quotations, Schama 459, 460
men were not strong enough: WRP 37, quoting Maillard
the beating down of gates: Ozouf 126
the sycophant Lafayette . . . slit their throats: The next quotations, *WRP* 44, 45
The town is . . . the female mob: Morris I, 242–3
Motion of the . . . Who Sell Fish: Schama 457
Every eye was turned: Staël *Considerations* I, 339
You must not be seen: Boigne 58
had been forced to march: La Tour du Pin 130
Habits of formality . . . uttering wild cries: The next quotations, Boigne 58
horrid yells and . . . advantages of education: Paulson 80
to bring back the queen's head: WRP 48
We suffer more . . . across our shoulders: The next quotations, Gutwirth 245, 244
Since that time . . . Watch with more exactitude . . . unworthy of us: The next
    quotations, WRP 159, 67
women were neither too weak . . .: Kennedy I, 90
at Creil . . . and Limoges: Villiers 28, 88, 89, 91, 102
all politics and . . . electrified hearts: WRP 85
We want to save: Dupuy 63
a Frenchwoman inflamed with love: Villiers 70
we do not venture to come: Roudinesco 88
in Tonneins, the local Jacobins . . .: Kennedy I, 92
Your predecessors deposited . . . raised to the ranks . . . fatherland in danger: The
    next quotations, WRP 72, 73, 74

Chapter 3 · CLUBISTE

the colour of blood: Roudinesco 197, quoting Lamartine
amante de carnage: Baudelaire, *Sisina*
the fatal beauty . . . vaillante, infortunée Liégoise: The next quotations, Michelet,
    Femmes 153, 147
suspended between literary bohemianism: Roudinesco 9
covered in diamonds: Roudinesco 10, quoting Thomas d'Espinchal
general effervescence: Ernst 87
descending into the . . . multitude: Kelly 11
did not witness the main: Ernst 88, 105
to play the role: Ernst 89
How the months, the days: Rosa 19
set up the tricoloured cockade: Yonge I, 126
professional coquette: Roudinesco 201
the kept woman . . . a free person: Schama 463
What most impressed . . . a heroic air: Roudinesco 5
My devotion to . . . the most worthy . . . public: The next quotations, Ernst
    90, 82

We should bear . . . are those of . . . the liberty of . . . with Spartan pride: The next
  quotations, Roudinesco 38, 39, 39, 28
because of my patriotism: Ernst 91
One might call . . . National embryo . . . unrest was greatest: The next quotations,
  Roudinesco 30, 32, 31
The reign of . . . with private virtues: Gutwirth 286
as the whirlwind attracts: Roudinesco 196
It is care-free and so: Schama 525
incompatible with liberty: Ernst 92
As soon as they began: Kotzebue II, 112
It is the Queen: Michelet *Femmes* 150
Mlle Théroigne and those of: Roudinesco 42
women were the soul of: Aulard *Histoire politique* 97
reading and interpreting the decrees: Villiers 43
He who votes . . . catch a cold: Roudinesco 46
the club of women: Cerati 25
the tyranny which men exercise: Roudinesco 71
there being a woman in . . .: Ernst 95

Chapter 4 · MONDAINE

The tranquillity of France: Gower I, 28
sans joie comme sans chagrin: Bourquin 57
her good and . . . profound immorality: Marcourt 42
of all the . . . prostituted: Frénilly 154
Even the men . . . taught to respect: Herold 69
What social disaster . . . were considered provincial: The next quotations, La Tour
  du Pin 17, 27
There is nothing in love: Goncourt 112
adultery in itself was nothing: Rousseau *Confessions* 190
dethroned . . . delicious: Bourquin 71
but extremely en beau: Bickley 64
no more beautiful . . . radiant femininity: La Tour du Pin 196–7
of caressing magic: Lacour 66
When they converse . . . Everything tiresome . . . than to listen: The next
  quotations, HMW 1790 70, 74, 43
A list of putative members . . .: Ernst 105
women of the . . . shocking and ridiculous: The next quotations, Genlis IV, 93, 92
The Revolution naturally descended: Staël *Considerations* I, 347
comme dans une . . . Dame de Fontenay: Houssaye 37
The following summer, a similar . . .: Cobban I, 168
inspired by the same spirit: HMW 1790 7
I honour no less: Ozouf 47
Ladies took the instruments: HMW 1790 7

victim to an excess: Herold 101
to be faithful forever to: Dowd 46
The French revolution is cemented: HMW 1790 15
What is it to me: Schama 512
no fatal gap had yet: Ozouf 35
This memorable day was: Mercier *New Picture* I, 47
the most sublime spectacle: HMW 1790 2
individual joy embodied . . . of the people: The next quotations, Ozouf 57, 51, 60
Every man seems at pains: HMW 1794 I, 172
We were transformed into: Ribeiro 141
had inflamed more souls: Dowd 2
the destruction of . . . destruction of despotism: Genlis IV, 90
I have found . . . by the world: HMW 1794 I, 143
altogether a most embarrassing person: Herold 52
To avoid the . . . powerful, useful men: Talleyrand I, 124
Though her eyes and smile: Vigée-Lebrun 321
One praise I . . . well on horseback: The next quotations, Genlis I 149, 167
derived less from Rousseau than . . .: Bruce 18
corrupted everything within his reach: La Tour du Pin 83
had a real esteem: Genlis IV, 87
had never been . . . food against famine: Frénilly 100
which they desired . . . to stop them: Berry I, 347–8
when age and ill health make: Roland, *Memoirs* 151
emigration became all the vogue: La Tour du Pin 116
an act of . . . dead or faithful: The next quotations, Staël *Considerations* II, 2, 4
stronger, more distinct and more: Berger 51
and at night, everybody: Herold 106
a little too . . . resist his eloquence: The next quotations, Bourquin 59, 63, 67
On Tallien and Thérésia's first meetings: Houssaye 39, 32
curieuse mythomanie: Marcourt 52; also Bourquin 36

Chapter 5 · RÉPUBLICAINE

yawning over the papers: Roland *Lettres* I, 653
But how can . . . to public affairs: The next quotations, Roland *Lettres* II, 10, 56
I had hated kings since: Roland *Memoirs* 249
Let them tremble . . . demand . . . petit comité . . . in our house: The next
    quotations Roland *Lettres* II 53, 220, 754, 253
an expression of . . . attachment to liberty: HMW 1796 I, 195–6
warm friend to liberty: Hill 219
the true heroes of humanity: Brissot *New Travels* 15
admired his devotion . . . wasting his time: Roland *Memoirs* 80
only the witness: Cobban I, 178
bons et: Jullien 35

I knew the proper role ... their time ... I loved political ... the astute Lameth: The
   next quotations Roland *Memoirs* 58, 58, 80, 57
very well satisfied ... applauded with delight: Roland *Lettres* II, 248
plain, undistinguished people ... a menial task: The next quotations, Roland
   Memoirs 125, 137
I should have been born: Rosa 19
a new strength ... They can kill me ... individuals ... in the future: The next
   quotations, Roland *Memoirs* 133, 133, 174, 175
If souls were pre-existent: May 29
a scene where feeble-minded people: Roland *Memoirs* 147
I cannot digest, among other: May 31
the possibility of domestic happiness: Roland *Memoirs* 217
it is right to exclude: Kelly 35
I am avid ... in the background: Roland *Memoirs* 93
I have not read of: Outram 138–9
Life was to her: May 65
I knew that I was: Roland *Memoirs* 164
unbearable contrast between the grandeur: Rousseau *La Nouvelle Héloïse* 72
*having concerned myself ... the external ... married in a ... without crying ...
   But of course ... the world ... I did not dare ... no sex ... as an affectionate
   ... in remaining virtuous*: The next quotations, Roland *Memoirs* 199, 245,
   245, 173, 170, 140–41, 163, 243, 246, 170
in truth, we are people: Roland *Lettres* I, 394
virtue produces happiness: Rudé *Robespierre* 95
the birthday of a new: Paine 65
under the simple and rustic: Brissot *Life* 7
greatly superior to ... circumstances are favourable: Paulson 12
I desire you ... voice or Representation: Applewhite and Levy 181
We regret this promised land: Roland *Lettres* II, 80
disgust with the revolution: Tocqueville 209
We must make ... lack, but soul: The next quotations, Roland *Lettres* II, 274, 276
500 heads would have sufficed: Gottschalk 121
was not just an unfortunate: Schama 447
infamous treason ... of these monsters: WRP 159
asked what was meant: Roland *Memoirs* 82
superfluity: Bizardel 86
keeping the king ... an indescribable enthusiasm: The next quotations, Roland
   Lettres II, 310, 325
On the royal family's return to Paris: Schama 557
the Jacobins passed ... incompatible with liberty: The next quotations, Roland
   Lettres II, 309, 325, 305, 317, 313
women, sisters, and Roman women: WRP 79
comme tous les bons: Applewhite and Levy 81

without interruption: WRP 159
I need to see my: May 195
Paris is as still: Jullien 41
as absolute, moral concepts: Outram in Porter 121
who desecrate words merely: Berger 105
one whose energy . . . justice from individuals: May 195–6
Roland, née Phlipon: Roland *Lettres* II, 388
had already singled . . . intimate and unbreakable: Roland *Memoirs* 84
Women are now . . . from the revolution: WRP 87–96
Although I am . . . to be geese: WRP 99
rushing around from nine o'clock: Staël *CG* II, part 2, 310
What a triumph . . . not their dupe: Fairweather 124
to the most . . . were equally distinguished: Staël *Considerations* II, 40
Ah! You overwhelm me: Gay III, 51
Imagine, my Lord, no buckles: Roland *Memoirs* 61

Chapter 6 · AMAZONE

*provoked and irritated . . . ineffectually . . . So much . . . left side . . . the famous . . .
    betray their secrets*: The next quotations, Roudinesco 64, 65, 64, 65, 55
particularly dangerous for . . . the French revolution: The next quotations, Ernst
    39, 42
*how it was . . . grave political crimes . . . the delightful person . . . As far as politics
    . . . This tyranny . . . This vision . . . prisoner's sworn enemies*: The next
    quotations, Roudinesco 58, 58, 58, 71, 71, 71, 62
the accused seems to be: Ernst 206
luminous and surprising . . . to her principles: The next quotations, Roudinesco 75,
    79
I can announce . . . the women's tribune: Ernst 249
president of her . . . long a time: The next quotations, Roudinesco 92, 96–7
for having escaped . . . they are citoyennes: Applewhite and Levy 90
she will serve her: Villiers 76
to find their household: Roudinesco 100
Women have shared . . . to both sexes: WRP 123
our most illustrious . . . celebration of insurrection: The next quotations, Dowd 56, 64
provide a mirror in which: Ozouf 23
Plant a stake crowned with: Dowd 81
I was there . . . festival of the people: Jullien 67
Whatever one may say: Ozouf 66
The pikes of the people: Applewhite and Levy 89
Jacobins' strumpet: Roudinesco 94
a manhunter, mad for men: Ernst 256
république: Landes 21
our shameful institutions . . . range the forests: Plutarch III, 426

the women who . . . all their scars: Roudinesco 105
Since we cannot find men: Ernst 263
constantly undermined the arrangements: Roland *Memoirs* 87
aimed at a . . . to their friends: The next quotations, Staël *Considerations* II, 28, 30
at the centre . . . me no rest: The next quotations, Roland *Memoirs* 62, 89
I hope only to be: May 212
an ardent lover . . . your mortal enemies: Roland *Lettres* II, 417
proved his lack . . . for the Republic: Roland *Memoirs* 89
will be accomplished . . . revolutions become necessary: Schama 605
the most pure language: Gidney 12
I would never . . . was worth something: The next quotations, Roland *Memoirs* 91, 97, 98
the tree of liberty grows: Paulson 24
in the most profound . . . What a triumph: Jullien 134
the heart of . . . this play-acting: Schama 607
la femme du roi was: Jullien 139
like a last cry: Yalom 154
He seemed a sacred victim: Staël *Considerations*, II, 53
the pleasure of . . . in actual possession: Gower I, 46
Let us strike this colossus: Schama 612
Pauvre Louis . . . but of them: The next quotations, Jullien 206, 194, 217
They all seemed . . . mirth and enjoyment: Moore *Journal* I, 5
monotonous, mournful and rapid: Staël *Considerations* II, 66
citoyennes without citizenhood: Godineau 122
stabbed, sabred, stoned and clubbed: Schama 615
to fight the . . . in my place: WRP 159
Citizens, the National Assembly: Roudinesco 113
carrying one of his children: Moore *Journal* I, 32
Day of blood: Jullien 217

Chapter 7 · ÉMIGRÉE

as much distinguished by his: Moore *Journal* I, 117
that men were born equal: Brissot *Life* 7
no longer possible: Staël *CG* II, part 2, 354
Not a carriage was: Frénilly 115
with death in . . . an equal footing: Staël *Considérations* II, 68
At last I can hope: Staël *CG* II, part 1, 1
You have saved my life: Staël *Lettres à Narbonne* 51
A little English phlegm: Moore *Journal* I, 63. Moore was actually writing about the debates at the National Assembly for exactly this period
Applauders and murmurers are: Moore *Journal* I, 126
a man devoted to public: Jullien 120
distinguished herself in the action: Moore *Journal* I, 70

Citizens, no nation . . . have been over: Schama 628

ravening wolves: Roland *Memoirs* 68

the first battle we shall: Schama 630

rise and let the blood: Gottschalk 124

good citizens to . . . departure of citizens: The next quotations, Schama 630, 630, 631

une heure un . . . in his vanity: Staël *Considérations* II, 71

All Paris saw . . . easily have prevented: Roland *Memoirs* 71

profound and sombre silence: Schama 634

the terrible details . . . torn to pieces: Loomis 83

naked, quivering bodies: Cobb *The French* 143

nothing but cutting . . . of the massacre: The next quotations, Gutwirth 309, 339, 340

asking for it: Linda Orr in Melzer and Rabine, 124

a swarm of . . . under a vault . . . sink into it: The next quotations, Staël *Considerations* II, 71, 73, 77

dying of hunger, of thirst: Staël *Considérations* II, 77

with their arms . . . on our minds: The next quotations, Staël *Considérations* II, 73, 78

Is it possible . . . lamenting their fate: The next quotations, Moore *Journal* I, 184, 185, 199

three years of . . . know the French: The next quotations, Jullien 285, 298

Anarchy is rampant . . . will enforce it: Bouloiseau 11

he was neither . . . they blew cold: Hardman 54

Kings are to the moral: Roudinesco 121

She shared all my fears: Ferrus 137

symbols of despotism: Houssaye 54

designated victims: Bearne 125

woman of rank: Moore *Journal* I, 255

The visible signs of patriotism: HMW 1796 I, 193

a tailor of the ancien: Loomis 276

poudré, frisé, parfumé: Ribeiro 84

Toi suits citizen . . . of good manners: Soboul *Parisian Sans-Culottes* 227

a mutual estimation: Tomalin 165

gay ornamental drapery: Landes 131

very disagreeable: Wollstonecraft 220

Do not kill . . . evil you do: The next quotations, Staël *CG* II, part 1, 16, 51

There can be nothing imagined: Burney 235

I love you . . . kind of doubt: The next quotations, Staël *CG* II, part 1, 41, 35, 95–6

Chapter 8 · FEMME POLITIQUE

Ferocious in face . . . evil reputation: The next quotations, Roland *Memoirs* 65 (trans. Loomis 201), 171, 65, 64

If the gratification: Moore *Journal* II, 148

and that there was no: Roland *Memoirs* 64

generous ideas . . . obstinate assurance: Barras I, 104

They had no . . . use her pen: Roland *Memoirs* 66

had been unable either to: Roland *Mémoires* (ed. Roux) 20

Most of them thought: Roland *Memoirs* 69

You know that I do: Loomis 76

that fanatical: Roland *Mémoires* (ed. Roux) 124

I don't give a damn: Roland *Memoirs* 44

necessary to appease the people: Schama 633

this personal predicament enabled: Roland *Memoirs* 72

see my husband's glory intact: Roland *Lettres* II, 756

had nothing to lose: Roland *Memoirs* 67

the unfortunate and almost ridiculous: Tocqueville 209

honnêtes gens: Bouloiseau 50

dispatch them in advance: Furet *Interpreting* 68

very vigorous measures . . . virtue and vice: The next quotations, Moore
    Journal II, 17, 215

No one is more fair: May 231

It was past midnight: Loomis 218

His only object . . . this is one reason . . . menace, or contempt: The next quotations,
    Moore *Journal* II, 145, 144, 101

Do you want a Revolution: Schama 649

as much enlivened . . . their mutual animosity: The next quotations, Moore
    Journal II, 181, 206

sweet as a . . . than from love: Jullien 342

He retires before . . . in his heart: The next quotations, Moore *Journal* II, 212, 146

solitary rebel: Arasse 50

Louis must die: Hardman 74

He knows that he is: Moore *Journal* II, 358

The blood, even of the: Kelly 81

To kill a king, you: Roudinesco 126

Who'll bid me . . . demand first refusal: Stevenson ii

amphibious animal: Roudinesco 125

neither the physique nor: Stevenson ii

I die content that: Schama 672

donned its costume and borrowed: Yonge I, 232

flocked to their . . . out the candle: Todd 216. The entry in her diary is dated 26
    Dec. 1792 but this must be a mistake since she is clearly describing the day
    of Louis's execution, 21 Jan. 1793

At half past ten: La Tour du Pin 177

it would be . . . a brilliant court: Arasse 60

to protect my honour: Roland *Memoirs* 37

if we did not possess: May 253

because he was not prepared: Roland *Memoirs* 28
retired from office: HMW 1794 II, 146
I am ashamed . . . my own house: May 252
theatre where she . . . recover her empire: Roland *Mémoires* (ed. Perroud) II, 475
great deal: Roland *Memoirs* 54
He adored me . . . chagrins domestiques: The next quotations, Roland *Lettres* II,
    757, 680, 759
it must be feared that: Schama 714
he is evidently a republican: Plutarch II, 225
repeated discussions about foodstuffs: WRP 126–7
thirty thousand women might assemble: Cerati 24
To provoke trouble . . . stirring up trouble: The next quotations, WRP 130, 140
I believe that . . . hard and unpitying: George 418
he will always prevent: Gottschalk 177
notary and curé: Soboul *Parisian Sans-Culottes* 245
the Jacobins and their supporters: Roland *Memoirs* 30
entirely personal: Roland *Lettres* II, 760
corrupt deputies: Shulim 270
a confusion of sounds inexpressibly: HMW 1790 4
saw at once . . . of the guilty: The rest of the quotations in this chapter, Roland
    Memoirs 32–5, 39–40

Chapter 9 · MARIÉE

all the calm . . . is Mlle Bernard: Letter reprinted in full in English in Herriot I,
    11–13, and in French in Wagener 504–5
singulièrement jolie: Wagener 17
play some great part: Herriot I, 3n.
to the great satisfaction of: Wagener 18
little doll: Roland *Memoirs* 136
was never anything . . . charmed his eyes: Lenormant *Memoirs* 7
respected her sensibilities: Herold 287
without the least worry: Wagener 36
as of a kind friend: Mohl 6
mother of warriors: Christiansen 103
we must not make too: Cobb *The Police* 91

Chapter 10 · ACTIVISTE

glorious . . . pay it homage . . . of the Republic: The next quotations, WRP 159,
    156–7, 159
On average only a tenth . . .: Palmer *Twelve* 27
to instruct themselves . . . Robespierre [and] Marat: The next quotations, WRP
    161–5, 159
exclusively: HMW 1796 I, 139

Fellow citizens, let . . . for their age: Roudinesco 132–4
Brissotine . . . incredible fury: The next quotations, Ernst 280, 277
le fouet: Duhet 80
depraved societies . . . of their sex: The next quotations, Cerati 55, 26
intoxicated Bacchanalians . . . drunk with blood: Melzer and Rabine 93
Vive la Montagne . . . Equality . . . domestic animals: The next quotations, Cerati
    56, 57, 54
evil influences, under: Hufton 30
Who rang the tocsin . . . We did: George 422
troupe de furies, avide: Hufton 31
in the passages: HMW 1796 I, 73
Their zeal is . . . coquines of Paris: The next quotations, Cerati 93, 55
firmness and intrepidity . . . themselves doubly useful: WRP 176–7
The vices of our education: Roudinesco 130
women are far from being: Soboul *BHÉSRF* 19
It would seem that, born: Gutwirth 293
joy and satisfaction . . . Constitution: WRP 160
Let Marat's head . . . them all guillotined: The next quotations, Schama 730, 736
assassinated by a . . . that great man: Petrey 73
Her beautiful face . . . with Charlotte Corday: Schama 741
She has killed us: Kelly 101
This woman being . . . race of Caen: The next quotations, Petrey 74, 72
There is no . . . sovereignty is enemy: Brooks 56
the red priest of: Hufton 27
A state is . . . belong to everyone: The next quotations, Soboul *Parisian
    Sans-Culottes* 63, 61
Victory is assured when women: Mathiez *Vie* 132
apostle of liberty: George 419
be replaced by the energy: Hufton 32n.
It is your . . . glory awaits you: WRP 175
director of the knitters . . .: WRP 166–71
grace and beauty: Plutarch I, 25 et seq.
O Women! Liberty . . . women of France: Schama 749
In making yourselves more motherly: Gutwirth 178
cold and indolent . . . I had hoped: Roland *Memoirs* 38
the nectar of the age: Applewhite and Levy 61
charmante nourrice: La Tour du Pin 206
We are all . . . the people life: The next quotations, Sennett *Flesh and Stone* 310,
    291

Chapter 11 · PRISONNIÈRE

men stood up . . . without curtains . . . capable of mastering: The next quotations, Roland *Memoirs* 41, 45, 42

since the national representation: HMW 1796 I, 172

Folly and crime have triumphed: Roland *Memoirs* 49

The evil sans-culottes . . . in the provinces: Roland *Lettres* II, 759

My conscience spoke to me: Brissot *Life* 75

How many times . . . of your valour: The next quotations, Roland *Lettres* II, 481, 484

With a smooth . . . like a homing pigeon . . . Citoyenne Roland . . . You would have thought . . . Commissioners . . . indecent curiosity . . . one of those . . . Gesture supplies . . . if my conscience . . . these dregs of . . . This is where . . . a cutlet . . . All they had done . . . These tyrants . . . the man who . . . of the people: The next quotations, Roland *Memoirs* 109, 110, 110, 111, 111, 112, 115, 115, 171, 115, 115, 113, 113, 115, 116, 82

believed nothing good could: Loomis 201

the thing that has struck: Roland *Memoirs* 97–8

to the degree that power: Outram in Porter, 125

This seemed my . . . my moral and political . . . the fire myself: The next quotations, Roland *Memoirs* 33, 75, 75

Here, behind bars and bolted: May 264

can I complain . . . my last sigh: Roland *Lettres* II, 492–3

overcome the contradiction: Outram 138

How I cherish the bars: Roland *Lettres* II, 500

chains that honour . . . no-one can see: May 265

this sweet image: Roland *Lettres* II, 499

How immediate . . . my ardent kisses: Rousseau *La Nouvelle Héloïse* 215–6

a loving soul . . . to practise it: Roland *Mémoires* (ed. Perroud) II, 437

pleasant little . . . unpatriotic talk: Roland *Memoirs* 121

I would hardly have believed: Roland, *Mémoires* (ed. Roux) 290

Chapter 12 · RÉVOLUTIONNAIRE

une petite crise . . .: Caron I, 94

The cockade . . . movements too much: Caron I, 150

Two citizens cannot whisper: Mercier *Waiting City* 121

and the queue represented: La Tour du Pin 194

Our husbands made the revolution: Caron I, 150

rage and despair . . . A Single heart . . . The most delicate . . . my own eyes: The next quotations, Yalom 199, 182, 182, 183

Who dares to . . . by bonnes rêpublicaines: The next quotations, Cobban I, 236, 165

coward: George 426

You are infatuated . . . pale and tremble: WRP 178–81

unanimous judgement: George 427
the doubly advantageous . . . to crush tyranny: Hufton 33
She claimed that one didn't: WRP 187
advocates of tyranny or federalism: Blanc xii
cockroach eyes . . . women to him: The next quotations, WRP 189, 189, 187, 190
It is these . . . not watch out: Hufton 35
*Citoyenne Lacombe . . . if they wanted . . . À bas . . . The first one . . . The tumult
. . . We found nothing . . . All the ills . . . ill of you*: The next quotations, WRP
191, 183, 192, 192, 183, 196, 193, 191
by their rudeness . . . desire to share . . . One can put it . . . citoyennes patriotes: The
next quotations, Caron I, 92, 154, 192, 162
very much an . . . being an aristocrat . . . aristocracy to wear them: The next
quotations, WRP 202, 203, 207
Down with red bonnets!: WRP 209–12
but adventurers, knights errant: Soboul *BHÉSRF* 26n.
violence and threats . . . the public safety: These next quotations, WRP 213–17
to organise in clubs: Landes 145
occasioned by a false report: George 436
Impudent women who . . . of the Fatherland: The rest of the quotations in this
chapter, WRP 219–20, 160, 160

Chapter 13 · VICTIME

I can feel . . . to be confined: The next quotations, Roland *Memoirs* 154, 156, 75,
156, 126, 156, 162, 163
How Robespierre loves blood: Roland *Mémoires* (ed. Roux) 302
I cannot go . . . nearer to you: The next quotations, Roland *Memoirs* 252, 254, 258
sincere and ardent . . . longer reign here: Roland *Lettres* II, 522–3
made no defence: HMW 1796, I, 155
Romans again: Outram 95
We are accused . . . are our functions: Palmer *Twelve* 71
in such a . . . his country's shame: HMW 1796 I, 163
sorte de joie: Roland *Mémoires* (ed. Perroud) II, 484
My God I am sorry: Schama 804
resolving to wait the appointed: HMW 1796 I, 162
displayed a villainous . . . the greatest consternation: Blanc 65
conspiring against the unity: Roland *Memoirs* 259
As for me . . . my unhappy husband: Roland *Lettres* II, 529
seemed absorbed in profound meditations: Roland *Mémoires* (ed. Perroud) II, 493
misfortunes and a long confinement: May 280, quoting Riouffe
No woman could . . . had met death with . . . The tender and . . . his own heart:
The next quotations, Yonge I, 175, 175, 174, 178
It is for . . . see me pass: The next quotations, Roland *Mémoires* (ed. Perroud) II,
489, 491

Long live the Republic: Roland *Memoirs* 259
You find me . . . they have shown: Roland *Mémoires* (ed. Roux) 37
a certain joyfulness: May 285
It suits you . . . fresh, calm, smiling: Roland *Mémoires* (ed. Perroud) II, 494
O Liberté, que de crimes: Roland *Mémoires* (ed. Roux) 38; Mercier *New Picture* I,
    206. Another version is 'O Liberté, comme on t'a jouée!', Christiansen 115
What more than Roman fortitude: HMW 1801 II, 63
he had died . . . covered with crimes: May 290–1
She is no . . . you have lived: Roland *Mémoires* (ed. Perroud) II, 269–70
the sword of . . . proud device: The next quotations, Arasse 75, 74
familiarized, domesticated and commodified: Stuart 134
It was not the love: Arasse 89
she showed very . . . alarmed the mob: Elliott 114
ambitious, without genius: Stevenson iii
Children of the Fatherland: WRP 259
Oh fatal aspiration to fame: Arasse 113
abnormal sexuality: Melzer and Rabine 115
Marie-Antoinette was . . . of her sex: Brooks 59
in so strange, so shocking: Kotzebue II, 172, records Julie Talma's account of
    Manon's last night in prison
the faithless subject . . . was an author: Plutarch III, 391
character renders beauty respectable: Kelly 129
The Goddess: on a person: Agulhon 30
that he had expelled: Mercier *New Picture* II, 81
In Pau, the women of . . .: Ozouf 101
Reason as the Supreme Being: Schama 779
Republican woman, preserve . . . me to suffer: Blanc 18

Chapter 14 · MAÎTRESSE

met a woman so endowed: Gastine 113
Thérésia and I, happy as: Abrantes *Salons* III, 191
the roving représentant . . . the great man: Cobb *The Police* 190
Between October and December Tallien . . .: Vivie II, 143
Bleed the purses and level: Ferrus 30
severe and sweet at: Bourquin 128
You think that . . . moi vous embrassons: Ferrus 117
He had rendered her some: La Tour du Pin 196
for having intimate . . . fall into discredit: Ferrus 165
*as good as . . . You will be safe . . . encouraged by . . . All these enemies . . . importune
    you further*: The next quotations, La Tour du Pin 196, 196, 196, 198
Thérésia stayed in the forbidding . . .: See Ferrus 158 on whether she really was in
    prison in Bordeaux; it seems likely, but there is no conclusive evidence
Consider my terror . . . shrugged her shoulders: La Tour du Pin 202

Such is the fate of: Gilles 105
une étrangère . . . question than Tallien: Ferrus 187
His heavy and monotonous style: Abrantes *Memoirs* I, 248
enemies to moral . . . will soon disappear: Ferrus 196 et seq.
At intervals the expression: Abrantes *Memoirs* I, 249
I risked my life: Gilles 142
stopping for neither . . . a pathetic scene: La Tour du Pin 203
You are an . . . I love Tallien: Bickley 64
divine, heavenly libératrice . . . devotion until death: Gilles 127
loved gold: Lage de Volude 172
these new Luculluses: Ferrus 208
Luxury suits neither my principles: Gilles 115
believe in the esteem: Ferrus 216
with all the grace: La Tour du Pin 209
spitting blood . . . was paying dear . . . that she had . . . Hand me . . . He did not
  speak . . . Believe me . . . a sort of honour . . . I will not . . . have been useful:
  The next quotations, Lage de Volude 171, 172, 174, 175, 175, 183, 185, 186, 176
so out of . . . first she wanted to show . . . tears of joy: The next quotations, La
  Tour du Pin 216, 216, 219
Anarchy from within . . . into the world: Palmer *Twelve* 5
If the mainspring . . . and inflexible justice: Bienvenu 33
We seek an order: Shulim 274
The grocers continue . . . haven of happiness: Bienvenu 71–2
Some wish to . . . tempest be steered: Palmer *Twelve* 129
dangerous weakness . . . tears of repentance: HMW 1796 II, 164
A revolution like ours: Bouloiseau 37
the most daring courage: HMW 1796 I, 13
who were not . . . of the earth: Gilles 136
I cannot look at: Ferrus 281
not to become . . . saluer mon papa: The next quotations, HMW 1796 II, 28; III,
  186
Adieu Loulou, adieu . . . going to die: Schama 820
Among the victims . . . of its tenderness: HMW 1796 I, 213
One can no . . . talk so loud: The next quotations, Blanc 64, 63

Chapter 15 · LIBÉRATRICE

Bordeaux seems to . . . portion of the . . . petite, menton rond: The next quotations,
  Gilles 148, 149–50 (excerpts from the document), 152
All the papers relating to: Gastine 22
Never did Robespierre pursue: Gilles 158, quoting Taschereau
silent streets and barricaded doors: Frénilly 124
Everyone seemed to slip through: Lacretelle 129
Women did not . . . doors securely closed: Frénilly 125

to see what sort of: HMW 1796 II, 67

impairing the purity of: Schama 837

Arbitrary power against which: Staël *Considerations* II, 33

crowded with commissaries and soldiers: HMW 1796 I, 10

an important component: Cobb *The French* 17

Let her look in: Gilles 165

The true priest . . . and feeling hearts: Schama 831

proclaim himself king, open: Hortense I, 36

When we are mothers: Ozouf 116

You may kill . . . round with iron: Yonge I, 180

United by the . . . No, he wants nothing . . . to the scaffold: The next quotations
    HMW 1796 I, 19; II, 102; II, 102

unworthy of a . . . any political matter: WRP 231

he who would have been: Hortense I, 34

A natural sentiment and: WRP 160

state of madness . . . suspect remarks: Ernst 283

If you are . . . would second me: Roudinesco 147

neither in his . . . of the people: Gilles 172

was the Terror itself: Barras I, 264

incapable of personal . . . at an end: Staël *Considerations* II, 142

Tallien contended for two lives: Fouché I, 16

that is to say . . . courage; calm yourself: Ouvrard I, 18

I will go to my: Ferrus 406

almost touching the guillotine: Bienvenu 234

I am from no faction: Gilles 183

It's the blood of Danton: Houssaye 5

Until now I . . . of the traitors: Gilles 185

Do you suffer, your majesty: Lyons 125

when the Thermidoreans killed Robespierre: Bienvenu 3

victory of representative . . . most tragic discourse: The next quotations, Furet
    Interpreting 58, 61

too near a . . . oppose nor govern: Fouché 15

at last, France is free: Aulard *La Réaction* I, 6

To finish the revolution: HMW 1796 IV, 172

Tallien! Thou raised thyself: Mercier *New Picture* II, 89

still pleased with . . . openness of heart: Wollstonecraft 259

I would prefer . . . weapon of tyranny: The next quotations, Bienvenu 234, 305

Terror is a . . . of the soul: Lajer-Burcharth 16

Je me porte . . . me porte bien: HMW 1796 III, 181

the most beautiful day: Gilles 191 (letter to Charles de Pougens)

Chapter 16 · ÉPOUSE

No-one was unaware . . . heart to everyone: Gilles 201
She seemed to us: Lacretelle 196
evil genius: Bienvenu 333
burst forth with uncontrollable energy: HMW 1796 III, 2
Life began again: Lacretelle 200
Men's hearts and minds: Gastine 121, quoting Lacretelle
The theatres, the public walks: HMW 1796 III, 190
absolutely indispensable: Gilles 200
an unheard-of impoliteness: Frénilly 129
Tallien loves you . . . and very busy: Gilles 200
The greatest of all miracles: Mercier *New Picture* v
We demand from Tallien: Bourquin 259
Villain, I have . . . of the people: Gilles 195
the entire audience was standing: Stuart 153, quoting Pasquier
The men who had taken: Bienvenu 335
The new revolution which: Herold 156
strange character of uncertainty: Tocqueville 222, quoting Meister
That woman is capable of: Gilles 203
Subsistence is always the subject: Aulard *La Réaction* I, 340
universal brocantage: Meister 124
Nothing was either . . . was a conspiracy: Frénilly 129
When one comes through: Gilles 133
We speak of . . . affection and respect: Ferrus 154
This, citizens, this is: Gilles 214
I would like so much: Jullien 314
a necessary introduction to good: HMW 1796 III, 2
People speak of patriotism: Meister 190
that peach-blossom dress you: Ducrest I, 270
l'idole du jour: Bourquin 272
Never had fashion . . . rules and boundaries: Tocqueville 198
adding that it was not: Gastine 303
with inimitable grace: Abrantes *Salons* III, 145
One could not be more: Lacour 66
The beloved is always pictured: Kotzebue III, 149
fecund belles: Meister 127
intoxicated by the speed: Bruce 83
Despairing of escape from: Tocqueville 197
collective cultural mourning: Lajer-Burcharth 6
What do they do: Almeras 266
enjoyed the only role fitting: Bienvenu 328
the beautiful Mme Tallien always: Gay III, 83

Contracts might be for anything: Bruce 81, quoting Kotzebue
not the main . . . procured for others: Barras II, 65
It is impossible, no matter: Bienvenu 331
une nouvelle Antoinette: Gilles 213
The airs of a courtesan: Aulard *La Réaction* I, 374
to rebellion and . . . most violent excitement: The next quotations, Applewhite and
    Levy 74, 76
If you go . . . are all suckers: WRP 283
One hundred and forty-eight . . .: Hufton 47
hotbed of insurrection: Soboul BHÉSRF 23
inconveniences that might result: WRP 308
assess the revolution . . . far too high: Hufton in Johnson 166
But for me . . . so intoxicated me: Bourquin 295
To forget mistakes: Houssaye 8
Tallien's company . . . thirst for success: Gilles 133
a lion sharing a cell: Lairtullier II, 298
with nothing in the way: Bienvenu 342
Tallien incapable of rising: Barras I, 391
Too much blood . . . repelled by him: Gilles 225
another attempt to realise: Furet and Richet 258
À demain les affaires: Gay III, 184
beautiful as in old romances: Girod de l'Ain 73
So, my friend, you have: Gilles 234
unconquerable passion: Barras II, 68

Chapter 17 · RETOURNEÉ

joyeuse, sur la route: Staël *CG* III, part 1, 332
Talking seemed everybody's . . . of her life: Boigne 190
to begin life anew, but: Herold 153
*There is, in . . . the most beautiful eyes . . . and inflicts his unhappines . . . with the
    desirable*: the next quotations, Fairweather 183, 199, 200 (and Staël *CG* III,
    part 1, 158), 202
If France crumbles . . . they will win: Herold 158
honourable and unexpected . . . wife is arriving: The next quotations, Fairweather
    205, 207
What things a man could: Herold 161
What do they do at: Almeras 266
frankly republican . . . talent, her principles: Bienvenu 329
Like the muse of history: Gastine 127
flesh-coloured pantaloons: Herold 168
We hear about . . . do the opposite: Fairweather 216 (slightly reworded)
graceful flattery . . . them to themselves: Staël *Considerations* II, 149
the principles of the revolution: Staël *Ten Years* 20

They hate you more: Herold 163

To speak of . . . their own use: Furet and Richet 262

would see to it that: Bruce 143

a corrupter of all those: Staël *CG* III, part 2, 43

ready-made: Barras II, 70

inventing a thousand . . . in your bed: Ouvrard I, 121

How could you . . . way with Bonaparte: Elliott 148.

got rid of her by: Frénilly 154

except from motives . . . they seemed, so to speak . . . It was a known fact . . . of her temperament: The next quotations, Barras II 66, 67, 67, 66

has not taken vows: Gower I, 177

I love you and will: Bruce 254

chère Thérésita . . . baisers bien tendres: Catinat 41

and see who is on: Abrantes *Memoirs* I, 250

a woman of so many: Turquan 103

Moved to tears at this: Gastine 207n.

Her humanity is . . . to be pitied: Gower I, 135

How shall a pure: Berger 179

by far the . . . admired at Paris: The next quotations, Gower I 138, 141

nothing but anarchy tempered by: Tocqueville 191

indifferents, who . . . like tragedy heroes: the next quotations, HMW 1801 II, 8, 3

seriously dignified and truly: Hunt 80

I still love . . . one's own country: Staël *CG* IV, part 1, 23

When in public . . . 9th of Thermidor: Frénilly 136

No man could equal: Bruce 35

Who has asked . . . both at once: Herold 179

Far from contesting . . . themselves men's duties: Barras I, 104

entirely neglected: Gutwirth 381

men had found it politically: Berger 185

they perceived that there was: Mercier *New Picture* 31

Never have women . . . kill your revolution: Lajer-Burcharth 242

beautiful Athenian: Abrantes *Salons* III, 171

to the greatest . . . of the government: Gilles 271

breasts uncovered, heads tossing: Mercier *Waiting City* 76

to his wishes in order: Gower I, 135

all powerful . . . with the royalists: The next quotations, La Tour du Pin 304, 309

we will all perish by: Bruce 190

The end of the letter: La Tour du Pin 311

the best republican in France: Herold 178

tone of noble . . . of military violence: Staël *Ten Years* 4

bestowed very little attention: Talleyrand I, 196

constantly . . . act upon him: Staël *Considerations* II, 196

not like a . . . to do so: The next quotations, Staël *Ten Years* 5, 9

Genius has no sex: Herold 181
that he did not, and: Hortense I, 49
son and hero of the: Herold 180
Madam, I love . . . number of children: Fairweather 240
political rights: Herold 182
with an appearance of friendship: Chastenay 258
notre charmante Chaumière . . . the unfortunate Tallien: Gilles 284
The baroness among . . . see her again: Herold 183
in the shape of exile: Staël *Corinne* 29

Chapter 18 · ICÔNE

brilliant with youth . . . heart of gold: Constant *Intermédiaire* 873
She speaks of her caboche: Bourquin 305
reigned in peace until Juliette: Herriot I, 29
Afterwards, Juliette and Thérésia . . .: portrait seen by the author at the château de Chimay
her fine figure . . . in the shade: Herriot I, 29
Are not her . . . and ridiculous expressions: Plutarch I, 139–40
Avenge thus the arrogance: Houssaye 7
the perfect woman: Boigne 177
was the least of her: Herriot I, 44
wholly beautiful . . . she was seen: Boigne 167
a vain coquet . . . being so beauteous: Plutarch I, 145
seemed anxious to conceal: Ducrest I, 59
You intoxicate yourself: Lenormant *Memoirs* 56
to electrify the world: Lajer-Burcharth 344, quoting Bernadotte
the enthusiasm that I excited: Herriot I, 64
threw her a look of: Lenormant *Memoirs* 11
At each of . . . this fleeting pity: The next quotations, Herriot I, 47, 61, 62, 50
struck by the beauty of: Wagener 64
An expression at one: Levaillant 38
to portray a . . . I should use: Lenormant *Madame Récamier, les amis . . .* viii
Do not have a greater: Herriot I, 80
Say to me . . . to my heart: Faderman 80
Why, whether in love: Herold 289
I thought of nothing but: Wagener 64
The speed with which one: Fairweather 262
The wealth of France had: Hortense I, 56
In all her . . . no one else: Staël *Corinne* 91
recalling the legend of Psyche . . .: Lajer-Burcharth 278
beautiful white shoulders . . . full of men: Gower I, 377
bewildered by her isolation: Brookner 144
into a palace of rubies: Mercier *New Picture* II, 125

perpetual circle of . . . dangerously fascinating: Trotter 226–7

these enchanting places: Almeras 98

surrounded and almost overpowered by: Trotter 341

kissing and chewing the train: Lajer-Burcharth 258

If one is happy to: Abrantes *Salons* III, 154

the Directory fell by: Talleyrand I, 203

waiting for the first master: Roland *Memoirs* 155

I do not . . . all of those: Hunt 184

two powerful passions: Fouché 72

but that he . . . owes me everything: Bruce 283

What can be done: Fouché 76

with charming vivacity: Barras IV, 104

on the happiness . . . drafted by . . . positive . . . follow one's convictions: The next quotations, Herold 185, 220, 220, 221

merely a question of dates: Loomis 104

I live with . . . tired of being . . . supervision of everything: The next quotations, Herold 225 (Fairweather 264), 245, 221

was once my . . . keep her out: The next quotations, Gastine 249, 246

Do you still . . . they are polite: Bruce 337

oriental etiquette: Staël *Considerations* II, 393

I hope that . . . of Citoyenne Bonaparte: Stuart 270

To have once loved Mme: Bruce 429

who was so timid without: Lenormant *Memoirs* 44

It was often . . . except its workings: Berger 46

every quality of . . . a gambler's fervour: Stuart 160

Enamoured of the lubricities: Sade *Zoloé* 17

the baptism of the personal: Stuart 274

In short . . . what I think: Berger 4

Advise her not . . . yes or no: The next quotations, Herold 230, 228

A woman distinguished . . . laws of nature: Fairweather 341

You are right . . . know the reason: Staël *Considerations* II, 201

which is and always has: Gilles 304

Few women had had it: Gower I, 402–3

glittering, radiant beauty: Vigée-Lebrun 238

They say she talks about: Christiansen 133

the tyranny of public opinion: Fairweather 286

Women . . . all social institutions: Herold 238

He fears me . . . not my will: Fairweather 279

like an Irishman who kept: Herold 251

No, no, there is no: Fairweather 293

could never appear . . . bear life elsewhere: The next quotations, Herold 290, 245

What I want . . . stick to knitting: Fairweather 349

We need the notion of: Bruce 313

Public education is not suitable: Stuart 271
had not her first husband: Plutarch II, 311
It is all very well: Gastine 304
Nay, God forbid . . . in her hand: Kotzebue I, 219
He has not yet met: Lenormant *Memoirs* 53
I am not Mme Récamier's: Levaillant 84

Chapter 19 · FEMMES

If I should deign: Houssaye 13
I own, madame: W. Russell, *Extraordinary Women* (London 1857) 211
revolutionary Fury: Roudinesco 152
expanded the soul: Lajer 17
What is most: Michelet 282
that received for humanity: Rosa 239
Although women were silenced: Landes 106
succeeded perfectly in carrying out: Outram in Porter 133
whether they . . . of the Republic!: The next quotations, HMW 1801 II, 52, 55
The Emperor has done: Fairweather 448

BIBLIOGRAPHY

PRIMARY SOURCES

Abrantes, L., *Memoirs* London 1883

——, *Histoire des salons de Paris* Brussels 1838

Applewhite, H., et al. (eds), *Women in Revolutionary Paris 1789–1795* Chicago Ill. 1979

Aulard, A. (ed.), *Paris pendant la réaction thermidorienne* Paris 1902

Barras, P., *Memoirs* London 1896

Berger, M. (ed.), *Madame de Staël on Politics, Literature and National Character* London 1964

Berry, M., *A Comparative View of the Social Life of England and France* London 1828

——, *Social Life in England and France from the French Revolution in 1789 to that of July 1830* London 1831

——, *Extracts from the Journals and Correspondence, 1783–1852* London 1865

Bickley, F. (ed.), *The Diaries of Sylvester Douglas (Lord Glenverbie)* London 1928

Boigne, E., *Memoirs* London 1907

Bonaparte, L., *Memoirs* London 1836

Brissot, J.-P., *New Travels in the USA Translated from the French* London 1792

——, *Life* London 1974

Burney, F., *The Diary and Letters of Madame D'Arblay* London 1931

Caron, P. (ed.), *Paris pendant la Terreur* Paris 1910

Catinat, M. (ed.), *Impératrice Joséphine: Correspondance 1782–1814* Paris 1996

Chastenay, V., *Mémoires* Paris 1987

Constant, C., in *Intermédiaire des chercheurs et des curieux* 20 Dec. 1898

Ducrest, G., *Memoirs of the Empress Josephine* 1894

Dumouriez, C.F., *Memoirs* London 1795

Elliott, G.D., *Journal of My Life during the French Revolution* London 1955

Ernst, O., *Théroigne de Méricourt* Paris 1935

Fouché, J., *Memoirs* London 1892
Frénilly, Baron de, *Recollections of Baron de Frénilly, Peer of France* London 1909

Gay, S., *Celebrated Saloons* Boston 1851
Genlis, F. de, *Memoirs* London 1825–6
Gérando, Baron, *Lettres inédites et souvenirs biographiques de Mme Récamier et Mme de Staël* Paris 1868
Gouges, O., *The Rights of Woman* London 1989
Gower, G.L., *Private Correspondence, 1781–1821* London 1916
Gronow, R.H., *The Reminiscences and Recollections of Captain Gronow* London 1870

Hall, H.J., *Napoleon's Letters to Josephine 1796–1812* London 1901
Hays, M., *Dictionary of Female Biography* London 1803
Hortense, Queen, *Memoirs* London 1928

Jullien, R., *Journal d'une bourgeoise pendant la révolution* Paris 1881

Kotzebue, A., *Travels from Berlin to Paris in 1804* London 1805

Lacretelle, C. de, *Dix années d'épreuves pendant la révolution* Paris 1842
Lage de Volude, B.-E., *Souvenirs d'émigration 1792–1794* Évreux 1869
La Tour du Pin, H.-L., *Memoirs* London 1999
Lenormant, A., *Memoirs and Correspondence of Madame Récamier* Boston Mass. 1867.
——, *Madame Récamier, les amis de sa jeunesse* Paris 1872
Luyster, I.M., *Memoirs and Correspondence of Madame Récamier* 1867

Meister, H., *Souvenirs de mon dernier voyage à Paris* Paris 1795
Mercier, L.-S., *The Waiting City. Paris 1782–1788* London 1933
——, *New Picture of Paris* London 1800
Méricourt, T., *Aux 48 Sections* Paris 1792
Mohl, M.E., *Madame Récamier, with a Sketch of the History of Society in France* London 1862
Moore, J.M., *A Journal during a Residence in France* Boston Mass. 1794
Morris, G., *A Diary of the French Revolution* London 1939

Ouvrard, G., *Mémoires* Paris 1826

Paine, T., *Basic Writings* New York 1942
Plutarch (pseud.), *The Female Revolutionary* London 1808

Reichardt, J.-F., *Un hiver à Paris sous le Consulat* Paris 1896
Roland, M., *Oeuvres* ed. L.A. Champagneux Paris 1799

——, *Lettres de Madame Roland* ed. C.L. Perroud Paris 1902
——, *Mémoires de Madame Roland* ed. C.L. Perroud Paris 1905
——, *Mémoires de Madame Roland* ed. P. de Roux Paris 1986
——, *The Memoirs of Madame Roland* (trans. E. Shuckburgh) Mount Kisco NY 1990
Rousseau, J.-J., *The Confessions* London 1953
——, *La Nouvelle Héloïse* University Park Pa. 1968
——, *Émile* London 1993

Sade, D. (attributed), *Zoloé et ses deux acolytes* Paris 1913
Staël, G., *Considerations on the Principal Events of the French Revolution* London 1818
——, *Considérations sur les principaux événements de la Révolution française* London 1818
——, *Ten Years of Exile* De Kalb Ill. 2000
——, *Letters on the Writings and Character of Jean-Jacques Rousseau* London 1814
——, *Réflexions sur le procès de la reine* Montpellier 1994
——, *Correspondance générale* ed. B.W. Jasinski Paris 1962
——, *Corinne, or Italy* London 1998
——, *Delphine* De Kalb Ill. 1995
——, *Lettres à Narbonne* ed. G. Solovieff Paris 1960

Talleyrand, C.-M., *Memoirs* London 1891
Tocqueville, A., *The Old Regime and the Revolution* Chicago Ill. 2001
Todd, J.M., *A Wollstonecraft Anthology* Bloomington Ind. 1977
Tourzel, L.-F.-J., *Memoirs* London 1886
Trotter, J.B., *Memoirs of the Latter Years of the Right Honourable Charles James Fox* London 1811

Vigée-Lebrun, É., *Memoirs* trans. S. Evans London 1989

Williams, H.M., *Letters Written in France in the Summer of 1790 to a Friend in England* London 1790
——, *Letters from France* London 1794
——, *Letters Containing a Sketch of the Politics of France* London 1796
——, *Sketches of the State of Manners and Opinions in the French Republic* London 1801
Wollstonecraft, M., *Collected Letters* ed. J.M. Todd London 2003

Yonge, C.M. (ed.), *Life and Adventures of Count Beugnot* 1871

SECONDARY SOURCES

Adams, W.H., *The Paris Years of Thomas Jefferson* New Haven Conn. 1997

Agulhon, M., *Marianne into Battle* Cambridge 1981

Almeras, H., *La Vie parisienne sous la révolution et le directoire* Paris 1909

Applewhite, H., and D. Levy (eds), *Women and Politics in the Age of Democratic Revolution* Ann Arbour Mich. 1990

Arasse, D., *The Guillotine and the Terror* London 1989

Aulard, A., *Histoire politique de la révolution française* Paris 1900

Bearne, C.M., *Heroines of French Society* London 1906

Bertaut, J., *Madame Tallien* Paris 1946

Bienvenu, R., *The Ninth of Thermidor: The Fall of Robespierre* Oxford 1968

Bizardel, Y., *The First Expatriates: Americans in Paris during the French Revolution* New York 1975

Blanc, O., *Last Letters: Prisons and the Prisoners of the French Revolution* New York 1987

Blanning, C.W., *The French Revolution: Class War or Culture Clash?* Basingstoke 1998

Boudet, M., *Julie Talma* Paris 1989

Bouloiseau, M., *The Jacobin Republic* Cambridge 1983

Bourdin, I., *Les sociétés populaires à Paris pendant la révolution* Paris 1937

Bourhis, K., *The Age of Napoleon: Costume from Revolution to Empire 1789–1815* New York 1989

Bourquin, M.-H., *Monsieur et Madame Tallien* Paris 1987

Brookner, A., *Jacques-Louis David* London 1980

Brooks, P., *Body Work: Objects of Desire in Modern Narrative* Cambridge Mass. 1993

Bruce, E., *Napoleon and Josephine: An Improbable Marriage* London 1995

Brunel, F., *Thermidor: la chute de Robespierre* Paris 1989

Byrne, P., *Perdita: The Life of Mary Robinson* London 2004

Caro, E.-M., 'Deux types de femmes de l'autre siècle' *Revue des deux mondes* XCII 15 Mar. 1871

Censer, J.R., and J. Popkin, *Press and Politics in Eighteenth-century France* Berkeley Calif. 1987

Cerati, M., *Le club des citoyennes révolutionnaires républicaines* Paris 1966

Chimay, E., *La Princesse de Chimères* Paris 1993

Chimay, Princesse, *Madame Tallien* Paris 1936

Christiansen, R., *Romantic Affinities: Portraits from an Age 1780–1830* London 1994

Clemenceau-Jacquemaire, M., *The Life of Madame Roland* London 1930
Cobb, R., *The French and their Revolution* London 1998
——, *Death in Paris* Oxford 1975
——, *A Sense of Place* London 1975
——, *The Police and the People* Oxford 1970
Cobban, A., *A History of Modern France 1715–1799* London 1961
Conner, C.D., *Jean-Paul Marat: Scientist and Revolutionary* Atlantic Highlands NJ 1997
Cooper, D., *Talleyrand* London 1932

Dauban, C., *Études sur Madame Roland et son temps* Paris 1864
Davis, N.Z., *Society and Culture in Early Modern France* Stanford Calif. 1975
Dolan, B., *Ladies of the Grand Tour* London 2001
Dowd, D.L., *Pageant-Master of the Republic: Jacques-Louis David and the French Revolution* Lincoln Nebr. 1948
Duhet, P.-M., *Les femmes et la révolution 1789–1794* Paris 1971
Dupuy, R., 'Les femmes et la contre-révolution dans l'Ouest' *Bulletin d'Histoire Économique et Sociale de la Révolution Française* Vol. 11 1979

Faderman, L., *Surpassing the Love of Men: Romantic Friendship and Love between Women from the Renaissance to the Present* London 1985
Fairweather, M., *Madame de Staël* London 2005
Ferrus, M., *Madame Tallien à Bordeaux* Bordeaux 1933
Furet, F., *Interpreting the French Revolution* Cambridge 1981
Furet, F., and D. Richet, *The French Revolution* London 1970

Gallet, M., *Paris Domestic Architecture of the Eighteenth Century* London 1972
Gastine, L., *Madame Tallien, Notre Dame de Thermidor: From the Last Days of the French Revolution until her Death as Princesse de Chimay in 1835* London 1913
Gay, P., *The Enlightenment: An Interpretation* New York 1966
George, M., 'The Républicaines-Révolutionnaires' *Science and Society* 40 (1976–7)
Gershoy, L., *Bertrand Barère: A Reluctant Terrorist* Princeton NJ 1962
Gidney, L., *L'Influence des États-Unis d'Amérique sur Brissot, Condorcet et Madame Roland* Paris 1930
Gilles, C., *Madame Tallien* Biarritz 1999
Girod de l'Ain, G., *Désirée Clary* Paris 1959
Godineau, D., *Citoyennes tricoteuses* Aix-en-Provence 1988
Goncourt, E. and J., *The Woman of the Eighteenth Century* London 1928
Gottschalk, L.R., *Jean-Paul Marat: A Study in Radicalism* Chicago 1967

Gutwirth, M., *The Twilight of the Goddesses: Women and Representation in the French Revolutionary Era* New Brunswick NJ 1992

Hampson, N., *A Cultural History of the French Revolution* London 1963
Hardman, J., *Robespierre* Harlow, Essex 1999
Harris, J., 'The red cap of liberty: a study of dress worn by French Revolutionary partisans 1789–94' *Eighteenth-century Studies* 14 (1981)
Herold, J.C., *Mistress to an Age* London 1958
Herriot, E., *Madame Récamier* London 1906
Hibbert, C., *Napoleon's Women* London 2003
Hill, B., *The Republican Virago: The Life and Times of Catherine Macaulay, Historian* Oxford 1992
Houssaye, A., *Notre dame de Thermidor* Paris 1867
Hufton, O., *Women and the Limits of Citizenship in the French Revolution* Toronto 1992
Hunt, L., *Politics, Culture and Class in the French Revolution* Berkeley Calif. 1984

Isambert, G., *La vie à Paris pendant une année de la révolution* Paris 1896

Johnson, D. (ed.), *French Society and the Revolution* Cambridge 1976
Jumièges, J.-C., *Madame Tallien* Paris 1967

Kelly, L., *Women of the French Revolution* London 1987
Kennedy, M., *The Jacobin Clubs in the French Revolution: The First Years* Princeton NJ 1982
——, *The Jacobin Clubs in the French Revolution: The Second Years* Princeton NJ 1988

Lacour, L., *Grand monde et salons politiques de Paris après la Terreur* Paris 1861
Lairtullier, E., *Les femmes célèbres de 1789 à 1795 et leur influence dans la révolution* Paris 1840
Lajer-Burcharth, E., *Necklines: The Art of Jacques-Louis David after the Terror* New Haven Conn. 1999
Landes, J.B., *Women and the Public Sphere in the Age of the French Revolution* Ithaca NY 1988
Lee, V., *The Reign of Women* London 1975
Levaillant, M., *The Passionate Exiles: Madame de Staël and Madame Récamier* London 1958
Lizin, A.M., *Théroigne de Méricourt* Brussels 1989
Loomis, S. *Paris in the Terror, June 1793–July 1794* New York 1964

Lyons, M., 'The 9 Thermidor: motives and effects' *European Studies Review*, 1975, pp.123–46

Marand-Fouquet, C., *La femme au temps de la révolution* Paris 1989
Marcourt, A. de, *La véritable Madame Tallien* Paris 1933
Marquiset, A., *Une merveilleuse: Mme Hamelin* Paris 1909
Mathiez, A., *The Fall of Robespierre* New York 1968
——, *La Vie chère et le mouvement social sous la Terreur* Paris 1927
May, G., *Madame Roland and the Age of Revolution* London 1970
Mayne, E.C., *A Regency Chapter: Lady Bessborough and Her Friendships* London 1939
McNair-Wilson, R., *The Gypsy-Queen of Paris* London 1934
Melzer, S.E., and L.W. Rabine, *Rebel Daughters: Women and the French Revolution* Oxford 1992
Michelet, J., *History of the French Revolution* London 1967
——, *Les femmes de la révolution* Paris 1988
Moore, J.M., *The Roots of French Republicanism* New York 1962

Outram, D., *The Body and the French Revolution* New Haven Conn. 1989
Ozouf, M., *Festivals and the French Revolution* Cambridge Mass. 1988

Palmer, R.R., *Twelve Who Ruled: The Committee of Public Safety during the Terror* Oxford 1989
——, *The Age of Democratic Revolution* Princeton NJ 1969
Paulson, R., *Representations of Revolution 1789–1820* New Haven Conn. 1983
Petrey, S. (ed.), *The French Revolution 1789–1989* Lubbock Tex. 1989
Porter, R. (ed.), *The Social History of Language* Cambridge 1987

Ribeiro, A., *Dress and Morality* London 1986
——, *The Art of the Dress* London 1995
Rosa, A., *Citoyennes: les femmes et la révolution française* Paris 1988
Roudinesco, E., *Théroigne de Méricourt* London 1991
Rudé, G., *The Crowd in the French Revolution* Oxford 1959
——, *Robespierre: A Portrait of a Revolutionary Democrat* London 1975

Sainte-Beuve, C.-A., *Portraits des femmes* Paris 1886
Savine, A., and F. Bournand, *Le 9 Thermidor* Paris 1907
Schama, S., *Citizens* London 1989
Sennett, R., *Flesh and Stone. The Body and the City in Western Civilisation* London 1994
——, *The Fall of Public Man* Cambridge 1977

Shulim, J.I., *Liberty, Equality and Fraternity: Studies on the Era of the French Revolution and Napoleon* New York 1989

Soboul, A., *The Parisian Sans-Culottes* London 1964

——, 'À propos de l'activité militante des femmes dans les sections parisiennes en l'an II' *Bulletin d'Histoire Économique et Sociale de la Révolution Française* 1979

Squire, G., *Dress, Art and Society 1560–1970* London 1974

Stevenson, V., *The Rights of Woman* London 1989

Stuart, A., *Josephine: the Rose of Martinique* London 2004

Sutherland, D.M.G., *France 1789–1815: Revolution and Counterrevolution* London 1985

Sydenham, M.J., *Girondins* London 1961

Tomalin, C., *The Life and Death of Mary Wollstonecraft* London 1974

Tulard, J., J.-F. Fayard and A. Fierro, *Histoire et dictionnaire de la révolution française* Paris 1987

Turquan, J., *La Citoyenne Tallien* Paris 1898

Villiers, M., *Histoire des clubs* Paris 1910

Vivie, A., *Histoire de la Terreur à Bordeaux* Bordeaux 1877

Wagener, F., *Madame Récamier* Paris 1986

Woronoff, D., *The Thermidorean Regime and the Directory 1794–1799* Cambridge 1984

Yalom, M., *Blood Sisters: The French Revolution in Women's Memory* London 1995

SECONDARY FIGURES

Full names and dates are given wherever I have been able to find them.

Laure, duchesse d'ABRANTES (1783–1834): memoirist; wife of one of Napoleon's generals, Jean-Andoche Junot, duc d'Abrantes

ALEXANDRE: secretary to Louis de Narbonne in 1792 and to Jean-Lambert Tallien in Bordeaux in 1793–4

André AMAR (1755–1816): Jacobin lawyer who sat on the Committee of General Security, 1793–4

'Reine' (Queen) AUDU: market woman; heroine of the women's march to Versailles in 1789

Jean-Sylvain BAILLY (1736–93): celebrated scientist and astronomer before the revolution, the liberal Bailly was elected mayor of Paris in July 1789, but his moderate views and his association with Lafayette earned him the distrust of the royalist party and the hatred of the republicans

Charles BARBAROUX (1767–94): prominent Girondin from Marseille, closely allied to Manon Roland and her friends

Bertrand BARÈRE (1755–1841): civilized and popular deputy to the National Assembly and then the Convention; one of the few Jacobins who managed to remain on good terms with many Girondins; on the Committee of Public Safety, 1793–4

Antoine BARNAVE (1761–93): one of the great orators of the first years of the revolution whose early liberalism gave way to support for the monarchy

Paul BARRAS (1755–1829): Provençal *vicomte* who became a deputy to the National Convention, *représentant en mission* to the Alps during the Terror, and held the post of Director throughout the Directory

Jeanne du BARRY (1743–93): mistress of Louis XV

Eugène and Hortense de BEAUHARNAIS: Rose's children by her first husband Alexandre de Beauharnais

Rose de BEAUHARNAIS (1763–1814): friend of Jean-Lambert and Thérésia Tallien; later, as Joséphine BONAPARTE, Empress of France

Lord BEDFORD: English visitor to Paris during the Terror; probably Lord John Russell, later Duke of Bedford (1766–1839)

Jean-Baptiste Jules BERNADOTTE (1763–1844): one of the most successful
generals of the Directory, with Jacobin sympathies; brother-in-law to
Napoléon (his wife was Joseph Bonaparte's sister-in-law); later Marshal
of the Empire (in 1804) and later still (1813) King of Sweden

Mary BERRY (1763–1852): English author, famous for her journals and
correspondence

Harriet, Lady BESSBOROUGH (1761–1821): sister of Georgiana Duchess of
Devonshire, and mistress during this period of Lord Granville Leveson
Gower

Jacques-Claude, comte de BEUGNOT (1761–1835): moderate deputy imprisoned
at the same time as Manon Roland; later a government minister under
Napoléon and a supporter of Louis XVIII; ennobled by Louis-Philippe
in 1831

William BIDOS: Thérésia Cabarrus's loyal manservant

François de BLANC: Austrian civil servant who dealt with Théroigne de
Méricourt's case at Kufstein in 1791

Adèle, comtesse de BOIGNE (1781–1866): memoirist

Joseph BONAPARTE (1768–1844): Napoléon Bonaparte's older brother, who
became King of Spain in 1808

Lucien BONAPARTE (1775–1840): Napoléon's younger brother, the most
sincerely radical of the three

Napoléon BONAPARTE (1769–1821): revolutionary general who became French
emperor

Renée BORDEREAU (1770–1824?): peasant woman who fought in the royalist
army of the Vendée

Augustin BOSC D'ANTIC (1759–1828): mineralogist, botanist and provincial
postal inspector before the revolution; friend of the Rolands from 1780,
associated with the Girondin circle in Paris in 1792–3

Nicolas-Edmé Restif de la BRETONNE (1734–1806): radical, licentious novelist
and social observer

Jacques-Pierre BRISSOT (1754–93): journalist and deputy to the National
Assembly; friend of the Rolands; unofficial leader of the Girondin party
(politically opposed to Robespierre's Jacobins), 1792–3

Guillaume BRUNE (1763–1815): printer and journalist turned National
Guardsman by the revolution, General Brune was stationed in Bordeaux in
the late autumn of 1793; he became one of Napoléon's closest allies

Georges-Louis Leclerc, comte de BUFFON (1707–88): scientific polymath best
remembered for his monumental, 44-volume *Natural History*; an habitué of
Mme Necker's salon

Fanny BURNEY (1762–1840): English novelist and diarist

François (or Francisco) CABARRUS (1752–1810): Thérésia's father, a financier
from Bayonne who became banker to the King of Spain, creating the Banco

San Carlos (forerunner of the Bank of Spain); after two years in prison (1793–4) he was restored to favour, and when Joseph Bonaparte became King of Spain he became Finance Minister

Luc-Antoine de CHAMPAGNEUX (1744–1807): Lyonnais lawyer, publisher and politician; friend of Jean-Jacques Rousseau and the Rolands; published Manon's memoirs in 1795

Victorine, comtesse de CHASTENAY (1771–1855): memoirist

François-René, vicomte de CHATEAUBRIAND (1768–1848): writer and diplomat, considered the founder of French romanticism; a gourmand, he gave his name to the chateaubriand cut of beef

Pierre-Gaspard CHAUMETTE (1763–94): radical, atheist Jacobin member of the Paris Commune, voice of the sans-culottes, with a special hatred for prostitutes

André CHÉNIER (1762–94): less radical than his younger brother Marie-Joseph and an opponent of the Jacobins, Chénier (a poet) was guillotined two days before Robespierre fell

Marie-Joseph CHÉNIER (1764–1811): Jacobin playwright who, with Jacques-Louis David, helped shape the philosophy, festivals and aesthetics of the early revolution

François-Joseph de Camaran, comte de CHIMAY (1771–1843): Thérésia Cabarrus's third husband

Mlle CLAIRON (1723–1803): celebrated actress who tutored Germaine Necker and Fabre d'Églantine in oratory, and was the mistress of Éric Magnus de Staël, Germaine's husband

Stanislas, comte de CLERMONT-TONNERRE (1757–92): liberal aristocrat and friend of Rousseau; orator on behalf of the constitutional party, 1789–91

Aimée de COIGNY (1769–1820): *merveilleuse*, and friend of Thérésia Cabarrus

Jean-Marie COLLOT D'HERBOIS (1749–96): actor before the revolution, he became a radical Jacobin sitting with Robespierre on the Committee of Public Safety

Anne COLOMBE: Marat's publisher

Antoine de Caritat, marquis de CONDORCET (1743–94): mathematician, rationalist philosopher and social reformer associated with the Girondins who helped write the constitutions of 1791 and 1793

Sophie de CONDORCET (1764–1822): bluestocking salonnière, friend of Germaine de Staël and wife of the marquis de Condorcet

Benjamin CONSTANT (1767–1830): Swiss writer and politician in France during the Directory and again after Napoléon's fall

Charles de CONSTANT (1762–1835): man of letters and Benjamin's cousin

Charlotte CORDAY (1768–93): young woman from Normandy of Girondin sympathies who murdered Jean-Paul Marat

Georges DANTON (1759–94): with a personality to match his enormous frame, Danton was a Parisian lawyer who rose to popular fame through the Cordeliers' Club, becoming one of the most prominent Jacobins

Jacques-Louis DAVID (1748–1825): celebrated artist before the revolution; patronized by the king; he became a radical Jacobin responsible alongside the lyricist Marie-Joseph Chénier for the festivals and iconography of the early 1790s

Camille DESMOULINS (1760–94): lawyer by training and journalist by profession, the sociable Desmoulins was at the centre of a group of radical middle-class Jacobins including Danton and Robespierre

Lucile DESMOULINS (1770–94): his adored and adorable wife

Denis DIDEROT (1713–84): writer and philosopher who edited the great *Encylopédie*; habitué of Mme Necker's salon

Charles François DUMOURIEZ (1739–1823): pro-war Girondin general and Foreign Minister in the spring of 1792 who successfully commanded the Army of the North in the winter of that year; defeat at Neerwinden in March 1793 prompted him to turn his forces towards Paris hoping to overturn the revolutionary government; repulsed, he fled to Austria with the future king Louis-Philippe, son of the duc d'Orléans

Alexandrine des ÉCHEROLLES (1777?–1843?): daughter of a Lyonnais army officer of gentle birth, she kept a diary during the siege of Lyons

Philippe François Nazaire Fabre d'ÉGLANTINE (1750–94): actor, poet and playwright turned Jacobin orator; prominent member of the Cordeliers' and close to Danton, Desmoulins and Marat; one of the creators of the revolutionary calendar

Grace Dalrymple ELLIOTT (1754?–1823): 'Dally the Tall', as she was known, was a Scottish courtesan whose lovers included the Prince Regent in London and the duc d'Orléans in Paris; she was an ardent royalist who just survived the Terror

Constance ÉVRARD (1768?–?): Parisian cook, Pauline Léon's friend and neighbour; I was able to find no connection between Constance and Simone despite their similar political views and identical names

Simone ÉVRARD (1764–1824): Marat's common-law wife, nurse, co-writer and editor

Adèle de FLAHAUT (1760–1836): official mistress of Talleyrand at the start of the revolution, unofficial mistress of Gouverneur Morris; fled Paris about 1791 and became a novelist

Jean-Jacques Devin de FONTENAY (1762?–?): rakish first husband of Thérésia Cabarrus

Théodore de FONTENAY (1789–1815): Thérésia's eldest son

Joseph FOUCHÉ (1759–1820): brutal, radical, anticlerical Jacobin who helped bring Robespierre down and became Napoléon's Minister of Police

Antoine FOUQUIER-TINVILLE (1746–95): principal revolutionary judge during the Terror

Claude FOURNIER L'AMÉRICAIN (1745–1825): violent radical agitator; one of the *vainqueurs* of the Bastille, member of the Cordeliers', an organizer of the popular risings of the summer of 1792; one of the few men known to have encouraged, profited by and participated in the prison massacres that September

Henry FOX (1773–1840): English Whig politician who visited France in 1802

FRENELLE: Thérésia Cabarrus's maid

Auguste-François Faveau, marquis de FRÉNILLY (1768–1828): memoirist

Stanislas FRÉRON (1754–1802): radical deputy and journalist, schoolfriend of his one-time associates Camille Desmoulins and Maximilien Robespierre; after Robespierre's fall (which he helped initiate) Fréron became ringleader of the *muscadins*

Félicité de GENLIS (1746–1830): educator, novelist and mistress of the duc d'Orléans, to whose children she was governess

Joseph-Marie de GÉRANDO (1772–1842): French philosopher of Italian descent

Antoine-Joseph GORSAS (1752–93): Girondin deputy and journalist who had (like Manon Roland) been one of Robespierre's early admirers; especially loathed by Marat

Olympe de GOUGES (1748–93): actress, playwright and probable courtesan before the revolution, she became a feminist activist with a soft spot for the beleaguered king and queen

Citoyenne GOVIN: member of the Société des Républicaines-Révolutionnaires

Granville Leveson GOWER (1773–1846): British politician and statesman who visited Paris in the late 1790s

Catherine GRAND (1762–1835): Talleyrand's mistress and later his wife

Sophie GRANDCHAMP: friend of Manon Roland

Citoyen GRANDPRÉ: Parisian prison inspector appointed by Jean-Marie Roland in 1792

Fortunée HAMELIN (1776–1851): sexy Creole *merveilleuse*

Jacques HÉBERT (1757–94): radical, anticlerical, *enragé* journalist, sitting well to the left of Robespierre

Lazare HOCHE (1768–97): general (and lover of Rose de Beauharnais while they were both held in Les Carmes prison in spring 1794) whose brilliant career was cut short by his early death

Arsène HOUSSAYE (1815–96): critic, poet, novelist and first biographer of Thérésia Tallien

Thomas JEFFERSON (1743–1826): third president of the United States and author of its Declaration of Independence; lived in Paris 1785–9 as US envoy

Marc-Antoine JULLIEN (1775–?): Robespierrist son of Rosalie and Marc-Antoine

Jullien de la Drôme; *représentant en mission* who replaced Tallien in Bordeaux in 1794

Rosalie JULLIEN DE LA DRÔME: wife of the Jacobin deputy Marc-Antoine Jullien de la Drôme (1744–1821)

Claire (called Rose) LACOMBE (1764–?): provincial actress who arrived in Paris in 1792 and set up the Société des Républicaines-Révolutionnaires with Pauline Léon

Charles de LACRETELLE (1766–1855): moderate monarchist journalist during the period following Robespierre's death; later a historian and memoirist

Gilbert du Motier, marquis de LAFAYETTE (1757–1834): French aristocrat who gained early fame as a member of the revolutionary American army; moderate constitutional monarchist and head of the National Guard in the early years of the revolution; declared a traitor to France in August 1792 and fled the country, only to be taken prisoner by the Austrians; returned to France in 1799 and to public life after Napoléon's fall

Béatrix, marquise de LAGE DE VOLUDE (1764–1842): fled France in July 1789 and returned on a false passport in 1792 to see her family in Bordeaux

LAMARCHE: the forger who went to the scaffold with Manon Roland in November 1793

Alphonse de LAMARTINE (1790–1869): romantic poet and historian

Marie-Thérèse, princesse de LAMBALLE (1749–92): friend of Marie-Antoinette

Alexandre de LAMETH (1760–1829): the most intelligent of the three liberal Lameth brothers

Charles de LAMETH (1757–1832): liberal aristocrat who fought alongside his brothers and Lafayette during the American War of Independence; fled France in the autumn of 1792; married to Marie-Anne

Marie-Anne, marquise de LAMETH (née Picot): Dondon (as she was known at the convent she attended with Thérésia Cabarrus) was Thérésia's best friend in the early years of the revolution

Théodore de LAMETH (1756–1854): the least politically involved of the Lameth brothers; lived at Juniper Hall in Surrey in the spring of 1793

Étienne de LAMOTHE (?–1836): young soldier who met Thérésia in the summer of 1793

François LANTHENAS (1754–99): trained as a doctor, Lanthenas was an old friend of the Rolands and became associated with them politically during the revolution; he was also Tom Paine's translator

Louis La REVELLIÈRE (1753–1824): although loosely affiliated to the Girondins, La Revellière survived their fall and rose to prominence during the Directory, first as president of the Council of Ancients and then as a Director; an ardent promoter of the new religion of theophilanthropy, a rationalized form of Catholicism

Lucy, marquise de La TOUR DU PIN (1770–1853): lady-in-waiting to

Marie-Antoinette who fled France in early 1794, making a new life for herself and her family in the United States before returning to Napoléon's France; wonderful memoirist

Théophile LECLERC (1771?–?): son of a provincial engineer, Leclerc spent the early years of the revolution in the army before arriving in Paris in the spring of 1793 where he became a radical *enragé*

Louis LEGENDRE (1752–97): Saint-Germain butcher (apparently Germaine de Staël, who lived nearby, bought her meat from him) turned popular political activist; closely allied with Danton

Amélie LENORMANT (c.1810–93): Juliette Récamier's niece, adopted daughter and memoirist

Félix LEPELETIER (1767–1837): following his brother Michel, a fervent revolutionary; lover, during the early years of the revolution, of Thérésia de Fontenay

Michel LEPELETIER (1760–93): perhaps the most radical of the liberal aristocrats who welcomed the coming of the revolution, Lepeletier was a Montagnard Jacobin who voted for the execution of Louis XVI and consequently was assassinated in a Palais Royal restaurant by a royalist who saw him as a traitor; he became a revolutionary martyr

René LEVASSEUR (1747–1834): ardent Jacobin devoted to Robespierre

LOUIS XVI (1754–93): the weak, pious, stubborn king removed from his throne in 1792 and executed six months later

Jean-Baptiste LOUVET (1760–97): Girondin novelist and publisher whose newspaper *La Sentinelle* was funded by Roland; after fleeing Paris in June 1793, assisted in his flight from Bordeaux by Thérésia Cabarrus, he returned to Paris, journalism and politics after Robespierre's fall

Stanislas MAILLARD (1763–94): National Guardsman, one of the *vainqueurs* of the Bastille, who accompanied the women of Paris to Versailles in October 1789

Louis-Pierre MANUEL (1751–93): writer, briefly imprisoned in the Bastille before the revolution, became prosecutor of the new Parisian government, the Commune, after August 1792; despite his Jacobin links, he publicly condemned the September massacres, voted against the execution of the king – and was guillotined for his moderation

Jean-Paul MARAT (1743–93): Swiss-born scientist and doctor, he became during the revolution an irreverent, fanatical, often bloodthirsty writer and publisher of *L'Ami du Peuple*, whose aim was to attack anyone in power; he saw himself as the 'wrath of the people'

MARIE-ANTOINETTE (1755–93): Louis XVI's unpopular Austrian queen

Louis-Sébastien MERCIER (1740–1814): chronicler of Parisian life and moderate revolutionary imprisoned in 1793 and released after Robespierre's fall

Jules MICHELET (1798–1874): prolific, romantic, republican historian

Honoré-Gabriel, comte de MIRABEAU (1749–91): extravagant, eloquent, womanizing, sometimes violent, always controversial orator and politician of genius, the young Mirabeau was imprisoned three times (for seduction, attempted abduction and duelling) under the ancien régime; a constitutional monarchist during the revolution, he tried to bring about a compromise between the royalists and the revolutionaries; at his death he was hailed a hero, but when it was discovered that he had accepted money from the king in return for advice, his remains were removed from the Panthéon

Antoine MOMORO (1756–94): radical Parisian printer and bookseller credited with coining the phrase 'Liberté, Égalité, Fraternité'

Sophie MOMORO: Antoine's beautiful wife, one of the women who played Liberty at the 1793 Festival of Reason

Femme MONIC: member of the Société des Républicaines-Révolutionnaires; haberdasher; said to have been one of the ringleaders of the *tricoteuses* who sat knitting beneath the guillotine

Mathieu de MONTMORENCY (1766–1826): fought with Lafayette in the United States and proposed the abolition of aristocratic insignia in June 1790, but became disillusioned with the revolution after seeing several members of his family killed during the Terror; he returned to politics when the monarchy was restored to France in 1814

John MOORE (1729–1802): Scottish doctor and writer

Jean Victor MOREAU (1763–1813): celebrated republican general who supported Napoléon at the coup of Brumaire 1799 but later turned against him

Gouverneur MORRIS (1752–1816): lived in Paris 1789–94 (as US Minister Plenipotentiary to France from 1792); despite his pride in being a US citizen and his co-authorship of the US Constitution, where France was concerned Morris was a convinced royalist

Louis, comte de NARBONNE (1755–1813): liberal aristocrat in the early years of the revolution whose affection for and loyalty to the royal family triumphed over his political ideals; he escaped France in August 1792 and returned in 1801, later serving Napoléon as a soldier and diplomat

Jacques NECKER (1732–1804): rich Swiss financier, father of Germaine de Staël, married to the salonnière SUZANNE, Necker became Finance Minister to Louis XVI in 1776, was dismissed in 1781, recalled in 1788, dismissed again in July 1789 and recalled later that month; he finally resigned in 1790 and spent the rest of his life in retirement near Geneva

Philippe-Égalité, duc d'ORLÉANS (1747–93): liberal, debauched cousin of Louis XVI whom, it was believed during the early years of the revolution, he hoped to replace on the French throne as a constitutional king (although he made no attempt to gain the throne); he voted for Louis's death and followed him to the scaffold within the year

Gabriel OUVRARD (1770–1846): immensely rich self-made businessman and
financier who was the navy's official supplier in 1797 and continued to fund
the French government through its successive administrations (except for a
brief period in prison, 1810–13) until his death

Tom PAINE (1737–1809): author of the incendiary 1776 pamphlet *Common Sense*,
he arrived in Paris in 1791 and was hailed as an honorary French citizen,
even being elected to the National Convention in 1792 where he sat with
the Girondins; his association with them led to his imprisonment from
December 1793 until November 1794; he did not return to the United States
until 1802

Etta PALM D'AELDERS (1743–99): Dutch feminist and sometime spy who lived
in Paris 1773–92

Jérôme PÉTION (1756–94): handsome, eloquent, reformist lawyer and writer,
one of the heroes of the early revolution; mayor of Paris 1791–2, first
president of the National Convention and one of the most prominent
Girondins

Louis PRUDHOMME (1752–1830): bookseller and publisher of the Jacobin
newspaper *Les Révolutions de Paris* who became a Bonapartist after 1800 and
a royalist after 1815

Jacques-Rose RÉCAMIER (1751–1830): Lyonnais merchant and financier who
funded the governments of the Directory, the Consulate and the Empire
and became one of the first governors of the Bank of France; married
Juliette Bernard in 1793

Jean-François REUBELL (1747–1807): a left-leaning deputy to the National
Assembly and the National Convention, Reubell was one of the first five
Directors elected in 1795

François (1762–1826) and Louise (1758–1821) ROBERT: editors of the *Mercure
national* 1789–91 and prominent members of the progressive Social Circle
founded in 1790

Maximilien ROBESPIERRE (1758–94): lawyer from Arras, who lost his parents
at a young age, Robespierre was celebrated as a deputy to the National
Assembly for his austere radicalism; he became the leader of the left-wing
deputies of the National Convention, using the Jacobin Club as his
power-base and the Committee of Public Safety as his administration

Eudora ROLAND (1781–1858): Manon Roland's daughter; married Léon
Champagneux, son of her mother's publisher, in December 1796

Jean-Marie ROLAND (1734–93): at the start of the revolution Roland was an
inspector-general of manufactures based in Villefranche; married Manon
Roland in 1780

Gilbert ROMME (1750–95): trained as a mathematician and doctor, before the
revolution he served as tutor to the Russian soldier Pavel Stroganoff; initially

allied to the Girondins, from 1792 he was a convinced Jacobin; he helped create the revolutionary calendar; having survived Robespierre's fall (he was away from Paris at the time), he was sentenced to death in the aftermath of the Prairial risings in 1795 but stabbed himself as he left the courtroom with the words, 'I die for the republic'

Jean-Jacques ROUSSEAU (1712–78): Enlightenment philosopher, novelist and educationalist whose ideas exalting simplicity, virtue, nature and love transformed the mindset of eighteenth-century France and inspired countless revolutionaries including Manon Roland, Germaine de Staël and Maximilien Robespierre

Pierre-Joseph-Alexis ROUSSEL: French writer

Jacques ROUX (1752–94): priest who arrived in Paris in 1790 and became a member of the Paris Commune in 1792, growing more and more radical in his demands on behalf of the city's poor

Donatien Alphonse François de SADE (1740–1814): libertine philosopher–pornographer freed from the Bastille when it fell in 1789; possible author of *Zoloé*, a 1799 pamphlet attacking Napoléon and Joséphine Bonaparte and their circle

Louis SAINT-JUST (1767–94): so-called Archangel of the Terror, Saint-Just was a devoted Robespierrist and sat alongside him on the Committee of Public Safety in 1793 and 1794 before being guillotined alongside him

Charles-Henri SANSON (1739–1809): chief executioner 1778–95

Antoine SANTERRE (1752–1809): rich brewer from Saint-Antoine, Santerre was made head of the National Guard in August 1792 and in this capacity accompanied Louis XVI to the scaffold in January 1793, ordering a drum-roll that would drown out his attempt to make a final speech; he was imprisoned after Robespierre's fall

Emmanuel Joseph SIEYÈS (1748–1836): despite his authorship of the influential 1789 article 'What is the Third Estate?' and co-authorship of the Declaration of the Rights of Man and the Citizen, ex-priest Sieyès was a reserved, self-effacing politician who disapproved of the excesses of the early 1790s but re-emerged as a significant political force during the Directory

Éric Magnus de STAËL (1749–1802): on-and-off Swedish ambassador to France 1786–96; married Germaine Necker in 1786

François SULEAU (1757–92): vitriolic royalist journalist

Elizabeth, Countess of SUTHERLAND (1765–1839): wife of George Granville Leveson Gower, first Duke of Sutherland, British ambassador to France 1790–2

Charles-Maurice de TALLEYRAND-PÉRIGORD (1754–1838): brilliant and self-serving French politician and diplomat who, except for a brief period of exile between late 1792 and 1796, worked continuously for each successive

French regime until his death; described by Napoléon as a 'shit in a silk stocking'

Jean-Lambert TALLIEN (1767–1820): revolutionary journalist who sat in the National Convention and was sent to Bordeaux as a *représentant en mission* in October 1793; the challenge he addressed to Robespierre in July 1794 led to Robespierre's fall

François-Joseph TALMA (1763–1826): the greatest actor of the revolutionary period; Napoléon adored his work

Julie TALMA, née CARREAU (1756–1805): Talma's first wife, an actress, who presided over a celebrated salon

Paul Auguste TASCHEREAU-FARGUES: Committee of Public Safety spy in the spring of 1794, a friend of both Robespierre and Tallien; imprisoned following the Thermidor coup

Alexis de TOCQUEVILLE (1805–59): historian and political thinker who championed democracy and liberty

Louise-Élisabeth de TOURZEL (1749–1830): intimate friend of Marie-Antoinette and governess to the dauphin

Jean VARLET: popular *enragé* imprisoned in autumn 1793

Pierre VERGNIAUD (1753–93): perhaps the greatest of the Girondin orators

Élisabeth VIGÉE-LEBRUN (1755–1852): artist (and memoirist) patronized by Marie-Antoinette

Helen Maria WILLIAMS (1761?–1827): British novelist, poet and social commentator who lived chiefly in France from 1790 until her death

Mary WOLLSTONECRAFT (1759–97): English writer, known for her radical political views and feminism, who lived in Paris during the revolution; she was the mother of Mary Shelley, her daughter by the philosopher and political theorist William Godwin

Claude YSABEAU (1754–1831): former priest sent to Bordeaux as *représentant en mission* with Tallien in autumn 1793; he sat in the Council of the Elders during the Directory

WORDS AND PHRASES

À bas . . . ! Down with . . . !

à la in the style of

amazone a women's masculine-cut riding habit, or a female soldier

ami/e friend

ancien régime the old regime (before the revolution)

baiser to kiss

bonnet rouge red Phrygian cap once worn by freed Roman slaves; revolutionary
   symbol of liberty

beau/belle handsome/beautiful

bon/bonne good

bourgeois/e member of the middle class, generally urban

cahier notebook

'Ça Ira' revolutionary anthem; the chorus translates as 'It will go our way!'

caisse box; crate; fund

chemise de la reine a simple white dress; literally, the queen's dress

cher/chère dear

ci-devant former

citoyen/ne citizen/citizeness

clubist/e a frequenter of clubs

cocarde rosette, cockade

comité committee

commissaire police officer, commissioner

Commune the popularly-elected Parisian government from 1789 until 1795

Conventionnel member of the National Convention

coup d'épée sword blow

cour court

cul noir rough pottery (literally, black-bottomed)

curé priest

dauphin heir to the French throne

décadi tenth day of the new revolutionary calendar, equivalent to a Sunday

Department one of the 83 administrative areas into which France was divided
   in 1790

deputy   member of the National Assembly
droit   right

émigré   someone who fled revolutionary France, usually aristocratic
enragés/enragées   a group of populist extremists prominent in the summer of
  1793
épouse   wife
Estates-General   the French representative assembly, composed of three
  estates, or classes (clergy, nobility and commons); it was called by the king
  in 1788 (and met in May 1789) for the first time since 1614
étranger/étrangère   foreigner, stranger
étrenne   gift, money

faubourg   suburb; traditionally, a working-class area like Saint-Antoine just
  outside Paris's walls
faux   false
fédérés   National Guardsmen from all over the country who gathered in Paris
  in summer 1792 for the Fête de la Fédération in July, and were instrumental
  in the storming of the Tuileries in August
femme   woman, wife
femme de chambre   maid
femme publique   prostitute; literally, public woman
fête champêtre   a rural village festival
Feuillants   club of constitutional monarchists, mostly aristocratic liberals,
  created in July 1791; met in the convent of the Feuillants on the rue
  Saint-Honoré; most of its members left Paris before or during the
  September massacres of 1792
fille de joie   prostitute
fournée   literally, batch; large groups of prisoners dispatched to the guillotine
  during the Terror

garde française   an elite force, founded in 1563, stationed in Paris in 1789 and
  highly susceptible to the incendiary revolutionary idealism prevalent there;
  dissolved in September 1789, with most of its men joining the new National
  Guard
garde nationale   a patriotic, voluntary National Guard formed in July 1789
gendarme   policeman
gens   people
Girondin   deputy from the Gironde region around Bordeaux; the word came
  to be used for a group of progressive, federalist deputies opposed to
  Robespierre and to the dominance of Paris in revolutionary politics; also
  known, after one of their prominent members, as Brissotins
guerre   war

guillotine   machine used to behead convicted criminals swiftly and humanely; it took its name from the doctor and deputy to the National Assembly who recommended its use

haut monde   high society
honnête   honourable, honest
hôtel   large town-house, either a private residence or an establishment renting out rooms and apartments
Hôtel de Ville   town hall

infortuné/e   unlucky; ill-fated

Jacobin   member of the Jacobin Club, especially a follower of Maximilien Robespierre
jeunesse dorée   gilded youth; a name given to the *muscadins* of 1794–5
joie/joyeuse   joy/joyful
joli/e   pretty
journée   day

lanterne   lamppost; '*à la lanterne!*' meant 'string them up!'
lettres de cachet   royal writs of pardon, imprisonment or exile; literally, stamped or sealed letters; the king needed no authority to issue them, and they became a hated symbol of his arbitrary power
libérateur/libératrice   rescuer
liberty trees   trees planted by groups or individuals as symbols of liberty and decorated with tricolour ribbons and red bonnets; perhaps 60,000 were planted in 1792
Liégois/e   person from Liège
Lyonnais/e   person from Lyon

mairie   town council or town hall
maisons de santé   temporary revolutionary holding-houses or prisons
manège   hall; a former indoor riding arena attached to the Tuileries palace, in which the National Assembly, the National Convention and the Council of Five Hundred successively sat; destroyed in 1802
marais   area of central Paris, literally meaning swamp; the name derives from the boggy land it was built on
marchand/e   shopkeeper or stall-holder
mariée   bride
'Marseillaise'   the marching song of the Rhine army, composed in 1792 by Rouget de Lisle, which was declared the French national anthem in 1795
mère   mother

merveilleuses   literally, the wonderful ones; the women of Directory high
    society
mondain/e   socialite
Montagnard   the name given to the most extreme left-wing deputies to the
    National Assembly, generally Jacobin supporters of Robespierre, because of
    the high seats they took on the left-hand side of the *manège*
mouchard   spy or informer
muscadin   dandy

Notre Dame   Our Lady, generally referring to the Virgin Mary
nourrice   wet-nurse

observateur   spy
oeil de vigilance   literally, a vigilant eye

pain   bread
patriote   patriot, but carrying with it the implicit meaning of a supporter of the
    revolution
patrie   the homeland
pauvre   poor
peuple   people
pierrot   a short woman's shift
pique   pike; a simple weapon used by common people and thus a symbol of
    their independence and patriotism
poissard/e   literally, rogue; also refers to the rough slang spoken by the market
    people of Paris
propriété nationale   national property; the slogan daubed on to émigrés'
    abandoned houses that had been confiscated by the revolutionary
    government
protecteur/protectrice   protector
putain   slut

quartier   area of Paris

régicide   a deputy who voted for Louis XVI's execution
reine   queen
représentants en mission   envoys appointed by the National Convention to
    maintain order in the French provinces
rivière   necklace; literally, river
roi   king

salon   drawing-room; or, more often here, the regular parties held in a
    drawing-room

salonnière   the hostess at a salon

sans   without

sans-culottes   lower-class Parisian radicals who, instead of aristocratic breeches or culottes, wore trousers, often striped red and white

Septembrist   someone implicated in the September massacres of 1792

sections   from May 1790, the 48 wards of Paris, each with its own popularly elected government

tendresse   tenderness

toilette   outfit; the process of getting dressed

tous/toute   all

tribune   visitors' gallery at the *manège* or convention hall; or the speakers' rostrum

tricoteuse   literally, knitter; women making socks for their husbands and sons fighting in the revolutionary army were the most regular (and savagely vociferous) observers of the guillotine

tutoyer (noun, *tutoiement*)   to address someone using the informal second-person-singular *tu* rather than the politer second-person-plural *vous*

tyran   tyrant

vainqueur   victor; applied as an honorary epithet to those men who sacked the Bastille on 14 July 1789

valet de chambre   gentleman's gentleman

vaillant/e   brave

veuve   widow

ACKNOWLEDGMENTS

This book has been wonderful to write, firstly because the subject matter was so enthralling, secondly because it involved frequent visits to Paris where I tortured librarians at countless *bibliothèques* with my appalling French, and finally because everyone who helped me with it was so delightful and so enthusiastic. Many, many thanks to: the staff of the British and London Libraries in London and the Archives Nationales and the Richelieu, Mitterand and Arsenal Libraries in Paris; Elisabeth, princesse de Chimay, for taking the time to dicuss Thérésia with me; Sybille de Rosée, for putting me in touch with the princesse and having me to stay for such a lovely evening; Anne Colette, for being so patient with my French over countless breakfasts; everyone at the Milk Studios for making me feel so welcome; Sophie Richard; Andrew Stock; my sisters, Corina and Sophie, who made my stay in Paris so much fun; the wonderful Tif Loehnis, Eric Simonoff, Rebecca Folland, Christelle Chamouton, Mollie Stirling and everyone at Janklow & Nesbit; and the fantastic team at Harper Collins, including Arabella Pike, Terry Karten, Annabel Wright, Vera Brice, Alice Massey, Helen Ellis, Caroline Hotblack, Leslie Robinson and John Bond, as well as Sue Phillpott for her immaculate copy editing (the mistakes which remain are all my own) and Douglas Matthews for the index. Thank you for putting so much into this project and giving me such warm encouragement. I'm really looking forward to working on the next one with you. Finally I'd like to thank my husband, Justin, who nobly commuted to Paris while I was staying there and to whom this book is dedicated. We'll always have Louis . . .

INDEX

P.S.

Ideas,
interviews
& features ...

Q and A with Lucy Moore

What drew you to this subject?
I had always been interested in the French
Revolution, ever since school. I was interested
in French women in general because of the
idea that you could be beautiful and still be
taken seriously, which isn't at all an English
idea. My father's second wife was French,
which I think is part of the reason for the
fascination. My parents split up when I
was 18 months old and, from 7 to 13, my
stepmother was a glamorous, intimidating
influence in my life. She'd been a model and
a ballet dancer and was rigidly disciplined
about her appearance. For a long time she
had been the champion on the French version
of *Countdown*. She had a Carol Vorderman
mind without her approachableness. I think
I was interested because it was so different.
My mother, who I think is much more
beautiful, has never worried about what she
wears, never wears makeup, is determined
not to judge others or be judged by external
appearances. In the end, the French women
I studied weren't really like my stepmother,
or particularly how I had expected them to
be; they didn't fit any mould, as people never
do when you look at them closely. When I
finished the book I felt it was a lament for an
idealism which doesn't exist now. I found
myself almost wishing that I lived in those
times, feeling that deeply about politics. What
really attracted me to the subject throughout
was the idea of looking at a period in which
people really genuinely believed the world
could be changed by their actions.

Did you find yourself drawn to any particular woman?
Madame de Staël is wonderful because she is so vulnerable. In her letters her heart pours out on to the page. She genuinely was, as she believed, this superior woman who was being discriminated against by society. She's maddening as well, because of that. She and Manon Roland, because they wrote the most, come to life the most. They are huge egos, but maybe you need that to really effectively communicate yourself on paper. Manon Roland is very self-righteous, smug almost, but so sincere.

What is your earliest memory?
My parents lived in Italy from when I was 9 months to 18 months old. I remember our house there. I went back with my father when I was 18 and the rooms had all been changed round and I immediately knew they were in the wrong place. When they split up, my mother and I went to stay with her great-aunt in Portugal and I remember being there, too. I don't remember things happening at these places, just being there, but I know the memories are to do with the fact that there was so much going on between my parents. You think children aren't taking anything in, but they get everything.

What was your childhood like and can you link it to what you are doing now?
Because of my parents divorcing and me being an only child until I was nine, I read a ▶

> ❝ What really attracted me to the subject was the idea of looking at a period in which people genuinely believed the world could be changed by their actions. ❞

LIFE
at a Glance

BORN
....
London, 1970.

EDUCATED
....
Faulkner House, London;
Williston Northampton
School, Massachusetts;
MA in History at
Edinburgh University.

CAREER
....
Lucy has written several
books, including the
bestselling *Maharanis*.
She also writes book
reviews for newspapers
and presents history
programmes on
television.

LIVES
....
In west London with
her husband, Justin, an
Australian who works in
the wine business.

Q and A *(continued)*

◄ great deal. I think that has a lot to do with
me wanting to write later. They were not
married for very long but one of the things
they shared was a real love of books and
poetry. It would have been hard to be as
bookish as I was without parents who
were encouraging me and wanting to talk
about the books that I'd read. Even now, if
something is wrong the first thing I want to
do is go back to a book I love and lose myself
in it. It's so soothing. I feel so sorry for people
who don't read.

What have you read most recently?
I've just finished *Mother's Milk* by Edward
St Aubyn. I loved the sense of trying to
remember things, being very clear that
memories are what define you. A huge
part of my childhood was that sense of life
slipping away and trying to hang on to it.
I haven't read another writer who has
captured that.

**Do you think you might try and write
fiction?**
I sort of vaguely think I might try and then
I get fearful about whether it would be
good. I'd quite like to leave a manuscript
in a drawer when I'm 85 and not have to deal
with it being edited or published. The nice
thing about writing non-fiction is it is
something you can view as a job. Obviously
you throw yourself into it, but it's easier
to separate yourself from your writing
even though of course the subjects you
choose are so determined by your own
preoccupations.

How do you manage to fuse scholarship with narrative in your writing?
I really want my books to be readable. With this one, I hoped the narrative of the revolution would take over, which is why I'm still not quite happy with the beginning. It's so hard to get readers into it when they don't know your characters. That's something that happens successfully in fiction and is incredibly hard to do with non-fiction, but once you've got to grips with who they all are I hope it has a proper novelistic feel.

Which other historians do you admire?
I think Stella Tillyard is one of the best writers today. She, Claire Tomalin and Jenny Uglow, those would be my big three. They are really skilful at what they do, writing with such a breadth of understanding and compassion. They always have that sense of narrative, but it's done in a very subtle way. My favourite non-fiction writers are mostly women, I'm not sure why. It may have to do with their lack of ego, which perhaps is a more feminine trait – allowing the subject to speak more loudly than the author.

If you didn't live in Britain, where would you live?
As a child I refused to learn French because of my stepmother, but now I'm a complete Francophile. I want to go and live in Paris. Not for ever, but maybe five years. I just think it's so civilized. I like the old-fashionedness of it, that you go into a toy shop and spend £5 on a child's toy and they wrap it up beautifully ▶

Q and A *(continued)*

◀ with ribbon without you even asking. Politeness is important in life and I'm not sure people in Britain are as polite as they could be. It's been bred out of us somehow. London has become like New York was, in terms of people being interested in how much money you have. I know it's old-fashioned but I still feel embarrassed when I ask what people do. I'm always astonished by those conversations about how much people's houses are worth. I don't know if France would be better, but I have this fantasy that it would be. ■

Top Ten
Favourite Books

The Great Gatsby
F. Scott Fitzgerald

Footsteps: Adventures of a Romantic Biographer
Richard Holmes

Speak, Memory
Vladimir Nabokov

War and Peace
Leo Tolstoy

Middlemarch
George Eliot

Secrets of the Flesh: A Life of Colette
Judith Thurman

A Long Way to Go
Marigold Armitage

Franny and Zooey
J. D. Salinger

Everybody Was So Young
Amanda Vaill

The Letters of Nancy Mitford and Evelyn Waugh
Nancy Mitford and Evelyn Waugh

A Writing Life

When do you write?
About nine to five. I try vaguely to keep office hours, although if I really need to get something done, first thing in the morning is best.

Why do you write?
To tell a story. And because it's my job.

Pen or computer?
Computer for work, longhand for personal things like letters or writing in my diary, and I take notes in longhand on index cards. I love a certain kind of Papermate biro that my mother sends me from the US.

Silence or music?
Generally silence. Sometimes Radio 1 as background. Radio 4 is far too distracting.

How do you start a book?
The research is always the first thing, and I can't contemplate starting to write until I've exhausted all my research leads.

And finish?
With a stiff drink! There's usually about a month when you think you've finished, but little things that need doing keep cropping up. Then suddenly one day you wake up and there's nothing more to do, which takes a little while to get used to.

Do you have any writing rituals?
Because I have a desk at home, I can't settle down to work if there's laundry or dishes to be done – so my house is always ridiculously tidy.

What or who inspires you?
My subjects – I find their stories endlessly
fascinating. That was especially true of
Liberty. I found myself completely swept
away by the idealism of the revolutionary
period and the courage of the women I was
writing about.

If you weren't a writer, what would you do?
Although I love my job, for years my fantasy
was being a florist; at the moment, it's being
an interior designer. Or a food writer.

What's your guilty reading pleasure?
Favourite trashy read?
Early Jilly Cooper, anything by Georgette
Heyer, Nancy Mitford or my new favourite,
Tilly Bagshawe. And back copies of *World of
Interiors*. But you can't feel guilty about it –
reading a good trashy novel with a nice cup
of tea and a pile of ginger nuts is one of life's
great pleasures.

Paris Streets

by Lucy Moore

AFTER I'D DONE as much research as I could in London, I went to Paris for a couple of months to look at the original sources. I had known it would be a magical time, but I had no idea quite how lovely it would be. Something about being alone in an unfamiliar place allows you to bury yourself completely in work: the telephone doesn't ring, the postman doesn't call, there is no one to have tea with or to speak to in the evenings – no one to resent for intruding on your fantasy world. The fact that it was Paris in the spring only heightened my sense of living in a dream state.

When I first arrived, I stayed in a sixth-floor room in an antiquated hotel on the Ile de la Cité. Their breakfast of milky chicory coffee, baguette and apricot jam just compensated for having to run down five flights of stairs to get the key to the shared bathroom. The best thing about being in the Place Dauphine was that it backed on to the red-brick, seventeenth-century building in which Manon Roland had grown up, and was perhaps two hundred metres from the medieval towers of the Conciergerie where she had been held before being guillotined. When she knew her death was certain she had asked her friend Sophie Grandchamp to stand on the corner of the Pont-Neuf, which she had looked out over as a daydreaming child, to watch her tumbrel pass by on the way to the bloody Place de la Révolution.

I found a tiny flat beside a Senegalese restaurant on a back street in the Marais. It was a couple of blocks away from the Musée Carnavalet which, by happy coincidence, was showing an exhibition entitled *Au temps des merveilleuses*, dedicated to the lives and circles of, among others, Thérésia Tallien and Juliette Récamier. I went there as often as I could to look at their portraits and pore over their possessions, including the warrant Robespierre signed in his minuscule spidery writing for Thérésia's arrest in the spring of 1794, her inlaid mahogany *nécessaire à jeux*, and the cobalt-blue-upholstered furniture designed by the Jacob brothers for Juliette.

My flat was also very close to the site of the prison (no longer standing) in which Thérésia had been held prisoner in the last days of the Terror. I used to buy milk and almonds from an Algerian shop on the corner of the rue Pavée, and think of Tallien standing outside La Force, longing for the sight of her. He had lived with his mother on the rue de la Perle, a five-minute walk north. Although his section of the street had long since been demolished, I walked along it nearly every day (it led to the Archives Nationales), and the shabby local bar became my favourite. It was this street which Robespierre's spy complained was too narrow for him to follow Tallien unobserved, and here where six months later Tallien was shot and wounded in the autumn of 1794 by a Jacobin still loyal to Robespierre's memory.

The Palais Royal is perhaps the most perfectly intact place to conjure up the ghosts of the revolution. It was there that Camille ▶

❝ The best thing about being in the Place Dauphine was that it backed on to the red-brick, seventeenth-century building in which Manon Roland had grown up. ❞

Paris Streets *(continued)*

◀ Desmoulins leapt on to a table and roused the crowds which would sack the Bastille; there that Théroigne de Méricourt was first inflamed by the new philosophies of liberty and equality; there that the duc d'Orléans and Félicité de Genlis – or Philippe Égalité and Citoyenne Brûlart, as they called themselves – tried to get into bed with the populist ideals that would one day destroy them; there that Charlotte Corday bought the kitchen knife with which she would stab Marat, and the new black hat with a green rosette that she wore for the occasion.

Although walking the streets held its own pleasures, the most intense moments of my time in Paris were spent in libraries. Most of the Bibliothèque Nationale's collection is now housed in the monumental Mitterrand building, but its manuscripts are still in the fabulous seventeenth-century site Richelieu (which I suspected, but couldn't confirm, may once have been the hôtel Richelieu where the *bals des victimes* were held). It contains some of Théroigne's papers, files of love letters written to Juliette Récamier, both available only on microfilm, and the journals Manon Roland secretly kept while she was in prison for the six months before her death. These were the originals: thick, poor-quality paper, yellowing or pale greenish grey, with her sharp, sure handwriting skimming over the pages. Even though I had read these words in printed sources hundreds of times over the past year, holding something she had had with her during her traumatic months in prison and thrown herself into with such passion was overwhelming.

Even more moving was the single, closely covered document in the Archives Nationales which Pauline Léon had written in prison in the summer of 1794. The statement was intended as an outline of her political career, her defence against accusations of being unrevolutionary, but because she was writing from the heart about her life and what had been important to her, it reads as a summary of her whole self. Barely anything else of her survives – the records of the Société des Républicaines-Révolutionnaires were destroyed; neither she nor her family and friends wrote letters or kept diaries that would have been saved, let alone published; after her release from prison a month after writing this document, she faded out of official notice entirely – and so this one faded, blotched page is an unbelievably poignant record of an entire life.

After finishing my other books, I found it fairly easy to shake off my subjects' hold on me and move on to the next project. The six women in *Liberty*, and revolutionary Paris in general, have had a much more tenacious grip. I just can't work out how to persuade my editor to let me go back to Paris and write the book all over again. ■

> ❛Although walking the streets held its own pleasures, the most intense moments of my time in Paris were spent in libraries. ❜

Have You Read?

Other books by Lucy Moore

The Thieves' Opera: The Remarkable Lives and Deaths of Jonathan Wild, Thief-Taker, and Jack Sheppard, House-Breaker
The story of the two early-eighteenth-century celebrity criminals Dickens used as the inspirations for Fagin and the Artful Dodger.

'Lucy Moore . . . vividly recreates the turbulent underworld of the 1720s, and reminds us that crime never really changes'
Mail on Sunday

Con Men and Cutpurses: Scenes from the Hogarthian Underworld
An anthology of eighteenth-century crime writing.

'A fascinating introduction to the criminal world of our ancestors'
Times Literary Supplement

Amphibious Thing: The Life of a Georgian Rake
The life of Lord Hervey, a politician and memoirist at the court of George II, whose worldly successes belied his private unhappiness.

'A highly intelligent, supremely enjoyable biographical study of the life and times of a celebrated rake and a brilliant picture of eighteenth-century aristocratic life in all its brittle artifice'
Observer

Maharanis: The Lives and Times of Three Generations of Indian Princesses
The story of India's long struggle towards Independence, told through the lives of four extraordinary women.

'Fascinating, engrossing, absorbingly intelligent and thoughtful'   *Sunday Times*

If You Loved This,
You Might Like…

The French and Their Revolution
Richard Cobb
Cobb is the great British revolutionary historian of the twentieth century, with an unforgettably idiosyncratic voice described by Julian Barnes as 'archival, anecdotal, discursive, button-holing, undogmatic, imaginatively sympathetic, incomplete, droll; sometimes chaotic, often manic, always pungently detailed'.

A Place of Greater Safety
Hilary Mantel
A brilliantly imagined, indescribably compelling novel set during the revolution, with the journalist Camille Desmoulins and his wife Lucile taking centre stage.

Memoirs
Madame de la Tour du Pin
Moore used these memoirs for much of the background detail that went into *Liberty*. She wished that Mme de la Tour du Pin had been in France during more of the main events of the revolution so that she could have made her one of her central figures.

The Life and Death of Mary Wollstonecraft
Claire Tomalin
Mary Wollstonecraft only lived in Paris for a few years during the 1790s, but she